Corporate Transformation

Ralph H. Kilmann
Teresa Joyce Covin
and Associates

Corporate Transformation

Revitalizing Organizations
for a Competitive World

J o s s e y - B a s s   P u b l i s h e r s
San Francisco   •   London   •   1989

CORPORATE TRANSFORMATION
Revitalizing Organizations for a Competitive World
by Ralph H. Kilmann, Teresa Joyce Covin, and Associates

Copyright © 1988 by: Jossey-Bass Inc., Publishers
350 Sansome Street
San Francisco, California 94104
&
Jossey-Bass Limited
28 Banner Street
London EC1Y 8QE

Library of Congress Cataloging-in-Publication Data

Kilmann, Ralph H., date.
   Corporate transformation.

   (The Jossey-Bass management series)
   Bibliography: p.
   Includes index.
   1. Organizational change.   2. Corporate reorgani-
zations.   I. Covin, Teresa Joyce, date.
II. Title.   III. Series.
HD58.8.K496   1988   658.4'063   87-45427
ISBN 1-55542-060-5

Manufactured in the United States of America

The paper in this book meets the guidelines for
permanence and durability of the Committee on
Production Guidelines for Book Longevity of the
Council on Library Resources.

JACKET DESIGN BY WILLI BAUM

FIRST EDITION
First printing: October 1987
Second printing: January 1989

Code 8731

The Jossey-Bass Management Series

Consulting Editors
Organizations and Management

Warren Bennis
University of Southern California

Richard O. Mason
Southern Methodist University

Ian I. Mitroff
University of Southern California

To Ines Martin and Jeff Covin
for their friendship and love

Contents

Preface

Members of every organization have heard the message: The world has changed. Yesterday's protected marketplace made the world seem stable and predictable; today's global marketplace makes the world appear dynamic and turbulent. Now, new competitors, technologies, government policies, tax laws, and social values affect organizations dramatically, overnight, all over the world.

Organizations designed to provide goods and services in yesterday's world are discovering that what made them successful in the past no longer applies. An exclusive emphasis on efficiency within the organization is not enough. A renewed focus on being innovative, market-driven, adaptive, and competitive in the outside world is now mandatory for success. Such a fundamental change in approach requires a major effort toward corporate transformation. Every familiar procedure involved in creating, designing, producing, and selling a product or service must be reexamined using a new set of guidelines.

Corporate transformation is a process by which organizations examine what they were, what they are, what they will need to be, and how to make the necessary changes. Implementing those changes affects both psychological and strategic aspects of an organization. The term *corporate* is used to convey the comprehensive effort required, in contrast to a piecemeal or single-division effort. *Transformation* indicates the fundamental nature of the change, in contrast to a mere linear extrapolation from the past. Corporate transformation is serious, large-scale change that demands new ways of perceiving, thinking, and behaving by all members of the organization. This volume provides the latest ideas, insights, strategies, and methods regarding corporate transformation. Leading academics who study transformation, experienced consultants who facilitate transformation, and visionary executives who direct transformation have all contributed their wisdom.

From October 22 to 25, 1986, the Program in Corporate Culture in the Joseph M. Katz Graduate School of Business at the University of Pittsburgh sponsored a conference on managing organizationwide transformation. The objective of the conference was to gather material for a comprehensive volume on this important topic. A summary of what transpired before, during, and after the conference may illustrate how an orchestrated approach can produce a wealth of information on a complex topic.

The Program in Corporate Culture at the University of Pittsburgh was founded in September 1983 in order to develop new knowledge concerning the impact of culture on organizational effectiveness and to disseminate this knowledge so that managers could increase the effectiveness of their organizations. The first major event sponsored by the program was a conference, held in 1984, on the topic of corporate culture, which, like the more recent conference, resulted in a book, *Gaining Control of the Corporate Culture* (1985). Because the topic of transformation is a direct outgrowth of examining corporate culture, we felt that the next major event should be to assemble the experts in corporate transformation and to compile the knowledge on that topic.

Experts were chosen in two ways. First, we made a list of individuals who, in our view, had demonstrated a keen understanding of the topic through academic research or by direct involvement in organizational efforts at corporate transformation. In this way, ten individuals—some academics and consultants who had facilitated transformation efforts and managers and executives who had acted as leaders during their organizations' transformations—were invited to present papers at the conference. Second, we mailed a conference announcement and call for papers to more than 25,000 professional societies and corporations whose members could be expected to have interest in the topic, including the Academy of Management, the American Psychological Association, the Institute of Management Sciences, the American Society for Training and Development, and several corporations. We expected that this search process would uncover important research and reports not yet published. Our expectations were more than realized: A total of sixty papers covering a wide range of material on corporate transformation were submitted as a result of our call for papers.

The submitted papers were subjected to a thorough review. Each paper received at least two independent reviews and was evaluated on the basis of four criteria: (1) innovativeness in approach to the topic, (2) quality in developing the approach, (3) practical usefulness in guiding management action, and (4) clarity of expression for a broad audience. In cases of disagreement, the paper was reviewed by a third person, and a discussion among the editors resolved any differences in opinion. This review process allowed the editors to select the best twelve from the total sixty papers. Editorial recommendations for revision were then sent to all authors. The invited authors' papers were subjected to the same review procedures to help them fine tune their ideas and improve their style as well.

The review process did not end with the editors, however. At the three-day conference, all authors delivered their papers to an audience of both academics and practitioners with thirty minutes for presentation and twenty minutes for discussion. This encouraged the authors to clarify their thoughts for a broad audience and allowed them to benefit from active debate and immediate feedback. Moreover, since all the papers presented during the conference concerned the topic of corporate transformation, there was ample opportunity for each author to learn from the presentations and discussions of the other papers. As editors, we were delighted to see the thinking evolve as the conference progressed. In fact, after reviewing the revised papers, which were submitted *after* the conference took place, we could observe the impact of the conference experience on each paper. As a result of this comprehensive editorial and interactive review process, the chapters in this book offer original ideas whose arguments are clearly conceived and well developed.

We expect that both academics and practitioners will find this book an invaluable resource. The practitioners who may be especially interested in this book include chief executive officers; senior operating executives; vice-presidents of corporate organization, planning, and development; human resource managers; personnel administrators; general managers; project managers; plant superintendents; management consultants; organizational development practitioners; management training and development practitioners; and administrators and directors of nonprofit organizations. The academics who may be especially interested in this book include faculty specializing in organizational theory, organizational behavior, organizational science, organizational development, sociology, anthropology, psychology, social work, health care, public administration, and educational administration.

Overview of the Contents

The twenty-two chapters in this volume are organized into four major parts that are especially designed to facilitate learning about corporate transformation—a field of management thought that is in some sense still emerging. It is best to read the chapters in order, or at least to review material from one part to the next, since the arguments build throughout the book.

In Chapter One, the Introduction, the editors discuss some key themes that recur throughout the book. These themes represent areas of both agreement and disagreement regarding what corporate transformation is and should be.

Part One provides an overview of what corporate transformation is and why it is particularly important at this point in time. The three chapters in this part define the theoretical as well as the practical considerations involved in managing corporate transformation.

Part Two includes six chapters that explore some of the

most critical issues in planning and organizing a corporate transformation effort. The topics of these chapters range from the role of the chief executive to that of lower-level employees in major change efforts. The authors also discuss potential problems that may lead to program failure and suggest strategies for increasing the probability of success.

The six chapters in Part Three consider specific methods and strategies for actually conducting corporate transformation. Based on their participation as researchers and consultants, the authors outline tested methods of implementing and evaluating change in organizational settings — such as creating a corporate vision and evaluating the long-term results of a transformation effort.

Part Four includes five case studies, some written by senior executives who have initiated and managed an entire corporate transformation. Organizations highlighted in this part include National Steel Corporation, Lutheran Health Systems, Westinghouse Electric Corporation, and the Minnesota Department of Labor and Industry. These case studies illustrate why a major change was needed, how it was accomplished, and what was learned from the process.

In the concluding chapter, the editors suggest steps for furthering the knowledge and practice of corporate transformation. Although this book focuses mainly on the psychological aspects of change, other perspectives must be explored to add to our understanding of the strategic, economic, financial, educational, governmental, and international considerations.

Furthermore, corporate transformation is presently viewed as a finite process, with an identifiable beginning and end. Because dynamic environmental changes will undoubtedly continue, transformation must become an ongoing way of managing.

Acknowledgments

Many people played a key role in making possible both the conference and this book. H. J. Zoffer and Andrew R. Blair at the University of Pittsburgh provided the impetus to form the

Program in Corporate Culture and to embark on these major projects. Vee Babyak, administrative assistant for the Program in Corporate Culture, managed all the conference and book arrangements efficiently and effectively, including conference registration and all correspondence. Jeanette Engel worked successfully with the hotel personnel to ensure a smooth operation. Doctoral students Amy Fried, Joyce Shelleman, and Brian Uzzi were invaluable in reviewing manuscripts and managing aspects of the conference.

Finally, we would like to express our appreciation to all the contributors to this book for their ideas and insights and to acknowledge the involvement of the two hundred participants at the conference who asked important and probing questions at every session.

September 1987

Ralph H. Kilmann
Pittsburgh, Pennsylvania

Teresa Joyce Covin
Atlanta, Georgia

The Authors

Ralph H. Kilmann is professor of business administration and director of the Program in Corporate Culture at the Joseph M. Katz Graduate School of Business, University of Pittsburgh. He received both his B.S. and M.S. degrees in industrial administration from Carnegie-Mellon University and his Ph.D. degree in management from the University of California, Los Angeles. Since 1975, he has served as president of Organizational Design Consultants, a Pittsburgh-based firm specializing in the five tracks to organizational success.

Kilmann has published more than one hundred articles and books on such topics as organizational design and strategy, conflict management, and organizational change and development. He is the developer of the MAPS Design Technology and codeveloper of several diagnostic instruments, including the Thomas-Kilmann Conflict Mode Instrument and the Kilmann-Saxton Culture-Gap Survey. One of his publications, *Beyond the Quick Fix: Managing Five Tracks to Organizational Success* (1984), describes his complete program for creating and maintaining an organization's high performance and morale. More recently, Kilmann coauthored *Gaining Control of the Corporate Culture* (with Mary Jane Saxton, Roy Serpa, and Associates, 1985), which integrates the expertise of academics and practitioners in a comprehensive volume on managing culture.

Teresa Joyce Covin is a doctoral candidate at the Joseph M. Katz Graduate School of Business, University of Pittsburgh.

She received her B.A. degree from Saint Bonaventure University and her M.B.A. degree from the University of Pittsburgh. Her research interests include the identification of critical issues in large-scale change efforts and the role of organization development techniques in major change programs. Since 1985, Covin has been affiliated with Organizational Design Consultants in Pittsburgh. She has served on the faculty of Saint Bonaventure University and currently resides in Atlanta, Georgia, where she serves on the faculty of Kennesaw College.

A. Lee Barrett, Jr., is a vice-president and consultant for Responsive Organizations, Inc. He received his B.S. degree in engineering from Purdue University and his M.B.A. and M.P.A. degrees from Harvard University. His interests and skills include organization development, large-systems change, strategic planning, and management systems design and implementation in both the private and public sectors. He has worked with all organizational levels, with both line and staff functions, in blue-collar and white-collar settings, and with both management and union organizations. His most recent clients include Atlas Crankshaft Corporation, American Can Company, and the World Bank.

Richard Beckhard is the executive director of Richard Beckhard Associates, where he is a consultant to a number of industrial and business firms and government agencies in the United States, Europe, and Latin America. Beckhard earned his B.A. degree at Pomona College and served on the faculty of the Sloan School of Management, Massachusetts Institute of Technology, from 1959 to 1984. His current research interests focus on the management of family-owned firms.

Michael Beer is professor of business administration at the Harvard University Graduate School of Business. He received his B.A. degree from Queens College, his M.S. degree from North Carolina State University, and his Ph.D. degree from Ohio State University. Beer was director of organizational research and development at Corning Glass Works from 1964 to

1975. Currently, he is chair of an executive business program, "Managing Change," which is based on his own theory and research on human resource management and organizational change. He is the author or coauthor of numerous books and articles, including *Managing Human Assets* (1984).

William P. Belgard is organization development manager with the Instruments Group at Tektronix, Inc. He earned his B.A. degree in psychology from Chapman College and his M.A. degree in human resources from Pepperdine University. He has gained extensive experience in human resource management through his participation in the Navy Human Resource Management programs, as a private consultant, and as an internal consultant and human resource manager at Tektronix. Presently, Belgard is working with a number of organizations on various corporate transformation issues, including the development of organizational cultures that will permit continuous rapid improvement.

Mary Elizabeth Beres is associate professor of management in the School of Business and Economics at Mercer University in Atlanta, Georgia. She received her B.S. degree in mathematics from Siena Heights College and her Ph.D. degree in organizational behavior from Northwestern University. Her current interests include applying the results of comparative culture research to management practice. She has made numerous presentations on the topics of empowerment, leadership, and organizational transformation.

Michael O. Bice is president and chief executive officer of Lutheran Health Systems, a multi-institutional health care management firm that operates more than seventy hospitals, nursing homes, chemical dependency units, and retirement living programs in thirteen states. He is a graduate of the State University of New York, Binghamton, and received his M.H.A. degree (in hospital administration) from the University of Michigan. Bice has served as a faculty member in the Department of Family and Community Medicine and the College of Professional Studies at the University of Massachusetts. He has also lectured at Clark University, Boston University, Concordia College, and the University of Minnesota.

Robert R. Blake is chairman of Scientific Methods, Inc., a behavioral science firm specializing in education and organization development. He holds a B.A. degree from Berea College, an M.A. degree in psychology from the University of Virginia, and a Ph.D. degree in psychology from the University of Texas, Austin, where he was a professor until 1964. Blake has lectured at Harvard, Oxford, and Cambridge universities, and he is the author or coauthor of numerous articles and books, including *Spectacular Teamwork* (with Jane Mouton and Robert Allen, 1987).

James L. Bowditch is a faculty member at the Boston College School of Management. He received his B.A. degree from Yale University, his M.A. degree in psychology from Western Michigan University, and his Ph.D. degree in industrial and organizational psychology from Purdue University. His current research interests include the quality of work life and the behavioral consequences of corporate mergers. Before his academic career, Bowditch was an officer with the Army Security Agency. Since joining the faculty of Boston College in 1969, he has served as chair of the Department of Organizational Studies and acting dean of the Graduate School of Management.

David E. Bowen is assistant professor of management and organization at the School of Business Administration, University of Southern California. He received his M.B.A. and Ph.D. degrees from Michigan State University. His present research interests focus on models of staff effectiveness and on the definition, measurement, and implementation of service quality. Bowen's recent publications can be found in *Research in Organizational Behavior*, *Academy of Management Review*, and *Organizational Dynamics*.

Anthony F. Buono is associate professor of management at Bentley College. He received his B.S. degree from the University of Maryland and his M.A. and Ph.D. degrees in industrial and organizational sociology from Boston College. Prior to joining the faculty of Bentley College, Buono was an instructor in the Department of Organizational Studies at Boston College. His current research interests include organizational transformation, mergers and acquisitions, and quality of work life. He is the author or coauthor of several books and articles, including recent articles and review essays in *Human Relations* and *Personnel Psychology*.

Anthony F. Chelte is on the faculty of the Department of Management of the School of Business at Western New England College. He earned his Ph.D. degree in industrial sociology from the University of Massachusetts. His dissertation and subsequent research interests have focused on quality of work life, absenteeism, productivity, commitment, leadership, and organizational behavior. Chelte has published articles in the *Journal of Work and Occupations* and *Monthly Labor Review* and has been a consultant for IBM, Digital, and Combustion Engineering.

Katharine Esty is a founder and chairman of the board of the IBIS Consulting Group, an affiliate of Goodmeasure, Inc. She received her B.A. degree from Smith College and her Ph.D. degree in social psychology from Boston University. Over the past fifteen years, Esty has worked as a consultant, manager, and trainer with a wide array of organizations. She has specialized in the areas of large-systems change, innovation, affirmative action, work-group effectiveness, downsizing, and flexible work options. She has been a professional member of the National Training Laboratories Institute for the last nine years and a research associate at Boston University's Center for Applied Social Science.

Russell Fanelli is on the faculty of the Department of Management at Western New England College. He received his Ph.D. degree from Rensselaer Polytechnic Institute and was a visiting fellow in Organizational Behavior at Yale University in 1985 and 1986. Fanelli is a consultant in communication and

1985 and 1986. Fanelli is a consultant in communication and organizational behavior and a founding member and instructor for the Springfield Leadership Institute cosponsored by the Springfield Chamber of Commerce and Western New England College.

William P. Ferris is director of the Resource Center at Western New England College. He earned his B.A. degree from Dartmouth College and his Ph.D. degree from Rensselaer Polytechnic Institute. He has held the position of visiting fellow in Organizational Behavior at the Yale University School of Management, and he is currently a vice-president of the Eastern Academy of Management. Ferris's research and consulting interests include teambuilding, communication, and organization development in business, public schools, and health care organizations.

Michael Finney is an independent management consultant who assists organizations in strategic redesign efforts. He received his B.A. degree in psychology from the University of Arkansas and is currently a Ph.D. candidate at the University of Southern California, where he teaches courses in interpersonal skills and leadership and in designing high productivity organizations. Finney is actively involved in research designed to improve the development and training of international managers. He has been a consultant to AT&T, Medtronic, and First Interstate Bankcorp.

K. Kim Fisher is currently an organization development consultant with Tektronix. He earned his B.A. degree in humanities and his M.O.B. degree (in organizational behavior) from Brigham Young University. He has been a manager and consultant to managers for several years. His other work experience has included production management responsibilities at Procter & Gamble's innovative technician plant in Lima, Ohio, and consulting support for organizational transformations in both unionized and nonunionized settings. Fisher is the author of several articles, including "Management's Role in the Implementation of Participative Management Systems," which appeared in *Human Resource Management.*

Paul Gergen is a clinical psychologist and partner in Organization Technologies, a consulting firm that specializes in assisting organizations undergoing major change. He received his B.A. degree from Fresno State University and his M.S. and Ph.D. degrees from the University of Washington, Seattle. His current research and consulting interests include exploring organizational transformation and examining how individuals deal with large-scale change. Gergen's recent articles (co-authored with Maggie Moore) can be found in *O.D. Practitioner* and *Training and Development Journal.*

Karin Harrington is an associate with Bill Veltrop and Associates. Her work has included documenting the field application of the organizational planning and development process she presents in this volume. She is currently researching strategies that make a lasting impact on organizations and is involved in documenting technologies and developing materials that support organizationwide transformation. Harrington received her B.A. degree in psychology and her M.B.A. degree from the University of California, Berkeley.

Peter Hess is associate professor and chair of the Department of Management at Western New England College, and he has held the position of visiting fellow at Yale University. Hess received his B.A. degree in psychology from Georgetown University and his Ph.D. degree from the University of Massachusetts. His research and consulting interests include leadership, planning, and organizational change.

Edward E. Lawler III is professor of management and organization and director of the Center for Effective Organizations at the University of Southern California. He received his B.A. degree from Brown University and his Ph.D. degree from the University of California, Berkeley. His areas of expertise include the changing work scene; unions and their power base;

productivity; work motivation, pay systems, and organizational change; and participative management strategies. In 1984 Lawler was ranked by his peers as belonging to the nation's top ten leaders in the field of organization development. He is the author or coauthor of more than one hundred fifty articles and fifteen books, the most recent of which is *High-Involvement Management: Participative Strategies for Improving Organizational Performance* (1986).

John W. Lewis III is on the faculty of the Department of Organizational Studies at Boston College. He received his B.A. degree from Ohio Wesleyan University and his Ph.D. degree in organizational behavior from Case Western Reserve University. Before joining academia, Lewis spent eleven years as a human resource executive with TRW, Inc. He has been a consultant to the General Electric Company and Pan Am World Services. His research has focused on building a theory of managerial effectiveness and examining the human aspects of corporate mergers.

Jeffrey K. Liker is assistant professor of industrial and operations engineering at the University of Michigan. He received his B.A. degree in industrial engineering from Northeastern University and his Ph.D. degree in sociology from the University of Massachusetts. He has consulted for many industrial and service organizations on the topic of organizational improvement and is currently conducting research on engineering productivity and the management of new technology. Liker is the author of more than twenty-five articles and chapters in various books.

Howard M. Love is chairman and chief executive officer of National Intergroup, Inc. He received his B.A. degree from Colgate University and his M.B.A. degree from Harvard Business School. He began his career in 1956 as a sales trainee at the Great Lakes Steel division of National Steel Corporation. In 1980 he became chief executive officer of National Steel Corporation. Love has served as a member of the President's Commission on Industrial Competitiveness and is a trustee of Colgate University and the University of Pittsburgh. He is a director and member of the executive committee of the American Iron and Steel Institute.

Maggie Moore is a partner in Organization Technologies and has been an organizational consultant for seven years. She received her B.A. degree in public administration from the University of Oregon and her M.A. degree in organization development from International College of Los Angeles. Moore is the codeveloper (with Paul Gergen) of the Organizational Norms Questionnaire and the Individual Tendencies Scale, instruments designed to assess risk taking in organizations. Her current research and consulting interests include using a risk-taking theory base to assist in the implementation of innovation and transformation.

Jane Srygley Mouton is president and cofounder of Scientific Methods, Inc., and codeveloper of the Managerial Grid, a widely known theory of leadership. Mouton received her B.A. degree in mathematics from the University of Texas, Austin, her M.A. degree in psychology from Florida State University, and her Ph.D. degree in psychology from the University of Texas, Austin, where she was also a faculty member. She is the author or coauthor of numerous books and articles, including *Executive Achievement* (with Robert Blake, 1985).

Thomas J. Murrin is president of the Energy and Advanced Technology Group of Westinghouse Electric Corporation. He received his B.S. degree in physics from Fordham University. He served on the President's Commission on Industrial Competitiveness, and, as a member of the Defense Policy Committee on Trade (DPACT), he is presently serving as chairman of DPACT's Subcommittee on Trade Relations with Japan. Murrin is a member of the National Academy of Engineering and the Aerospace Industries Association, the director of the Atlantic Council, and the chairman of Mercy Hospital in Pittsburgh.

Stephen J. Musser is associate professor of management at Messiah College. He received his B.A. degree from Albright College and his M.A. degree in labor economics and his Ph.D. degree in organizational behavior from Temple University. Musser's current research interest is the role of ideas in power redistribution within organizations. He has published articles in the areas of conflict management and labor relations and he is the editor of the *Newsletter of the Conflict Management Group*, a publication for individuals interested in conflict management.

David A. Nadler is the president of the Delta Consulting Group, which specializes in organizational research and consulting. Previously, he was an associate professor in the Graduate School of Business at Columbia University. Nadler received his B.A. degree in political science from George Washington University, his M.B.A. degree from the Harvard Business School, and his Ph.D. degree in organizational psychology from the University of Michigan. He is the author of numerous books and articles concerning organizational behavior and change.

William H. Newman is professor and research director at the Management Institute, Graduate School of Business, Columbia University. He earned his Ph.D. degree from the University of Chicago and served on the faculty of the Wharton School at the University of Pennsylvania prior to joining the faculty of Columbia University. Newman has been a management consultant for more than thirty-five years and has held many management positions in government and industry. He is a fellow and past president of the Academy of Management and the author or coauthor of numerous books and articles, including *The Process of Management*, 6th ed. (1987).

Lee M. Ozley is founder of Responsive Organizations, Inc. (ROI). Prior to founding ROI, he spent twenty years in the field of organizational consulting as a third-party consultant and in various operational and staff positions in both corporations and labor organizations. He was executive director of the American Center for Quality of Work Life, where he was involved in some of the pioneering work in participative management, labor-management cooperation, and quality-of-work-life activities. Ozley earned his B.S. degree in economics and psychology at Auburn University and his M.S. degree in industrial psychology at the University of Wisconsin.

Christine M. Pearson is a lecturer in the areas of management and organization and academic area coordinator at the Management Effectiveness Executive Program, Graduate School of Business Administration, University of Southern California. She is also completing her Ph.D. degree at the University of Southern California. Her current research focuses on the sociopsychological impact of organizational change and the effects of the interaction between work and family on employees and family members. As a management consultant, Pearson's clients include American Honda Motor Company, the State of California, and the Small Business Administration.

Steven R. Rayner is a senior organization development consultant with Tektronix, Inc. He received his B.A. degree from Lewis and Clark College and his M.S. degree in organization development from Pepperdine University. He is the author of *New Excellence: The Forest Grove Project*, which examines the high-involvement management practices introduced at the Tektronix circuit board plant in Forest Grove, Oregon. In addition, Rayner is the editor of *The Progressive Organization*, a newsletter dedicated to assisting organizational leaders in managing complex change.

David O. Renz is executive director of the Metropolitan Council of the Twin Cities, an intergovernmental organization for planning and coordinating regional development and growth, headquartered in Saint Paul, Minnesota. He received his B.S. degree in communications, his M.A. degree in industrial relations, and his Ph.D. degree in organizational theory and behavior from the University of Minnesota. Renz's chapter in this volume was written while he was the assistant commissioner of the Department of Labor and Industry, State of Minnesota.

David B. Roitman is a researcher and project manager at the Center for Social and Economic Issues, Industrial Technology Institute (ITI). He received his B.A. degree in psychology from the University of Arkansas and his M.A. and Ph.D. degrees in psychology from Michigan State University. He has conducted research and consulted on a variety of projects involving the implementation of advanced manufacturing technology. Roitman is the author of more than twenty-five articles, reports, and papers on innovation, organizational change, and technology transfer.

Ethel Roskies is professor of psychology at the University of Montreal. She received her B.A. and M.A. degrees in political science from McGill University, and a second M.A. degree in psychology and a Ph.D. degree in clinical psychology from the University of Montreal. She was a visiting scholar at the Institute for Social Research, University of Michigan, where she became involved with the project she discusses in this volume. Her current research concerns the effects of job insecurity on individual well-being and job performance. Roskies's book, *Stress Management for the Healthy Type A: Theory and Practice* was published in 1987.

Caren Siehl is assistant professor of management and organization at the School of Business Administration, University of Southern California. She received her Ph.D. degree in organizational behavior at the Graduate School of Business, Stanford University. She is currently conducting research on the impact of organizational culture on mergers and acquisitions and on the use of cultural artifacts to improve the provision of quality service. One of Siehl's most recent publications, "After the Founder: An Opportunity to Manage Culture," appeared in *Organizational Culture* (1985).

Michael L. Tushman is professor of management at the Graduate School of Business, Columbia University, and vice-president of the Delta Consulting Group. He received his B.S. degree from Northeastern University, his M.S. degree from

Cornell University, and his Ph.D. degree from the Massachusetts Institute of Technology. His current interests are in the areas of organizational innovation, research, and development, and strategic organizational adaptation. Tushman is the author of numerous books and articles and has worldwide consulting experience.

Bill Veltrop is a management consultant who specializes in large-systems development, redesign, and renewal and a principal with Bill Veltrop and Associates. He worked at Exxon Corporation for thirty-three years, during which time he played a principal role in the successful Baytown Refinery Renewal effort and initiated the organization development function at Exxon Enterprises, Inc. Veltrop also served as the internal consultant to the Rotterdam Refinery organizational renewal effort. He is a member of Certified Consultants International and the Organization Development Institute.

Corporate Transformation

Ralph H. Kilmann
Teresa Joyce Covin

1

Introduction: Key Themes in Corporate Transformation

Corporate transformation is a new phenomenon. Never before in the history of the world have so many organizations had to question their very purpose, strategy, structure, and culture as they have had to do in the 1980s. No senior executives of any organization today could or would dispute that one of their major responsibilities is to revitalize their organizations for a competitive world. There is thus a critical need for theories and methods that will allow organizations to conduct transformations efficiently and effectively. Without this knowledge base, mere trial-and-error learning will exact too high a price: American companies will experience severe economic and psychological hardships while other countries reap the benefits of their competitive advantage in the global economy.

It is hardly an overstatement to suggest that the fundamental cause of economic prosperity is a function of organized effort. Organizations and institutions, in fact, must be considered the greatest invention of all time. If human beings could not transcend their own physical, biological, social, and mental limitations through organized action, other great inventions — including everyday products and services — could not have been created and brought to the marketplace. But it now seems that the major trading and producing nations are fighting an eco-

1

nomic war: life-and-death competition based on who has the best organizations for providing goods and services to the people of the world.

To learn about, plan for, and implement major organizational change where needed thus becomes the highest priority for long-term survival and prosperity. Businesses and governments must take this challenge seriously. In a regulated environment, organizations can live with inefficiencies for quite some time. In a competitive environment, organizations can and will die quickly. As a contribution to solving this critical problem of national well-being, this book seeks to provide academics, consultants, and practitioners with state-of-the-art knowledge about corporate transformation.

As the various chapters in this book will attest, each author has a somewhat different way of defining organizational transformation. While we view transformation as a systemwide change in an organization that demands new ways of perceiving, thinking, and behaving by all its members, full consensus on this concept among academics and practitioners cannot be expected at this time. Nevertheless, the objective of this introductory chapter is to summarize some areas of agreement and disagreement concerning the meaning and practice of corporate transformation. These themes emerged from our review of conference papers and from our attendance at conference presentations and debates (a more elaborate description of the review process and the conference proceedings is provided in the Preface).

Areas of Agreement

A recurring discussion at the conference concerned the difference between corporate transformation and the three-decade-old field of organization development. If, in fact, transformation is only different in degree and not in kind, then there would appear to be little justification for adding one more academic term to the already jargon-filled social sciences. The general consensus, however, is that transformation *is* qualitatively different from organization development and, even more importantly, that to keep the new ideas of transformation under the rubric of organization development would be to give them "the kiss of death." Essentially, organization development relies on such focused techniques as teambuilding (as an outgrowth of the T-group movement) and is typically applied to isolated parts of the organization with little awareness or support on the part of top management. As will be seen below, transformation must be conducted quite differently if organizations are to be fundamentally changed for today's competitive world versus being fine tuned for yesterday's world. In any event, the following ten areas of agreement were identified at the conference:

1. *Transformation is a response to environmental and technological change by different types of organizations.* There was strong consensus that forces in the environment have provided the impetus for transformation efforts (Tushman, Newman, and Nadler in Chapter Six). In some cases, it seemed that the organization had absolutely no choice but to make fundamental changes to adapt to a very different business environment (Love, Barrett, and Ozley in Chapter Seventeen). It generally was acknowledged that the early efforts at organization development were often spurred on by special advocates or by interest in experimenting with new management methods — but not for the prime reason of survival in a changed world. In addition, it was recognized that transformation is now taking place in many different types of organizations — in different ways *because of* different environmental demands. For example, Renz (Chapter Twenty) examines change in a government bureaucracy; Roitman, Liker, and Roskies (Chapter Ten) consider a manufacturing organization; Beres and Musser (Chapter Eight) explore changes in an organization of nuns in the Roman Catholic church.

2. *Transformation is a new model of the organization for the future.* Since transformation is generally viewed as revolutionary rather than evolutionary, organizational members — particularly top management — must be able to envision a new reality for their organization: an ideal state that is fundamentally different from the present state. Otherwise, members will not under-

stand the reasons for undergoing such a concerted effort if fine tuning and incremental change appear to be sufficient, as they have been in the past. Breaking out of the old ways of viewing an organization (Nadler in Chapter Four) and formulating new blueprints for action (Finney, Bowen, Pearson, and Siehl in Chapter Twelve) were seen as a prerequisite to any transformation effort. For some, creating a new vision is the most important part of the process.

3. *Transformation is based on dissatisfaction with the old and belief in the new.* Before top executives and organizational members will commit themselves to upsetting their customary ways of behaving, there must be dissatisfaction and discontent. Typically, the performance of the organization has been disappointing and morale has been fading. It seems that the old ways of doing business just do not work anymore (Lawler in Chapter Three). A realization of this predicament by key executives, however, is not enough. There must be some consensus that a new organization *can* be created to replace what is experienced as inadequate now. It is one thing for a top management group to provide a vision, it is another for the key players to *believe* that this vision is viable and obtainable. Unless this belief is widespread, members will not give up the present for some ill-defined fantasy in the future.

4. *Transformation is a qualitatively different way of perceiving, thinking, and behaving.* There seems to be strong agreement that members throughout the organization must function quite differently if the transformation effort is to be successful. Specifically, it may be necessary for members to perceive multiple causes of performance problems, to think in dialectical, paradoxical ways, and to enact more trusting and risk-taking behavior. Just changing the documents, such as job descriptions, rules, regulations, and policies, is not enough to ensure such a fundamentally different way of functioning. Only if the changes in documents result in changes in *behavior* has a true transformation taken place (Buono, Bowditch, and Lewis in Chapter Twenty-One). It must be understood, however, that the tremendous pressure for behavior change is also very painful to organizational members. Lawler (Chapter Three) considers how much

it hurts for top managers to give up a role they have been playing for so long; Love, Barrett, and Ozley (Chapter Seventeen) emphasize how difficult it was to leave "steel" behind in the transformation of National Steel Corporation; Buono, Bowditch, and Lewis (Chapter Twenty-One) underscore the anxiety provoked by an upcoming merger or acquisition; Moore and Gergen (Chapter Sixteen) go so far as to propose a method for easing the pain of change. It might be said, in fact, that if all members in the organization do not experience some amount of anxiety and pain, it is unlikely that a real transformation is underway.

5. *Transformation is expected to spread throughout the organization at different rates of absorption.* The transformation is not intended to occur for just one or a few divisions in the organization, as is typically the case for organization development efforts. The expectation is that the entire organization will be affected — that transformation will be organizationwide or systemwide. It is recognized, however, that one or more pilot projects might be conducted first to test out the chosen strategies and methods of transformation and that a plan then be developed for transferring the results of the pilot project to the remaining organizational units. Also, since different business units might require different degrees of transformation and may have different capacities for learning and change, the rate of absorption in each unit will be different. Some units will be transformed sooner and more easily than others, but *all* units will be significantly affected in some way. However, failure to recognize the different capacity and willingness to change across different organizations and units within an organization can lead to unhappy results. Hess, Ferris, Chelte, and Fanelli (Chapter Nine) and Roitman, Liker, and Roskies (Chapter Ten) describe unsuccessful transformations that resulted from unrealistic expectations and from overly ambitious efforts to change things too fast.

6. *Transformation is driven by line management.* While most organizational development efforts seem to be led by human resource, human relations, industrial relations, personnel, or similar staff groups, transformation should be led by line management, preferably by top management. With top management

behind the change effort, the necessary resources and commitment to conduct transformation will be available. Furthermore, with top management leading the charge, the necessary priority will be given to the transformation effort in spite of all the pressures to concentrate on here-and-now business problems and operational issues (Bice in Chapter Eighteen).

7. *Transformation is ongoing, endless, and forever.* Most traditional improvement efforts are characterized by a well-defined time frame. In the extreme case, such efforts are viewed as the "program for the year"—management by objectives, quality circles, small venture groups, special recognition plans, and intrapreneuring. In contrast, a transformation effort is much more ill defined and may last anywhere from three to ten years. When transformation is "complete," the organization would once again concentrate on fine tuning its operations and incremental change; but conference participants wondered whether transformation would ever end. Since no one has been able to point to a complete transformation, the present belief seems to be that the world will never sit still long enough to bring any transformation program to completion. In fact, some felt that transformation should not be referred to as a program—with a finite beginning and end—but as the new way of managing today's organizations. Managing change in a proactive, continuous, and evolutionary manner might enable organizations to stay in tune with a dynamic environment, thereby avoiding the pain and disruption of a more reactive, acute, and revolutionary catch-up effort.

8. *Transformation is orchestrated by inside and outside experts.* While top management is responsible for leading the transformation effort, there was consensus that outside experts should be used to facilitate at least some parts of the process. Because of all the transformation efforts that have been initiated in the past few years, there is a wealth of knowledge that goes beyond what any one organization has learned on its own. Outside experts may have more experience dealing with different types of clients than inside consultants working with only one or a few organizations. Moreover, outside experts may have more detailed knowledge of change techniques (for example, how to build commit-

ment, diagnose organizational problems, and spread change) than line managers. Even in cases where internal organizational development practitioners are available, the special kind of credibility and lack of vested interest on the part of outside experts does argue for their use. The ideal case, undeniably, seems to be a *team* effort involving line managers, external consultants, and internal consultants. Such a team effort allows the greatest probability of understanding the strengths and weaknesses of the organization and of overcoming the limitations of viewing the organization from one point of view.

9. *Transformation represents the leading edge of knowledge about organizational change.* Since cases of "complete" transformation are rare, there is little knowledge derived from evaluating whole, large-scale, organizationwide corporate transformations. Thus, what is known about organizational transformations is rapidly evolving. Transformation, then, requires risk taking and experimentation. The frontiers of knowledge in this field are pushed forward every time some significant and qualitatively different form of organization is revitalized. This state of affairs also means that organizations requiring transformation cannot wait until the knowledge base is firm and predictable. Such questions as "can you prove to me that this process will work?" cannot be answered in the affirmative. Perhaps one answer is to work together and try to make it happen with what is now known. Actually, any organization that plans to wait for the methods for transformation to be proven effective is probably writing its own epitaph.

10. *Transformation generates more open communication and feedback throughout the organization.* While there was considerable uncertainty regarding the "end state" of transformation, experience indicates that many different methods and approaches have one common goal: to increase the flow of information across all levels of the hierarchy and across all organizational units as a result of a transformation effort. Such an increase in communication and feedback seems to foster better problem-solving efforts (because each person knows more about what is going on inside and outside the organization) and a commitment to be more efficient, effective, and competitive (because

people can commit to excellence if they know what needs to be done and why). Thus, such spreading and sharing of information may be a by-product of any transformation effort beyond the other benefits that can be expected. At the same time, this widespread sharing of information enables both managers and consultants to monitor the impact of their change efforts and to make the necessary adjustments to improve the process of implementation.

Areas of Disagreement

While the forgoing themes received considerable support at the conference, there were also a number of issues that resulted in some disagreement. These issues were discussed at length at the conference but could not be completely resolved. In most instances, they involved more detailed concerns while the issues on which agreement was reached were more general in nature. Seven unresolved issues are briefly presented as questions below, indicating that the answers require considerably more research and discussion:

1. *How much top management commitment and involvement are necessary in any transformation effort?* This question concerned just how much priority should be given to organizational change and how much direct time and effort of top management are necessary for success. Some participants in the audience felt that transformation should be given the highest priority while others felt that such a commitment is unrealistic. Numerous business issues surface from time to time that demand the full attention of the top management group — for example, a hostile takeover bid. Others felt that the role of top management is to ensure that transformation takes place under any set of circumstances. Examples were cited showing that many "excuses" can be and have been given to retreat from transformation in the face of new business issues. Perhaps if transformation proceeded as the top priority, all other issues would be more easily managed in time. Regarding direct involvement by the chief executive officer (CEO) and other senior executives, the debate was divided into what management activities should or should

not be delegated to others and what signals would be sent if top management "talked transformation" but did not actually take part in the process. Is the involvement of top managers sufficient if they make sure that everyone else will be transformed or do they need to ensure that they *themselves* will be transformed along with everyone else — as active participants in all aspects of the transformation effort.

2. *Is charismatic leadership required for successful transformation?* The debate on this issue often hinged on whether the CEO must provide charismatic leadership in order to spearhead corporate transformation. What if the CEO is not Lee Iacocca of Chrysler or Jack Welch of General Electric? To have an "ordinary" CEO attempt to communicate the necessary enthusiasm and vision for the whole corporation seemed to be asking too much. But if not the CEO, what about a charismatic senior executive? For some individuals at the conference, this seemed plausible *if such a person was available*. The major concern was whether transformation could take place without a charismatic top manager. It seemed that most of the popular examples of transformation in process had a rather dynamic person in charge. Clearly, the role of the leader in driving such a change effort, as well as his or her particular management and personal style, is open to further exploration.

3. *Where should transformation start? Does it matter?* This issue centers on such distinctions as top-down versus bottom-up efforts at change. It seems that organization development experts are more likely to endorse a bottom-up, participative approach to transformation (Belgard, Fisher, and Rayner in Chapter Seven; Beres and Musser in Chapter Eight). Those individuals who focus on the strategic aspects of transformation (in contrast to the human aspects) seem more inclined to start with a top-down approach (Beckhard in Chapter Five; Bice in Chapter Eighteen). Perhaps a simultaneous top-down and bottom-up approach will ensure the necessary involvement and commitment by all members of the organization. Furthermore, the issue of where transformation should start involves a determination of which division or business unit should be chosen as the pilot project. Some feel that the core business unit should be

chosen as a sign of the importance of the effort and to serve as a suitable role model for the remaining organizational units (Beer in Chapter Two). Others believe that, given the limited experience base and therefore the sizable risks involved in transforming organizations, one of the more inconsequential units should be chosen for the transformation "experiment." The question of whether or not it makes a difference where one starts the effort, however, was also left unresolved, if for no other reason than that there have not been enough transformation efforts documented to make such comparisons.

4. *Must transformation involve changes in all aspects of the organization?* This issue received more debate than perhaps any other, since this question seems to pit one expert's target of change (both a theory and an action lever) against another target of change. While there was considerable agreement that transformation requires major changes in several aspects of organizational behavior, can such fundamental changes be accomplished by a training and development program, by a new reward system, by strategy and structure modifications, by documenting a new set of corporate values, by a new union contract? It seems that each inside and outside expert has his or her favorite intervention method and thinks that fundamental change can occur by that method alone. Those consultants who specialize in reward systems believe that changes in the pay-for-performance relationship will cause significant changes in behavior. Line managers who pride themselves on clear communication believe that well-written memos and ongoing conversations will convince people to change. Several "levers" for change are discussed by authors in this volume. For example, Esty (Chapter Fifteen) concentrates on the development of group structures, Murrin (Chapter Nineteen) focuses on organizational culture, and Blake and Mouton (Chapter Eleven) emphasize the importance of the power and authority system as a starting point for change. Kilmann (Chapter Thirteen) and Veltrop and Harrington (Chapter Fourteen) argue for a combined set of interventions to address several aspects of organizational behavior.

5. *Can organizational transformation take place without per-*

sonal transformation? If organizational transformation requires that most organizational members begin to perceive, think, and behave in fundamentally different ways, do members themselves, as individuals, need to be radically transformed as well? Some in the conference audience suggested that transformation may involve a personal crisis for the individuals affected by it. Think, for example, of senior executives who made it to the top after struggling for twenty years to master corporate politics. Now they are asked to forget what made them so successful and to begin perceiving, thinking, and behaving in altogether different ways. Such executives might very well panic if asked to question the basis of their self-esteem, self-confidence, and sense of competence. Corporate transformation, therefore, might well be associated with deep personal traumas requiring serious self-reflection, internal conflict, and personal resolution before an organizational transformation can really be evident. But others in the audience suggested that such personal transformation is very much a separate and distinct issue and would not be brought about by the transformation effort itself. For persons holding this view, the belief seems to be that organizational members should keep their personal struggles removed from their jobs and positions; significant change can occur in the organization without major upheaval in the lives of its members. In essence, this unresolved issue seems to be focused on whether such a separation can be made between person and organization, and whether the requirements of organizational change will necessarily result in personal change.

6. *How can top managers and others be encouraged to anticipate change instead of reacting to crisis situations?* Most or all efforts at transformation seem to stem from significant environmental changes that have gradually caught the organization off guard or have taken the organization completely by surprise. Thus, transformation becomes a *reaction* to environmental change, a necessary adjustment in order to survive in a competitive world. Many persons in the conference audience and much discussion in the conference papers highlighted the reactive nature of human beings in general and the special problems created by an organization's traditions and inertia. Others in the audience

and some of the authors, however, emphasized that top management must be *proactive* and learn to anticipate environmental changes before their organizations are caught in a bind (Nadler in Chapter Four). This proactive stance would provide the organization with the time to carefully plan and implement corporate transformation under noncrisis situations—a seemingly more desirable circumstance in all ways. At the very least, if transformation does change the attitudes and behaviors of top managers and others, then these individuals would be more likely to be proactive in the future. Whether a proactive style can be encouraged *before* any major transformation is conducted is what the debate on this issue seems to be about.

7. *What is the role of the human resources function in the transformation effort?* Previous efforts at organization development were often led by persons in human resource, human relations, industrial relations, employee relations, or personnel departments. However, if transformation is to be driven by top management, as most members of the conference audience and most authors in this volume think it should be, what is the *new* role for these staff groups? While most of the discussion on this issue outlined the greater support role that human resource individuals would play in recruiting, allocating, training, counseling, developing, and inspiring organizational members to fit the transformed organization, there was considerable uneasiness—especially among the human resource experts in the audience—about "losing" critical functions to top management. How much of this uneasiness and discomfort was based on protecting a traditional domain versus genuine concern about what is best for the organization, is hard to say. Nevertheless, there was some discussion at the conference that recognized what is truly meant by transformation: *everybody's* job and function would undergo significant change and not just the job and function of the human resource professionals; *everybody* would feel that he or she was losing some of the power, control, and security enjoyed in the past. Perhaps an important step in the early stages of transformation is to show people what both they and the organization can gain from the *outcome* of the effort so that the focus is not exclusively on the costs of the process.

Otherwise, resistance and anxiety about the process might prevent transformation from taking hold.

Conclusion

Ten areas of agreement about corporate transformation and seven areas of disagreement have been summarized in this chapter. These themes represent a capsulated view of the current thinking in the field and highlight some areas that clearly deserve further exploration. The following chapters examine these key themes either directly or indirectly and thus provide the reader with a comprehensive story of how many organizations are addressing the problems and opportunities associated with transformation.

Part One

Defining and Understanding Corporate Transformation

Part One provides an overview of what corporate transformation is and why it is of crucial importance at this point in time. The following three chapters provide a theoretical grounding, as well as some practical considerations, for managing organizationwide transformation.

In Chapter Two, Michael Beer examines the change efforts of six companies and, in contrasting successful and unsuccessful efforts, draws important lessons for companies that are considering major transformations. The author emphasizes the importance of determining the tasks essential for success, so that the organization can select the critical path for change. His discussion of why some organizations succeed in the difficult task of transformation while others fall short provides an overview of many of the issues discussed in more detail in later chapters.

Edward E. Lawler III then describes the paradigm shift in management styles that is taking place in today's organizations. Lawler describes the types of changes now occurring, the reasons for these changes, and what must be done in order for these changes to be successful. The author suggests that more and more organizations are shifting from a bureaucratic, control-oriented managerial style to an approach that is based on commitment and involvement, and he argues that much more can be done to encourage this kind of shift. While the movement toward involvement and commitment may cause a great deal of pain for many members of the organization, Lawler cites examples from several industries to show that this type of transformation has many potential benefits.

David A. Nadler concludes this introductory section by presenting a framework of various types of large-scale organizational changes based on his many years of experience with such changes. He discusses re-creation, reorientation, adaptation, and tuning as four distinct types of change that an organization might experience. The author suggests that the change efforts of today are quite different from those of the 1960s and 1970s.

This overview will provide the reader with a macroview of some of the key issues in corporate transformation. Part Two of the book will provide a more in-depth discussion of the critical issues that should be considered when a company plans and organizes for major organizational change.

2

Michael Beer

❦ ❦ ❦ ❦ ❦ ❦ ❦ ❦

The Critical Path for Change: Keys to Success and Failure in Six Companies

The pressures of global competition and deregulation have led many corporations in industries such as autos, rubber, steel, consumer electronics, airlines, and banking to search for ways to compete more effectively. At stake is their very survival. The search is leading corporations to transform their means of organizing and managing their human resources. This chapter is about the *strategy for corporate change* employed by companies that have made significant progress in the difficult task of transformation. That choice of strategy proved to be far more important to their success than the particular model for managing human resources that they applied.

A paradigmatic shift is now underway. Historically, corporations have relied on *control* from the top to achieve results. The new, but still emerging, model relies on developing employee *commitment* (Walton, 1985). Traditionally, corporations used clear lines of authority, rules, procedures, and the division of work to maintain control, to ensure *stability* and predictability. On the shop floor or in the office, jobs were narrowly defined. Employees were expected to commit their hands but seldom their hearts and minds. At the management level, corporations

17

tended to have too many organizational layers, to be organized functionally, and to rely on large corporate staff groups to act as watchdogs. Information flowed to the top, and all important decisions were made there. Decisions were then communicated down the channels for implementation by individuals and groups whose responsibilities were clearly prescribed by job descriptions and procedures developed over many years.

The competitive environment of the 1980s, however, has caused corporations to search for a different model, a more effective way of organizing and managing people. Although still being shaped by practicing managers in response to the competitive pressures of today's environment, the new model appears to place a greater premium on *adaptability*, that is, on the organization's capacity to respond to a dynamic business environment. Thus, employees in factories are being given broader responsibilities and are increasingly involved in decisions. This is taking the form of ad hoc problem-solving groups, better employee communication, and organization of work groups around "whole" tasks with responsibility and accountability to accomplish the job. The result is a significant shift in authority for day-to-day decisions from managers and plant staff groups to production employees.

In unionized companies this transformation depends on the cooperation of unions. Adversarial union-management relationships are giving way to more cooperative ones. In some companies union leaders are consulted about personnel, manufacturing, and marketing policies that are outside the collective bargaining process. Such involvement is often a quid pro quo for wage and work-rule concessions that unions have granted to help companies survive.

At the management level corporations are becoming flatter, leaner, and less functionally oriented. Levels of management are being eliminated and corporate staffs are being reduced or devolved to decentralized business units. Responsibility, power, and accountability are being shifted to executives in charge of focused business units. As these changes take place, effort is being directed to improving coordination between interdependent functions and related business units. Task forces, product and business teams, general management boards, and key account teams, which cut across historically impervious organizational lines, are created in an effort to add value to products and services (Porter, 1985).

Competitive advantage in industries under pressure from global competition or deregulation depends in part on the rapidity, efficiency, and effectiveness with which companies can move to this new model. The transformation underway is nothing less than a *cultural revolution*. Top managers now have to be able to assume the role of change agents, something never required in less competitive environments. Zane Barnes, CEO of Southwestern Bell, a company heavily impacted by deregulation, put it this way: "My point is simply this . . . managing organizational change is a topic American business needs to examine and understand. Because fundamental change will be the order of the day for the foreseeable future. And, obviously, the company that can adapt its culture to change — quickly and successfully — will have a powerful competitive advantage" (Barnes, 1985). An examination of six companies attempting to make the transformation described above indicates that such changes are difficult to make. Not all the companies were equally successful. Consider the most successful company (corporation A) and the least successful company (corporation F) in the sample:

> Corporation A, with $10 billion in sales, largely a single product, began a transformation in 1977. Experiencing competitive pressures and a long strike, the CEO commissioned a project to build a new nonunion plant. With the help of a newly hired corporate director of organization development, the plant became a highly successful and visible example of the emergent model for organizing and managing. Under the leadership of its chief operating officer (COO) and vice-president of manufacturing, the company began to spread the new model to other new plants and to a number of older, unionized plants. Several domestic and

international subsidiaries, as well as the company's
research and development center, also undertook
to transform themselves. By 1986 about one-third
of the corporation's plants were far along in the
transformation. Approximately another third were
underway but less advanced, and a third were not
yet engaged in a transformation. Top managers at
headquarters talked knowledgeably and consistently about the type of changes being made and
the new breed of manager required. While the
change process had not yet touched most of the
corporate staff, transformation of the corporation's
approach to organizing and managing was a well-
established competitive strategy.

Corporation F, with $4 billion in sales in
related product lines, began the transformation
process in 1979. After hearing about innovations in
organizing and managing, the then executive vice-
president in charge of domestic operations formed
a motivation committee composed of several top
managers to evaluate and later introduce new approaches. The vice-president saw these approaches
as a vehicle for transforming a lethargic and medi-
ocre company (in terms of financial performance)
into a dynamic and profitable one. Consultants
arrived to educate top management. A new director of education and organization development
was brought in to help stimulate and encourage
change. Under the leadership of another executive
vice-president, a new model plant was started up in
1981. By 1986 the executive vice-president who
started the change process had become the CEO.
However, in an interview he admitted the corporation had not been successful in making the cultural
transformation envisioned in 1979. The model
plant did not perform well and therefore failed to
establish the efficacy of its innovative approaches

to organizing and managing. The director of education and organization development had left the company three years earlier, and his corporate staff group disbanded. While the company had substantially reduced corporate staff and had a number of plants organizing and managing people in a more innovative manner, no systematic, centrally orchestrated strategy for transforming the corporation existed. Top managers at headquarters did not speak knowledgeably and consistently about a new model of managing. Indeed, one top manager said the senior management eduation program had failed to transform the company. The CEO, with some concern, candidly described the new COO he was about to appoint as a traditional manager who did not have much sympathy for the new management model.

How could two corporations undergoing transformation in organizing and managing human resources at approximately the same time achieve such dramatically different results? Both efforts had top management support. Both used the same consultants. Both established a corporate staff group to stimulate and support innovations in management by the line. Both more than adequately resourced the transformation effort in the early years with time, money, and visible involvement of top management. Why, then, did one succeed and the other fail?

The remainder of this chapter is devoted to examining this question. Conclusions are based on an intensive study of six corporations that have been engaged in an effort to change the organization and management of their human resources (Beer, Eisenstat, and Spector, 1986). The six companies studied are all large corporations with sales ranging from $3 billion to $10 billion. Companies A and C are single-product companies in the rubber industry and steel industry, respectively. Company F is a manufacturer of container products that require the use of various materials and technologies. Companies B and E are multibusiness firms serving the aerospace, computer, power generation, broadcasting, and control system markets. Company D is a large multinational bank. All the manufacturing companies are unionized, although only the steel company bargains nationally.

Findings from the six companies were supplemented by contact that the investigators had with a dozen other corporations undergoing similar transformations. The six corporations were selected on the basis of their known efforts to transform the way their human resources were organized and managed. As the investigation proceeded, it became clear that two companies (referred to as A and B) had made significant progress in the scope and extent of the transformation when judged by the following criteria:

1. Innovativeness in approaches to organizing and managing
2. Penetration of the change throughout the corporation
3. Making the transformation more than the sum of the changes in the corporation's various subunits. The companies were engaged in a synergistic transformation, not simply a number of unconnected subunit transformations.

Companies C and D were judged to have made only moderate progress when the criteria above were applied, and companies E and F were seen to have made relatively little progress. Conclusions can be drawn about the essential ingredients in corporatewide transformations by examining differences between the corporate change leaders and laggards as well as cases of success and failure within subunits of all six corporations.

The Fallacy of Programmatic Change

When asked about the transformation going on in their company, corporate human resource executives typically began to describe the series of programs that were being implemented. They discussed programs such as quality circles, a new compensation system, a new performance appraisal system, or a widely attended educational program. Though each of these programs still had enthusiastic supporters at corporate headquarters, most line managers saw them as ineffective. In no instance did line managers indicate that these programs were playing a major role in the transformation. At the time of their implementation these programs were heralded as the centerpiece of the transformation. They received the ringing endorsement of top management and were more than adequately resourced with money, management time, and consulting resources. Consider the following examples:

Management Education. Company F instituted an advanced management program designed to expose its high-potential middle managers to ideas about business strategy, organizing and managing people, leadership, and interpersonal relations. This program was so well received that participants asked their bosses—senior managers—to go through a similar program, and about 100 senior managers did complete a shortened version of it. Although many participants told us they learned a significant amount about organizing and managing people, they also acknowledged that the program had surprisingly little impact on the corporation's culture. Five years after the program had been completed a top manager who had been through the shortened version and whole heartedly supported the transformation said, "The program had absolutely no impact on the company!"

Quality Circles. Company E utilized the quality circle as an early strategy for change. A productivity and quality center was created to coordinate the spread of quality circles throughout the corporation. Top management held lower-level managers accountable for the number of quality circles in their unit. Despite this interest by top management, the program received negative evaluations. Managers pointed to top management's interest in the *number* of circles rather than in the fundamental cultural transformation they were intended to spur. Managers also complained that quality circles did not necessarily address their most pressing business problems. The imposition of quality circles, intended to improve manufacturing efficiency, actually took energy away from more important customer service problems in one business unit.

Mission and Philosophy Statements. An extensive year-long effort involving task forces composed of one hundred managers was launched to develop consensus on strategy and management philosophy in one company not in our original sample of six companies. The outcome was an extremely sophisticated statement of assumptions about people, as well as explicit guidelines for managerial behavior consistent with the goals of the transformation. The CEO's top management team, composed of all heads of the major business units, signed on to the final product, a strategy and mission statement that was disseminated throughout the company. When the corporate human resource staff tried to engage these executives and their organization in a transformation effort, however, they met with resistance. This happened despite the fact, or perhaps because of the fact, that in two units a transformation effort consistent with the management philosophy was already underway.

Culture Programs. In company D, one of the companies making only moderate progress in its transformation, a year-long effort to define a new culture and communicate it to all employees failed to stimulate significant change, despite top management's involvement in examining the old culture and defining the new one. Two years after the completion of this program, corporate human resource executives were troubled by the lack of any real changes in the behavior of managers, even though the managers had given considerable verbal support to them.

Why Do Programs Fail?

There are many other examples of programs that fail to develop momentum even though initiated at the top of the corporation. Many are excellent in conception and gain early and enthusiastic support of managers, only to be evaluated later as contributing little to transforming the corporation's culture.

One executive summed it up this way: "I had witnessed some very disturbing experiences the past several years with programs such as zero defects, quality circles, and so on. So often these programs were seen as gimmickry by the working people and as magic by the managers. In most cases they were implemented through management edicts and directives. I am not interested in just another short-lived program." Serious questions should be raised about the value of high-profile corporate programs for revitalization when one considers that company A, a change leader in the sample of six companies, *never* developed a mission statement, defined a philosophy, initiated a quality circle program, or tried to launch any other corporate program!

But should major corporate programs having top-level support fail to develop momentum for change? By the very fact that they are conceived and implemented from the top, corporate programs are often not relevant to the most pressing business problems facing different plants, branches, and divisions. At best these programs are a response to a general diagnosis of corporate problems, not a specific diagnosis of the highest-priority problems facing a given subunit. At worst these programs are fads imported without a proper diagnosis of the strategic problems facing the company and the changes in organization and management methods required for their solution. Their top-down character makes it difficult for employees to feel a sense of ownership in the program. The purpose, even if potentially relevant to the organizational unit, is too easily dismissed as not useful when it originates at the top.

Corporate programs tend to be unidimensional. They cannot change the many aspects of an organization—structure, systems, managerial style, people and politics—required for behaviors and attitudes to change permanently. Moreover, programs are often time bound, a week's training program or a monthly award. Effective organization requires follow-up over an extended period of time, not one week and a slogan.

In addition, programs are seldom targeted at behavior. Instead, they use words transmitted in classes, memoranda, speeches, and glossy booklets. Employees have difficulty translating these words into behavioral changes. Nor does mastery of the words mean that managers have mastered the new skills. Consider a conference of key executives on the theme of quality. Executive after executive makes an impressive and sophisticated presentation regarding programs for transforming his or her division's culture by removing "unquality" decisions and methods. When asked, however, human resource managers confide their doubts that much real change is occurring. The executives themselves profess uncertainty about how the quality theme can be translated into action in their own divisions. These executives knew how to talk about the new way to manage but did not have the knowledge and skill to implement it. Such skills can only be learned by doing, by being placed in a situation that requires a manager to try the new way.

If managers perceive that these programs are not addressing high-priority problems, is it surprising that they become cynical about the energy diverted from their primary task—running a business to make a profit? As a result, top managers and human resource staff members associated with the program lose credibility, making it more difficult for them to arouse commitment to the corporate transformation. Moreover, future programs aimed at furthering the transformation are likely to be greeted with skepticism from the start, making it unlikely that managers will invest much time or energy in them.

If programs do not work, why are they used so often as a strategy for creating change? Programs are easy to talk about and promote. They have a definite beginning and an end. Their content is specific and the activities prescribed are actionable. Furthermore, compliance with programs such as quality circles and management education is easily measurable, making it possible to hold managers accountable. Unfortunately, corporate revitalization is a considerably more subtle and elusive matter. Finally, programs do not threaten the power of top managers, union leaders, supervisors, or departments, because they do not deal with fundamental problems that underlie the need for revitalization. No one gets hurt, and lip service has been paid to the ideal of change.

If creating programs is not the way to implement a human resource transformation, what is the alternative? By contrasting companies A and B (the change leaders) with companies E and F (the change laggards) and by observing successful and less successful change efforts in business units within all six companies (there were examples of less successful change efforts even in companies A and B), we can draw some conclusions about the character of successful systemwide transformations.

Achieving Effective Corporate Transformation

Pressures, both external and internal, were the trigger for change in all six companies. In most cases, changes in the external environment were threatening the profitability and competitiveness of the company. Company A, for example, faced the introduction of a superior product by a European competitor in the early 1970s—a product with the potential to cut deeply into the company's market share. Later, in the mid 1970s, the entry of a Japanese competitor began placing cost pressures on the company. At approximately the same time the company experienced a long and costly strike. By 1977 the CEO had set the change agenda: build a nonunion, low-cost plant that would compete successfully with the impending Japanese threat. Simultaneously, several existing plants began to experiment with new approaches to managing—for example, open communication, employee involvement, and gains sharing. The transformation was underway.

External or internal pressures are prominent in all six attempts to transform, but the severity, scope, and timing of the crisis seem to be critical to the success of the transformation. Simultaneous external and internal pressures are necessary to trigger change. Moreover, transformations that start when the threat is clear to employees more effectively mobilize energy for change. Starting a transformation in advance of a crisis and without sufficient top management consensus about impending problems, as company F did, raises the likelihood that it will become just another program. Starting the transformation too late makes the effort a turnaround with greater emphasis on cost reduction than on innovative management approaches. This is what eventually happened in company F when the recession of 1982 made rapid change necessary.

Mobilizing Energy for Change. Environmental pressures can alert management to the need for change, but these pressures are seldom felt or clearly understood by lower-level managers, union leaders, and workers. Organizations that successfully transformed themselves had leaders gifted in translating these complex environmental demands into employee commitment to change. The four primary strategies that they used follow:

1. Providing employees with information and thereby putting them in touch with the realities of the competitive environment was the basic strategy most widely utilized. In most cases this activity was preceded by trust building, although the process of information sharing itself built trust between management, workers, and unions. Successful methods included sharing information about cost and quality in relation to competitors, employee trips to customers, and trips to Japan by union-management teams.

2. Setting high standards of performance for individuals and organizational subunits was another means for mobilizing energy to change. When this is accompanied by trustworthy information about the competitive crisis, employees and union will accept such demands. In company A the executive vice-president for manufacturing created a new set of quality specifications for the company's major product line. All products that did not meet these specifications had to be scrapped. Many plants had no hope of achieving these tighter specifications without completely rethinking their manufacturing process and the way they organized and managed employees.

Company A also took a tough stand with managers and unions and made it clear that the company's various plants were in competition for capital resources. Investments would be made only in plants that demonstrated superior performance. Those that did not perform would be closed. The CEO described his predecessor's encounter with union leaders: "We brought in the labor council and sat them down in this room to make the announcement that this was what we were going to do

[transfer operations to another state]. It wasn't a thing for negotiations. . . . The union leader pleaded for two more days,
which [the former CEO] gave him, and he came back two days
later and gave everything that was on the list and threw two more
in if we'd keep the plant here. . . . The jobs that they lost they got
back and they got competitive." While such tactics may create
resentment and have the potential to backfire, properly applied
they can create the climate needed for change.

3. Creating innovative models of organizing and managing people in new plants or businesses will also mobilize energy
for change. In fact, without a tangible model, managers and
union leaders will not be able to visualize what the new ways will
require of them or develop confidence that they can actually be
implemented. Company A's and company B's success can be
traced to an effective early model, while company F's failure can
be traced to a model plant that did not live up to expectations. It
became a negative symbol. Those opposed to the transformation used the model plant's failure to buttress their argument
that new management approaches would not work.

A person can also be a model. A senior executive in
company B spoke of wanting to adopt the people-oriented management approach of a former boss and senior executive. The
same company created an award for excellence in managing
and named it after this executive. Thus, he became a symbol of
the desired style of management for more than one person. For
other managers, the experience of working for an autocratic
manager served as an important example of what not to do.
Sometimes consultants can help shape the vision of the future,
providing a new way of thinking and behaving. Many of the
companies relied on the same small circle of consultants to
educate them about new approaches and help them in developing their model organization.

4. Finding a theme with which people can identify and
from which they can derive meaning is useful in mobilizing
support for change. "Quality" was a theme that served most
companies well, probably because it is the one theme that
all stakeholders — workers, management, unions, and shareholders — can support. Managers and professionals, however,

sometimes had difficulty identifying with the theme and saw it as more appropriate in manufacturing organizations. Company F provides an example of how lack of a meaningful theme can prevent commitment. The CEO addressed employees in an effort to rally their support for improving corporate performance. He stressed the need for improvements in profits and return on equity. The goal was to make the company an industry leader. Feedback, however, was very negative. The speech had failed to arouse enthusiasm for the CEO's cause. As one employee succinctly put it, "I can't get excited about 15 percent return on equity."

In mobilizing energy for change, therefore, leaders must translate warnings from the environment into clear messages about the new approaches to organizing and managing that will be required if a company is to compete effectively. Information, tough standards of performance, symbols, living models, and meaningful themes that will be perceived as credible and relevant to improving performance are the first steps on the "critical path" to change.

The Critical Path to Change. It is this path that helps the organization accomplish its core task, the task essential to its success. An organization aspiring to transform itself, be it a corporation, business unit, plant, or branch, must first diagnose its situation and identify the one or two things it has to do well to succeed. That may be product innovation in one instance, it may be customer service in another or low-cost production in still a third. In instances where there are several key success factors, it is important that they be prioritized. Their relative importance will depend on the maturity of the market as well as on the strategy of the organization in relation to its competitors.

The six corporations in our study are in the process of transforming themselves because their environments have changed as a result of global competition or deregulation. This change in the environment has caused a change in what these corporations must do to be successful—in the tasks they must perform to survive and prosper. Unfortunately, the competence, behavior, and attitudes of their employees are still geared to the tasks defined by their previous, less competitive environment.

Not all the corporations studied approached the transformation process with the kind of analytic clarity we have been recommending here. Less successful transformations tended to be defined by the kind of management desired—participative management or employee involvement—rather than by the task that had to be accomplished to be successful. Employees became frustrated by the emphasis on style unconnected to substance. Consider the following examples:

The transformation of company D, a multinational bank, started in two very different ways, one more successful than the other. The first strategy set out to change the culture of the bank. The bank hired consultants to interview employees about what they thought hindered effectiveness and to analyze the history of the bank to identify the beliefs and value system of its founder. Feedback meetings were held with top management to make them aware of how employees felt and how the current culture deviated from the culture of earlier years. Top management then set about defining the new culture and communicated the ensuing description through speeches and educational programs.

The second strategy involved a consultant who took a quite different approach. He pushed management at various levels to identify present markets and to define the profitable market segments that they wanted to serve. Task forces were established to carry these investigations forward. Management teams in relevant parts of the organization were then asked to define the organizational structure and management process that would best support the objectives defined earlier. The result was a change in the structure and systems of the bank that realigned responsibility and accountability. The bank created a matrix that gave product/market managers responsibility for performance in the products and services sold in the bank's numerous branches; this approach significantly changed the role of branch managers.

Executives in the bank felt that the second strategy for change was much more effective than the first. But why should

two change efforts in the same bank, both initiated and supported by top management, yield such different outcomes? The
answer lies in the relative alignment of these change strategies
with the core task of the organization. People were frustrated by
the apparent lack of relevance of the first strategy, which emphasized means, desired attitudes, and behaviors, but did not directly address the immediate problems of the bank. The second
thrust enabled the bank to move forward in dealing with its
immediate business problems, even though the consultant's
style came under criticism. This approach was successful in
diagnosing the problems of the business.

Examination of transformations in several other subunits
of the six companies studied supports the conclusion that a
diagnostic process involving organizational members is very
important in keeping a transformation focused on the critical
path. Consider a research and development center in company
A struggling to transform itself. For two years the center made
various efforts to apply concepts of employee involvement that
had been successfully applied in the company's plants. Employee task forces were formed to identify barriers to career
development in response to employee complaints about lack of
career progression. (A committee of employees was also formed
to recommend what art should be hung in the center's atrium.)
The center's director and his staff had many meetings with their
internal consultant to define and implement a transformation,
something clearly valued by company A's top management. Two
years after these efforts began, however, many managers were
frustrated with the meager results that their efforts had yielded.

The only bright spot on the horizon was a task force that,
with the help of a consultant, was analyzing why new-product
development projects were not meeting a major customer's
needs. The result was a recommendation to organize a project
team that would overlay the functional organization and facilitate integrated decision making between functions that dis-
trusted one another and spent too much time protecting their
own "turf." A second consultant then confronted management
with his own diagnosis: the core task of the center, developing
new products, was being impeded by strict functional lines and

a lack of teamwork. The top team undertook to verify this diagnosis with an internal process that involved lower-level managers. The result was the implementation of a number of project teams for developments in a broad product category. The change effort was finally moving, according to the internal consultant and top management.

The center had adopted a project organization, structurally and culturally. This meant that more delegation and participation, teamwork, and employee involvement would be needed. These management methods, which had previously been advocated as ends, were now tied to an understanding of how they would solve coordination and delay problems that were impairing the center's capacity to accomplish its core task.

Causes of Failure. Here, we might ask, Why do so few transformations follow the critical path?

First, managers in the six companies were generally unable to link analysis of their business with the organizational arrangements and behaviors that require change. That weakness can be attributed in part to poor training in making this link. A stable environment does not require these skills. It is interesting to note that companies A and B had leaders who were better in making this link than were their counterparts in the other companies.

Second, managers are generally reluctant to confront the difficult relationship and power issues that underlay existing management practices. This is particularly true if changes suggested by a diagnosis involve the manager's own role, power, or behavior. We found this reluctance in all the companies we studied, but it was more pronounced in company F than in the others. Here the CEO and his staff members were protected from first-hand feedback by management practice (they made relatively few visits to operating units) and an office building layout that limited employee access (the executives had separate elevators and a restricted top-floor location). In company A, by contrast, the COO and executive vice-president visited plants regularly.

Third, effective diagnosis can only be accomplished by an

effective top team. Where such a team is not in place, as it was not in the research and development center, it is impossible to get difficult issues on the table and examine them openly from the perspective of all functions.

Fourth, early success in transforming a plant, department, or division can, ironically enough, lead a corporation off the critical path when the successful model is imposed on other organizational units. This is a particular problem in decentralized firms with diverse businesses. A successful model for organizing and managing in one division will not necessarily apply to another division in a different business. Since most transformations in manufacturing companies start in plants, a problem also develops in moving the transformation to the division and corporate level. The plant model is not perceived to be relevant by managers, a problem apparent in the research and development center that we studied.

Finally, if line managers do not themselves have the skills to diagnose barriers to organizational effectiveness, they will sometimes turn to human resource specialists. Unfortunately, such specialists are also typically weak in making diagnoses that link organizational and behavioral changes to business requirements. They lack knowledge of the business and the general management perspective required for such an analysis.

Top managers in the six companies who had the ability to link changes in organizing and managing to business realities typically got to the top through a career in manufacturing or operations. The COO of company A came from manufacturing, the CEO of company F from finance, personnel, and planning. Operating experience seems to provide the perspective needed to make the link. The successful transformations described above stayed on the critical path because they were rooted in a diagnosis of the company's problems. However, they were also helped, in the case of the bank and the research and development center, by structural changes that demanded new behaviors.

Creating Demand for New Behavior and Supporting It

Those who implement successful transformations focus on behavior change rather than simply talk about it. While diagnosis can help identify the individual, group, and inter-group behavior needed to accomplish the organization's core task, getting and staying on the critical path require that appro-priate behaviors be stimulated and sustained over time. This cannot be done through training or through speeches exhort-ing employees to change. Only a change in the context—struc-ture, systems, staffing patterns, and management process—in which employees function can stimulate and sustain new man-agement approaches. Managers in company A, the most suc-cessful in transforming itself, coined the term *forcing strategy* to capture the essential point that organizational arrangements that demand or enable new behaviors must lead the change process. Softer approaches such as persuasion, education, and counseling may be helpful, but only if they follow changes in context.

Structural Change. Changing structures and systems is a powerful intervention because it alters the information that employees are exposed to, the roles they play, the relationships they form, the interactions they must manage, and the responsi-bility and accountability they feel. Of course, simply changing structures will not accomplish this unless such action is sup-ported by communication from the top about the purpose of the change and the management approach expected. Our thesis is that attitude change follows and reinforces behavior change, which is itself brought about by the new organizational arrange-ments. For instance, successful unit-level transformations in the six companies included reducing levels of management, intro-ducing project teams and other structural overlays that force communication and cooperation, decentralizing into divisions or semiautonomous work teams, and introducing information systems to which people must respond.

The executive vice-president of manufacturing in com-pany A, who was a change leader, had learned about the impor-tance of structural change early in his efforts to manage change. As plant manager of an old unionized plant, he had introduced a number of changes that regressed after his departure. He attributed this to the absence of changes in structure. As executive vice-president, he advocated structural changes in his plants that would reduce levels and devolve plant staff to business centers, which were relatively self-sufficient departments. Each business center would have its own staff. His vision: the plant manager and remaining plant staff would support business centers, not dictate to them. While he allowed each plant manager to approach this general vision in his own way, he also pushed for changes in structure. After a plant had designed its new structure and begun to implement it, managers and supervisors were sent to a specially developed corporate training program that taught them how business centers were supposed to function.

How a structural change is introduced is very important to its ultimate success. Changes imposed from the top without the involvement of the managers and employees affected by them usually fail. Consider the case of company A's CEO who, convinced that global product strategies would be important in the future, wanted to improve integration between domestic and international operations. By unilaterally consolidating some staff, he incurred resentment and resistance from managers in the international division who experienced job changes without warning.

Structural changes are best implemented in two stages. First, bring together on a committee or task force those people who might ultimately work together. Give them the task of examining interdependencies between their departments and ask for recommendations for managing those interdependencies. The result may be a recommendation to restructure, if that is indeed the appropriate solution. For example, a functionally organized company, not one of those in our sample of six companies, regionalized its manufacturing and selling functions only after creating informal task teams of manufacturing and sales managers in each region. The assignment was to "study how effectiveness of the business might be increased by regionalization and recommend if and how we should proceed."

To reiterate, forcing required behaviors by structure and system changes is an important first step in keeping a transformation on the critical path, but involvement of those affected, as well as support for skill and style development, is necessary for this forcing strategy to work.

Essential Role of Leadership. In companies A and B key leaders at several levels played important but different roles. Thus, the top managers in company A and company B had very different styles. They varied widely in the extent to which they were participative or autocratic. Their personalities were quite different; a few were charismatic leaders and had the capacity to arouse enthusiasm in employees, but most of them did not have this ability. Many gave dull speeches. Only one had deeply held values about how people should be managed. The rest were more pragmatic in their reasons for supporting the transformation. Almost all the top managers showed inconsistencies between espoused beliefs and actual management style. But if the style of transformational leaders at the top is not crucial, what is?

It is important to differentiate between the role of CEOs in transforming a company and that of other top managers. Typically the CEOs understood and accepted that transforming the corporation's approach to organizing and managing would enhance competitiveness, but in five of the six companies they did not take the lead in conceptualizing this question. In companies A and B the COOs or executive vice-presidents in charge of major business units or functions led the transformation in their own areas and helped spread it throughout their companies. They did this by encouraging lower-level managers to transform their own units, not by dictating a particular approach to management. It is remarkable how often this point was stressed by the COO of company A, the company that underwent the most successful transformation. To be able to give this kind of encouragement, top managers had to have *a commitment to a general vision* of how things might be. That vision was shaped by a successful experience with new approaches to organizing and managing, by a people-oriented boss, or by a personal experience that touched them deeply. The vision was continually modified and enriched by successful and unsuccessful transformations of subunits within their organization.

Senior transformational executives in the successful companies also understood how to manage companywide change. They recognized that it was an incremental, unit-by-unit process. Companies E and F lacked a sufficient number of senior executives with the experiences and skills needed to effect this kind of change. In company E, there was only one such senior executive and he lacked the full support of the CEO or the understanding of how to transform a company. In company F, as already mentioned, the new COO was a traditional manager, and an executive vice-president who supported innovations in management was taking early retirement. Perhaps most important, transformational leaders at the top provided adequate resources for subunit transformations, including money for training and consultants, their own time, staff support, and effective managers who could lead the transformation.

The importance of replacing key managers — the single most important change tool top managers possess — is illustrated by the following example from company A. Because the COO of this company was committed to transforming it, he prevailed on the president of the international division to begin a change in the methods of organizing and managing people. With the help of the organization development staff and an outside consultant, a worldwide diagnosis of the organization was undertaken. The finding was that the organization was overmanaged by headquarters. The president's lack of commitment to change became apparent during the feedback meeting when he failed to strongly endorse or support the finding. Subsequently, he undermined the transformation by writing a letter to all key executives around the world in which he criticized the consultant's finding and reiterated his support for current values and practices. The transformation bogged down until a new president was appointed. He was in favor of the delegation and decentralization indicated by the diagnosis, and his backing ultimately led to a speedup of the transformation without any support from consultants.

The opposite was true of company F, where the failure of a model plant was acknowledged to have occurred because the best managers had not been transferred there. This is also the company in which a newly promoted COO was uninterested in new approaches to organizing and managing. A manager's most powerful change tool, particularly at the top of the corporation, is the placement and promotion of managers who support the transformation with what they do, not just with what they say. The dramatic turnaround in the transformation of company A's international division following a leadership change also illustrates the importance of a subunit leader's beliefs, values, and skill in moving along a transformation. Companies A and B simply had more of these middle-level transformational leaders, although even in these companies they were in short supply.

Effective middle-level transformational leaders were typically more consistent in the beliefs they espoused and how they actually managed than were their more traditionally minded counterparts. Their effectiveness as change leaders depended on their ability to model the new approaches in day-to-day interactions with workers, union leaders, and subordinate managers. Many described a significant personal experience in management that led to a transformation in their beliefs about how one should manage. One felt that his energy for transformation, when contrasted with that of top management, came from blending idealism and pragmatism in equal amounts. Successful transformational leaders at this level, however, never confused means and ends. They were tough and task oriented in their application of participative management. Subunit leaders who failed typically stressed means, communication, and participation at the expense of ends, productivity, and profitability.

The picture that emerges is one of transformational leaders at all levels who are more instrumental than inspirational. They keep the transformation on the critical path by recognizing that the new model of organizing and managing is a means for achieving competitiveness, not an approach to management to be pursued for its own sake. They keep the transformation on the critical path by pushing a general vision, not a specific management practice or program, and by providing adequate resources for the task at hand.

Mobilizing a Network of Supporters. Despite the essential role that leaders played, they could not transform a corporation all by themselves. Successful transformations were characterized by a network of supporting actors, consultants, human resource executives, internal consultants, and union leaders. These people played a major role in providing ideas, advice, training, and political support. Without them, leaders would have been unable to define the vision for transformation or to implement it.

External consultants were used by all the companies in our study. They brought new ideas that helped educate managers who were leading the transformation. Indeed, the more successful transformations were guided by consultants who kept them on the critical path. They did this by insisting that the client define the business or task-related reasons for change and that the new model of management fit that definition. In almost every case, the diagnosis led to a redefinition of the problem. In company A, for example, the CEO's directive to build a non-union plant was redefined with the help of a new director of organization development as well as consultants. The objective was no longer simply one of avoiding unions. It was to develop an organization that would yield higher productivity through employee involvement. Effective consultants tended to have a general management perspective while less effective consultants tended to be specialists, delivering a program, procedure, or way of looking at problems that precluded them from helping managers define the critical path to change.

A staff of internal consultants, that is, an organization development department within the human resource function, was developed and nurtured within companies A and B. In company A this staff was augmented by a network of line managers trained to consult with managers attempting to make changes. In company B human resource specialists were trained as consultants and facilitators. An innovative division of 600 employees required seven such consultants in the first six months of the transformation. Training, coaching, and advising, these "facilitators" were thought to be crucial to the division's success in transforming itself. In contrast, companies E and F had no internal consulting staff as of 1986. Company E never had such a staff. Company F disbanded its staff when the director left the company due to lack of support.

In both company A and company B the director of organization development—the key staff person concerned with the transformation—had good access to top management. In company A, for example, the director had an office very close to those of the top executives in the firm. In company B the director had a second office in the executive building that allowed him reasonable access to top management.

A strong human resources executive who is an advocate of new approaches to organizing and managing helps move a transformation forward. When he has access to top management, the human resource executive can ensure consistency between corporate policies and transformation objectives. He can educate top executives in order to protect resources required for the transformation against reductions for economic or political reasons. In times of tight budgets, it is often inevitable that constituencies opposed to the transformation will argue for such reductions.

Company B and, to a lesser extent, company A had a human resource executive who advocated change. Each executive had replaced a more traditional labor relations executive. In company B the human resource vice-president was a member of the top management committee. He played a key role in protecting the human resource development department, which provided staff support for the transformation, from cuts during a budget squeeze. In contrast, company E had a human resource executive with a traditional labor relations background. When asked about innovations in management within the company, he spoke about compensation and labor relations, not about new approaches to organizing and managing. Company F had changed its human resource executive three times in six years. The last two supported innovation in human resources but were forced out of the organization by unsupportive top management.

Union leaders able to step outside their traditional adversarial role played an important part in successful transformations. In companies that bargained nationally, support by a top official in the international union was important. Consider the essential leadership role that Irving Bluestone and Don Ephlan of the United Auto Workers played in the transformation of General Motors. They worked to get the support of their union and often helped Stephen Fuller, the ranking human resource executive at General Motors in the 1970s, to convince line managers of the need for change. Ephlan later played a similar critical role in the transformation of Ford Motor. Transformational leaders spend time mobilizing the support of these union leaders, always being careful to recognize the fine line that the latter have to tread between supporting change and representing the interests of their members. They can support the transformation if management helps them establish the need for change with their members.

Company B involved union leaders in a series of conferences on quality in which mutual understanding about the problems facing the company was developed. This was followed by similar conferences at lower levels. Company C used joint labor-management teams to discuss problems at various levels. With this type of process as a backdrop, union leaders were able to support management initiatives for changes in work practices and wage and benefits. Tough and consistent messages about the concessions required for survival—the effective tactic of the CEO in company A—also made it possible for union leaders to ask members to grant such concessions. However, if this approach is not accompanied by efforts to build a relationship of mutual trust and an understanding by union leaders of the business problems facing the company, the cooperation achieved in this way will probably be short-lived. In company A, such a relationship was not fully developed because of the particular adversarial stance of a union leader. Union leaders who want to help shape a transformation must find a different way to relate to management.

Starting at the Periphery and Moving to the Core

The traditional wisdom is that change must start at the top and filter down through the organization. But comparing the actual experience of successful and less successful companies suggests the need for a very different pattern.

The successful transformations that occurred in company A and company B involved a synergistic interaction between initiatives from the top and from the bottom. Active experimentation with new approaches to organizing and managing started at the periphery of these organizations, that is, at a new plant and at a troubled business unit. Company A opened an innovative plant at the request of the CEO, but the CEO did not play an active role in its development nor did he have a vision of how the plant should be managed. In company B, a division in trouble applied new approaches to management with the approval of top management but not with its involvement or understanding of the innovations. When these early models proved successful, other organizational units began to apply the same methods. As momentum increased, initiatives became more innovative and even began to appear in older unionized plants and corporate headquarters.

Even in relatively successful transformations, top management does not necessarily become involved in the process until it is well underway, and sometimes this is years after the first initiative. Six years after the transformation started in company A, the COO and the executive vice-president of manufacturing were leading the transformation. They had succeeded to positions in the company from which such leadership could be exerted, and they had learned enough about the new approaches to form a commitment to change and a vision of what their company could be like.

However, top management in company A had yet to apply new approaches in organizing and managing to the corporate staff and the marketing function, whose traditional approaches frustrated the manufacturing people in innovative plants. Moreover, top management had not reexamined its own inconsistent style of management. As the reader can imagine, this led to much cynicism at lower levels and in organizations at the periphery where innovations were being applied. Top management in the most advanced group in company B was further along. Its executive vice-president started an examination of the relationship between the group and its divisions. This led to feedback about his management style, as well as to the formation of a general managers' board that was to involve itself in major decisions. Many saw this development as a breakthrough. The EVP himself commented: "Until now I didn't know these approaches could be applied to us [at the top]. Now that we are doing it I recognize that perhaps we should have done it sooner."

If a lagging top management can cause difficulties in the transformation, so can a top management that is too far ahead of the rest of the organization. Consider company D, a multinational bank, where change started with involvement by top management. During the three years in which top management studied the bank's culture and its own management process, however, the transformation failed to spread to lower levels. No model organization had emerged to help shape top management's vision or to provide a subculture in which managers could learn to manage in a different way.

The lesson to be drawn is that successful transformations involve a reciprocal learning process between the top and bottom and between the periphery and the core. The transformation may start at the top or the bottom, the core or the periphery. But if reciprocity does not develop, the transformation will stray from the critical path. If the transformation starts at the top, the role of top managers must be limited to giving permission to innovate in approaches to management that they may not fully understand. Anything more directive than this will turn the transformation process into a program. A change effort at the top that confronts core values too early is likely to allow those who oppose the change to mobilize resistance before success can be demonstrated. If the transformation starts at the periphery and top managers do not ultimately learn from successful innovations, they will not become committed to a vision and are precluded from leading the transformation, encouraging its spread to the organization's core, and speeding adoption of new approaches in all its parts. This will prevent middle managers from learning about the new approaches from experience in subunits that have already institutionalized the new approaches. Without a continually growing circle of middle-level managers who have this kind of experience, the company will lack the most crucial resource for a successful transformation, namely, managers who have internalized the new model of organizing and managing and can themselves lead a transformation.

A top manager who wants to transform the corporation's approach to organizing and managing as rapidly, effectively, and efficiently as possible must orchestrate the organizational learning process described in this chapter. There are no short cuts to this developmental process. An understanding of it can enable top managers to keep the transformation on the critical path by avoiding the fallacy of top-down programs, by mobilizing the energy of unit managers to initiate change that are consistent with the key success factors of their business, and by supporting those changes with resources, particularly with bosses and subordinates who solidly back the transformation efforts.

References

Barnes, Z. Talk delivered at the symposium "Managing Organizational Change: Leadership, Structure, and Values," at the 45th annual meeting of the Academy of Management, San Diego, Aug. 1985.

Beer, M., Eisenstat, R., and Spector, B. "Revitalizing American Corporations." Symposium conducted at the 46th annual meeting of Academy of Management, Chicago, Aug. 1986.

Porter, M. E. *Competitive Advantage: Creating and Sustaining Superior Performance.* New York: Free Press, 1985.

Walton, R. E. "From Control to Commitment in the Workplace." *Harvard Business Review,* 1985, *63* (2), 76–84.

3

Edward E. Lawler III

Transformation from Control to Involvement

The premise of this chapter is that major changes in the way organizations are managed are not chance happenings. They are produced by motivated actions on the part of organizations. These actions come about as a result of a complex combination of the characteristics of these organizations and the business environments they face. The focus here is on when and why organizations make a particular shift in their management approach—that is, when and why they move from a control-oriented bureaucratic management approach to one based on commitment or involvement (Walton, 1985). Once we have analyzed these questions, we will consider what actions can be taken to encourage an organization to make this shift. First, however, we need to look at the two competing management paradigms of control and involvement.

Basically, a paradigm is a set of assumptions about how the world works; these assumptions produce a congruent and often tightly interconnected system of policies and practices in an organization. When new paradigms arise, they have to compete with the older, more established ones for acceptance. Typically, for a new paradigm to triumph over an old one, there must be a fundamental restructuring of people's thought processes and the way they operate (Mohrman and Lawler, 1985).

46

This is certainly true when there is a shift from the control-oriented paradigm to the involvement-oriented paradigm.

The control-oriented paradigm assumes that organizations can best get people to perform their tasks by using formal reward and punishment systems to motivate them. It emphasizes such practices as describing jobs in detail, carefully measuring job performance, and handing out rewards on the basis of achievement. In the control approach lower-level members of the organization are assumed to be primarily in a performing role and are not asked to participate actively in the planning, scheduling, controlling, and strategy issues that arise in every organization. Their actions are coordinated through rules, procedures, and supervisory direction. It is typically assumed that their major interactions are the ones that they have with their supervisor, who provides them with direction and control and administers rewards and punishments.

The involvement approach, which is becoming increasingly popular, makes a very different set of assumptions about what produces organizational effectiveness (Walton, 1985). It assumes that most employees can figure out the right thing to do if they are properly trained and informed. It also stresses that they can be intrinsically motivated to see that the organization performs effectively and that they are capable of a considerable amount of self-control and self-direction. Finally, it believes that most employees are capable of producing important ideas about how the business should be operated. It calls for such practices as quality circles, teams, skill-based pay, and flat, lean organizational structures (Lawler, 1986). It is based on decades of research and writing and includes notable early contributions by Likert, McGregor, Argyris, and a host of others concerned with organizational theory.

In the past, many of the ideas that are part of the involvement paradigm were taught in business schools but were not practiced in the real world. Recently, however, a number of large corporations have adopted involvement-oriented management styles. Notable among these corporations are Honeywell, Mead, Xerox, Ford Motor, Motorola, and some of the smaller steel companies. But why is it that, after years of little change, the involvement paradigm has finally begun to catch on?

Motivation for Change

If we assume that changes in management style are examples of motivated behavior, then we can use some of our knowledge about motivation to help explain shifts from the control paradigm to the involvement program. Expectancy theory has proven to be the most useful approach to understanding organizational behavior (Lawler, 1973). This theory argues that people's tendency or motivation to behave in a particular way is a result of the attractiveness of the rewards or outcomes that are attached to that particular behavior as well as of the perceived probability that the behavior can be accomplished. In short, for a person to behave in a particular way that person needs to feel that he or she can accomplish the behavior and that the behavior will be rewarded.

In many situations people have the opportunity to choose among a number of alternative behaviors, most of which have some attractive and some unattractive outcomes attached to them, and the difficulty of achieving these behaviors usually varies. Essentially, expectancy theory argues that when people have to choose among alternative behaviors, they will choose that behavior that is most likely to produce the best mix of positive and negative outcomes. In many cases this causes people to continue to perform well-learned behaviors if those behaviors are producing a reasonable mix of outcomes.

Known behaviors are seen as achievable, and the positive results associated with them are seen as high-probability occurrences. By contrast, new behaviors may be perceived as difficult to accomplish, and the connection between them and positive outcomes may be in doubt. What all this argues, of course, is that individuals and organizations are unlikely to change their behavior if their present behavior is producing a relatively satisfying mix of rewards. Indeed, the literature would suggest that they are not even likely to begin a search for alternative behaviors if they are obtaining a satisfying level of rewards from their present behavior (March and Simon, 1958).

A management style paradigm change is particularly difficult and costly to accomplish because of the systems issues involved. Numerous researchers have stressed that organizations are composed of many interconnected systems and that effectiveness is achieved only when the systems are in alignment (see, for example, Katz and Kahn, 1966; Galbraith, 1973; Nadler, 1987). Changing the management style of an organization, therefore, is not a simple matter of changing an individual's behavior or of changing a single part of an organization such as the reward system. Making a major paradigm shift involves changing the behavior of a large number of individuals as well as virtually all the systems in an organization (Lawler, 1986).

Writers who have advocated the involvement-oriented approach call for new organization structures, cultures, reward systems, information systems, supervisory behaviors, and human resource management systems. Because such massive change is needed, it can be very costly to move to an involvement-oriented approach. Not only are significant amounts of training needed, but major organization design changes are also needed. New pay systems, job designs, and career tracks are needed. In the case of the involvement approach, making these changes is particularly difficult because some of the technology to support them has not yet been developed. It is not always clear how to run an effective selection system, pay system, and information system when the involvement paradigm is used.

To some extent, developing the technology to support a new paradigm is a classic chicken and egg problem since development requires testing but testing cannot take place unless someone believes that the new paradigm will work. Just the opposite is true with respect to the control approach; it has been practiced for so long that knowledge about how to implement it is well developed. Many consulting firms are available to help organizations use the control approach, and it is the approach advocated by most management textbooks.

Another complication of major organizational change is the effect that a paradigm shift may have on the key individuals in an organization. It is one thing to argue that the organization will be better off after a paradigm shift, it is quite another to argue that a given individual will be better off. This issue is particularly pertinent with respect to a shift from control- to involvement-oriented management. This shift has the potential of making the quality of work life better for many individuals in the organization, particularly the lower-level participants who gain a greater degree of authority and responsibility. The same, however, may not be true for middle-level managers and executives. In some cases they may become redundant, and in others they may lose power and certain perquisites and rewards because of the kind of egalitarian power sharing that the involvement paradigm emphasizes. Thus, executives and middle managers often perceive that they have more to lose than gain from a shift to involvement-oriented management. Given that leadership for this type of shift best comes from the top (Tichy and Devanna, 1986), it is not surprising that shifts toward employee involvement still are relatively rare.

From what we have said so far, we can make some predictions about when a major paradigm shift is likely to occur. First and foremost, it is likely to occur only when the present paradigm is seen to be significantly inferior to the new paradigm. One common way to conceptualize this is to think of dissatisfaction with the present as ranging from zero to one and the attractiveness of the new as ranging from zero to one (see, for example, Beckhard and Harris, 1977). Conceptually, we can imagine these two as having a multiplicative relationship—to produce motivation for a paradigm shift. In this approach, if either dissatisfaction with the present or the attractiveness of the new is zero, the prediction would be that no shift will occur. Stated another way, shifts are likely to ,occur when the new approach is very attractive and considerable dissatisfaction exists with the old one. Little motivation for change is likely to exist if it is simply a matter of the appearance of an alternative paradigm or simply a matter of a high level of dissatisfaction with the present situation.

Although the multiplicative idea is intriguing, the expectancy theory approach does not necessarily agree with it. Expectancy theory argues that people are motivated to perform the behavior that is most attractive. Thus, if an extremely attractive new paradigm presents itself, it may be adopted even if the existing one is not a source of dissatisfaction. Also, if there is great dissatisfaction with the existing paradigm, even an unproven and undeveloped new approach may be chosen if it lacks obvious weaknesses. At this point in time, however, it is impossible to reject either the expectancy argument or the multiplicative one since little data exist to support either in the area of organizational change. Perhaps the most important point is that they both argue that change is most likely when a new, attractive alternative is competing with a relatively unattractive old alternative.

Organizational Effectiveness as a Competitive Advantage

What is likely to produce dissatisfaction with an old management paradigm? The answer here seems relatively straightforward: poor organizational performance. Ultimately, poor performance in the marketplace has negative effects not only for the organization but also for all individuals in the organization because their intrinsic rewards are diminished as are their security and financial rewards. Thus, when an organization's performance falters badly, we can usually predict that there will be a high level of dissatisfaction with the existing management paradigm.

The attractiveness of a new paradigm is very much related to its potential effectiveness. To put it simply, a paradigm will be attractive to the degree that it is perceived as a way of increasing organizational performance; this might be the case when a new paradigm is already being used by a competitor and that competitor is performing effectively. As long as a paradigm is simply a textbook description of what can be done, its perceived attractiveness is likely to be limited because there will be a lack of confidence in its ability to produce promised results. In addition, it may be unclear how to implement it and what practices are needed to make it effective.

Both the involvement and the control styles can be implemented in effective or ineffective ways. Figure 3-1 illustrates a hypothetical distribution of organizations in terms of their management styles and their effectiveness in implementing them. It shows that organizations can be managed on a continuum from control to involvement and that they can range from high to low in how effectively they utilize a management paradigm.

Many more organizations are managed toward the control end of the continuum than toward the involvement end. Because this distribution shows more companies below than above average, it suggests that many of the organizations managed with the control approach are perhaps less than optimally effective. This is an increasingly difficult style to implement in the United States, given the kind of work force and social conditions that prevail. Evidence continues to accumulate that general societal conditions are becoming increasingly favorable to the involvement approach because it fits with the democratic values and education level of the current work force (Lawler, 1986). Finally, the figure shows that, on the average, organizations that practice involvement do not do it as well as those that practice control. No doubt, this is related to the fact that we still know relatively little about how to design and manage an involvement-oriented organization: the experience simply does not yet exist.

When an organization wants to improve its performance, it essentially has two ways it can change. It can try to improve its performance by doing a better job of implementing the management paradigm it has been using or it can choose a new management paradigm. I think it is fair to say that most organizations choose the first approach. As a result, they end up making only marginal changes in their basic systems and practices. In essence they try to move up the vertical axis in Figure 3-1 in the hope of improving organizational performance. Occasionally an organization—Motorola is one example—chooses to move to the right on the continuum in order to increase organizational effectiveness. It is just this kind of paradigm shift behavior that is both unusual and important to understand.

As has been stressed already, any explanation of why an

Figure 3-1. Distribution of Management Styles.

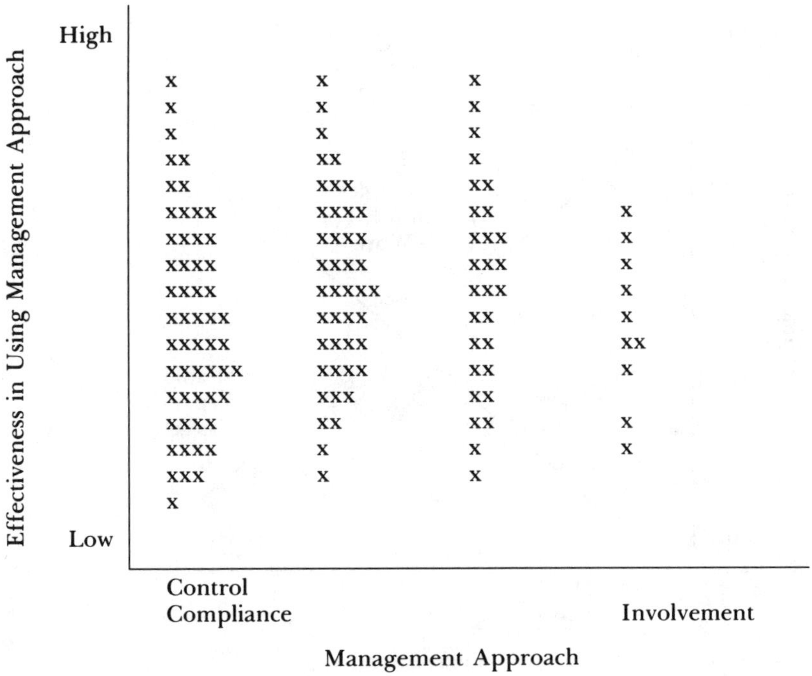

```
High
      |
      |   x        x        x
      |   x        x        x
      |   x        x        x
      |   xx       xx       x
      |   xx       xxx      xx
      |   xxxx     xxxx     xx       x
      |   xxxx     xxxx     xxx      x
      |   xxxx     xxxx     xxx      x
      |   xxxx     xxxxx    xxx      x
      |   xxxxx    xxxx     xx       x
      |   xxxxx    xxxx     xx       xx
      |   xxxxxx   xxxx     xx       x
      |   xxxxx    xxx      xx
      |   xxxx     xx       xx       x
      |   xxxx     x        x        x
      |   xxx      x        x
      |   x
Low
      |_____

          Control                     Involvement
          Compliance

               Management Approach
```

(vertical axis label) Effectiveness in Using Management Approach

organization chooses the involvement paradigm has to look closely at its potential effectiveness. Research suggests that this paradigm tends to be particularly good at producing improvements in product quality, facilitating problem solving, attracting and retaining highly talented individuals, and helping an organization remain flexible and responsive (Lawler, 1986). In contrast, the control approach tends to be effective in getting repetitive, reliable behavior from individuals at a relatively low labor cost.

Given the kind of performance it produces, contingency approaches to organization design suggest there are certain kinds of work situations particularly amenable to the involvement approach (see, for example, Burns and Stalker, 1961; Galbraith, 1973). Figure 3-2 captures some of this thinking by making predictions about the relative performance effective-

Figure 3-2. Performance Effectiveness of Management Approaches.

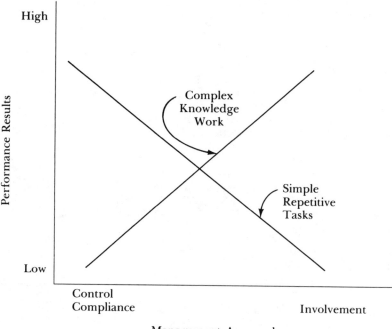

ness of the different management paradigms. Essentially, it suggests that the more knowledge work an organization does, the more advantage it gains from using the involvement paradigm. Knowledge work is found in many high-technology organizations, universities, and professional firms. It is usually the province of highly trained individuals who expect to control the way they carry out their tasks.

Similar effectiveness relationships probably exist with respect to work flow interdependence and environment stability. We can predict that

1. the more interdependent that the work of individuals is, the more effective the involvement approach is likely to be.
2. the more dynamic the environment in which the organization operates, the more effective the involvement approach is likely to be.

Interestingly, this line of reasoning suggests that an organization can be less effective in implementing an involvement approach than its competitors are at implementing the control approach and still be more effective. This will occur if the organization has picked the superior management paradigm for its particular technology and business situation. Of course, the reverse of this can also be true: when the situation favors control, even a good involvement-oriented organization may lose out.

Predictions Concerning Change

Our discussion of the costs of adopting a new paradigm leads to an interesting prediction: adoption of a new paradigm is most likely to occur when a new organization starts up. A new organization does not have a heavy investment in an existing paradigm. Thus, when it compares the control paradigm with the involvement paradigm, it is likely to see the involvement paradigm as the more attractive one. In contrast to an existing organization, it does not have to invest in retraining and in the dismantling of old systems. There is good reason to believe that the involvement paradigm can be made operational much more rapidly in a new organization because the old system and behaviors do have to be unlearned (Perkins, Nieva, and Lawler, 1983). In the new situation, key managers also often do not feel that they have as much to lose, so they are more agreeable to trying the new paradigm.

Our discussion of competitive advantage leads to some interesting predictions about what kinds of organizations are particularly likely to adopt the involvement paradigm. The competitive advantage analysis suggests that organizations that face dynamic environments and perform complex interdependent work are particularly likely to adopt the involvement-oriented paradigm. One qualification is in order here, however.

Even though the involvement approach may lead to greater effectiveness, it does not follow that organizations will necessarily adopt it. Indeed, they may be in a position to gain from the involvement approach but still maintain the control approach. The key here is how effective they perceive their present approach to be. If they think that they are doing reasonably well, then the probability of change is relatively low. But if they feel they are not effective, then there is likely to be a strong motivation to adopt the involvement approach. But how do organizations judge their effectiveness/ineffectiveness? There are of course a number of absolute financial measures (for example, return on equity), but perhaps the most compelling is the relative performance of the organization, that is, how the organization compares to its competitors.

There are two developments that can cause an organization to be at a competitive disadvantage. First, a company in a different part of the world may have a cost structure that allows it to deliver a product or service much more effectively. This by itself can stimulate the adoption of a new paradigm, although it may simply encourage the organization to strive for better utilization of its existing paradigm.

A good guess is that one of the issues that determines how an organization responds to a foreign competitive disadvantage is the size of the improvement that it feels it needs. Only if a major improvement is needed is a paradigm shift likely. The logic for this statement is that most organizations feel that they can improve by 15 to 20 percent without a major shift. They can accomplish this kind of improvement by the typical cost-cutting and top-down edicts that are characteristic of the control model. Thus it may take a perceived need for a 30 to 50 percent improvement for serious consideration to be given to a paradigm shift. Also, if the organization does the kind of work that on the surface seems amenable to the new paradigm, it is much more likely to shift paradigms in order to become competitive. In sum, when an organization's dissatisfaction with its present state is stimulated primarily by foreign competition, a new paradigm is likely to be adopted if the new paradigm fits the organization's situation and a significant performance improvement is needed.

The situation is different when the issue is a competitive disadvantage that is produced by a local competitor. Here it matters both what kind of management style the competitor uses and how significant a disadvantage the organization feels it has. As it would do with an offshore competitor, an organization is particularly likely to choose a paradigm shift if it is at a large performance disadvantage. However, in the case of a domestic competitor, the key to understanding the response may be the management paradigm used by the competitor.

If an onshore competitor not only has a significant advantage but is seen as obtaining it by using a new paradigm, then the motivation of an organization to adopt the new paradigm will be particularly strong. In essence, there will be a high level of dissatisfaction with the existing state of affairs and a high level of attractiveness associated with a new paradigm. When a domestic competitor uses a new paradigm, it establishes that it can be made to work under similar conditions, thus dealing with the "can do" issue in expectancy theory. It also helps to solve some of the technology development problems mentioned earlier that go along with pioneering a new paradigm.

This point leads to one last observation about changes that are motivated by foreign competition. The nature of these changes may depend on a combination of the type of paradigm used by the foreign competitors and the perceived similarity between their culture and the domestic culture. At least initially, practices from very different cultures are unlikely to be adopted even though they lead to high levels of effectiveness in competing organizations. They are easily dismissed as not being applicable. This argument was used for a long time by American companies with respect to many of the practices in Japan. It was even used to discount some of the initial American successes with high-involvement management (Lawler, 1986). Successful high-involvement plants in rural areas, for example, were dismissed as not being significant because it was thought that this approach would not work in other environments.

The discussion so far suggests that a domino effect may occur: the more that competitor organizations adopt a new paradigm and succeed with it, the greater will be the motivation for the remaining organizations to adopt it. This point leads to an additional nonobvious prediction about change within organizations. In those organizations that operate in multiple businesses, the paradigms they use on a business-by-business basis may be more influenced by what is going on in particular industries than what is occurring in other parts of the same organization. Thus, if you want to predict the paradigm that part of an organization will use, it may be more important to know what their competitors are doing than what other parts of their organization are doing.

Finally, one other situation needs to be mentioned, namely, the one in which an organization simply decides that the best way to be effective in the business world is to adopt a new paradigm. In short, an organization perceives that it can gain a competitive advantage by going to the involvement paradigm. This is the least likely scenario for change, although one that cannot be ruled out completely, particularly if the technology and organizational situation seem to strongly favor the involvement paradigm.

In conclusion, predictions about whether a particular organization will switch paradigms can be made if we know its age, its current performance effectiveness relative to its competitors, the kinds of work it does, its technologies, the environment it faces, and the investment it has made in the existing paradigm. The greatest probability of a paradigm shift exists when an organization needs to make large improvements, faces onshore competitors who are successfully using the new paradigm, and has little invested in the old paradigm. At the other extreme situation we find an older organization using the traditional paradigm quite effectively, with everyone else in the industry following suit. In between these extremes are a variety of situations that potentially could lead to paradigm shift.

Patterns of Change

With the discussion so far in mind, let us look at some of the changes that are taking place in the American economy. It is, of course, extremely difficult to characterize the paradigms that organizations use, much less those that whole industries are using. Nevertheless, we can at least make some general observation about what seems to be going on in the United States.

First of all, however, we should note that there are four key reasons why the involvement approach had trouble winning acceptance when it was first advocated in the 1950s:

1. Most business organizations in the United States were performing well.
2. Little proof existed that the involvement approach produced superior results.
3. Many of the details of how to install and implement the involvement approach were unknown.
4. Top management, which had to lead any change to involvement, saw itself as better off under the control approach.

In short, it is hardly surprising that for decades business schools taught about involvement but that few of these teachings were implemented. What is perhaps surprising is that some people expected that the involvement approach would be implemented simply because it was taught in the schools and there was some evidence of its effectiveness. Given the current competitive problems that some American businesses are having, it is also not surprising that change is finally taking place.

The paper industry represents a particularly interesting example of a paradigm shift. About twenty years ago Procter & Gamble introduced the involvement paradigm into the domestic paper industry. It seems that this change came about largely because Procter & Gamble happened to have a manager who was a strong advocate of the new paradigm at the very time when it was experiencing poor manufacturing performance in its unionized facilities. In addition, it was a new business for Procter & Gamble, so the company had little investment in the existing paradigm in that industry. Finally, the company discovered that some Scandinavian paper companies were using the involvement paradigm successfully, as were some other parts of Procter & Gamble itself.

Part of the willingness of Procter & Gamble to change may also have been based on the technological fit between paper making and the involvement paradigm. Much of paper making involves knowledge work and requires high levels of interdependency. In short, Procter & Gamble wanted to gain a competitive advantage and chose to adopt a new paradigm. This is understandable given offshore competition, the nature of the work, the newness of the business to Procter & Gamble, and the presence of a charismatic individual who was willing to work for the new paradigm.

Over the years since Procter & Gamble has introduced the involvement paradigm, the company appears to have gained a competitive advantage and to have motivated most other paper companies to adopt it. Mead, Weyerhaeuser, Kimberly-Clark, Scott Paper, and James River, for example, have all adopted an involvement approach to managing their businesses. This pattern is consistent with the arguments that have been made so far. Thus, we have the case of a domestic competitor gaining a competitive advantage through a new management style. This produced a great deal of dissatisfaction with the existing approach, a clear example of how to do it differently, and clear evidence that doing it differently had strongly improved organizational effectiveness. Given all this, it is hardly surprising that most paper companies have adopted some version of the involvement approach. However, not all parts of the companies in the paper industry have adopted the involvement paradigm. For example, Procter & Gamble does not use it in its nonmanufacturing areas, and other companies do not use it in their nonpaper businesses.

The situation in the automobile industry is somewhat different but nevertheless worth examining. Until approximately ten years ago the American automobile companies competed with each other strictly in terms of their effectiveness in implementing the traditional paradigm. There was no great level of dissatisfaction with that paradigm, and the three major auto companies had no clear vision of a new paradigm, despite the fact that Volvo and Saab were utilizing involvement to an increasing degree. In fact, the U.S. auto companies denied the applicability of the Volvo and Saab experiment with the involvement paradigm to their own situation because of the different cultures involved and continued to compete by trying to implement the traditional paradigm more effectively.

Matters started to change, however, when the Japanese

made strong inroads into the U.S. auto market. They appeared to use a different management paradigm approach, but, more importantly, they increased the level of dissatisfaction with the old one. They had quality and cost advantages that were large and perhaps unachievable through better execution of the traditional paradigm. Indeed, General Motors, which was often cited as an excellent implementer of the traditional paradigm, must have felt considerably at sea. The company was supposedly good at what it was doing and yet was orders of magnitude too ineffective to compete in the domestic marketplace. Not surprisingly, this situation set off a search for a new paradigm that continues to this day.

The New United Motor Manufacturing Incorporated (NUMMI) plant of General Motors in northern California and its proposed Saturn plant are examples of how one company is trying to implement the involvement paradigm in order to close the gap between itself and the Japanese. Change, however, has been relatively slow, partly because the involvement paradigm is not fully developed for the auto industry, despite the early work of Saab and Volvo. In addition, some of the work in the industry is really not knowledge work and does not require a high degree of interdependence. Finally, as many critics of the American auto companies have pointed out, senior executives have a great deal to lose if the involvement paradigm were to be adopted. They have a long tradition of control-oriented management, and this paradigm is a source of special benefits and perquisites for them (O'Toole, 1985). Thus, it is perhaps not too surprising that the auto industry has been slow to change. In many ways the conditions in the rubber, steel, and glass industries are very similar to those in the auto industry. Foreign competition is forcing a change in paradigm, but it is occurring slowly because of the lack of well-articulated alternative paradigms and the heavy hand of tradition in those industries.

Producing Change

The arguments made here suggest some things that can be done to stimulate paradigm shifts. First, dissatisfaction with the existing state can be elaborated, clarified, or even produced. Two approaches suggest themselves here. The first is bench marking performance relative to the competition. This has been used extensively by Xerox in its paradigm shift efforts and has proven to be a very valuable tool. It has served to highlight just how big the gap is between Xerox and some of its competitors and has heightened dissatisfaction with the company's tradi- tional approach to management. Very much related to this is the idea of contrasting the existing to an ideal state. If people can be shown that the current system is producing results far short of what they desire, then motivation for a shift can be produced. Finally, improving the performance measures that are used by an organization can often help clarify the shortcomings of the existing paradigm. Surveys, measures of human resource ac- tivities, quality indexes, and so on can all help point to the shortfalls in the existing paradigm and increase dissatisfaction with it.

In short, perhaps the best way to increase dissatisfaction with the existing situation is to be sure that all the consequences of it are known and to compare the organization's performance to that of its competitors. There is one danger in setting out to increase dissatisfaction, however. This tactic may result in a counterproductive, defensive reaction on the part of organiza- tional members. There is very little evidence on when and why this happens, but a good guess is that it is particularly likely to occur when there is a strong suggestion that the problems are due to poor performance on the part of employees or to overly conservative behavior. Less defensiveness might be expected if people are made to feel good about their past behavior but are also made to realize that environmental or technological changes require a paradigm shift (Nadler, 1987).

Finally, working on the dissatisfaction side of change is not likely to be effective if an organization is doing well relative to its competitors but is falling far short of its potential because it is simply using the wrong paradigm. The major hope for stimulating a desire for change here is to increase the attrac- tiveness of the new.

There are a number of things that can be done to increase

the attractiveness of a new paradigm. Simply educating people in the new paradigm can be useful. This can include visiting locations that use the new paradigm, reading about it, attending conferences, and trying it out on a limited basis. Emphasizing to people that they are going to have the option to invent their own version of it can be particularly effective. There is no question that participation in the invention of a paradigm is a powerful way to presell it in an organization (Nadler, 1987).

Also important in increasing the attractiveness of the new is the role that leadership can play in creating a vision of what the company might become (Bennis and Nanus, 1985). Most successful large-scale organizational change programs are led by an individual who is clearly able to articulate a positive vision of how the new paradigm will operate. Basic to a positive vision of the involvement paradigm is the combination of values such as democracy, individual growth, and justice with arguments concerning organizational effectiveness.

Critical also to the attractiveness of the new is providing people with some sense of security about their own position in it. To allow them to participate in the design is, of course, one way to accomplish this. However, it may also be necessary to guarantee them employment, guarantee them their current wage levels, and perhaps even reward them for adopting the new paradigm (Lawler, 1981). If the issues of personal security and careers are not at least taken into account, it is natural to expect considerable resistance to the new paradigm on the part of management. In some cases management resistance may simply be unavoidable, and the assumption must be made that turn-over will occur in this group. Where possible, however, it is highly desirable to try to reduce resistance through a combination of providing personal security and rewards for a change.

In summary, a number of things can be done to encour-age paradigm shifts, but all of them involve both decreasing employees' satisfaction with the existing paradigm and increas-ing the attractiveness of the new. To a degree, paradigm shifts can be stimulated and motivated by change agents and indi-viduals. But the situational arguments made earlier suggest that such shifts are going to be effective only if certain environmental conditions exist and if the organization is operating with technologies and work situations that favor the involvement paradigm. When the skills of internal change agents, the type of technology used by the organization, and the external environment all come together to support change, then the kind of paradigm shift that involves moving from control to commitment can occur.

References

Beckhard, R., and Harris, R. T. *Organizational Transitions*. Reading, Mass.: Addison-Wesley, 1977.

Bennis, W. G., and Nanus, B. *Leadership: Strategies for Taking Charge*. New York: Harper & Row, 1985.

Burns, T., and Stalker, G. M. *The Management of Innovation*. London: Tavistock, 1961.

Galbraith, J. *Designing Complex Organizations*. Reading, Mass.: Addison-Wesley, 1973.

Katz, D., and Kahn, R. L. *The Social Psychology of Organizations*. New York: Wiley, 1966.

Katz, D., and Kahn, R. L. *The Social Psychology of Organizations*. (2nd ed.) New York: Wiley, 1978.

Lawler, E. E. *Motivation in Work Organizations*. Monterey, Calif.: Brooks/Cole, 1973.

Lawler, E. E. *Pay and Organization Development*. Reading, Mass.: Addison-Wesley, 1981.

Lawler, E. E. *High Involvement Management*. San Francisco: Jossey-Bass, 1986.

March, J. G., and Simon, H. A. *Organizations*. New York: Wiley, 1958.

Mohrman, A. M., and Lawler, E. E. "The Diffusion of QWL as a Paradigm Shift." In W. G. Bennis, K. D. Benne, and R. Chin (eds.), *The Planning of Change*. New York: Holt, Rinehart & Winston, 1985.

Nadler, D. A. "The Effective Management of Organizational Change." In J. Lorsch (ed.), *Handbook of Organizational Behavior*. Englewood Cliffs, N.J.: Prentice-Hall, 1987.

O'Toole, J. *Vanguard Management*. New York: Doubleday, 1985.

Perkins, D., Nieva, R., and Lawler, E. E. *Managing Creation.* New York: Wiley, 1983.

Tichy, N. M., and Devanna, M. A. *The Transformational Leader.* New York: Wiley, 1986.

Walton, R. E. "From Control to Commitment in the Workplace." *Harvard Business Review*, 1985, *63* (2), 76–84.

4

David A. Nadler

❧ ❧ ❧ ❧ ❧ ❧ ❧ ❧

Organizational Frame Bending: Types of Change in the Complex Organization

The past decade has witnessed the attempt of more and more well-known organizations to manage large-scale planned change. Some of these cases have been dramatic and have captured public attention — AT&T, Chrysler, and Apple Computer come to mind. Others, while involving equally profound changes, have received somewhat less attention (for example, Corning Glass Works, Xerox, Citicorp, and GTE).

The concept of planned organizational change has been around for some time (Bennis, Benne, and Chin, 1961). This most recent generation of changes, however, is somewhat different from earlier ones. First, these changes typically have been initiated by the leaders of the organizations themselves rather than by behavioral scientists, consultants, or human resource specialists (although these types of individuals have played significant roles in some cases). Second, the changes have been closely linked to strategic business issues, not just to questions of organizational process or style. Third, most of the changes can be traced back rather directly to certain external events (rather than to internal factors), such as new sources of competition, new technology, deregulation or legal initiatives, maturation of product sets, or changes in fundamental market structure. Finally, while the list of companies includes successes, failures, and those still in process, there are now more large visible examples of successful planned organizational change than there have been in the past.

My work has brought me into contact with a number of these situations. They have, in general, been changes that encompass the whole organization, that have occurred over a number of years, and that have involved fundamental changes in the way of thinking about the business, the organization, and how the organization is managed. My experience has included changes that both internal and external observers would rate as successes, some that have been described as failures, and some that are still in process. The material in this chapter is based on observations of approximately twenty-five organizations over the past five years, and specifically on close work with the most senior levels of management in planning and implementing significant multiyear strategic level changes in six organizations.

My purpose here is to share some insights, generalizations, and hunches about these large-scale organization changes, working from a perspective of close-in participant observation. The chapter will build on earlier work on organizations and change (Nadler and Tushman, 1977, 1980, 1986; Nadler, 1981). I will begin by reviewing some basic concepts of organization and change that have shaped the way we think about and observe these types of events. Second, I will briefly describe an approach for thinking about types of organization change — how one change may differ from another. Third, I will spend most of the chapter developing a set of observations about a particular type of large-scale change (which I refer to as *frame bending*) in complex organizations.

Basic Concepts of Organization and Change

As a starting point, let us view organizations as open systems that, in the context of an environment, an available set of resources, and a history, produce outputs (see Nadler and Tushman 1977, 1980, for a more detailed description and dis-

Figure 4-1. Organization Model.

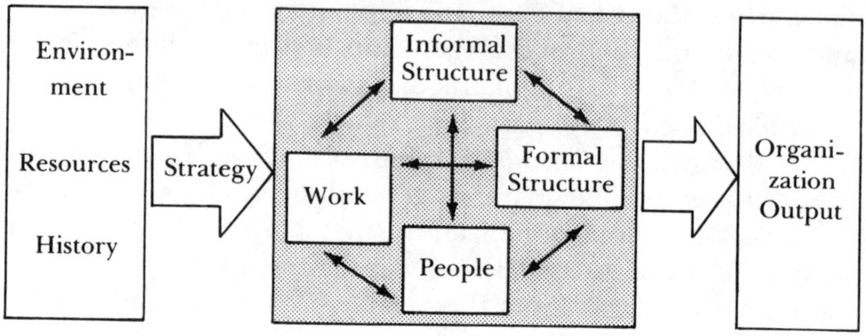

cussion of this model). The specific systems model has two major elements (Figure 4-1). The first is strategy, the pattern of decisions that emerges over times about how resources will be configured against environmental opportunities and threats. The second is organization, the mechanism that is developed to turn strategy into output. It includes four core elements—work, people, formal structures and processes, and informal structures and processes. The fundamental dynamic is congruence among the elements. Effectiveness is greater when the general pattern of organization matches or fits the strategy. Effectiveness will also be achieved when the four components are more congruent, consistent, or have greater "fit" with each other. The model emphasizes that there is no one best way to organize. Rather, the set of most effective ways of organizing is determined by the nature of the strategy as well as by the nature of the work (in most cases), the nature of the individuals who are members of the organization, and the nature of the informal processes and structures (including culture) that have grown up over time.

While the model emphasizes congruence as a desirable state, it is, in fact, a double-edged sword. In the short term, congruence of organizational elements seems to be related to effectiveness and performance. A system with high congruence, however, can also be one that is resistant to change. It develops ways of buffering itself from outside influences and may be unable to respond to new and unique situations.

From time to time, however, organizations are faced with the need to modify themselves. The required change may involve one or more pieces or elements of the organizational system, or it may involve a realignment of the whole system (affecting all the key elements—strategy, work, people, formal and informal processes and structures). A core problem is how to maintain congruence in the system while implementing change, or how to help the organization move to a whole new configuration and a whole new definition of congruence. There has been a growing literature on organization change management and methods of implementation (see, for example, Pennings, 1985; Goodman, 1982). At the most basic level, some observers of change have proposed that organization changes can be thought of as a move from a current state to a future state, moving through a transition state (Beckhard and Harris, 1977). Others have suggested that the critical issues in managing such changes include (1) managing the political dynamics associated with the change, (2) motivating constructive behavior in the face of the anxiety created by the change, and (3) actively managing the transition state (Nadler, 1981).

While these approaches have been useful for managers and implementers of organizational change, they have limitations when applied to the type of large-scale, complex organization changes described above. Specifically, these larger-scale changes seem to have some of the following characteristics:

- *Multiple transitions.* Frequently the changes are not confined to one transition; rather, there is a whole set of different transitions. Some of them may be explicitly related to one another, but others may be unrelated.
- *Incompleted transitions.* Many of the transitions that are initiated do not get completed. Events overtake them, or subsequent changes subsume them.
- *Uncertain future states.* In many cases, it is difficult to predict or define exactly what the future state will be. Sometimes there are many unknowns that limit the ability to describe a future state. At other times, although a future state can be

described, there is a high probability that events will change the nature of that state before it is achieved.

- *Transitions over long periods of time.* Many large-scale organization changes take long periods of time to implement—in some cases anywhere from three to seven years. The dynamics of managing change over this amount of time are different from those needed to manage a change with a discrete beginning and end and of short duration.

Through discussing these issues, one sees the need to extend the concepts and frameworks of organizational change to deal with these additional challenges.

Types of Organizational Change

As a first step toward understanding large-scale organizational change, we have attempted to develop a way of thinking about the different types of changes that organizations face (Nadler and Tushman, 1986). Change can be thought about on two dimensions. The first dimension concerns the scope of the change—whether it involves pieces of the organization or the entire system. Changes that are focused on individual pieces or components, with the goal of maintaining or regaining congruence, may be called incremental changes. Changes that are addressed to the organization as a whole—to most or all of the organization's components, including strategy—may be called strategic changes. These changes frequently involve breaking out of the current pattern of congruence and helping the organization to move to a completely new configuration. Incremental changes are those that are made within the context or "frame" of the current set of organizational strategies and components. They do not address fundamental changes in the definition of the business, shifts of power, alterations in culture, and similar issues. Strategic changes, however, address the context or frame of the organization itself. Thus we think of incremental changes as being within the current organizational context, paradigm, or frame, while strategic changes involve changing that frame, either shaping or bending it, or (in the extreme) breaking it.

Figure 4-2. Types of Organizational Changes.

	Incremental	Strategic
Anticipatory	Tuning	Reorientation
Reactive	Adaptation	Re-creation

A second dimension for thinking about change concerns the temporal positioning of the change in relation to key external events. Some changes are clearly in response to an event or series of events that occur. These are called reactive changes. Other changes are initiated, not in response to events, but in anticipation of external events that may occur. These are called anticipatory changes. This approach can best be described through the use of a figure illustrating types of changes (see Figure 4-2). Four types of change are described:

- *Tuning.* These are incremental changes that are made in anticipation of future events. These changes are similar to the incremental adjustment of an engine, which seeks to find ways to increase efficiency but is not done in response to any immediate need or problem.
- *Adaptation.* These changes are also incremental but they are made in reaction to external events. Actions of a competitor, changes in market needs, new technology, and so on make it necessary for the organization to respond, but the response is not one that involves fundamental change across the organization.
- *Reorientation.* This is strategic change, but change made when and where the external events that necessitated change were anticipated. These changes do involve fundamental

redirection of the organization but are frequently put in terms that emphasize continuity with the past (particularly values of the past). Since the emphasis is on bringing about major change but without a sharp break with the existing organizational frame, we talk about these types of change as frame-bending changes.

- *Re-creations.* These are strategic changes necessitated by external events, usually those that are life threatening to the organization. Such changes necessitate radical departure from past practices and include shifts in senior leadership, in values, in strategy, in culture, and so forth. These changes, therefore, can be thought of as frame-breaking changes.

Building on this classification scheme, we can describe these different types of change in terms of their intensity (Figure 4-3). Intensity is the degree of strength or severity of the change and, in particular, the degree of shock, trauma, or discontinuity created by the change throughout the organization. Strategic changes are obviously more intense than incremental changes, which can frequently be implemented without alterations to the basic management processes of the organization. Reactive changes are more intense than anticipatory changes since they create the need to pack a lot of activity into a short period of time without the opportunity to position or prepare people to deal with the resulting traumas. There also is less room for error and correction because threats to survival are involved.

An additional factor in thinking about changes involves the characteristics of the organization being changed. It appears that organizations become more difficult to change as they increase in their complexity—complexity being determined by (1) size of the organization in terms of employees and (2) the diversity of the organization in terms of number of different businesses, geographical dispersion, and so on. Smaller organizations with a few highly related businesses are easier places to implement changes than are larger, highly diverse organizations. If we put these concepts together, we get a mapping of the difficulty of the organizational change task (Figure 4-4). The least difficult changes are those that are low

Figure 4-3. Relative Intensity of Different Types of Change.

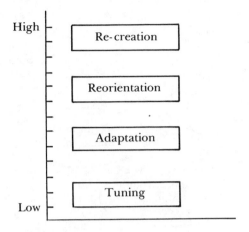

intensity and in fairly noncomplex settings. The most difficult changes are those that are high intensity (strategic) and occur in high-complexity organizations.

With this classification scheme in mind, we want to now turn to some of the observations on managing changes. Our focus will be on the upper end of the diagonal space in Figure 4-4, although we will concentrate on the reorientations rather than the re-creations. The re-creations pose a very specific set of concerns and issues. Our assumption also is that most managers would rather avoid the costs and risks associated with re-creation. The challenge, then is, how to manage the reorientations or the frame-bending changes in very complex organizations.

Effective Organizational Frame Bending

As mentioned above, the observations we will make are still in an early stage of formulation. Rather than creating an elaborate theoretical framework, we will merely list them as a set of "principles" for managing these types of changes, keeping in mind that each of them really is no more than a tentative observation that will need to be tested and refined over time.

Figure 4-4. The Difficulty of Organizational Change.

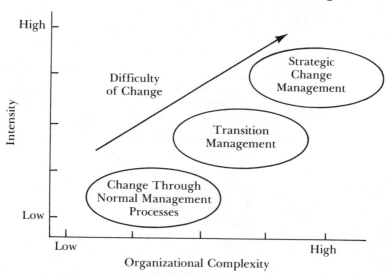

The Management of Pain Principle. Much of the organizational change literature talks about pain as a necessary antecedent to change. While this is true, there are additional issues to consider in organizational frame bending. It appears to be true that for people in organizations to consider significant change, they must feel some degree of pain with the current state. The larger and more intense the change, the more extreme the pain must be in order to mobilize individuals to consider doing things differently. The problem is that pain can create energy that motivates different types of behavior. The consequences of pain can be dysfunctional behavior as well as functionally directed action.

The first part of the task is the creation of pain. Large organizations develop means of buffering themselves and their people from pain. Size and inertia help people to ignore what might otherwise be painful information. In addition, the task of reorientation or frame bending by definition takes place in anticipation of external events that might create pain. Thus, part of the job of change management is either to focus people on potential sources of pain or to create some sense of urgency around the changes that are being advocated.

At the same time, the manager of change needs to be on guard against dysfunctional responses to pain. Negative information can lead to such defensive reactions as denial, flight, or withdrawal. To the extent that the organization is characterized by pathology, the creation of pain or urgency may stimulate maladaptive responses. Successful long-term changes seem to be characterized by creation of a sense of urgency right at the limits of tolerance—just at the point where responses may start to become defensive. At the same time, efforts are made to track dysfunctional or pathological responses and to find ways to redirect the energy in positive directions.

The Centrality Principle. For a change to engage the organization, it needs to be clearly and obviously linked to the core strategic issues of the firm rather than being seen as peripheral. The positioning and labeling of the change are critical. Successful long-term changes are positioned as strategic imperatives that are therefore compelling to members of the organization. Usually, the connection is so clear and has so much face validity that the relationship of the change to company health and survival is obvious. Where changes are not seen as central to the survival, health, or growth of the organization, they tend to be transient in nature, existing only as long as the perceived interest of senior management lasts. For a change to "catch on," people need to be able to easily see its connection with core organizational and individual outcomes.

To the degree that the change is central, it also raises another dilemma. If the organization has been successful and has built some degree of congruence over the years, people may resist wholesale changes in the way that things are done. In many of the successful long-term changes, managers worked to make sure that the core themes of the change had organizational resonance, that is, that the core themes of the change seemed related to and consistent with some of the historical core values of the organization. A related problem is how to find themes with strategic centrality when there is great diversity in an organization. It appears to be more difficult to find such themes across sets of widely diverse businesses in large organizations. Successful attempts here seem to involve basic or generic themes (such as quality or competitiveness) that can be positioned across the businesses but that can also be related with specificity to the situation of each particular business.

The Three-Theme Principle. While a strategic change may involve a large number of specific activities, initiatives, programs, or actions, most managers of change find it necessary to identify sets of themes that can serve to communicate and conceptualize the changes going on. Themes provide labels, a language, and a means for people to understand and find patterns in what is happening around them. At the same time, however, organizations and people in organizations seem to be capable of integrating only a limited number of themes in the midst of all the other transactions that make up daily life. People are bombarded with different programs, messages, and directives in large organizations. In many situations individuals cope by figuring out which messages to ignore and which to attend to. More are ignored than are listened to. The successful long-term changes seem to be characterized by a careful self-discipline that limits the number of major themes or initiatives. It appears that, as a general rule, managers of a change may only be able to initiate and sustain three (plus or minus one) key themes during any particular period of time.

The dilemma in this area is to create enough themes to get people truly energized around what needs to be changed, while limiting the number of themes. The toughest part of this is facing up to the decision not to initiate a new program, communication, or initiative that by itself, has great merit, because of the possibility of diluting the themes. Successful cases appear to be characterized by consistency of themes over time. There seems to be great value in stability and repetition. It is the consistency of the theme that is significant in getting people to believe that the theme is credible. The dilemma, then, is how to manage the evolution of themes over time as conditions change (and hopefully progress is made), while maintaining the consistency of themes.

The Magic Leader Principle. All the successful reorientations we have observed are characterized by an individual leader who is able to serve as a focal point for the change and whose presence, activity, and touch have some special feel or magic. Large-scale organizational change appears to require active, dynamic, and visible leadership to help articulate the change and to capture and mobilize the hearts and minds of the people in the organization (Bennis and Nanus, 1985; Tichy and Devanna, 1986). In our experience, these leaders display some of the following characteristics:

- *Distinctive behaviors.* Leaders engage in three types of distinctive behaviors that appear to be related to getting people to act in ways consistent with the change. One type of behavior is envisioning; this includes acts that help to create a picture or vision of a future state that is engaging and inspirational. A second type of behavior is energizing— creating or stimulating energy to act through personal demonstration, rewards and punishments, and the setting of high standards. A third type of behavior is enabling, which involves creating the processes, resources, or structures to enable individuals to do the things that they have been motivated to do. The successful large-scale change leaders seem to exhibit elements of all three of these types of behavior.
- *Creating a sense of urgency.* The individual leader seems to be critical in creating the sense of urgency that is so important to organizational changes of this type. As discussed above, the leader is a key actor in the creation and management of pain.
- *A mix of styles.* The leaders of large-scale changes also appear to display an interesting mix of management styles. On one hand, they appear to be directive, uncompromising, and even autocratic in the direction or objectives that they set for

the change. On the other hand, they appear to be very participative and spend lots of time getting people involved in shaping how the change will occur. This balanced mixture of arbitrariness and participation appears to be critical to success.

- *Guardianship of the themes.* The leader is the guardian of the themes of the change. He or she is the one individual who can make sure that the themes survive. Successful change managers appear to exhibit great tenacity (or even stubbornness) in the articulation of themes over a period of years, keeping everyone's attention focused on them in the face of both good times and bad times.

The dilemma in this area is that while the individual leader is a necessary element of successful change, continued dependence upon him or her can lead to the death of the change. The change becomes too personalized, nothing happens unless that individual stakes personal sponsorship, and the next levels of management may become disenfranchised on a de facto basis. Furthermore, when the leader makes mistakes (as he or she inevitably does), the "magic" may fade. The heroic leader finds it difficult to live up to the fantasies that organization members create around him or her. Thus, the dilemma for this individual is to fulfill the need for a leader while at the same time allowing the organization to grow beyond that need.

The Leadership Is Not Enough Principle. While strong individual leadership is necessary, it cannot by itself sustain a large-scale change. The successful changes appear to be those in which a broader base of support is built, with other individuals acting first as followers, second as helpers, and finally as co-owners of the change. The device for doing this usually is the senior management team of the organization. Successful changes seem to be characterized by a large amount of investment in the senior team, both as individuals and as a group. The senior team needs to share and own the vision over time to become more visible as champions, and to come to grips collectively with the task of managing today's business while also managing the change to position tomorrow's business. While the senior team is usually a focal point, it clearly is not the only point where leadership can be broadened. Other sets of people or groups (ranging from middle management, to labor unions, to boards of directors) also are candidates for expanded ownership of the change.

The No Free Lunch Principle. Large-scale significant organization change requires significant investments to make it occur. These are investments of time, effort, energy, dollars, and so on. While change may yield significant positive results, it is not cost free. Successful changes are characterized by a willingness to invest all the resources that will be needed to make change occur. The most scarce resource appears to be senior management time. Organizations engaging in large-scale change find it necessary to get senior managers involved in a wide range of activities, including senior team meetings, presentations, attendance at special events, and education and training. The broadening of ownership, mentioned above, also requires a significant investment of time, particularly on the part of members of the senior team. The less successful changes seem to be those where the investments of time were put off or avoided because senior managers felt so overloaded with change activity that they could not do their everyday work. In the successful cases, the change was seen as an integral part of that work.

The dilemma here is that investment of time by the senior team is needed, and yet this may cut into the time that the team needs in its role as leader of the rest of the organization. This may lead to charges that the senior team is too insular, too inward looking, too absorbed in its own processes. Again, the challenge is to find a balance between these two demands.

The Check Is in the Mail Principle. Large-scale organization change takes time. As the complexity of the organization increases, the time required to change it also increases. Each level of the organization engaged in the change takes its own time to understand, accept, integrate, and then subsequently own and lead change. In many cases, it becomes important to sell and resell the change throughout many levels of the organization. Each level has to go through its own process of comprehending the change and coming to terms with it. Organizations seem to pass through predictable states as they come to grips with a change and a set of themes:

- *Awareness.* People within the organization first become aware of the need to change and the dimensions of the change. They work to come to grips with this need and to understand what the change is all about.
- *Experimentation.* Small-scale efforts are made to experiment with the changes in a bounded and manageable setting. Efforts are made to see if the change will really work in "our unique setting."
- *Understanding.* The experimentation leads to increased understanding of the change, its consequences and implications. At this point, people begin to realize the "full horror" of the change and what it may involve.
- *Commitment.* The leadership recognizes the need for change and decides to move forward by making a significant and visible commitment to take action.
- *Education.* People invest time formally to acquire skill and information to be able to implement the change. This may involve training or other investments to transfer skills.
- *Application to leveraged issues.* The new approach, perspective, or skills are applied to key issues or specific situations where there is leverage. This is done consciously, and even a bit awkwardly.
- *Integration into ongoing behavior.* The new changed behavior starts to become a way of life. People naturally (unconsciously) are working in new ways.

Obviously, a change rarely follows these steps exactly as described above. Also, each level of the organization may go through each stage at its own pace. But, at some time, each part of the organization must come to grips with each of these issues in some form. As a result, large-scale reorientations in complex organizations probably take from three to seven years to be substantially implemented. The efforts may be characterized by false starts, derailments, and the necessity to start over in some places or in some elements. In addition, significant payoffs may not be seen until after two years at a minimum. Again, there is a dilemma. People need to be convinced to invest personally in the change while there still is no evidence that it will pay off, either to the organization or to them personally. Their motivation is needed for success, but success over time is needed to get their motivation. Hence, there is a need to be able to demonstrate (through experiments, through personal example, or through "face validity") that the change will ultimately pay off.

The Nuts and Bolts Principle. Assuming that all the other principles are adhered to, the organization ultimately will have to come to grips with the need to adjust its infrastructure to be consistent with and supportive of the change. As all the other work is being done, there is the less glamorous but still critical work of building the processes and structures to support, enable, and reinforce the changes. This is tough, detailed, and sometimes tedious work, but it is required. Some of the things that need to be addressed include:

- Standards and measures of performance
- Rewards and incentives
- Planning processes
- Budgeting and resource allocation methods
- Information systems

The dilemma here is one of timing. This work cannot get out too far ahead of the change, yet it cannot lag too far behind. In practice, it may be ignored and seen as a bothersome detail. But successful changes are characterized by skillful use of these processes to support and in some cases drive the change over time.

Conclusion

This chapter has focused on the regularities of change — on the consistencies that seem to characterize the more suc-

cessful attempts at large-scale, long-term organizational reorientation. But it would be a mistake to end this chapter without
commenting on the very important, critical, and central "irreg-
ularities" of organizational life and how these impact on change.
Two elements are greatly intertwined with the implementation
of such change—power politics and pathology. All organizations are political systems, and changes occur within the context
of both individual and group aspirations. Thus, strategic
changes become intertwined with ideological issues (what type
of company should we be), as well as personal issues (what is
going to be the impact on my career). These are not aberrations;
they are a normal part of organizational life. However, they will
be magnified, and indeed may "play themselves out" through the
change. It is difficult to provide general guidance, rules, or
principles for dealing with this phenomenon, since the issues
vary greatly. However, the successful change manager seems to
work hard at understanding what these dynamics are, to try to
predict their impact on the change and the impact of the change
on the dynamics, and to work to shape the situation to make use
of these dynamics positively.

　　Not all organizational life is normal, healthy, and adaptive. Organizations, like people, have their dark sides—their
destructive or maladaptive responses to situations. Organizations develop stylized responses to problems or situations over
time. These responses may be elicited by the intensity of a
strategic change. An organization that has ignored environmental threats may become more insular. An organization that
engages in collective despair may become still more despairing.
Again, it is the leader who needs to be able to understand the
extant organizational pathology and attempt to bound it or, in
some cases, raise it up to consciousness so that it can be
confronted.

　　We have attempted here to share some initial views on a
particular subset of organizational changes that we think are
particularly significant. More and more organizations seem to
be facing the need to undergo such changes as global competitive pressures increase. As such, this chapter is just a first

step in trying to understand these changes and provide guidance to those who are called upon to lead these organizations.

References

Beckhard, R., and Harris, R. T. *Organizational Transitions*. Reading, Mass.: Addison-Wesley, 1977.

Bennis, W. G., Benne, K. D., and Chin, R. *The Planning of Change*.
New York: Holt, Rinehart & Winston, 1961.

Bennis, W. G., and Nanus, B. *Leadership: The Strategies for Taking
Charge*. New York: Harper & Row, 1985.

Goodman, P. S., and Associates. *Change in Organizations: New
Perspectives on Theory, Research, and Practice*. San Francisco:
Jossey-Bass, 1982.

Nadler, D. A. "Managing Organizational Change: An Integrative
Perspective." *Journal of Applied Behavioral Science*, 1981, *17*,
191–211.

Nadler, D. A., and Tushman, M. L. "A Diagnostic Model for
Organization Behavior." In E. E. Lawler and L. W. Porter
(eds.), *Perspectives on Behavior in Organizations*. New York:
McGraw-Hill, 1977.

Nadler, D. A., and Tushman, M. L. "A Model for Diagnosing
Organizational Behavior." *Organizational Dynamics*, 1980, *9*,
35–51.

Nadler, D. A., and Tushman, M. L. *Managing Strategic Organizational Change: Frame Bending and Frame Breaking*. New York:
Delta Consulting Group, 1986.

Pennings, J. M. *Organizational Strategy and Change: New Views on
Formulating and Implementing Strategic Decisions*. San Francisco:
Jossey-Bass, 1985.

Tichy, N. M., and Devanna, M. A. *The Transformational Leader*.
New York: Wiley, 1986.

Part Two

Planning and Organizing for Corporate Transformation

This section explores some of the critical issues in managing corporate transformation. The focus of the chapters in this section ranges from the role of CEOs in corporate transformations to the role that lower-level employees can play in major change efforts. The authors also discuss potential problems that might lead to program failure and suggest strategies for increasing the probability that a change effort will be successful.

Richard Beckhard begins the section with an outline of several issues that general managers should consider when attempting major change. The author discusses the meaning of transformation, the individual and organizational conditions necessary for change, and the behaviors necessary to accomplish change. He suggests that executives must take the major role in setting the stage for effective transformation and uses two cases to illustrate his central theme.

Next, Michael L. Tushman, William H. Newman, and David A. Nadler offer a broad view of patterns of organizational evolution. The authors draw on a large research base of well-known companies to show that organizational evolution is characterized by relatively long periods of incremental change punctuated by discontinuous systemwide change. Their focus is on the role of executive leadership in managing incremental change and in recognizing when systemwide change has become necessary. This analysis provides many lessons for executives who must guide their companies through both incremental and major change.

While it is clear that top managers often play the key roles in transforming organizations, lower-level employees also can influence the types of change that will take place. In fact, sometimes lower-level employees must take the first steps in initiating a change program. In Chapter Seven, William P. Belgard, K. Kim Fisher, and Steven R. Rayner describe how employees with limited power can impact the change initiatives that eventually make it to the agendas of key executives. The authors stress the importance of vision, opportunity, and tenacity in influencing top executives and describe the role of these three factors in the transformation of Tektronix, a Fortune 200 electronics company.

Mary Elizabeth Beres and Steven J. Musser continue the theme of bottom-up transformation by presenting a non-business case. In this chapter, the authors discuss how an organization of nuns within the Roman Catholic church managed to initiate a systemwide change, and identify three role behavior sets—those of visionary, orchestrator, and legitimator—that contributed to the successful transformation. The authors use this case to explore the differences between bottom-up and top-down change. The case clearly shows that the avenues and impediments to transformation may be quite similar across very different types of organizations.

The section concludes with two chapters on transformation efforts that were somewhat less than successful. Peter Hess, William P. Ferris, Anthony F. Chelte, and Russell Fanelli document the failure of a company to implement an employee involvement program. A lack of top management commitment, mixed messages about the importance of the program, and unrealistic expectations regarding the requirements and probable outcomes of the program plagued the effort from its initiation. The authors use expectancy theory as a framework for discussing the failure and suggest that consultants can do much to set the stage for successful transformation by providing a "realistic change preview" for clients.

David B. Roitman, Jeffrey K. Liker, and Ethel Roskies describe a failed change effort in a manufacturing environment. The authors document the attempted implementation of a computer-integrated manufacturing process through interviews with company employees both during and following the change project. The difficulties in this effort stemmed in part from a change that was expected to take place too quickly. Management attempted to implement radical changes "all at once," causing worker alienation and resistance. The authors discuss what can be expected during this type of transformation and the actions that can be taken to improve the odds for successfully implementing technological change.

Part Three will build on this general discussion of critical issues in managing corporate transformation by describing some specific strategies and methods designed to aid in the implementation of major organizational change and by offering suggestions for managing some of the problems encountered in the process of transformation.

5

Richard Beckhard

The Executive Management
of Transformational Change

In this chapter, I intend to focus on the *strategic* or *general* management of a change effort that takes place within a complex organization. I want to look at the issues that are *unique* to the management of a complex system-wide change, and I will examine these issues from the standpoint of the executive leadership of the change effort. The chapter will discuss what one needs to know, understand, and be able to do to optimize the management of such an effort.

Nature of Transformation

Let us start with the definition of transformation in Webster's dictionary—"a change in the shape, structure, nature of something"—and use this definition as the basis for our discussion of transformational change. The dictionary definition of change and the needs and practices of organizations involved in transformational change seem to coincide at this point in history. There is no question that there is an increasing need for organizations of all types, but particularly business organizations, to change their shape and character in order to cope with the rapidly changing environment.

But what, in fact, is the appropriate shape for organizations, given the dynamic world in which they now operate? Moving the boxes around and writing new role descriptions are simply not adequate to cope with this new environment. Note that the word *structure* in the definition applies to those basic parts of the organization, some tangible and some less tangible, that provide it with its character. A structure is not a matter of boxes and charts but of values, beliefs, reward systems, type of leadership, management style, and the like.

The environment in which organizations operate to-day—changing consumer interests and demands, a changing work force, changing technologies, competition of minds and money from countries all over the world, the normalness of ambiguity—means that their leaders must make significant reappraisals of the nature or character of their enterprises.

The above conditions all indicate that executive management not only has to reexamine its mission or reason to be; it must also generate a vision of what it wants to be at some point in the future, and it must work out the strategies that will move it toward that vision. These types of strategic issues are quite different from those involved in running the store more creatively or increasing the business or profits short term.

The types of changes that can be called transformational are:

1. Changes in what drives the organization—for example, a change from production driven or technology driven to market driven.

2. Fundamental changes in the relationship between the parts of the organization, that is, a redefinition of staff roles. This might mean moving from functionally driven to line-of-business driven, from centrally to decentrally managed, or from executive to strategic management.

3. Changes in the ways of doing work. Moving from low-technology to high-technology manufacturing systems; emphasizing the use of computers and telecommunications; and redesigning the customer interface by, for example, providing lap computers for salespeople so that they can interact directly with both customers and suppliers—these are transformational ways of doing things.

4. Basic cultural changes — that is, changes in norms, values, and rewards. For example, significantly rewarding people who produce an invention, whether it be a new business or changing to a system that rewards for flexibility, development, creativity of the organization and rewards teamwork as well as individual effort.

In this chapter the term *transformational change* always refers to a change in some complex system or organization. It is certainly possible for individuals and small groups to transform their shape or character, but that is not the focus of attention here. Rather, I am concerned with larger or more complex systems.

Generic Implications of Transformational Change

When a transformational change occurs, there is always imbedded in it the need for some, often significant, change in the behavior of those who play key roles in the organization. For example, the types of decision making that apply under a functionally controlled organization do not apply in a company that is business-area driven or has a matrix organization. One of the key members of an organization who has to modify his behavior or, in some cases, significantly change it, is the CEO. Frequently, if a major change is to occur, the top manager must behave in new ways that indicate strong commitment to the new state. Again, the goals, priorities, and even activities of human resource managers require major modification in many transformational changes. They need to move from control to facilitation modes, from providing services to assuming leadership of change; from being implementers of policies to being active initiators of new mechanisms such as improved reward systems.

Finally, for heads of major staffs a transformation can produce an agonizing change in power structures, expectations of performance, and control over events in their functional areas. New relationships need to be worked out between staff heads and business leaders, new rewards need to be negotiated, and new definitions of what constitutes good performance need to be worked out. From a position of being the "experts" in their staff function, heads of staff must now move to being supporters, facilitators, and leaders in long-range thinking.

There needs to be explicit communication of the vision, values, priorities, and rewards that will govern the new state or condition. This often means making commitments before all the details are filled in. There also must be a clear executive strategy for managing the *tension* between the need for stability (we still have to run the store) and the need for change. Perhaps most important, there needs to be acceptance and understanding of the fact that resistance will occur and is normal. There must be strategies for working with, not against, resistance. Many executive leaders look on those who resist change as "the other side" or "the enemy," whereas the reality is that no change can take place without resistance. It is a process of internalizing, of taking on and letting go, and of eventually moving into a new state.

Resistance to change is quite normal. For example, when learning to play golf, you are told that you must hold your hands around the golf club in a certain way. Once you try this "straight way" of holding the club, however, you induce a change into your muscular system. Your entire body mobilizes to resist that change and sends you a message called pain. This same tension between status quo and change is an inherent part of complex change processes and needs to be managed in an intelligent way. Mechanisms must be set up and managements identified for managing the change *process* — the getting from here to there.

Necessary Organizational Conditions

Following is a list that suggests the priorities when an organization embarks on a major change effort.

1. In the organization's top leadership, there must be one or more *committed* champions of the change. There may be a great deal of enthusiasm in various other parts of the organization, but unless and until key top leaders are willing to make real commitments, most changes will be ephemeral at best.

2. There must be a statement in behavioral terms of what the changed organization will look like: what its basic character,

policies, values, and priorities will be. This is not a statement of short-term objectives but a vision of the future.

3. There must also be a set of external conditions that make it difficult or impossible to maintain the status quo. Unless there is some significant pressure for change, inertia will not only cause difficulties but frequently will even prevent the change from taking place. People have to be hurting enough.

4. There must be a high potential that key people will get on board and support the change. It is essential to identify the key players, both inside the hierarchical system and in the immediate environment, who are critical to success.

5. Those involved in a change effort must have a medium to long time perspective, that is, the expectation that the change will take years, not months. Quick fixes tend to be just that—first-aid treatments that do not have a base. However, it is sometimes necessary in a turbulent environment to make very dramatic character changes very quickly. When this is the case, a trap is to assume that when the first phase of the change is over, the situation has really changed. In fact, this point only marks the beginning of the need for executive *management* of the change process.

6. Change leaders must be aware that they will encounter resistance, must take this resistance seriously, and must seek to understand why it is occurring.

7. There needs to be awareness of the need for educating a number of different people and groups. Education is one of the best tools for reducing resistance, providing understanding, and getting commitment.

8. A conviction must exist that the transformation is necessary, so that resources will be provided, an experimental attitude will come into being, operate, and the organization will stay with the effort. In particular, there must be commitment from the executive management to put its money where its mouth is.

9. The organization must be willing to use all kinds of resources—technical, consultative, and expert—to effect the change.

10. Also necessary is a commitment to maintaining infor-

mation flow among all parts of the organization—for example, between those who are running the store and those who are trying to replace it with something else.

Key Factors in Managing Change

I want to present here a model for diagnosing and managing the change process that has guided me in my own work and that I think is applicable to various kinds of transformational situations. Let us first state some postulates:

First, the function of an organization is to transform inputs (needs and raw materials) into outputs (goods and services). The work of the organization, therefore, should drive the way in which one organizes to do that work, the relationships of the people doing it, and the allocation of resources to do it.

Second, when a change in the environment, a change in values, a change in the work force, or a change in its mission forces an organization or institution to transform itself, it is, in fact, transforming the function and purpose of the organization.

Third, in any change there are three "states": the present state—things as they are; the future state—what the changed condition will be; and the transition state—between the first two states.

Fourth, the core of the model is that in a change process, one first designs the future state, which can be defined as the vision of the future and the strategic objectives of a change. One then does a diagnosis of the present state in the *context* of the future state. From this diagnosis one extrapolates what is necessary in the way of activities, resource allocations, relationships, and rewards to get to the future state.

Having defined what is necessary, one then looks at the *work* that occurs during that particular state—the transition state—and provides the kind of management organization needed to manage this unique work. This is where executive management comes in. Its function is to *manage the management*, not necessarily to manage the work.

Given these states, the planning activity then falls into (1) defining the future state, (2) diagnosing the present state in the context of the future state, and (3) defining the transition state.

Fifth, the future state consists of two parts, namely, the end state or vision and an intermediate state, such as halfway to an end state or "a year from now." The model assumes that for either the end state or the intermediate state, a scenario is needed—a written description of the actual behavior of the operation at some point in time. It is as if one were in a helicopter with a wide-angle camera that could take a picture for a week.

Sixth, the model suggests that, in diagnosing the present state, one needs to analyze the "constellation" of change problems imbedded in the defined change problem and to prioritize those in terms of "domino effects." In other words, is there any particular part of the change constellation that *must* be carried out first or would make a difference if it were carried out first?

Having defined the change problem, it is now necessary to define the *system* that is affecting the problem. So one now begins to identify a critical mass, the people inside and directly outside the organization who *must* be on board if the change is to succeed. The smallest number of people or groups is the optimum. Having identified such a critical mass, one takes a look at where each of its members are on two dimensions: their readiness to contribute to the change and their capacity to do whatever is required of them for the change.

Seventh, the next piece of analysis is to identify the power relationships and resources necessary to ensure that the change takes place.

Eighth, in the transition state, management needs to identify the major activities that must occur to get from "here to there." These should then be listed in sequence and some time frame put around them.

All this adds up to the work to be done. The next major step is to define the kind of general management or executive management necessary to manage this unique work.

A Multinational Chemical Company

To do this, we will examine a large organization that operates in over eighty countries and produces a variety of chemicals, from pharmaceuticals to heavy chemicals. It operates in a number of markets and thus has competitors all over the world. It is organized in about ten business areas, each having its own board of directors and its own CEO but all wholly owned by the parent company. The enterprise is governed through a board of directors, half of whom are executive directors — these make up the active leadership of the enterprise — and half of whom are outside directors who provide the more traditional board functions.

The organization has historically operated through executive management: executive directors served as the CEOs of each of the businesses, as well as heading the territories and functions such as finance and personnel.

The organization was a leading part of the economy of its home country. It also had a very traditional culture. It was highly people oriented, somewhat paternalistic, and, in general, a comfortable place to work. There were excellent relations with the trade unions. It was one of the first companies to start joint consultations with its unions.

It had become apparent to several members of both the main board and the heads of the businesses, however, that the technically controlled decentralized divisions, primarily local in nature, would not be the appropriate way of "going to market" in the future. Technical innovation had slipped, markets had been eroded in various ways, and some of the products were too mature for much growth. Clearly, the company was ailing.

Some of the younger members of the executive board began to rethink the organizational culture. They also saw a pressing need to revitalize the research and development efforts of the company and relate them more closely to the businesses. There would be only a small central research effort as opposed to the highly centralized effort that now existed.

For a number of years the efforts of those who were working toward this "vision" were blocked or negated by the majority, who were opposed to such a massive change. All the classic modes of resistance were used. Commissions and study groups were set up to study organizational changes and changes in board functioning. Through various tactics of postponing or sending reports back for further clarification, these efforts were effectively squashed.

A small number of the leaders saw themselves as having to provide executive leadership for the change and to develop a strategy for doing so. Two or three of them were on the main board. They worked carefully to obtain some support from some other members of the board, and they worked even harder on those people who were heads of the businesses and would soon be coming on board. Then over a period of time (six years) the board membership moved from a small minority of three who were for the change to a critical mass who were absolutely committed to the change and only concerned about how to accomplish it.

As some of the leaders of this effort moved into top positions, they began explicitly strengthening the divisional leadership and discussing the need for change in meetings with leaders of the businesses around the world. They engaged in goal-setting and visioning exercises and changed the methodology by which business heads reported to control groups from the center.

These leaders then began to institute the necessary changes.

First, they reduced the number of board members to seven or eight and widened the span of control of each so that it was impossible for anyone to grab too much power. Second, they redefined the role of the business head as that of a chief executive with control of all his or her resources. Third, they moved to a strategy management mode in which each of the business heads met with the entire executive board once a year to define strategic objectives and once a year to define budget. In between, there was not necessarily any contact with the board, although each business had a "friend" on the board for ongoing support and contact. Fourth, they revised the budget process. Fifth, they significantly reduced overhead by combining various subheadquarters of related businesses. They were able to reduce the work force by well over 20,000 people. With the new small board, they could get by with a smaller support staff. They physically moved their headquarters to a building half the size of the former one, thus providing one more visual symbol of the change in the culture.

However, those leading the transformation simultaneously supported and maintained values and ways of work such as joint consultation with the unions that had been productive in the past. They specifically defined the nature of the change management systems, whether it was a committee or a subset of the board or a special study group to manage the change. They monitored the change efforts closely.

In this case the driving force came from *within* the organization. Thus, for the last several years, it was the chief executive who was, in fact, the "project manager" of the entire change effort. He used his power in the top leadership position to bring along the critical mass that was necessary to make the change.

A Change Induced by Competitive Activity

In our second example, we will look at a large consumer goods enterprise that for many years had a virtual monopoly in its markets. It sold its products worldwide, was a household name, and had virtually no competition. It was driven primarily by technology and concentrated on maintaining high-quality products. The company had stores all over the world and a highly centralized distribution system. Most of its products were made in one giant plant. Research and development were very active in the company, and it was constantly upgrading the quality of its products. In recent years, it had started to manufacture some related types of products.

The bulk of the company's facilities were located in one city; and although it did business around the world, most of its manufacturing was done in the home city, and most of its employees resided there. The company had been a very humanistic, caring, and paternalistic organization, and it had a policy of never firing anyone. A job at the company was a career for life. It paid very well and had excellent benefits.

But the company's market share, which had tended to grow in line with the world economy, suddenly began to be eroded by the emergence of a Japanese competitor who managed not only to produce a price-competitive product but a quality-competitive and, in many cases, better quality product.

This was something that had never happened before. For a time the company "didn't believe it," but then the numbers began to get very serious. The response of management was to say that the company must "regroup," become leaner, and work differently. As is often the case, the first thing it planned to cut was the work force. Programs were instituted to reduce the number of employees by 20 percent. These were implemented in various ways, most of which were humanitarian.

The manufacturing entity, which had the largest number of employees, very creatively managed its change effort. It started a "people reduction" program and then moved to a productivity improvement program. It developed a transition management team composed of high-potential managers at the operating management level. These people went to the entire organization for suggestions for improvement and got several hundred. They condensed these down to approximately fifteen suggestions and set up study groups to design a new state for each of the fifteen. When those study group reports and recommendations were in and had been approved by the hierarchy, transition teams were established to *manage* the "getting from here to there."

The company was not only able to reduce its work force but also to improve its operations. With fewer employees, changes that had been considered impossible, such as combining major functions, had now, in fact, been accomplished. For example, five levels of management were cut. That sent a message to the work force that job reductions were not being made only at the bottom.

Other parts of the enterprise made cuts but not as radically. Top management became aware that making operations leaner, although necessary, was not attacking the basic problem, which was that the organization had been designed for another time in history and not for the competitive world in which it now functioned. Instead of the business driving the organization, the organization was driving the business.

It became apparent that the company needed to fundamentally reorganize. After consultation and planning, it set up the organization in fifteen or so lines of business, each one having a product line and each one with a general manager/ business head. Clusters of these lines of business reported to three group vice-presidents. The manufacturing, technical, sales, and other staffs were matrixed. Part of each functional staff now was dedicated to the new businesses, but significant parts were kept functional in order to achieve the synergy necessary for certain processes to occur.

As it is easy to imagine, this produced a whole new set of issues and relationships. It was necessary to develop a number of so-called change management organizations to cope with the various matrices and to implement some of the major changes that were necessary if the total change was to be optimized. In the process, several thousand new jobs have been created, there have been major changes in management, and the commitment of top management has been severely tested.

To get the critical mass, it was necessary to (1) make some changes in the center of the organization, (2) provide new and highly committed leadership that would coordinate all manufacturing efforts, and (3) make some changes in the leadership of the various parts of the manufacturing process, the sales process, the advertising process, and so on. A year was needed to train a group of people to function as general managers of businesses. A task force was set up to provide this education and training, mostly on the job.

While commitment for change was high at the top, the methods for achieving the change were confused, and there was not sufficient effort to bring along the people at lower levels. Each of the subparts was working on its specific concerns. No one analyzed what we have called the domino effect.

Later on the company centralized the change management and built in information linkages among the parts. Although there are still some problems, the company is clearly moving in the direction of systemwide management. Here again the critical dimensions were having a vision but not a clear enough one, or at least not a well-communicated one; focusing too much on cost reduction and not enough on developing a new state; not having adequate transition management structures; and not consciously intervening in the matrix management issues until they had become acute.

Challenges

In conclusion, I see the following challenges facing executive leadership any time a transformational change occurs. Although individuals who guide or assist this type of change may have their own models and biases, I believe the following issues must be considered before and during the process.

1. Securing the commitment of the CEO and other key leaders
2. Ensuring that adequate resources are allocated to support the change
3. Reaching an appropriate balance between managing the change and managing the stability of the ongoing organization, which includes managing the rate of change
4. Ensuring appropriate use of special roles, temporary systems, study groups, consultants, and transition teams
5. Carrying out ongoing evaluation (for planning improvement) of both the total effort and its various parts
6. Providing continuity of leadership of both the stable and change systems during the change process, so that momentum is maintained
7. Allocating rewards (and punishments) in ways consistent with the priority of the change effort
8. Using information technology and telecommunications in ways that will ensure adequate information flow among the various parts of the organization and also encouraging innovative use of these technologies in the change
9. Constant monitoring of the people systems to ensure that everyone in the organization knows what is going on and understands his or her part in the total effort

Michael L. Tushman
William H. Newman
David A. Nadler

6

Executive Leadership and Organizational Evolution: Managing Incremental and Discontinuous Change

A snug fit of external opportunity, company strategy, and internal structure is a hallmark of successful companies. The real test of executive leadership is keeping the organization in step with changing competitive conditions. Consider the Polaroid and Caterpillar corporations. Both firms virtually dominated their respective industries for decades, only to be caught off guard by major changes in the business environment. The same strategic and organizational factors that were so effective for decades resulted in complacency in the face of sharp technological and/ or economic changes.

Recent studies of organizations over long periods of time indicate that the most successful firms (1) establish and maintain a workable equilibrium for several years (or decades) and (2) are able to initiate and effectively implement discontinuous

This chapter builds on and extends Tushman, Newman, and Romanelli (forthcoming).

changes throughout the organization when environmental conditions shift. These organizational discontinuities redirect and otherwise add renewed vigor to the enterprise. Less successful firms, in contrast, get stuck in a particular pattern. These firms either do not see the need to reorient themselves or cannot implement strategic reorientations.

This chapter focuses on patterns in organizational evolution. Building on a growing research base, we demonstrate that organizational evolution is characterized by relatively long periods of incremental change punctuated by discontinuous, systemwide change. We concentrate on the role of executive leadership in managing incremental change, in recognizing the need to engage in discontinuous changes prior to organizational crisis, and in implementing discontinuous change. We will begin by describing four examples of incremental and discontinuous change patterns:

Founded in 1915 by a set of engineers from MIT, the General Radio Company was established to produce innovative and high-quality (but expensive) electronic test equipment. Over the years, General Radio developed a highly consistent organization to accomplish its mission. General Radio hired only the brightest young engineers, developed a loose functional organization dominated by the engineering department, and developed a "General Radio culture" (for example, no conflict, management by consensus, slow growth). Promotion was strictly from within the firm. General Radio's strategy and associated structures, systems, and people were very successful. By World War II, General Radio was the largest test-equipment firm in the United States.

After the war, however, increasing competition began to erode General Radio's market share. While management initiated numerous incremental changes, General Radio remained fundamentally the same organization. Indeed, in the late

1960s, Don Sinclair initiated strategic changes while leaving the firm's structure and systems intact. These changes were less than successful. In 1972, the firm incurred its first loss.

In the face of this sustained performance decline, Bill Thurston (a long-time General Radio executive) was made president, and he, in turn, initiated systemwide changes. General Radio adopted a more marketing-oriented strategy. Its product line was cut from twenty different lines to three; much more emphasis was given to product-line management, sales, and marketing. Resources were diverted from engineering to revitalized sales, marketing, and production functions. During 1973, the firm moved to a matrix structure, increased its emphasis on controls and systems, and went outside for a set of executives to help Thurston run this revised General Radio. To perhaps more formally symbolize these changes and the sharp move away from the "old" General Radio, the firm's name was changed to GenRad. By 1984 GenRad's sales had exploded to over $200 million per year (versus $44 million in 1972).

Thus, after sixty years of incremental changes around a constant strategy, Thurston and his colleagues (many new to the firm) initiated and implemented discontinuous systemwide changes in strategy, structure, people, and processes. While traumatic, these changes were implemented over a two-year period and led to a dramatic turnaround in GenRad's performance.

Prime Computer was founded in 1971 by a group of individuals who had left Honeywell. Prime's initial strategy was to produce a high-quality/high-price minicomputer based on semiconductor memory. These founders built an engineering-dominated, loosely structured firm that sold to original equipment manufacturers (OEMs) or through distributors. This configuration of strategy, structure, people, and process was very successful. By 1974, Prime turned its first profit; by 1975, its sales were more than $11 million per year.

In the midst of this success, Prime's board of directors brought in Ken Fisher to reorient the organization. Fisher and a whole new set of executives hired from Honeywell initiated a set of discontinuous changes throughout Prime. Prime now began to sell a full range of minicomputers and computer systems to OEMs and end users. To accomplish this shift in strategy, Prime adopted a more complex functional structure, with a marked increase in resources to sales and marketing. The shift in resources away from engineering was so great that Bill Poduska, Prime's head of engineering, left to form Apollo Computer. Between 1975 and 1981, Fisher and his colleagues consolidated and incrementally adapted structure, systems, and processes to best meet the strategy developed in 1975. During this convergent period, Prime's sales grew dramatically to over $260 million per year by 1981.

In 1981, in the midst of this continuing sequence of increased volume and profits, Prime's board again initiated a set of discontinuous changes. Fisher and his direct reports left Prime, while Joe Henson and a set of executives from IBM initiated wholesale changes throughout the organization. The firm diversified into robotics, computer-aided design/computer-aided manufacturing (CAD/CAM), and office systems, adopted a divisional structure, developed a more market-driven orientation, and increased controls and systems. It remains to be seen how this "new" Prime will fare. Prime must be seen, then, not as a fourteen-year-old

firm, but as three very different organizations, each
of which was managed by a different set of executives. Unlike General Radio, Prime initiated these
discontinuities during periods of great success.

The Operating Group at Citibank prior to
1970 had been a service-oriented function for the
end-user areas of the bank. The Operating Group
hired high school graduates who remained in the
back office for their entire careers at the bank.
Structure, controls, and systems were loose, while
the informal organization valued service, responsiveness to client needs, and slow, steady work habits. While these patterns were successful enough,
increased demand and heightened customer expectations led to ever decreasing performance during the late 1960s.

In the face of this severe performance decline, John Reed was promoted to head of the
Operating Group. Reed recruited several executives with production backgrounds, and with this
new top team initiated systemwide changes. Reed's
vision was to transform the Operating Group from
a service-oriented back office to a factory producing a high-quality product. Consistent with this new
mission, Reed and his colleagues initiated sweeping changes in strategy, structure, work flows, controls, and culture. These changes were initiated
concurrently throughout the back office, with very
little participation by employees, over the course of
a few months. While all the empirial performance
measures improved substantially, these changes
also generated substantial anxiety. Reed addressed
this issue only after the changes had been
implemented.

For over twenty years Alpha Corporation was
among the leaders in the industrial fastener indus-

try. Its reliability, low cost, and good technical service were important strengths. However, as Alpha's segment of the industry matured, its profits declined. Belt tightening helped but was not enough. Finally, a new CEO presided over a sweeping restructuring: cutting the product line, closing a plant, trimming overhead and then focusing on computer parts that call for very close tolerances, CAD/CAM tooling, and cooperation with customers on design efforts. After four rough years, Alpha appears to have found a new niche where convergence will again be warranted.

These four short examples illustrate periods of incremental change, or convergence, punctuated by discontinuous changes throughout the organizations. Discontinuous or *frame-breaking* change involves simultaneous and sharp changes in strategy, power, structure, and controls. Each example illustrates the role of executive leadership in initiating and implementing discontinuous change. While General Radio, Alpha, and Citibank initiated systemwide changes only after sustained performance declines, Prime proactively initiated systemwide changes to take advantage of competitive/technological conditions. These patterns in organizational evolution are not unique. The most successful firms both manage incremental change *and* are able to initiate and implement discontinuous changes prior to experiencing performance declines.

The task of managing incremental change or convergence differs sharply from that of managing frame-breaking change. Incremental change is compatible with the existing structure of a company and is reinforced over a period of years. In contrast, frame-breaking change is abrupt, painful to participants, and often resisted by the old guard. Forging these new strategy-structure-people-process consistencies and laying the basis for the next period of incremental change call for distinctive skills.

Because the future health, and even survival, of a company may be at stake, we first want to take a closer look at the nature and consequences of convergent change and at the differences imposed by frame-breaking change. We next explore when and why these painful and risky revolutions interrupt previously successful patterns and whether these discontinuities can be avoided and/or initiated prior to crises. Finally, we discuss what managers can and should do to guide their organizations through periods of incremental change and discontinuities over time.

In terms of our research base, we might note that written company histories and case studies abound. The more complete case studies track the evolution and various crises of firms in great detail—for example, Chandler's (1962) seminal study of strategy and structure at Du Pont, General Motors, Standard Oil, and Sears Roebuck. To bolster these in-depth case histories, new studies deal systematically with whole sets of companies and trace their experiences over long periods of time. For instance, a series of studies at McGill University covers over forty well-known firms in diverse industries for at least twenty years per firm (Miller and Friesen, 1980, 1984; Mintzberg and Waters, 1982). Another research program conducted by M. Tushman, E. Romanelli, B. Virany, and P. Anderson at Columbia University tracks the history of all sixty companies born between 1966 and 1971 in the minicomputer industry. Tushman and his colleagues are also gathering historical data on firms in the cement industry from 1880 to 1980 and the airline industry from 1934 to 1980 (see Tushman and Romanelli, 1985; Tushman and Anderson, 1986; Tushman, Virany, and Romanelli, 1985; and Virany, Tushman, and Romanelli, 1986). Their research, like the McGill research, finds that the most successful firms evolve through long periods of convergence punctuated by frame-breaking change. Poorly performing firms either do not engage in frame-breaking change or attempt these discontinuities too often.

The discussion that follows is based on the history of companies in many different industries in many different countries; it includes both large and small organizations and organizations in various stages of their product class life cycle. We are dealing with a widespread phenomenon—not just a few dramatic instances. Finally, we focus here on single-line companies or individual units of larger firms. The issues of corporate-level evolution or the evolution of conglomerates are left for another time. While a few of our examples may have become divisions of diversified corporations, they maintained their autonomy at least throughout the years that we studied them.

Building on Strength: Periods of Convergence

Successful companies wisely stick to what works well. At General Radio between 1915 and 1950, the loose functional structure, committee management system, internal promotion practices, and the high-quality, premium price, engineering mentality all worked together to provide a highly congruent system. These internally consistent patterns in strategy, structure, people, and processes served General Radio well for over thirty-five years.

Similarly, the Alpha Corporation's customer-driven, low-cost strategy was accomplished by strength in engineering and production and ever more detailed structures and systems that evaluated cost, quality, and new product development. These strengths were epitomized in Alpha's chief engineer and president. The chief engineer had a remarkable talent for helping customers find new uses for industrial fasteners. He relished solving such problems, while at the same time he was able to design fasteners that could be easily manufactured. The president excelled at the production of dependable, low-cost fasteners. The pair were outstanding role models and set a pattern that served Alpha well for fifteen years.

As the company grew, the chief engineer hired kindred customer-oriented application engineers. They developed new products in cooperation with innovative users and left more routine problem solving and incremental change to the sales and production departments. The president soon came to rely on a hands-on manufacturing manager and to delegate financial matters to a competent treasurer-controller. Note how well the organization of the company reinforced Alpha's strategy and how well the key people fit the organization. There was an excellent fit between strategy and formal structure. The informal structure was also appropriate—communications were open, the simple mission of the company was widely endorsed, and routines were well understood.

Convergence begins, as the General Radio example suggests, with an effective dovetailing of strategy, structure, people, and processes. For other strategies or in other industries, the particular formal and informal systems might be very different, but they would still add up to a winning combination. The formal system includes decisions about grouping and linking resources as well as about planning and control systems, rewards and evaluation procedures, and human resource management systems. The informal system includes core values, beliefs, norms, communication patterns, and actual decision-making and conflict resolution patterns. It is the whole fabric of structure, systems, people, and processes that must be suited to company strategy (see Nadler and Tushman, forthcoming, for a detailed discussion of congruence and effectiveness). As there is never a perfect fit between strategy, structure, people, and processes, convergence is an ongoing process characterized by incremental change. Over time, in all the companies studied, two types of changes were common: fine-tuning changes and incremental adaptations.

Converging Change: Fine Tuning. Even with good strategy-structure-process fits, well-run companies seek better ways of exploiting (and defending) their missions. Such efforts typically include one or more of the following strategies:

1. Improving policies, methods, and procedures
2. Utilizing increased volume to create more specialized sub-units, to refine coordination among subunits, and to exercise closer control
3. Developing personnel especially suited to the present strategy through improved selection and training and by tailoring reward systems to match strategic thrusts
4. Fostering individual and group commitment to the company mission and to the excellence of one's own department

5. Promoting confidence in the accepted norms, beliefs, and myths
6. Clarifying established roles, power, status, dependencies, and allocation mechanisms

These fine-tuning efforts fill out and elaborate the consistencies between strategy, structure, people, and processes, the kinds of changes described here lead to an ever more interconnected (and therefore more stable) social system. Convergent periods fit the happy situations romanticized by Peters and Waterman (1982).

Converging Change: Incremental Adjustments to Environmental Shifts. In addition to fine-tuning changes, shifts in the environment will call for some organizational response. Even the most conservative of organizations expect, even welcome, small changes that do not make too many waves.

A popular expression has it that almost any organization can tolerate a 10 percent change. At any one time, only a few changes are being made, and these changes are compatible or congruent with the prevailing structures, systems, and processes. Examples of such adjustments are an expansion in sales territory, a shift in emphasis among products in the product line, or improved processing technology in production. The usual elements of changes of this sort are well known: wide acceptance of the need for change, openness to possible alternatives, objective examination of the pros and cons of each plausible alternative, participation of those directly affected in examining possible alternatives, a market test or pilot operation where feasible, time to learn the new activities, established role models, known rewards for positive success, evaluation, and refinement.

The role of executive leadership during convergent periods is to reemphasize mission and core values and to delegate incremental decisions to middle-level managers. Note that the uncertainty created for people affected by such changes is well within tolerable limits. Opportunity is provided to anticipate and learn about the coming changes, while most features of the structure remain as before. The overall system adapts, but it is not transformed.

Converging Change: Some Consequences. For those companies whose strategies fit environmental conditions, convergent periods are associated with enhanced effectiveness. Incremental change is relatively easy to implement, and it optimizes the consistencies between strategy, structure, people, and processes. For example, at AT&T the period between 1913 and 1980 was one of incremental change that steadily bolstered the "Ma Bell" culture, systems, and structure and contributed greatly to developing the telephone network.

Convergent periods are, however, a double-edged sword. As organizations grow and become more successful, they develop internal forces for stability. Organizational structures and systems become so interlinked that they allow only compatible changes. Further, over time, employees develop habits, patterned behaviors begin to take on value, and employees develop a sense of competence in knowing how to get work done within the system. These self-reinforcing patterns of behavior, norms, and values contribute to an emphasis on organizational history. Heroes begin to emerge, as do certain not-to-be-questioned standards, and stories about the organization's past start to be passed along to new employees.

This organizational momentum is profoundly functional as long as the organization's strategy is appropriate. The culture, structure, and systems at AT&T, Citibank, and General Radio were critical to each organization's success. However, if (and when) strategy must change, this momentum cuts the other way. Organizational history is a source of tradition, precedent, and pride that is an anchor to the past. But a proud history often stands in the way of problem solving and may be a source of resistance to change. When faced with environmental threats, highly inertial organizations may not register the threat due to organization complacency and/or stunted external vigilance (for example, the automobile and steel industries); or if the threat is recognized, the response is frequently one of heightened conformity to the status quo and/or increased commitment to "what we do best." For example, the response of dominant firms to technological threat is frequently increased commitment to their obsolete technology. A paradoxical result of long periods of success may be heightened organizational complacency (see Schon, 1967).

Converging change is, then, a two-way street. The very social and technical consistencies that are key sources of success may also become the seeds of failure if environments change. The longer the convergent period, the more dominant these internal forces for stability become. This momentum seems to be particularly accentuated in the most successful firms in a product class (for example, Polaroid, Caterpillar, and Xerox), in historically regulated organizations (for example, AT&T, GTE, and financial service firms), and in organizations that have been traditionally shielded from competition (for example, universities, not-for-profit organizations, and government agencies and/or services).

On Frame-Breaking Change

What, then, leads to frame-breaking change? Why defy tradition? Simply stated, frame-breaking change occurs in response to (or in anticipation of) major environmental changes—changes that require more than incremental adjustment. The need for discontinuous change may spring from either discontinuities in a company's industry or from shifts in its product life cycle or from a combination of both.

First, sharp changes in legal, political, or technological conditions change the basis of competition within industries. Deregulation has dramatically transformed the financial services and airlines industries. Competence-destroying product technologies such as jet engines, electronic typing, and microprocessors or competence-destroying process technologies such as the planar process for semiconductors or float-glass in glass manufacture completely change the bases of competition within industries. Similarly, the emergence of industry standards, or dominant designs (such as the DC-3 or the IBM 360), signal a shift in competition away from product innovation and toward increased process innovation (see Tushman and Anderson, 1986). Finally, major economic change (for example, an energy crisis) and legal shifts (such as patent protection in biotechnology or trade/regulatory barriers in pharmaceuticals or cigarets) also directly affect bases of competition.

Second, over the course of a product class life cycle, different strategies are appropriate. In the emergence phase of a product class, competition is based on product innovation and performance, while in the maturity stage competition centers on cost, volume, and efficiency. Over a product class life cycle, patterns in demand and users change, the nature of required innovation changes, and the nature of competition changes. For example, the demand and nature of competition for minicomputers, cellular telephones, wide-body aircraft, and bowling alley equipment changed as these products gained acceptance and their product class evolved. Compounding these forces may be powerful international competition (Porter, 1980).

Whether due to discontinuous changes in competitive, legal, political, or social factors, major changes in environmental conditions can render previously successful strategies no longer so. Altered strategic contingencies demand fundamentally different strategies and, in turn, fundamentally different organizations. For example, in minicomputers, the advent of semiconductor memory and microprocessors shifted the basis of competition away from technology and toward marketing and selling to a broader array of end users. Those firms that hold on to existing (and previously successful) strategies in the face of different competitive contingencies suffer performance decline (see the example of General Radio). The most effective organizations proactively shift strategy and associated structure, people, and processes before being forced to do so by performance decline, and they thus reap the early-mover advantages—a good example here would be IBM's decision to bet the company on the 360 computer.

Frame-breaking change is driven by shifts in business strategy. As strategy changes so too must structure, people, and organizational processes. Quite unlike convergent changes, frame-breaking changes involve discontinuous shifts throughout the organization in a relatively short period of time. For example, the systemwide changes at Prime Computer and General Radio were implemented over time periods of eighteen to twenty-four months. Similarly, Reed's transformation of Citibank's back office was accomplished in a few months. Frame-breaking changes are revolutionary changes *of* the system as opposed to incremental changes *in* the system. The following elements are present in frame-breaking change.

Redefined Mission and Core Values. A strategy shift involves a new definition of company mission. Entering or withdrawing from an industry may be involved; at the very least, the way that the company expects to achieve excellence is altered. The revamped AT&T is a conspicuous example of this. Success on the new course may call for a competitive, aggressive strategy, as well as for a revised set of core values. Thus, the initial shift at Prime Computer reflected a strategic shift away from technology and toward sales and marketing. Core values also were aggressively reshaped to complement Prime's new strategy.

Altered Power and Status. Frame-breaking change always alters the distribution of power. Some groups lose in the shift while others gain. For example, at Prime Computer and General Radio, the engineering functions lost power, resources, and prestige, while the marketing and sales functions gained in all these areas. Such shifts in distribution of power reflect shifts in bases of competition and resource allocation. A new strategy must be backed up with alterations in the balance of power and status.

Reorganization. A new strategy requires a shift in structure, systems, and procedures. As strategic contingencies shift, so too must the choice of organizational form. A new direction calls for added activity in some areas and less in others. Changes in structure and systems are means to ensure that this reallocation of effort takes place. New structures and revised roles deliberately interrupt business-as-usual behavior.

Revised Interaction Patterns. The way people in the organization work together has to change during frame-breaking changes. Since the strategy of the company has changed, new procedures, work flows, communication networks, and decision-making patterns must be established. With these changes in work flows and procedures must also come revised norms and informal decision-making and conflict resolution procedures.

New Executives. Frame-breaking change also involves the appointment of new executives, who are usually brought in from outside the organization and placed in key managerial positions. Commitment to the new mission, energy to overcome prevailing inertia, and freedom from prior obligations are all needed to refocus the organization. A few exceptional members of the old guard may attempt to make this shift, but they will find it difficult to break habits and expectations of their associates. New executives are more likely to provide both the necessary drive and the enhanced set of skills appropriate for the new strategy. For example, frame-breaking changes at Prime, General Radio, Alpha Corporation, and Citibank were all spearheaded by a relatively small set of new executives from outside the organization or division.

Frame-breaking change is revolutionary in that the changes reshape the entire nature of the organization. The more effective examples of frame-breaking change were implemented rapidly (for example, at Prime Computer and Citibank). It appears that a piecemeal approach to frame-breaking change gets bogged down in politics, individual resistance to change, and organizational inertia (consider Sinclair's attempts to change General Radio). Frame-breaking change requires discontinuous shifts in strategy, structure, people, and processes concurrently — or at least in a short period of time. There are several reasons for rapid, simultaneous implementation of frame-breaking change:

1. *Synergy* within the new structure can be a powerful aid. New executives with a fresh mission, working in a redesigned organization with revised norms and values, can provide strong

reinforcement for change. The pieces of the revitalized organization pull together; by contrast, in the case of piecemeal change, one or more parts of the new organization may be out of "synch" with the old organization.

2. *Pockets of resistance* have a chance to grow and develop when frame-breaking change is implemented slowly. The new mission, shifts in organization, and other frame-breaking changes upset comfortable routines and precedent. Resistance to such fundamental change is natural. If frame-breaking change is implemented slowly, then individuals have a greater opportunity to undermine it, and organizational inertia works to further stifle fundamental change.

3. Typically, there is a *pent-up need for change*. During convergent periods, basic adjustments are postponed, and boat rocking is discouraged. Once constraints are relaxed, however, a variety of desirable improvements press for attention. The exhilaration and momentum of a fresh effort (and new team) make difficult moves more acceptable. Change is in fashion.

4. Frame-breaking change is an inherently *risky and uncertain venture*. The longer the implementation period, the greater the period of uncertainty and instability. The most effective frame-breaking changes initiate the new strategy, structure, processes and systems rapidly and then usher in the next period of stability and convergent change. The sooner fundamental uncertainty is removed, the better the chances of organizational survival and growth.

Frame-breaking changes are revolutions that shake an organization's foundation. These discontinuities trigger four generic change problems that hinder the smooth implementation of change. But if we understand the roots of these problems, we can more effectively bring about fundamental change within organizations (see Nadler and Tushman, forthcoming, for an extensive discussion of change management). A review of multiple cases of discontinuous change suggests that four factors arise whenever executives attempt to implement frame-breaking change:

1. Frame-breaking change always triggers *individual resistance to change* — resistance that is rooted either in anxiety or in

personal commitment to the status quo. Discontinuous change destroys familiar routines, threatens feelings of individual competence, and produces substantial anxiety among employees. Anxiety in turn, leads to narrowed attention spans, a decrease in communication, decreased problem-solving effectiveness, and an increased reliance on familiar routines and precedents. Highly anxious individuals hold on dearly to what is known and familiar, even though this refusal to change may itself become counterproductive. Individual resistance to change may, however, also be rooted in strong personal commitment to the status quo. Individuals may reflect back on years of consistent behaviors and remain strongly committed to previously successful patterns of interaction. Whether individual resistance is rooted in anxiety or personal commitment to the status quo, executives managing frame-breaking change must motivate individuals to act constructively and support the new organization.

2. Organizations are *political systems* characterized by compromise and accommodation between actors with different degrees of power. During convergent periods a political equilibrium is reached. Frame-breaking change disturbs this equilibrium; some actors or groups stand to lose, others to gain. Managers must expect that those powerful individuals and/or groups who see their power threatened will actively resist change. Hence, management must carefully shape the political dynamics of change.

3. *Control problems* always arise during frame-breaking change. As the organization is being transformed, executives no longer have systems, structures, or controls to help in managing the transition period or the new organization. Systems, roles, and responsibilities must be clarified if the transition between the old and new organizations is to be carried out effectively.

4. Frame-breaking change also impacts *external constituencies*. Suppliers, vendors, customers, and regulatory agencies develop expectations and standards that are always affected by frame-breaking changes (witness AT&T's problems in adjusting to deregulation). These revised working relations often meet with strong resistance by important external constituents. Re-

sistance to frame-breaking change from outside the organization must also be managed.

Frame-breaking change triggers resistance from multiple sources both inside and outside the organization. Convergent change does not stir up resistance of such intensity. The challenge for executive leadership is not only to decide on the when and the what of frame-breaking change but also on how the change is to be implemented to maximize the probability of success.

There has been relatively little study of the management of frame-breaking organizational change. But work by Nadler and Tushman (forthcoming), Beckhard and Harris (1977), and Quinn (1980) has been utilized by several organizations in managing discontinuous change. Their work provides action steps that help manage the four generic change problems discussed above. Briefly, action steps that seem to be important in managing frame-breaking change include:

Motivating Constructive Behavior. Individuals must recognize the need for major change. If they do not feel this need, they will be slow to change. Managers can involve their employees in data gathering and problem solving so that key individuals will come to see the need to engage in these transformations prior to the emergence of crisis conditions. Participation in both the content and process of change builds ownership, reduces felt uncertainty, and increases commitment to the change. Employee involvement linked with formal and informal reward systems also helps to motivate constructive behavior. Managers must help build rewards, controls, and incentives in support of the new mission. Without a revised set of formal and informal incentives and controls, individual behavior will not change.

Finally, discontinuous change is often experienced as a personal loss—particularly if the prior convergent period lasted for a long time, as it did at AT&T (sixty-five years) and at General Radio (fifty-five years). Employees need time and opportunity to disengage from the prior organization in order to fully commit themselves to the new organization. Moreover, they need to be

given the opportunity to be proud of their past accomplishments and to be freed up enough to accept the challenges of the
new organization.

Shaping Political Dynamics. Without the support of key individuals, frame-breaking change may be sabotaged. Management
can explicitly build coalitions in support of the change effort.
Diagnostic questions might include: Who are the informally
influential individuals in the system, what is at stake for them in
the change, and how can those key individuals who are against
the change be influenced? Methods to influence key individuals
include participation, rewards, incentives, and exchange ("let's
see if we can cut a deal"). If key individuals cannot be motivated
to support the change, then they may have to be transferred out
of the division or asked to leave the organization. Just as management can diagnose and shape communication networks, so too
must it diagnose and shape the political topography in the
organization.

An executive's own behavior has a major impact on the
political dynamics of his or her organization. Executives need to
clearly communicate every day what they stand for and where
the organization is going. If executives send out clear messages
about norms, values, rewards, and mission, the amount of negative political behavior will be diminished. But if they send out
inconsistent, tentative, or ambiguous signals, then the informal
organization may work to bolster the status quo.

Executives can infuse their organizations with value, direction, energy, and enthusiasm. They must be role models of
the behaviors expected in the new organization. Sustained attention to detail can provide substantial direction, energy, and
clarity, all of which are vital in reducing the uncertainty that a
discontinuous change will inevitably generate. Since strategy,
structure, incentives, and processes are potentially expensive
components of frame-breaking change, attention to this "mun-
dane behavior" is a vital, no-cost tool in the management of
discontinuous change. Finally, in a sea of change, executives
need to be clear as to *what is not changing.* For example, at IBM,
although the organization has evolved through several frame-

breaking changes, individuals can hold onto the trilogy of core values that are anchors to IBM's past and a link to its future (see Yavitz and Newman, 1982, and Peters and Waterman, 1982, for more detail on focused climate and change).

Managing Control During the Transition. Frame-breaking change introduces substantial uncertainty and turbulence into an organization. Management can work to maintain control during the transition period as the old organization transforms itself into the new organization. Executives can develop and communicate a clear image of the future organization. Without such an image, employees will opt for the certainty of the status quo. As frame-breaking change involves the entire organization, executives need to use multiple and consistent levers to reinforce the changes. Structure, systems, people, and processes must be concurrently managed so that they work together to support the new organization.

Organizational arrangements need to be developed to directly manage the implementation process. An executive with status and respect can be personally responsible for making the change happen (for example, Reed at Citibank, Thurston at General Radio). This person needs the resources to build a team that will together develop a formal implementation plan. It is this team's responsibility to spearhead the change and to gain commitment to it throughout the organization. This team needs to decide on educational and training programs, when and how to try pilot tests, how rapidly to implement the changes, and what human resources need to be developed. Given an implementation plan, this team can measure and evaluate how well the organization is meeting change targets and act to correct deviations from targets (as well as adapt targets to changing environmental conditions).

Managing External Constituencies. External constituencies can also be motivated to support frame-breaking change. Innovative customers, distributors, or suppliers may well be involved in the design or evaluation of new products or systems (see Von Hippel, 1978, on user needs). Incentives may have to be developed to motivate constituents to support the new mission. Management must learn how to present the merits of the new mission and vision to suppliers, vendors, and customers who are familiar with the old products and systems. Finally, organizations might build in feedback mechanisms to track the response of critical changes within the organization or to further attempt to shape key constituents.

These action steps for managing frame-breaking change are clearly not exhaustive. But they do represent the types of actions that can be taken to manage the four generic change problems. Note how difficult these action steps are and how the management of frame-breaking change runs counter to the organizational, individual, and group inertia that is so supportive of convergent change. The effective implementation of frame-breaking change is, however, vital. Brilliant ideas for new strategies, structures, and processes will not be effective unless they are coupled with thorough and insightful implementation plans. Since frame-breaking change is so difficult to implement, most organizations initiate dramatic changes only under financial duress. The most successful organizations, however, proactively initiate and implement discontinuous change to take advantage of competitive opportunities, as we saw, for example, in the case of Prime Computer. It is to this issue of executive leadership in initiating and implementing frame-breaking change that we now turn.

Executive Leadership and Organizational Evolution

Executive leadership plays a vital role in the evolution of organizations. It is only the executive (or executive team) who can mediate between internal forces that make for stability and incremental change, on the one hand, and external forces that call for fundamental change, on the other. The most successful organizations engage in frame-breaking change when environmental conditions shift; less successful organizations either do not recognize the need to reorient themselves or are unable to implement frame-breaking change. Only executive leadership can initiate and implement such change. It is the mark of inspired executive leadership to be able to manage both for stability during convergent periods and for discontinuous, frame-breaking change.

The role of executive leadership is very different during convergent periods than during periods of frame-breaking change. During convergent periods, it focuses on *maintaining* congruence and fit within the organization. Because strategy, structure, processes, and systems are fundamentally sound, the myriad of incremental substantive decisions can be delegated to middle-level management, which possesses the needed expertise and information. The key role for executive leadership during convergent periods is to reemphasize strategy, mission, and core values and to keep a vigilant eye on external opportunities and/or threats.

Frame-breaking change, however, requires direct executive involvement in all aspects of the change. Given the enormity of this kind of change and the internal forces that make for inertia, executive leadership must be involved in the specification of strategy, structure, and organizational processes, as well as in the development of implementation plans. During frame-breaking change executive leadership is directly involved in reorienting the organization. Whereas convergent change can be delegated, frame-breaking change requires strong, direct leadership from the top as to where the organization is going and how it is to get there. Tentative change does not seem to be effective — at least, this was certainly the case at General Radio.

But frame-breaking change does not only require substantial technical, social, and conceptual skills; it also requires visionary skills. Visionary executives are those executives who provide a new direction for their organizations and who can infuse that redirection with energy and value. Visionary skills include:

I. Envisioning
    A. Articulating a clear and credible vision of the organization and its future
    B. Setting new and difficult standards

      C.   Using and shaping history to generate pride in the past and enthusiasm for the current mission

II. Energizing
      A.   Demonstrating personal excitement
      B.   Becoming actively involved with individuals
      C.   Finding and using examples of success to create new energy
      D.   Modeling expected behaviors

III. Enabling
      A.   Providing resources
      B.   Using rewards to motivate behavior
      C.   Building an effective senior team
      D.   Building supportive executive practices

Beyond their role in change management, executives must make several kinds of decisions to steer organizations over changing industry conditions. Executives must decide *when* to initiate frame-breaking change, *what* the nature of the change is to be, *how* to implement the change, and *who* should be involved in managing and directing these organizational transformations.

When to Initiate Frame-Breaking Change. If the organization is successful and the environment is stable, then frame-breaking change is inappropriate and could become quite dysfunctional. If, however, the organization is facing a financial crisis or if the environmental conditions change (or will change) sharply, then frame-breaking change is vital. Executive leadership must be vigilant to major changes in legal, political, technological, and/ or competitive conditions.

The most effective executives are those who identify environmental threats before they adversely affect their firms. While some environmental shocks are unpredictable, in many cases companies have received substantial early warnings. The evidence is clear, however, that frame-breaking change is usually postponed until a crisis threatens. The momentum and frequent success of convergent periods seem to make executives slow to respond to new conditions, to breed complacency, and to encourage strong commitments to the status quo. Indeed, in the Columbia and McGill research programs, financial crisis was the dominant impetus behind frame-breaking change. However, the most effective firms in the Columbia project risked short-run success by initiating frame-breaking change to take advantage of technological and market events (for example, Prime Computer, Rolm, Datapoint, and Data General). Thus the mark of exceptional leadership is to initiate frame-breaking change proactively rather than to allow oneself to be forced into turn-around management situations.

What to Initiate. Quite apart from recognizing when to initiate frame-breaking change, executive leadership must decide on the nature of the new organization. Executives must make decisions as to the appropriate strategy and then, with the aid of their colleagues, build appropriate structures, systems, and processes. The content of frame-breaking change must hinge on critical environmental success factors. Since different environmental conditions require different strategies, we do not find that organizations always go through the same series of changes. Their strategies and associated organizational structures and systems will vary over time by industry and by executive vision.

How to Implement Frame-Breaking Change. Because frame-breaking change is so traumatic for an organization, executive leadership must help develop an implementation plan that takes into account individual resistance to change, the politics of change, the need to manage control during the transition period, and the need to manage external constituencies. Executive leaders must build a senior team to help manage the change and to spread direction, energy, and enthusiasm throughout the organization.

There is also the question of *who* should be involved in managing and directing these transformations. During convergent periods management can be effectively promoted from within, and incremental changes can be delegated to middle- and lower-level managers. Senior management must, however, manage frame-breaking change. Further, it seems as though external executives can facilitate the implementation of organizational discontinuities. During frame-breaking changes, therefore, organizations frequently go outside the system for executives with different skills and/or with a fresh perspective. External executives are unencumbered by prior commitments and organizational precedent.

At General Radio, Prime Computer, Alpha, and Citibank it took external executives to initiate and implement frame-breaking change. Tushman, Virany, and Romanelli (1985) found that executive succession occurred with frame-breaking change in over 80 percent of the changes. Further, when frame-breaking change was coupled with executive succession, organizational performance was significantly higher than when the frame-breaking change occurred without executive succession. In only six of forty cases was a current president (or CEO) able to initiate and implement multiple frame-breaking changes. In each of these six cases, however, frame-breaking change was coupled with major changes in those reporting directly to the senior executive.

Executive succession seems to be a powerful tool in managing frame-breaking change. It takes a fresh set of executives, unfettered by precedent and prior commitments, to provide the expertise and energy required to manage organizational discontinuities (see Hambrick and Mason, 1984, for more detail on executive characteristics and organizations). Note also that some executives who could not, or would not, implement frame-breaking changes, went on to become quite successful in other parts of the organization or in other organizations (for example, Ken Fisher at Encore Computer, Bill Poduska at Apollo Computer, Henry Kloss, Gene Amdahl, and so on). Executive succession can, then, be used both to revitalize organizations and to reassign executives to areas of the corporation that best match their distinctive competencies.

As environments change, executives must be able to manage both congruence and fit as well as frame-breaking change. In managing these organizational reorientations, executives must deal with systemwide inertia and transform those very structures, systems, processes, and relations that have been so successful in the past. Executive succession seems to be a powerful tool in adding the critical skills and energy needed to initiate and implement frame-breaking change.

The trauma of frame-breaking change calls for executives with extraordinary vision. Given the difficulties of these organizational reorientations and the scarcity of visionary executives, frame-breaking changes are usually initiated only under crisis conditions. The most successful firms (and executives) proactively initiate and implement these transformations to take advantage of competitive threats or opportunities.

Conclusion

Our historical analysis of organizations indicates that to remain competitive over changing environmental conditions, organizations must evolve through fundamentally different patterns in strategy, structure, people, and processes. The most effective organizations are those that evolve through relatively long periods of convergence in support of a given strategy, punctuated by concurrent and discontinuous changes throughout the organization. These frame-breaking changes are initiated either under crisis conditions or proactively in response to environmental changes. Given the strength of organizational inertia, frame-breaking changes are most frequently initiated during a financial crisis.

This metamorphic approach to organizational evolution puts a premium on executive leadership. Executive leadership must determine the nature of the frame-breaking change and decide when and how to implement it. The role of executive leadership shifts from reinforcing mission and core values and delegating incremental changes during convergent periods to directly managing concurrent shifts in strategy, structure, people, and processes during frame-breaking change. Frame-breaking change seems to be facilitated by an infusion of new executives who bring different skills and fresh energy to the enterprise.

The ability to initiate and implement frame-breaking

change *and* to manage convergent change over different environmental conditions marks the most successful executives. If environmental conditions change sharply, the following imperatives come into play:

1. Frame-breaking change cannot be avoided. These discontinuous organizational changes will either be made proactively or initiated under crisis or turnaround conditions.
2. Discontinuous changes need to be made in strategy, structure, people, and processes concurrently. Tentative change runs the risk of being smothered by individual, group, and organizational inertia.
3. There must be direct executive involvement in all aspects of the change, usually bolstered with new executives from outside the organization.
4. Strategy and, in turn, structure, systems, and processes must meet industry-specific competitive issues. There are no patterns in the sequence of frame-breaking changes.

Finally, our historical analysis of organizations highlights the following issues for executive leadership:

1. Need to manage for balance, consistency, or fit during convergent periods
2. Need to be vigilant to environmental shifts in order to anticipate the need for frame-breaking change
3. Need to effectively manage frame-breaking change
4. Need to develop core values that can be used as an anchor even as organizations evolve through frame-breaking change
5. Need to develop and use organizational history as a way to infuse pride in an organization's past and enthusiasm for its future
6. Need to bolster technical, social, and conceptual skills with visionary skills, which add the energy and direction and excitement so critical during frame-breaking change

References

Beckhard, R., and Harris, R. T. *Organizational Transitions*. Reading, Mass.: Addison-Wesley, 1977.

Chandler, A. *Strategy and Structure: Chapters in the History of American Industrial Enterprise*. Cambridge, Mass.: MIT Press, 1962.

Hambrick, D., and Mason, P. "Upper Echelons: The Organization as a Reflection of Its Top Management." *Academy of Management Review*, 1984, *9* (2), 193–206.

MacMillan, I., and McCaffrey, M. "Strategy for Financial Services: Cashing in on Competitive Inertia." *Journal of Business Strategy*, 1984, *4*, 58–73.

Miller, D., and Friesen, P. "Momentum and Revolution in Organizational Adaptation." *Academy of Management Journal*, 1980, *22*, 591–614.

Miller, D., and Friesen, P. *Organizations: A Quantum View*. Englewood Cliffs, N.J.: Prentice-Hall, 1984.

Mintzberg, H., and Waters, J. "Tracking Strategy in an Entrepreneurial Firm." *Academy of Management Journal*, 1982, *25*, 465–499.

Nadler, D. *Feedback and Organization Development*. Reading, Mass.: Addison-Wesley, 1981.

Nadler, D., and Tushman, M. *Strategic Organization Design: Concepts, Tools, and Processes*. Glenview, Ill.: Scott, Foresman, forthcoming.

Peters, T. J., and Waterman, R. H., Jr. *In Search of Excellence: Lessons from America's Best-Run Companies*. New York: Harper & Row, 1982.

Porter, M. *Competitive Strategy*. New York: Free Press, 1980.

Quinn, J. B. *Strategies for Change: Logical Incrementalism*. Homewood, Ill.: Dow Jones-Irwin, 1980.

Schon, D. *Technology and Change*. New York: Delacorte Press, 1967.

Tushman, M., and Anderson, P. "Technological Discontinuities and Organization Environments." *Administrative Science Quarterly*, 1986, *31*, 439–465.

Tushman, M., Newman, W., and Romanelli, E. "Convergence and

Upheaval: Managing the Unsteady Pace of Organization Evolution." *California Management Review*, forthcoming.

Tushman, M., and Romanelli, E. "Organization Evolution: A Metamorphosis Model of Convergence and Reorientation." In B. Staw and L. Cummings (eds.), *Research in Organizational Behavior*. Vol. 7. Greenwich, Conn.: JAI Press, 1985.

Tushman, M., Virany, B., and Romanelli, E. "Executive Succession, Strategic Reorientation, and Organization Evolution." *Technology in Society*, 1985, 7, 297–314.

Virany, B., Tushman, M., and Romanelli, E. "The Effects of Executive Succession." Working paper, Graduate School of Business, Columbia University, 1986.

Von Hippel, E. "Successful Industrial Products from Customer Ideas." *Journal of Marketing*, 1978, *42* (1), 39–46.

Yavitz, B., and Newman, W. *Strategy in Action*. New York: Free Press, 1982.

William P. Belgard
K. Kim Fisher
Steven R. Rayner

7

Vision, Opportunity, and Tenacity: Three Informal Processes That Influence Formal Transformation

What if you came to envision an appropriate large-scale transformation opportunity for your organization, but you were not in a position to make it happen? Should you simply dismiss the idea from your mind, assuming that you will never be able to make it a reality? On the contrary. We suggest that a number of people play significant roles in the evolution of organizations who do not have the formal authority to personally drive organizationwide transformation. These individuals focus their energy on influencing rather than sponsoring organization change. This chapter attempts to characterize their unique role as the influencers of change and describes how they operate through informal channels and strategies in helping to bring forth organizationwide transformation.

Formal Phase of Transformation

Much has been written about systematic, organizationwide change. It is typically described as a sequential process that

131

is managed in a top-down manner and requires a clear understanding of three unique states of transformation: the current
state, the desired future state, and the transition state (Beckhard
and Harris, 1977). Once these states have been defined, strategic
plans are developed that carefully outline major steps in the
transition. Ideally, these plans will be an accurate reflection of
all the necessary steps leading to the creation of the desired
future state. We refer to this change process as the formal phase
of organizational transformation since it is highly structured
and carefully planned and is, in addition, driven by the top
management of the organization.

When executed properly, the formal phase of organizational transformation can be highly effective and efficient. The
top-down focus provides the necessary support from key power
figures while the strategic planning element assures that the
effort is sequential and systematic. Change efforts that are attempted without these important prerequisites tend to be inef-
fectively supported and poorly executed. The result is often the
collapse of the change initiative.

We believe that this formal phase of organization transformation is essential in introducing long-term organizational
change. We can think of few examples where significant organizational transformation has occurred without clear direction,
effective planning, and, perhaps most important, top-level management support. A key point that is often overlooked in the
literature on organization change, however, is how lower-level
managers, professionals, and staff can influence the change
initiatives that eventually make it into the agendas of key executives. It is our belief that those who have never seen the
boardroom can still have a significant impact on corporate
direction. There is a key distinction between their role and that
of their hierarchical "superiors," however. They are "change influencers" rather than "change drivers."

As we use the term, change drivers are individuals who,
through their organizationally sanctioned position, have the
legitimate power to initiate and direct an organizationwide
change effort. These are individuals at the top of the organization who can require subordinates to execute major changes

and who authorize the allocation of resources and rewards to support such efforts. The focus of the change driver is to make sure that the change is initiated and implemented. The change driver is also the individual who formalizes the change initiative by publicly introducing it to the organization.

In contrast, change influencers are typically persons with limited hierarchical power. They are often lower-level managers or staff. They recognize that they cannot directly impact the decision-making process at the top levels in the organization so their focus is on how to influence key executives rather than on directly driving a proposed change initiative and holding people responsible for its execution. They not only generate ideas but also gather support for a future transformation through their ability to influence others.

Informal Phase of Transformation

Unlike the systematic, sequential planning process associated with top-down change, the approach used by change influencers is opportunistic and contextual and appears, at times, to be somewhat random. Their goal is twofold: (1) to get their change initiative into the agendas and discussions of members of the board and (2) to make sure, to the greatest extent possible, that there is movement toward the desired future state that they envision. We refer to these activities of the organizational transformation process as the informal phase.

But this informal phase of the transformation process is not simply a predecessor to the formal phase. Our experience indicates that the informal phase typically does precede the formalizing of the change initiative but that there are also a host of informal activities that continue to occur long after the change effort has been formalized. One way to picture this relationship is to imagine an amoebalike figure that represents the seemingly unsystematic and imprecise nature of the informal phase of the transformation. The amoeba begins forming before the change effort has been formalized and then continues to influence and help move the transformation effort forward through time. To pictorially represent the formalizing of the change initiative, we might imagine an arrow appearing from within the amoeba. This arrow represents the sequential, linear, and systematic nature of the formal phase of the transformation effort. The arrow continues to be surrounded and supported by the amoeba, which demonstrates the need for both formal and informal activities to occur concurrently during the entire course of the transformation.

Our experience suggests that major change efforts are often built on the foundations that have been laid by change influencers. While their work may be invisible to most organization members, it nevertheless plays a critical role in influencing and preparing the leadership of the organization for the challenges of managing the change initiative through time.

Naturally the "buck stops" with the person in power. It would be unrealistic to suggest that change influencers can impact change efforts if those at the top of the organization refuse to accept their ideas. It is equally unrealistic, though, to suggest that top-level managers will never listen to or act upon the ideas brought to them by mid-level managers and staff. Unfortunately, it is often the perception of those in the middle that they "have their hands tied"—that what they say cannot make a difference. Our experience suggests that their ideas can, and often do, have a significant impact on their organizations.

The manner in which the effective change influencer operates is difficult to characterize. To an outside observer it would probably appear that he or she initiates a series of loosely coupled activities that have little strategic or systematic orientation. Specific actions here might include conversations in the parking lot or local coffee shop, informal networking, writing, phone calls, a great deal of lobbying, and occasional blank stares.

Influencing Change

Although by all outward appearances the change influencers may seem to be operating in a state of chaos, randomly thrashing about as they attempt to get their ideas heard, we believe that among effective influencers there is "method to their madness." In fact, we suggest that there are three activity clusters where change influencers focus their time and energy: They create a vision of the potential future state of the transformed organization, they take advantage of every opportunity to discuss their vision, and they tenaciously support processes that facilitate the implementation of the vision while discouraging processes that inhibit it. We will refer to their activity clusters as vision, opportunity, and tenacity.

Vision. The term *vision* has become so overused in business circles that it has become a rather trite and meaningless expression. Its importance to the change influencer cannot be overemphasized, however. A vision is an attempt to articulate, as clearly and vividly as possible, the desired future state of the organization. The vision is the goal that provides direction, aligns key players, and energizes people to achieve a common purpose. It is a statement of an organizational dream — it stretches the imagination and motivates people to rethink what is possible. It is the most critical element of a successful organizationwide transformation.

Initially, the vision of a better future is all that change influencers have on their side. It is their most powerful tool in gaining the support of key figures in the organization, but it also represents a formidable challenge — visions are not easily articulated. It is, in our experience, critical that the vision of the desired future state be clear, concise, easily understandable, memorable, and exciting. This often demands a vision that is so tangible that it can engage the participant's senses. Common sense also dictates that it be consistent with the current and future needs of the organization and its stakeholders. The vision helps create a desire for change by making a possible future more attractive than the realities of the present.

Opportunity. We describe the second cluster of activities as opportunities. By opportunities we mean those sometimes planned, sometimes unplanned events that provide the change influencer with a chance to discuss his or her vision and gain support for it. This might be something as carefully planned out as structuring a series of formal networking meetings or as random as having a chance meeting in the corridor with a key executive. The point is that the opportunity is identified and used as a stage for further influencing key players.

Planned opportunities are typically those activities for which the change influencer has set an agenda, determined the appropriate membership, and created an event that will give him a chance to openly discuss his vision and receive feedback from key members in the organization. As these organization members become more personally involved with the vision through the iterative process of discussing it, providing feedback, and then reviewing changes, the vision becomes more and more solidified in their minds. The ideal outgrowth of this process is the beginning of a formal organizational change effort.

But unplanned opportunities can also have a tremendous amount of impact. We believe that effective change influencers are able to "leverage serendipity." In Kotter's studies (1982) of what effective managers really do, he found that the standard descriptors of management behavior, such as planning and controlling, were simply inadequate to describe how general managers spent their time. Rather than systematically operating from planned agendas, they often took advantage of chance occurrences to work toward their goals. Like the change influencers we have observed, they were, in fact, leveraging serendipity by taking advantage of even unplanned opportunities to move in the direction of the desired future state.

Our experience indicates that effective change influencers have working agendas that they always carry around in their heads. When likely opportunities present themselves, they are quick to act and take advantage of them. Change influencers seem to intuitively recognize that unplanned opportunities to influence change drivers often make a more powerful impression than carefully orchestrated events. If an executive happens to initiate a conversation in the lunchroom, for example, this might provide the perfect opportunity for a change influencer to introduce the key elements of his or her vision. These unplanned activities are one of the reasons that the informal phase appears to be so imprecise. Our experience indicates, however, that the precision and rationale for these various, seemingly unrelated activities are integrated by the internal work agenda of the change influencer. While the process is certainly not linear or systematic, it is rational.

Tenacity. The final activity cluster relates to simple tenacity, which suggests the kind of commitment individuals must feel toward the change initiatives that they are proposing. Since the legitimate, hierarchical power does not reside with the influencers, they must accept the fact that their ideas and initiatives are often going to be ignored or sidestepped. They may even come to feel that they are walking into a wall time after time after time. The key is to have the desire, commitment, and simple doggedness to keep walking into that wall until it finally collapses. We believe that effective change influencers exhibit a unique "stick-to-itiveness" that, over time, makes their vision salient and begins first to create and later helps to carry out the formal change process.

By behaving with tenacity, change influencers display their commitment to the vision they are advocating. They begin to be seen as people who really "walk their talk." This does not mean they pound on their desks and jump up on soap boxes — effective change influencers are also politically astute, recognizing that if they alienate change drivers, they will strangle the change initiative that they so passionately want to see implemented. They tend to operate with a kind of calculated audacity, taking full advantage of the opportunities that present themselves while politely sidestepping events that might block implementation of their vision. Thus, when obstacles do appear, change influencers immediately begin searching for new paths to achieve their desired ends. They seem to intuitively recognize that the path to organizational effectiveness is crooked and often unpredictable. They adapt, change directions, and explore new alternatives with ease.

Supportive systems and processes are, of course, important parts of the effectiveness of the emerging transformation. These changes are often the outgrowth of the tenacity of the change influencer. Often change influencers will focus their initial efforts on those pieces of the system that they can directly change. These small changes then become the foundation on which the organizational transformation is built. The change influencer nurtures this foundation, gets the attention of the change drivers, and, if all goes well, sees the systemwide changes that he or she advocates begin to materialize.

Although no model can adequately depict all the complexities involved in a major change effort, we feel that the vision, opportunity, and tenacity model is an important starting point for understanding how individuals can influence change. This belief is based on our observations of, and involvement in, the transformation of a major high-tech corporation. In reflecting on what has happened in that corporation to date, it has become increasingly apparent to us that change influencers have played, and continue to play, a critical role in its transformation. Examining this case will also help to further illustrate the vision, opportunity, and tenacity model.

Transformation in a High-Tech Company

The organization in transformation is Tektronix, a Fortune 200 electronics company with $1.5 billion in sales per year. It is a major producer of test and measurement, information display, and computer-aided products. "Tek," as it is known by most people, is headquartered in the so-called silicon rain forest of the Pacific Northwest; more than 80 percent of its employees work within a thirty-mile radius of headquarters.

Several divisions within Tektronix are in the process of transforming themselves from organizations that foster control over their workers to ones that foster their commitment (Walton, 1985). At the heart of this effort is the fundamental belief that enhanced performance and value for the customer can best be achieved by a work force that is honestly committed to producing superior results and meeting customer needs. Transformational leaders (Tichy, 1984) also believe that once committed, the work force will itself perpetuate the key elements of the business success more effectively than such external control measures as restrictive systems, policies, procedures, and supervision.

For Tek, this transformation toward high-commitment systems (Walton, 1980), or to what has also been referred to in the literature as sociotechnical systems (Trist and Bamforth, 1951; Trist, 1981; Cherns, 1976) or new design plants (Lawler, 1978), is a return to many of the fundamental values, thinking processes, and organizational structures of the early entrepreneurial venture. When interviewed for the company newspaper just a few months before his death in 1986, cofounder Howard Vollum was asked if he supported the first "green field" application of high-commitment systems in Tektronix. He replied, "Sure, but that's not new. It was here at the start. Then we kind of got away from it. I think it's very important that we get back to it." In its beginning, senior employees report, Tek was much like the organization that many of the divisions are being transformed into today. It was a place where information and decision making were widely shared and where people were committed to achieving business goals. It was unencumbered by multiple, restrictive job descriptions or other barriers to organizational responsiveness and employee contribution. Tek was composed of a handful of committed employees working with (not for) the founders Jack Murdock and Howard Vollum to satisfy customers through the relentless pursuit of technical excellence and concern for people.

During its periods of rapid growth, however, Tek followed the conventional management wisdom of the time and began to "act like a business" and less like the high-performance/high-commitment organization of its infancy. The management structure became highly centralized and bureaucratic. The resulting pyramid required narrowly defined, fractionated jobs and highly specialized departments. In 1980, when it became increasingly apparent that this monolithic structure could not adapt fast enough to the turbulent environment that the company was entering, a major restructuring was initiated. The result was the decentralizing of the company into four product groups and twenty-nine divisions. Although now decentralized, the control orientation of the centralized structure was still very much in evidence in virtually all the divisions. The new structure did provide the opportunity for more flexibility and experimentation, however. This, in turn, opened the way for change influencers who were committed to transforming the organization.

To illustrate how vision, opportunity, and tenacity have been used in certain Tek divisions, we will highlight a few of the informal activities and processes that we believe have significantly influenced the formal transformation to high-performance/high-commitment systems. The activities and processes presented here can be thought of as a kind of collage—there is no distinct, linear, or logical sequence that was followed. The change influencers pasted together their forward path, using what was available to them at any given time.

Developing a Vision

One of the primary challenges associated with a transformation of this magnitude is to get people to coalesce around a common vision. The earliest attempts to develop such a vision at Tektronix occurred in relatively small and fairly isolated groups. These initial efforts were conducted by mid-level managers who had reached the conclusion that, in order to maintain a competitive advantage in the current business environment, they had to move toward a commitment-oriented management design. Their work, and the success of their respective organizations, became the early foundation for the emerging companywide transformation effort.

Since much of the work of these first-generation visionaries occurred in relative isolation, it became increasingly apparent that, if the change was to gain momentum throughout the company, there needed to be some way to capture and more broadly communicate the key denominators of high-commitment systems. Early in 1984 a small group of change influencers created what they referred to as a *visioning tool*, which was designed to help people better understand the core characteristics of high-commitment systems (Fisher and Rayner, 1984).

In the development of this visioning tool, both the context

facing Tektronix and the history of the corporation were considered. It was becoming increasingly clear, for example, that the
high-commitment system was "an idea whose time had come"
because of the pressures currently facing several divisions of the
company. Among the pressures identified were the fiercely competitive nature of the company's markets, the increasing rapidity
of technological change, the changing expectations of a more
highly educated work force, the increase in job alienation, the
underutilization of the creative and intellectual power of employees, the need for increased organizational adaptability and
flexibility, and the desire to bring democracy back into the
workplace. In addition, the change influencers also took into
account the fundamental values of the company. At Tek these
values are very clear—respect for the individual, equality, and
partnership. The company founders instilled these values into
the organization over forty years ago, and they still remain a
motivating part of the cultural fabric, despite the introduction
of systems and structures over the years that run counter to them.

The visioning tool that was created describes several examples of what low-commitment and high-commitment organizations would look like in behaviorally oriented terms. For example, it describes the range of skills that would be seen, the
kinds of issues that people would talk about, and the kinds of
leadership that would be practiced in the two organizations.
The intent of highlighting the characteristics of both a low- and a
high-commitment organization was to better illustrate the profound nature of the emerging transformation.

More important than the completed visioning tool, however, was the process used to compile it and put it into operation.
The document went through numerous iterations with input
from a variety of sources. Input from change drivers and change
influencers within Tek, including sources as diverse as previous
employees of Procter & Gamble, Cummins Engine, and General
Foods, influenced the final version of the document. Managers
throughout the company have since used it as a way to begin
discussions about the transformation to high-commitment systems within their divisions. The outcome of many of these
discussions has been formulation of a commonly held vision

Table 7-1. Excerpts from the High-Performance/High-Commitment Systems Visioning Tool.

Low Commitment	High Commitment
1. Customer Orientation	
Most individuals within the organization have little knowledge of the needs of the customer or little commitment to meeting the needs of the customer.	Customer satisfaction is the key focus of all people within the organization. People actively introduce and operationalize ideas that enable the product to be more effective and profitable from the customer's perspective.
2. Technical Excellence	
People cannot explain key processes or technologies that do not directly impact the specific task they are doing.	People can explain the key processes and technologies that affect all members of their work group. They can draw diagrams that accurately explain the work flow of their products and can illustrate potential problems through the process. Everyone can list some acceptable alternative processes or technologies to the ones they are using to either market, produce, design, or maintain their products/services.
3. Shared Values	
Operational philosophies include: • The primary indicator of success is staying within budget. • Decisions should be made by management. • Disagreement is usually disruptive and should generally be avoided. • Successful risk taking is rewarded but unsuccessful risk taking is punished. • Information should be shared primarily on "need-to-know" basis.	Operational philosophies include: • The primary indicator of success is customer satisfaction. • Decisions should be made at the lowest possible level. • Constructive disagreement is OK and is encouraged. • People are rewarded for taking appropriate risks even if they fail. • Information is shared freely.

- Only people who have "proven track records" are respected.
- People need to be controlled and organized through job descriptions, work rules, direction of activities, and so on.
- The customer will be provided with the product and/or service that is produced.

- Everyone is respected.
- There should be no artificial barriers that limit a person's contribution to the organization.
- The customer will always be provided with the best value.

4. Performance Commitment

- Most people are seldom involved in suggesting activities that improve the business.

- A wide variety of people frequently champion their own or their team's ideas. It is common for these ideas to become operationalized.

5. Environmental Awareness

Everyone can state:
- The name of the area they work for
- The name of their manager
- Their job in the area

Everyone can state:
- Key business objectives
- Chief competitors and what differentiates their products
- Key cost data
- Main factors influencing product profitability and how these factors affect it
- Key customers
- How customers affect other parts of the business

6. Trust

In general, mutual feelings of distrust are more readily shown between people than are feelings of trust. This is evidenced by tight managerial control over operations and policies, on the one hand, and by continual attempts to "beat the system" or "game playing," on the other hand.

Mutual trust between all people is demonstrated by such things as lack of time clocks, flexible break hours, self-managing groups, joint problem-solving teams, and the discussion of potentially sensitive information.

Table 7-1. Excerpts from the High-Performance/High-Commitment Systems Visioning Tool, Cont'd.

Low Commitment	*High Commitment*
7. Reward Systems	
Rewards are based solely on the isolated performance of individuals and therefore may not take organizational performance into consideration.	Reward systems are consistent with organizational objectives and therefore are tied directly to customer satisfaction.
8. Work Autonomy/Job Flexibility	
Jobs are specifically and narrowly defined to ensure maximum control of the work.	Jobs are flexible and broad enough to allow people to make their maximum contribution to the business.
9. Organization Structure	
The main emphasis is on attempting to maintain organizational effectiveness with the minimal amount of energy. The maintenance of a "smooth" operation—the status quo—is the goal.	Considerable energy goes into examining ways to help the organization continually improve its overall effectiveness. This is an unending process that is considered extremely important for the continued growth of the business.
10. Leadership	
People say they feel limited or unduly constrained by those in management positions above them.	People say that they frequently feel empowered and motivated to accomplish business results. They frequently attribute this to effective leadership. They recognize the boundary conditions (time constraints, budget limitations, and so on) given to them as focusing rather than limiting their activities.

throughout the organization that has served as the catalyst for significant changes in management philosophy and practices.

Taking Advantage of Opportunities

Coinciding with the development of the visioning tool, a group of change influencers established a weekly network meeting of human resource professionals from throughout the corporation. These network meetings focused on the topic of high-commitment systems. The intent was to develop a coalition of people who would develop and share a common language to discuss and articulate the emerging transformation. These people would then be better prepared to support line management in formulating and leading the change.

This network became a key sounding board for the visioning tool. Its members provided valuable feedback that helped to further refine and improve the tool. Further, the vision document was used by network members when discussing the concepts of high-commitment systems with the change drivers in their own organizations.

Some of the most effective planned opportunities used by change influencers were presentations by consultants and visits to plants. External consultants helped in disseminating information about high-commitment systems while simultaneously giving the vision of change influencers additional credibility. Similarly, visits to high-commitment-oriented organizations both within and outside of Tektronix were used by change influencers as a way to help demonstrate to change drivers the tremendous potential of this management approach.

While carefully orchestrating opportunities was extremely important, it seemed that the most powerful and effective kinds of change influencing occurred through taking advantage of fortunate circumstances. For example, concurrent with the initiation of efforts to transform some production groups within Tektronix to high-commitment systems, a senior executive introduced a significant organizational improvement effort for achieving manufacturing excellence. Change influencers encouraged the inclusion of "people involvement" as one of the key target areas for attaining excellence in manufacturing. This provided credibility for much of the work that had already begun and helped to legitimize it as an appropriate response to the challenges being faced in manufacturing. In addition, the early work of the change influencers put them in a position to influence how "people involvement" was defined and described to managers throughout the company.

There were a variety of these kinds of unforeseen opportunities. As technology changes occurred, they often provided ideal means for accelerating the movement toward high-commitment systems. The unfreezing effect caused by the introduction of "just-in-time" manufacturing techniques, for example, provided an excellent opportunity to introduce the concepts of high-commitment systems to numerous manufacturing groups. Like many other companies, Tektronix had stockpiled "just-in-case" inventories to guard against unexpected fluctuations in manufacturing processes. The new just-in-time philosophy required the relentless elimination of waste and the rapid resolution of problems that, under traditional practices, would have remained hidden under excess inventory. Just-in-time practices suggested the need for increased teamwork and flexibility, cross-training activities, and the development of appropriate support systems to reward and encourage these behaviors, all of which were complementary to the standard practices in high-commitment systems. As just-in-time practices spread throughout the company so did the emphasis on introducing high-commitment systems.

Other opportunities popped up. For example, undesirable business results in some areas of the company made some change drivers search for viable organizational alternatives. People began asking tough questions about how they could make their unit operate more effectively. The result, in some instances was the emergence of leaders who became strong advocates of the high-commitment approach. Where and when they could, change influencers provided information and guidance to these individuals. When a few of these projects were deemed successful, more managers began examining high commitment as an improvement strategy. In effect, the snowball had begun to roll.

During the course of this effort we found that the most successful strategies for change were often those that did not seem like change at all. Rather, they were evolutionary changes that built on the good and strong elements of the current system rather than highlighting its weaknesses. We believe that this approach has had some benefits. First, it did not alienate those who had a vested interest in the way things were, and, second, it took advantage of the momentum of the status quo. It avoided the view that the "foolishness" of the past had caused the "ills" of the present — a view that might easily have led to the formation of opposed factions that would have focused more energy on challenging one another's views than on attempting to facilitate the transformation effort.

As time passed, the vision became increasingly salient to numerous change drivers within Tektronix. A high-commitment system no longer seemed like an abstract notion; it began to have a clear meaning that implied certain actions. Movement had begun. This was most evident in the emergence of division business plans with entire sections dedicated to transition strategies aimed at creating a high-performance/high-commitment organization. It was clear that the transformation effort had attained legitimacy in the eyes of many key executives.

Behaving with Tenacity

"Here today and here tomorrow" seems to be an appropriate slogan for change influencers who tenaciously demonstrate and perpetuate ongoing commitment to a transformation. In our observations of effective change influencers, we have found that brilliance in the transformation is less important than consistency and repetition. It is by being tenacious that change influencers at Tek have demonstrated their firm commitment to the vision of a high-performance/high-commitment organization. By constantly encouraging those activities and processes that facilitate the transformation, change influencers have helped change drivers make things happen. Here again their influencing power has come from repeated effort rather than from single bursts of energy. They stick with it.

We have found that ongoing training and education programs provide important examples of the tenacity required in this transformation effort. In addition to developing skills, such sessions reinforce and keep salient the transformation issues. Several change influencers, for example, have been teaching the same two-day workshop on "people involvement" every month for the last two years. While this may no longer be a new and exciting task, the change influencers involved recognize that these sessions serve the important purpose of providing a continuity of concept, a common vocabulary, and a networking opportunity for people.

Change influencers at Tek have also found that being involved in a major transformation requires a great deal of legwork. Influencers who once took advantage of chance opportunities to discuss a vision of a better future with various change drivers have exhibited the same kind of commitment and tenacity in addressing implementation issues. They have aggressively pursued such projects as the restructuring of the performance appraisal and job evaluation systems and have worked through the ongoing employee relations and business issues that follow transformations of any magnitude. Their support has played a key role in helping the transformation effort maintain its momentum.

This stage requires a great deal of energy and patience. Although it may not be as exhilarating as the creative process required during the initial stages of the transformation effort, the likelihood of organizationwide transformation success without it is minimal.

Summary

Although the transformation of organizations requires a formal change process—led by the change drivers of the organization—we would argue that it also requires an informal change process. Like the yin and yang of Taoist philosophy, the formal and informal processes may appear to be diametrically opposed to each other, but they actually work together to prepare and reinforce organizational transformation. Throughout the informal phase lower-level managers, staff, and professionals can have a significant impact on organizational transformation efforts by focusing their energy on three activity clusters: vision, opportunity, and tenacity.

Fundamentally, major transformations are born of visions — visions that ignite the imagination and help others rethink what is possible. This cornerstone of organization transformation can be put in place anywhere, at any level in the management hierarchy. Those who can make the vision of a new and worthwhile future tangible, communicable, motivating, and memorable have already begun the process of influencing change.

Armed with a vision of a better future, effective change influencers seek out opportunities to articulate this vision and get their message into the discussions and agendas of the key managers who can drive the change. They do this by looking for opportunities to influence these change drivers. Some opportunities are created through careful planning and orchestration. Others are random, chance occurrences that are spotted by the change influencer and quickly acted upon. Each opportunity that is utilized, whether it was a planned or unplanned event, helps the change initiative gain momentum.

The task of influencing change can be a frustrating one. Often managers will ignore or sidestep the key points that the change influencer is trying to bring to their attention. Hence the need for the kind of drive and tenacity that we found in those individuals who have significantly influenced the transformation that is currently underway at Tektronix. Their energy and spirit stem from a strong and unyielding belief in a better future for the organization.

In summary, when attempting to develop a broader perspective on the nature of organizational transformation, it is important to recognize the informal activities that typically accompany the formal change process. Our observations suggest that, when effectively executed, the activities that occur "informally" are often the catalyst for major change efforts. We have attempted to describe the three activity clusters—vision, opportunity, and tenacity—on which those who are effective at influencing change typically focus their time and energy. Our hope is that this model will become a first step in an evolving examination of the informal side of organizational transformation—a side that could be of significant help to managers involved in major transformation efforts.

References

Beckhard, R. *Organization Development: Strategies and Models.* Reading, Mass.: Addison-Wesley, 1969.

Beckhard, R., and Harris, R. T. *Organizational Transitions: Managing Complex Change.* Reading, Mass.: Addison-Wesley, 1977.

Cherns, A. "The Principles of Sociotechnical Design." *Human Relations,* 1976, *29* (8), 783–792.

Fisher, K. K., and Rayner, S. R. *The High-Performance/High-Commitment System Assessment Guide.* Beaverton, Ore.: Tektronix, 1984.

Kotter, J. P. "What Effective General Managers Really Do." *Harvard Business Review,* 1982, *60* (6), 156–167.

Lawler, E. E. "The New Plant Revolution." *Organizational Dynamics,* 1978, *6* (3), 3–12.

Rayner, S. R. *New Excellence: The Forest Grove Project.* Beaverton, Ore.: Tektronix, 1984.

Tichy, N. M., and Ulrich, D. O. "The Leadership Challenge—A Call for the Transformational Leader." *Sloan Management Review,* 26 (1), 1984, 59–68.

Trist, E. *The Evolution of Sociotechnical Systems: A Conceptual Framework and an Action Research Program.* Occasional Paper, no. 2. Toronto: Ontario Quality of Working Life Center, Ontario Ministry of Labor, 1981.

Trist, E., and Bamforth, K. W. "Some Social and Psychological Consequences of the Longwall Method of Coal-Getting." *Human Relations,* 1951, *4*, 3–38.

Walton, R. E. "Establishing and Maintaining High Commitment Work Systems." In J. R. Kimberly, R. H. Miles, and Associates,

The Organizational Life Cycle: Issues in the Creation, Transformation, and Decline of Organizations. San Francisco: Jossey-Bass, 1980.

Walton, R. E. "From Control to Commitment in the Workplace." *Harvard Business Review*, 1985, *63* (2), 76–84.

Mary Elizabeth Beres

Steven J. Musser

8

Avenues and Impediments to Transformation: Lessons from a Case of Bottom-Up Change

Missing the forest for the trees is a fairly common human experience. We often lose perspective on the whole picture as we step up close to study individual details. The progression of the organization development field from aspirations for system-wide change to fragmented studies of specialized techniques traces this familiar path. While organization developers have accumulated a great deal of specialized knowledge, results at the systemwide level have often failed to meet expectations.

This volume provides an opportunity to look once again at the big picture of systemwide transformations. There are three ways that such a forest can be brought back into focus. One is to wander within its boundaries, experiencing its motion, arrangement, climate, texture, color, and so on. Another way is to move outside and view the entire forest from a single vantage point. A third is to compare the forest to seas, prairies, deserts, or metropolises. In this chapter, we will follow the third path to understanding systemwide organization development. We will examine the top-management-sponsored, planned process of systemwide change by contrasting it to a bottom-up, spontaneously orchestrated, systemwide change. The presentation is

152

divided into two parts. The first part describes a particular organization, the changes that have occurred within it, and the change process that it has undergone. The second part suggests lessons to be learned about organization development; it discusses potential problems in top-management-sponsored, planned approaches and three role/behavior sets that contribute to effective corporate cultural change.

From a Centralized Hierarchy to a Collegial Network

The organizational transformation on which this study is based occurred in a women's religious congregation, part of an order of nuns founded at the beginning of the thirteenth century. It is one of many such organizations that provide educational, health care, and social services to the public. The members are educated, professional women who promise obedience to authority within the organization, relinquish the right to private ownership, and commit themselves to a celibate life. Obviously a religious congregation of women is an unusual organization in many respects. It is a nonprofit service organization based explicitly on Christian values. The members make lifetime commitments to the congregation, which itself operates within the framework of the Roman Catholic church. In spite of these differences, however, the congregation's transformation has followed the path of many for-profit corporations.

Actually, the congregation highlighted is not as different from other organizations as it at first seems to be. Some corporations, such as IBM and AT&T, also claim service as their mission, have members who identify personally with the corporation, and in many cases provide lifetime employment. Technologically, the congregation operates in the knowledge-based service sector that is central to the emerging information era. At the behavioral level, people in both types of organizations are products of similar sociocultural environments. In fact, members of religious congregations have educated some of the major leaders of industry. Thus, members of corporations and congregations share many behavioral characteristics. It is to this shared behavioral level that organization development is directed. Given these points of convergence, it may be that American corporations can learn as much from American religious congregations as they have from Japanese corporations.

For several specific reasons the systemwide transformation of the congregation can offer useful, general lessons for organization development. First, the changes in the congregation have penetrated to the very deepest level of the system and in the process have transformed relationships between members and the organization, redefined the nature and role of authority, and redistributed power. These changes correspond with the early aspirations of the organization development field (Shepard, 1965; Argyris, 1957) and have produced the kind of market-oriented, flexible, participative, loosely coupled structure being advocated for today's corporations (Peters and Waterman, 1982; Toffler, 1980). Hence, the experience of the congregation provides links between organization development's normative aspirations and the practical problem of reinventing American corporations (Naisbitt and Aburdene, 1985).

Second, the change process in the congregation has been underway long enough to produce operational results. The transformation described here began about twenty years ago. The process has passed beyond the trauma and excitement of the "charismatic" period and settled into a new routine. This new routine has been a matter of continuing adaptation as the organization develops its resources, analyzes the global situation, and receives new challenges from the environment. Thus, the case is an illustration of successful transformation from a centralized, stable, industrial age organization to a loosely coupled, pluralistic, dynamic information era organization.

Third, the organization's long history of successful adaptation to environmental change makes it a functioning laboratory for organization developers. The congregation is one of a very few modern organizations that began during the agricultural age and survived the upheaval of the industrial revolution. During this 750-year period the organization has demonstrated the flexibility and adaptability that many organizations seek today.

Nature of the Change. The change described here occurred in a congregation headquartered in the Midwest. Most of its members are dispersed across the United States, but a few are in other parts of the Americas and in Africa. Prior to the change, the organization had approximately 2,500 members working primarily in educational institutions. Authority was vested in the prioress general (CEO) and her councilors (executive board), who were elected during the General Chapter (Corporate Assembly) held every six years. Until 1960, the prioress general appointed all local superiors, staffed all missions, and oversaw the regulation of all convents. In 1960 the congregation was organized into geographical divisions. Responsibility for staffing was delegated to provincials (geographical division heads), with final approval of appointments being given by the prioress general. When the transformation process began, the congregation had been operating in this manner for about fifty years and there was no expectation of change.

Historically, the change described in this study is the most recent of several major transformations in the order. The order began as a group of independent houses of women who lived celibate lives of piety, prayer, and sacrifice in cloistered (completely closed) communities. The house from which the current organization descends was formed about 1230 in Bavaria, long before Germany existed as a nation (Ryan, 1967).

Following many cycles of growth and decline, the first transformation occurred in the early 1800s when the German house added education to its mission and opened an elementary school on its premises. The second transformation began about fifty years later when the organization began sending members to the people it served rather than requiring clients to come to the organization. For example, the German house sent women to teach German-Americans in the United States. This change in strategy soon led to a transformation in structure from autonomous local units to a centrally controlled, geographically dispersed organization. The change contributed to the prolific expansion of the order and was officially acknowledged at the close of the century. As the organization expanded across the

United States, regional groups were organized into geographical divisions. For various reasons, these divisions were later "spun off" (in modern terms) as independent organizations. The Midwest-based organization, on which this study focuses, became independent in the 1920s. It then grew rapidly into an international organization in its own right, much as the newly independent regional Bell companies are doing today.

The organizationwide transformation described in detail here occurred during the late 1960s and early 1970s. In the course of this transformation, the organization has radically changed its mission, priorities, strategies, and structures. Data sources for studies of the change (Musser, 1985; Beres, 1982, 1976) included extensive archival materials, surveys, and interviews. To facilitate description of the change, specialized congregation terminology has been translated into general organization language. Some of the main characteristics of the change are identified in Table 8-1.

The organization's general mission became one of outward service rather than inward development. Its specific mission broadened from particular areas of service to a general philosophy of service. Priorities were shifted from an emphasis on the works of the congregation to an emphasis on members as the primary vehicle for fulfilling the organization's mission. The corporate strategy was changed from growth in the education area by means of acquisition and internal development to divestiture of institutional commitments and diversification based on the needs of society and members' abilities. In business terminology, the organization has shifted from a product to a market orientation, using members' abilities to identify the markets that the organization is best equipped to serve.

Structurally, the organization has transferred much of its decision making from the executive hierarchy to collegial assemblies at local, divisional, and corporate levels. Changes in functional strategies reflect both the expanded concept of mission and the decentralization of decision making. Member initiatives affect local operations, job placement, the locations and types of work sites, and local financial management. The extent to which these changes have actually occurred is manifested in

Table 8-1. Prechange and Postchange Characteristics.

Characteristic	1962	1972
General Mission	Praise of God and self-transformation	Share Christian love with each other and all people
Specific Mission	Christian education, health care, and social service	Communication of the gospel individually and corporately
Corporate Strategy	Focus on education	Diversification based on social needs and members' abilities/interests
	Growth primarily through acquisition, some growth through internal development	
		Divestiture of institutional ownership
Structure	Centralized hierarchy	Decentralized network
	Major decisions made by executive officers	Major decisions made in collegial assemblies
Functional Strategies		
Operations	Centrally formalized processes administered by local authority	Dependent on local initiatives
Staffing	Assignment by regional unit head	Individual search in consultation with regional unit head
Marketing	CEO interacted with bishops and pastors to obtain schools to staff	Research on opportunities, information distributed to members
Finance	Compensation for members' services primary source of income	Compensation for members' services primary source of income, some investment income
	Finances managed centrally except for ordinary local expenses	Finances managed centrally except for ordinary local expenses
	All current income used for current operations	Income used for current operations and invested for future operations

the organization's formal documents, the behaviors of officials and members, and the outcomes of the organization's activities.

Formal Changes. The formal structure of the organization has changed from a centralized hierarchy to an open collegial network that fits Child's (1977) description of a "loosely coupled" system. Figure 8-1 shows major stages in the evolution of this change. Throughout the change process, the structure has included both executive positions and collegial assemblies. The change from the 1960s to 1980s is most apparent in the role and primacy of the order's hierarchies. Thus, in the 1960s, executive positions dominated the structure at the corporate, divisional, and local levels. The collegial assemblies at the divisional level could only raise issues for consideration at the corporate level. The corporate-level assembly elected the CEO and her executive board and had authority over extraordinary organizational matters. Deliberations in all collegial assemblies were secret. Elections were held in silence, and only the results of elections were communicated to the membership.

By the early 1970s, however, collegial assemblies had come to dominate the organization's structure at all three levels. These assemblies became open bodies with legislative authority over the organization's affairs. Their meetings were open to observers and extensively reported to the members. Executives' responsibilities were to carry out the decisions of the collegial assemblies. Executive positions at the local level were eliminated. In the early 1980s, collegial and executive hierarchies were merged into a corporate network. Individual members now choose the local group through which they link into the network. Officials elected at a lower level of the network constitute a collegial council at the next level in a "linking system" (Likert, 1961). The current structure is ambiguous about the relative authority of the CEO, the Corporate Council at the center of the network, and the collegial Corporate Assembly, which has been omitted from the organization's official chart.

We have assessed changes in the allocation of decision-making authority as the structure has evolved by using a modification of the Pugh, Hickson, Hinings, and Turner (1968) cen-

Figure 8-1. Prechange and Postchange Structural Configurations.

1960s

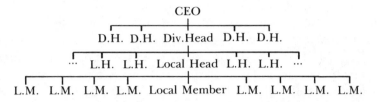

1970s

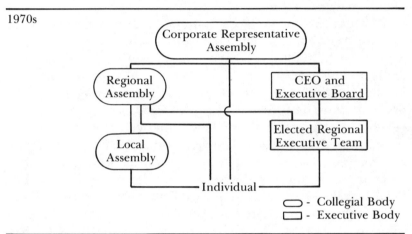

1980s

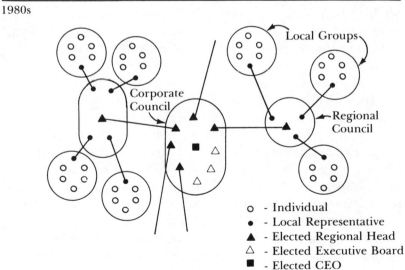

tralization measure. The Pugh measure contains a list of thirty-seven decisions, which range from how to allocate work to how to develop strategies. The list includes decisions in the areas of budgeting, staffing, organizational design, scheduling, pricing, purchasing, business strategy, and evaluation. For our study, Pugh, Hickson, Hining, and Turner's original list of decisions has been translated from a manufacturing to a service context, and a parallel hierarchy has been added to include the authority of collegial assemblies (Beres, 1976).

Figure 8-2 shows the decision-making profiles of the organization as its structure changed from an executive hierarchy to a collegial hierarchy to a network. The profiles indicate the levels at which decisions must receive final approval prior to implementation. The left side of each graph shows how many decisions must be approved at a centralized, executive level. The center of each graph indicates how many decisions are made at a decentralized, local level. The right side of each graph shows how many decisions are made at a centralized, collegial level. A comparison of the profiles shows that the major change has been a transfer of final authority from the executive to the collegial hierarchy. There has also been some decentralization to the local assembly. As the changes have occurred, the CEO has retained final authority over only three areas: recruitment and training of new members, relations with the hierarchy of the Roman Catholic church, and organization finances.

Behavioral Changes. The change in the congregation's formal authority has been reflected behaviorally in numerous ways. One rather interesting manifestation involves a linguistic change in letters sent to the membership by the CEO (Beres, 1976). Two different pronoun forms were used: a "you" form that reflects an implicit distinction between members and management, and a "we" form that reflects an implicit collaborative relationship. Prior to 1967 the "you" form of address was used more than two-thirds of the time. "You" and "we" forms were used in about equal proportion as the change attempt gained momentum. After the change was agreed upon, the "we" form was used approximately three-fourths of the time. Thus, pronoun

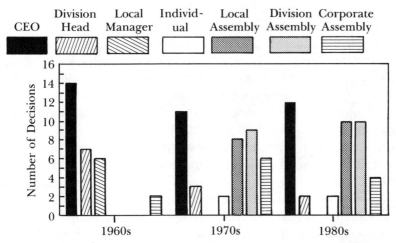

Figure 8-2. Decision-Making Profiles.

Note: Profiles show the levels at which final approval is needed prior to action.

usage reflects the shift from vertically differentiated authority to horizontally shared authority that took place in the congregation.

In addition, prior to the change in structure, all members' actions were prescribed by rules or directives. The structure in place after the change reduced the number of specific rules from approximately 600 to 90. It also gave members the right to participate actively in decisions that directly affected them. By 1972, nearly 75 percent of the members chose the residences in which they lived in a dialogue process with a regional team member. Over 90 percent of the members created their own local decision-making structures. About 70 percent of these structures were completely collegial (Beres, 1976).

Outcomes. The opening up of the organization's boundaries was one of the significant effects of members' exercise of choice. As the upper half of Table 8-2 indicates, members quickly adopted contemporary forms of dress, more conventional residence locations, and new areas of work. The new works ranged from farming, social action, and business services to pastoral ministries and counseling. Exercise of these options significantly improved members' morale. The transformation of the organization also had significant corporate outcomes. These are summarized in the lower half of Table 8-2. The organization is now smaller in size, its members are older, it owns fewer institutions, and it manages a larger corporate budget.

The transformation described here goes beyond the discontinuous change from one state to another, which was labeled *gamma change* by Golembiewski, Billingsley, and Yeager (1975). In this case, the changes are so extensive that they alter not only the system but also the dimensions along which measurement is meaningful. Prior to the change, for example, dress and residence were constants, now they are variables. Although attitudes and feelings varied before the change, measurement of them was neither permitted nor even considered because they were supposed to be subordinated to the organization's goals. Prior to the change every action was concretely defined, including such details as where people would sit, when they could talk, how they should walk. After the change, prescriptions were written in general, philosophical terms. Thus, the congregation has undergone a *delta change* in which the total transformation of the system has affected even the bases for assessing change.

Change Process

Because the congregation's transformation has been analyzed after the fact, it may seem that its various steps were clearly defined and distinctly recognized by members beforehand. In reality, however, the process was traumatic, highly ambiguous, and fraught with conflict and uncertainty. Focusing on the first three years of the transformation process, this section of the presentation has described some of the events that contributed significantly to the structural component of the change. This phase of the change process has been reconstructed from the organization's archival records and confirmed through retrospective interviews with some of the active participants (Musser, 1985). The chronology of events and data points for assessment of the change are presented in Table 8-3.

Table 8-2. Organizational Outcomes.

A. Opening of Boundaries and Effect on Morale

Year	Wear Modern Dress	Live in House or Apartment	Area of Work (for those employed)[a]				Report Being Very Happy
			Formal Education	Health Services	Organization Offices	Other, New Areas	
1968	0%	0%	96%	4%	[b]	0%	47%
1972	44%	25%	68%	3%	4%[c]	24%	61%
1977	65%	34%	54%	5%	3%	38%	63%
1981	73%	46%	47%	6%	2%	46%	73%

[a] Percentage of members actually employed; excludes retired and student members
[b] Figures not recorded
[c] Includes secretarial and clerical members; figures for 1977 and 1981 include only officers

B. Corporate Changes

Year	Number of Members	Median Age	Institutions Owned			Corporate Budget[d] (in millions)
			High Schools	Colleges	Hospitals	
1968	2,480		10	2	2	1.8
1972	2,030	47	7	1	2	4.3
1977	1,750	51	5	1	2	5.7
1981	1,600	55	4	1	2	7.2

[d] Excludes institution budgets and local operating budgets

Table 8-3. Chronology of the Change Process.

Major Events	Date	Data Sources	
Corporate Assembly, election of the CEO	June 1962	Constitutions as revised	
Convening of Vatican Council	Oct. 1962		
Distribution of "Decree on the Appropriate Renewal of Religious Life"	July 1965	Decree	
Pope Paul's norms for implementation of renewal	Aug. 1966	Norms	Letters of the CEO
Central Committee elected	Dec. 1966		
Central Committee meeting	June 1967		
Prechapter Commission elected	Oct. 1967		
Renewal Assembly proposals requested	Jan. 1968		
General voting on the Renewal Assembly proposals	Apr. 1968	Proposals	
Renewal Assembly, first session, election of new officials	June 1968		
	Apr. 1969	Membership survey	
Renewal Assembly, first session, business	Aug. 1969		
Renewal Assembly, second session	Aug. 1970	Renewal assembly report enactments	
	Apr. 1972	Membership survey	
Corporate Assembly, reelection of the CEO	Jan. 1974		
Corporate Assembly, business	Aug. 1974	Enactments	

One immediate stimulus for the change was a decree issued in 1965 by the Vatican Council of the Roman Catholic church. This decree, among other things, urged religious congregations to reexamine themselves and develop plans for renewal and adaptation of their founding spirit to contemporary problems. At the time of the decree the organization had been operating hierarchically for about one hundred years, and there were no particular indications that a change was about to occur. According to what they said in interviews, members many times felt frustration and emotional pain but gave little thought to trying to change conditions within the order. Members had apparently accepted the authoritarian norms of the existing organizational paradigm as inevitable. As one member said in an interview, only when members heard the idea of collegiality discussed at renewal meetings did many of them begin to seriously question the legitimacy of the existing authority structure. This new collegial organization paradigm provided impetus for the structural transformation. The processes by which the idea took hold in the organization are the processes through which change developed.

The first step was taken by the CEO. In response to the Vatican decree, she directed all members to nominate and elect members of their choice to regional renewal committees. These committees were charged with the task of developing plans for renewal, including the proposal of any constitutional changes for consideration by the Corporate Assembly in 1968. The committees began their work in 1966 by seeking members' ideas and preferences through the use of surveys, meetings, and discussions. Some, but by no means all, of the ideas and views they collected centered on governance. A growing number of members felt that the authority within the organization was too centralized. They believed that collegiality (more individuality and decentralization) was needed to make renewal meaningful. Several who felt this way were prominent members and chairpersons of the renewal committees.

During the summer of 1967, all the chairpersons of the renewal committees met for several weeks as a Central Committee to assimilate the ideas and suggestions collected from the entire membership. In the original plan, the Central Committee was to translate members' suggestions into specific proposals for the upcoming Corporate Assembly and then to disband. Once approved by the Corporate Assembly, proposals would be sent to Rome for approval before becoming part of the organization's constitutions.

One important accomplishment of the Central Committee was creation of a Prechapter Commission that would continue to involve members in the renewal process until the Corporate Assembly met in 1968. Without this innovation, direct member participation would have ended at the close of the Central Committee meeting. The idea of a Prechapter Commission was "sold" to the CEO on the basis of Vatican precedent and the need for continuation of the renewal "spirit." Specifically, the Central Committee argued that the Vatican had used a two-stage process to prepare for its own council. They had a *commissio ante-preparatorio* to which the Central Committee equated itself and then a *commissio preparatorio* to which the committee equated the proposed Prechapter Commission. What the committee did not state was that the *commissio preparatorio* controlled the agenda for the Vatican Council. Later the committee would argue unsuccessfully that, because of precedent, the Prechapter Commission should control the agenda for the upcoming Corporate Assembly, now called the Renewal Assembly.

Having established a successor committee, the Central Committee then proceeded to develop a proposal for a decentralized governmental structure (which was ultimately rejected by the CEO), an extensive communications plan to enable members to continue dialogue and exchange of ideas during the coming months, and plans for increased and broader member participation in the Renewal Assembly. At this point the Central Committee was dissolved and the Prechapter Commission replaced it. Membership of the two groups was essentially the same.

The first act of the Prechapter Commission was to seek membership control of the upcoming assembly agenda. By now the CEO was concerned that things were getting out of control. She felt that collegial government and decision making were not at all what the Vatican meant by "spiritual" renewal. She may have been right since several other organizations have not developed collegial governance as part of their renewal programs, and there was and is to this day Vatican concern over this type of governance.

As the Prechapter Commission increased its communications among members and fostered growing support for a more collegial governance structure through meetings and publications, the CEO brought in a very conservative church lawyer. He told the commission that Rome would never approve some of the governance proposals that members were suggesting nor would it approve their plan for controlling the assembly agenda.

Undaunted, in January 1968, the Prechapter Commission sent a representative to members across the country to share ideas and discuss a broad range of issues, including collegial governance. The CEO then withdrew funding from the commission, which responded by collecting its own funds from individual members. The momentum of the new ideas was given a further boost when the commission, in accord with established General Assembly requirements, collected proposals from members to be transmitted to the Renewal Assembly. In conjunction with this task, the commission also sought the right to use the proposals to set the Renewal Assembly agenda. This request was refused by the CEO, but her effort to retain control was really too little too late.

In order to communicate the feelings of members to the assembly delegates, the Prechapter Commission invited all members to express their opinions about each of the 1,060 proposals that had been submitted to it. Although there were only sixty-nine specific proposals on decentralized governance, they were relatively radical and wide ranging. They received strong support in the general voting (61 percent in favor, 24 percent opposed, 15 percent not sure). Thus, the idea of collegial governance had already gained tremendous acceptance among members. The results of the polling were included with the proposals when they were forwarded to the Renewal Assembly. By the time they met, the assembly delegates could see the strong desire by most of the membership for a redistribution of power.

Throughout this period there was intense conflict about what changes to make and how thoroughgoing these changes should be. It took until 1970 for the outlines of the new organization to become clear and for the organization to commit itself to radical transformation. In retrospect, however, the evolving commitment of the membership was evidenced in the replacement of the CEO and the election of three leading members of the Prechapter Commission to the organization's executive board at the 1968 session of the Renewal Assembly.

The final results of the assembly were new policies that stressed the rights of individuals, including the right of self-expression and the right to help shape decisions about congregational and work affairs; increased the emphasis on interpersonal relationships; broadened the definition of the congregation's mission; and freed members to enter forms of service suited to their talents. Policies that specified the behavior of individuals were eliminated, and authority was changed from a hierarchical to a collegial mode. Through the bottom-up, spontaneously orchestrated process that produced these changes, the operating norms of the organization were changed dramatically.

Lessons to Be Learned

Much can be learned from this case of organizational change. One very hopeful lesson is that contemporary organizations can be totally reconfigured, all the way from their global mission to their daily operating procedures. A more humbling lesson is that radical transformation can occur without the direct intervention of organization development specialists. The processes by which the change was accomplished have been explored elsewhere (Beres, 1976; Musser, 1985). Here the discussion focuses on some practical lessons that can be derived from the congregation's experience, and we believe that analysis of the case can provide relevant insights to several different types of users. Since it was a matter of a membership-orchestrated change, the case can offer guidelines to lower-level organization members who want to transform their organizations. At the same time, it can also supply top managers with information on how to block lower-level change initiatives. Neither of these groups, however, are the typical clients of organization development specialists. Organization development has focused instead on organization change sponsored by top management. To the more traditional organization developers, whether consultants or top managers, the bottom-up change process exemplified in our case offers practical information by way of contrast.

Indeed, a successful bottom-up transformation may provide insight into top-management-supported change in much the same way that Japanese management has shed light on U.S.

management practices. The view from "outside the forest" points to well-intentioned practices that may actually interfere with effective action. The study of an alternative approach also yields new methods that may be productively incorporated into the original system. Here, analysis of the case has identified three role/behavior sets that contribute to effective organizational transformation. The remainder of the discussion focuses on these cautionary and constructive lessons for top-management-sponsored organizational transformation.

Since its inception, we might recall, organization development has advocated a top-management-supported, planned approach to systemwide change. This emphasis reflects, in part, the environment into which organization development was born. In the 1950s and 1960s it was generally assumed that organizations were rigid, fixed entities that could only be changed by external change agents. Today, in life cycle theories of organization (for example, Kimberly, Miles, and Associates, 1980; Lippitt, 1969), there is a greater awareness of the dynamics inherent in organizational processes. As the case reported here illustrates, systemwide change can occur through the agency of internal, lower-level organization members who orchestrate processes that build upon spontaneous events. The success of the change described here points to three areas in which a top-management-sponsored, planned approach may be deflected. Thus, the case may help explain why organization development has not been as productive as expected.

The Power Problem. Haire (1964) clearly identified the power problem when he observed that managers often think others need to change, while in fact the need for change frequently lies in the managers themselves. Top-management change is particularly critical when the corporate culture itself is the object of change. The implicit norms and routines of an organization are a result of the prevailing management style. Because it sets the stage, either intentionally or through unintentional defensive responses (Argyris, 1985), top management is primarily responsible for the prevailing style. Thus, if corporate culture is to change, the behavior of top management needs to change.

There are, however, serious behavioral obstacles to such change. Basically, most top managers have internalized the existing system and use their power to hold in place at least the parts of the system within which they operate. Most top managers act this way for good reasons. Usually, they have received positive reinforcement from the existing system, including advancement to positions of power. These reinforcements have socialized top managers into behavioral habits that support the existing system, even though that system may now be inadequate. In addition, top managers are frequently faced with uncertainty and disagreement. To act at all under these conditions, they must have confidence in their own judgment. For many top managers confidence comes from the sincere belief that their approach is the best for the organization. Finally, the skills of top managers have been developed within the existing system. A new system may require skills that they lack and top managers may therefore fear that they will lose their positions with all the accompanying rewards. Cultural change, therefore, is a threat challenging many a top manager's success, values, confidence, and sense of self-worth.

To defend themselves from threat (Argyris, 1985), top managers can, and often do, use their positions of power to control, block, or sidetrack organizational transformations. This can be done through intimidation or through seemingly supportive manipulation (Argyris, 1985), as well as through the deployment of resources and the exercise of other kinds of decision-making authority. As a result, organizational change efforts often begin with minor tinkering and only escalate to transformations when less radical efforts have failed (Hage, 1980). At this point, unfortunately, it may be too late for the organization to survive.

In advocating a top-management-sponsored approach, organization development recognizes the need for top management to be involved in organization change, a need supported by empirical evidence (Nicholas, 1982). What is not always appreciated, however, is the kind of involvement required. In radical corporate culture change, top management itself often needs to be a primary target of change. This is an extraordinary demand to make of individuals who are successful and powerful. Some may not be able to make the necessary transitions. In this event, radical change will require replacement of top officials, as happened in the case presented here.

The Persistence Problem. The conservative, system-maintaining behavior of power holders is only one manifestation of the persistence of learned, habitual behavior. All members of an organization automatically repeat learned routines. Normally, the persistence of behavior is an asset, enabling people to act predictably and efficiently. When change is needed, however, persistent behaviors may become a significant impediment. Unconscious, reflexive habits maintain the status quo by functioning as inertial lines of least resistance.

During the early stage of the transformation process described here, those who did not want the change were quite persistent in their opposition. As the process continued, however, it became apparent that all members of the organization, even change advocates, needed to learn new behaviors. Various temporary systems, such as facilitator training, life planning, career counseling, and leadership training, were created to help members learn patterns of interaction consistent with the emerging system. Even now, members continue to struggle with old habits, including conflict avoidance, reliance on authority for initiating action, and the use of uniformity as the test of conformity. While space has precluded description of these later developments in the transformation process, it is important to recognize that neutral members and advocates, not only opponents, engage in behaviors that impede development of an organizational transformation. Deeply enculturated habits are highly resistant to change, even when individuals consciously want to act in new ways.

By contrast with the bottom-up process, in which members actively seek change, organization development efforts often pursue transformations that are neither understood nor desired by the people affected. This has led organization development to focus on resistance as the major impediment to change. The case presented here suggests, however, that overcoming resistance is not sufficient to bring about transformation. Because they are unconscious, reflexive triggers for behavior, habits internalized under the old system are at least as great a threat to change. To succeed, organization development efforts must identify and work to transform these unconscious, unintentionally persistent behavior patterns, even among advocates of the new system.

The Planning Problem. Not only do individuals internalize system-supporting behavior patterns, but systems themselves also institutionalize self-reproducing routines. The planning process is one of modern management's reproduction systems. Rooted in classical management theory, planning generally includes goal setting, strategy formulation, and a priori design of implementation processes. Goal setting usually means the selection of a desired, obtainable outcome state. For descriptive purposes, the classical planning process can be called outcome-driven planning. If, in advocating planned change, organization development uses the outcome-driven approach, then it will produce refinements of a system rather than true transformation. The problem is that outcome-driven planning reflexively perpetuates controlled, risk-aversive, stability-oriented routines. Such an approach contains three inherent impediments to innovative behavior:

First, outcome-driven planning is a risk reduction strategy that requires an understanding of the outcome prior to implementation. Because the organizational forms needed today are radically new, however, their eventual form cannot be anticipated. A development process is needed that encourages emergence rather than requires a priori design. Efforts that seek to control or predetermine the outcome of change will limit organization development to change in the levels of what already exists and block transformative change.

Second, outcome-driven planning approaches imply a "before-after" sequence, aptly captured in the terms *unfreezing*, *moving*, and *refreezing* (Lewin, 1947). The organizational forms being envisioned today, however, are fluid systems that institutionalize the "moving" state (Boyle, 1985). In the case described here, the organization continues to strive for transformation as an explicit objective even twenty years after the original push for reform. To create this kind of organization, "from now on" change processes are needed.

Third, in differentiated organizations, outcome-driven planning usually separates the initiators from the implementers, creating a "we-they" division. One group does things to or for the other. In organization development the two groups are called change agents and change targets. Collaborative structures, however, are "collective we" organizations in which members do things "with" each other. To create this kind of environment, the change process must use "collective we" approaches.

By relying on persistent routines from classical systems, outcome-driven planned change may actually delay or block the learning of innovative routines. At the very least, outcome-driven planning fails to model the new system (see Beer and others, 1985) when the objective of the change is to create an innovative, flexible organization. Innovation is a spontaneous process that requires an open-ended form of planning. The spontaneously orchestrated approach used in the organization described here offers an input-driven alternative. Planning was centered on the use and creation of opportunities to increase the active input of all members into the change process. The remaining section of the chapter describes how this input-driven process contributed to organizationwide transformation.

Crucial Role Behaviors

Although outcome-driven planning may impede development of innovative systems, this does not mean that transformations produced by other means have to be random, disorganized processes. Organization members must be capable of building upon spontaneous events that provide opportunities for transformation. Evidence from the case presented here suggests that three different sets of behaviors or roles help guide the

Table 8-4. Task Sets of Three Strategic Roles
in Organizational Transformation.

Visionary Role

1. Promoting skepticism toward the status quo
2. Advocating change in a bold or charismatic manner
3. Generating creative basic alternatives
4. Empowering members to refine and develop the change

Orchestrator Role

1. Promoting broad member involvement in developing and refining the emerging change
2. Creating extensive and effective communications networks
3. Establishing and maintaining effective decision-making structures appropriate to the emerging change
4. Treating information and decision making in a nonmanipulative, unbiased manner

Legitimator Role

1. Displaying firm commitment to the emerging change
2. Providing confidence and assurance concerning the change
3. Empathizing with the fears of members
4. Listening with respect to dissent yet remaining committed to the change

transformation process. Thus, the process by which the collegial paradigm spread among members of the organization was in large measure a function of three specific sets of role behaviors filled by members of the Central Committee and the Prechapter Commission: the visionary role, the orchestrator role, and the legitimator role (see Table 8-4).

The visionary role is characterized by skepticism toward the existing state of things, creativity with respect to generating alternatives, and boldness or charisma in presenting and advocating changes (Foy, 1985; Linder, 1985). The orchestrator role is primarily an administrative one. It includes creating communications networks that link all members and channeling the flow of information about the change among members in an unbiased, unfiltered manner. The orchestrator role is also concerned with behaviors aimed at establishing and maintaining decision-making structures that are both effective and consistent with the emerging organizational paradigm

(McLaughlin, 1985; Silverzweig and Allen, 1976; Edwards, 1983). Finally, the legitimator role is comprised of behaviors that lend credibility, legitimacy, and respect to the proposed change in the minds of organizational members. It also conveys confidence and assurance to those who are contemplating acceptance of the change. In the congregation studied, each of these roles was clearly identifiable in the change process.

Visionary Role. The visionary role was filled by several members, but most notably by SJ. After listening to members in her area and identifying their desires, she became an advocate of the needed changes. The renewal committee, of which she was chairperson, was the first to raise the issue of authority and was the most vocal in its opposition to the existing patterns of authority. Under her leadership the members of her region wrote the CEO "en masse" (a tactic rarely used before this) to ask for increased participation for members in the upcoming assembly. She encouraged members to reevaluate the meaning of a "spirit of obedience," seek to have all superiors elected rather than appointed, and consider the merits of a more collegial system of decision making within the governance structure.

At the Central Committee meetings, SJ was one of the major movers with respect to proposed decentralization of the governance structure. She was the "idea" person and seemed to generate ideas that always produced considerable debate. By her own admission, she spent a lot of time after the Central Committee meetings going to various other meetings and discussion groups to try to "sell" the collegial governance idea. She explained that many members initially viewed this idea with such suspicion that she had to do a great deal of persuading to gain acceptance for it. MP also filled the visionary role, although to a lesser degree than SJ. After leading the Prechapter Commission in establishing its collegial platform, she spent thirty days traveling across the country and holding meetings with all the members that she could reach to build support for the collegial organization paradigm.

The visionary role filled by these and other less prominent proponents of change was crucial to the acceptance of the

collegial paradigm among members. Their willingness to enthusiastically and publicly advocate the new paradigm contributed
greatly to the momentum of the change. Some members reported that they left meetings led by these individuals quite
excited and enthusiastic about the new ideas they had heard.
They had begun to internalize the vision.

Orchestrator Role. But exciting ideas presented in challenging ways were not the only means employed to maintain the
momentum of the change. In playing the orchestrator role, TR
determined that effective methods of communications and participative decision-making systems were needed. She believed
that the collegial paradigm being proposed by members
needed to be reflected in their planning for renewal. Hers was
the first renewal committee to use questionnaires for gathering
information from members in her area, and she urged their use
in other renewal committees as well. Perhaps the most important communications link in the early stages of the change
process was the expanded use of "idea stimulators" by TR. She
felt that interesting or challenging renewal ideas from members
of one renewal committee should be shared with the general
membership for debate, and she created a communications
vehicle for this purpose. TR was also the first to have members
express their individual satisfaction or dissatisfaction with ideas
being proposed and to share collective responses with members
to promote further discussion.

When the Central Committee met in the summer of 1967,
TR urged its members to keep members in each of their areas
up-to-date on the committee's activities. She recognized the
importance of the committee to all members of the order.
Unlike the preceding corporate assemblies, whose processes
were totally secret, she wanted the members to have knowledge
of and input into Central Committee decisions. She even created a newsletter during the several weeks that the committee
met. At the committee meeting, TR urged that it make expanded representation for members at the upcoming Renewal
Assembly its first priority.

When the Prechapter Commission replaced the Central

Committee, TR made sure, through frequent newsletters sent to all branches, that all members were aware of everything that was happening with respect to renewal. She helped develop the idea of sending MP on visits to the members for a month to discuss upcoming assembly issues, including the idea of collegiality, and to expand members' participation in the process. TR was instrumental also in the plan to collect agenda item proposals for the assembly from all members of the organization and then have everyone individually queried on their opinion about each proposal. Finally, when the Renewal Assembly was held, she had the idea of setting up teletypes at various sites across the nation to "open up" the actions of the assembly to the entire membership.

The successful fulfillment of the orchestrator role by TR was crucial to the momentum of the change. The extent of awareness and input offered to members through her actions was unheard of before this. The communications network she established produced clarification and confirmation of the nature of the proposed change and contributed greatly to the collective development and refinement of the collegial paradigm. Her use of and emphasis on participative decision making, a key element in the emerging paradigm, modeled the change and undoubtedly increased its acceptance. Perhaps most important of all, she saw her role as providing a conduit for spreading members' ideas. She never sought to personally control the outcomes of the process.

Legitimator Role. All this was still not necessarily sufficient for the change to permeate the organization. Strong norms of obedience to authority existed in the congregation. These norms were perceived by many to be essential for organizational coordination and were strengthened by the religious value of submission. Since members were aware of the existing hierarchy's lack of support for the collegial plan being proposed, it was necessary that someone who was greatly respected by both proponents and opponents of the new ideas assure members of the appropriateness and morality of the change. This person was MP.

MP fulfilled the legitimator role successfully because she

was highly respected, greatly admired, and well known among the membership. According to interviews, many members, particularly the conservative ones, would not have accepted collegiality or would have resisted it more strongly had it not been for MP's support of it. There were several factors that gave her such influence. She was respected intellectually, had worked closely with the existing hierarchy in the past, and possessed the uncanny ability to help others express their opposition while remaining firm in her commitment to the change. She was sensitive to the fears of some members about the change and helped to allay many of their concerns. She was also nonreactive. Her demeanor was cool, calm, and analytical, yet she was also sensitive to others. As such, she provided an air of stability and integrity that visionaries like SJ and orchestrators like TR could not. Some members expressed serious doubt that the change would have been as successful had MP's personal qualities not been imprinted on the change process through her chairmanship of the Central Committee and the Prechapter Commission.

In summary, then, SJ and other visionaries had the ability to capture the imagination of members. They boldly and passionately helped some members break down the pillars of tradition and open themselves to new vistas. They challenged members to get the change process started by taking public stands in support of collegiality. But it was TR, the orchestrator, who developed the infrastructure that made it possible to diffuse the change throughout the organization. Finally, MP provided the legitimizing force necessary to propel the change through the infrastructure.

These three roles can undoubtedly be generalized to the management of any bottom-up organizational transformation process. According to Lewin (1947), the status quo will inevitably become institutionalized or "frozen" in organizational members' norm structures. To get people to break out of their established, repeated patterns of behavior and to internalize change, someone or some group must present a basic change in such a way that it shatters their confidence in existing behavior patterns. This requires not only a good basic alternative but most likely a charismatic or transformational leader who will advocate the change (Bass, 1986). This is the essence of the visionary role. People filling this role in the change process need to be equipped not only with a high-quality basic alternative but also with the leadership ability to empower other members to become proponents of the basic change within the organization. These proponents then help in the diffusion of the change among other members.

A second necessary role for successfully managing organizationwide transformation is the orchestrator role. As described above, this role enables members not only to better understand the basic change but also to participate in its refinement and evolution. In the case discussed here, collegiality was specifically defined and implemented through an independent process of social interaction among members. Once the communications and decision-making structures were in place, members were able to autonomously and collectively form and mold the transformation to meet the needs of the organization. The distinctive characteristic of the orchestrator role, therefore, is a detached, value-free treatment of information and decisions. The orchestrator realizes that his or her role is limited to facilitating the evolution. In addition, it seems vital that the communications and decision-making mechanisms established by the orchestrator reflect the nature of the emerging change so that members can use their own interactions in the change process to test and refine transformation concepts as they develop. Such an ad hoc, yet thoroughly managed process, is perhaps the key to real norm change. This type of spontaneous, unbiased, unfiltered orchestration of participation, rather than outcome-driven planning, may be what is needed to create a true change in a corporate culture.

It is very likely that the legitimator role has been the most overlooked element in organizational transformations. Changes in an organization's norms involve a great deal of risk for members, regardless of the type of organization. This is particularly true in bottom-up transformations. Since most people are risk aversive, the legitimator must help members cope with some of the risk by assuring them that their engagement in the change process is not foolish, irrational, immoral, or illogical. In addition, if all members are to feel confident enough to participate in the specific refinement and evolution of the transformation, and if the transformation is to truly permeate the norms of the organization, legitimation will be crucial. In the case of the congregation discussed here, there appeared to be as much time, effort, and resources devoted to the fulfillment of this role as there were to the other roles.

Conclusion

According to Toffler (1980), organizations faced a wave of change as society moved from an agricultural era into an industrial age. Many organizations failed to transform themselves to meet the demands of this new age and, as a result, ceased to exist. Now, futurists tell us we are facing a new wave of change as we leave the industrial age and enter the information era. Organizations are again faced with the need to undergo significant transformations if they are to survive the demands of a new environment.

Because the organization studied here had the capacity to transform itself, it survived not only the change wave of the industrial age but also the initial change wave of the information era with its demands for individual expression and decentralization. The lessons learned from this case emphasize the critical importance of orchestrating spontaneous transformation. Such transformations make paradoxical demands on top management. These managers need to be actively involved in the change process, but at the same time, they must be willing to relinquish tight control in order that meaningful new change behaviors and norms can develop. This type of transformation also requires the successful filling of three crucial role/behavior sets—those of visionary, orchestrator, and legitimator—to facilitate evolution of the transformation. Thus, the process by which the organization studied experienced self-regeneration contributes a viable alternative in our efforts to evaluate and improve current organizational change strategies.

References

Argyris, C. *Personality and Organization.* New York: Harper & Row, 1957.

Argyris, C. *Strategy, Change, and Defensive Routines.* Boston: Pittman, 1985.

Bass, B. M. *Leadership and Performance Beyond Expectations.* New York: Free Press, 1986.

Beer, M., and others. "Managing Human Assets — Part 3: Management Values and HR Policy." *Personnel Administrator,* 1985, *30* (3), 74–81.

Beres, M. E. "Change in a Woman's Religious Organization: The Impact of Individual Differences, Power, and the Environment." *Dissertation Abstracts International,* 1976, *37,* 3671B (University Microfilms No. AAD77–01211).

Beres, M. E. "From a Hierarchical, Closed System to a Collegial, Open Network." Paper presented at 14th annual meeting of American Institute for Decision Sciences, San Francisco, Nov. 1982.

Boyle, R. J. "Why Wrestle with Jellyfish?: Lessons in Managing Organization Change." *National Productivity Review,* 1985, *4* (2), 180–183.

Child, J. "Organization Design and Performance: Contingency Theory and Beyond." *Organization and Administration Sciences,* 1977, *8,* 169–184.

Edwards, R. D. "The Cultural Crisis in Banking." *United States Banker,* 1983, *94* (10), 10–18.

Foy, N. "Ambivalence, Hypocrisy, and Cynicism: Aids to Organization Change." *New Management,* 1985, *2* (4), 49–53.

Golembiewski, R. T., Billingsley, K., and Yeager, S. "Measuring Change and Persistence in Human Affairs: Types of Change Generated by OD Designs." *Journal of Applied Behavioral Science,* 1975, *12* (2), 133–157.

Hage, J. *Theories of Organization.* New York: Wiley-Interscience, 1980.

Haire, M. "The Social Sciences and Management Practices." *California Management Review,* 1964, *6* (4), 3–10.

Kimberly, J. R., Miles, R. H., and Associates. *The Organizational*

Life Cycle: Issues in the Creation, Transformation, and Decline of Organizations. San Francisco: Jossey-Bass, 1980.

Lewin, K. "Group Decision and Social Change." In T. Newcomb and E. Hartley (eds.), *Readings in Social Psychology.* New York: Holt, Rinehart & Winston, 1947.

Likert, R. *New Patterns of Management.* New York: McGraw-Hill, 1961.

Linder, J. C. "Computers, Corporate Culture, and Change." *Personnel Journal,* 1985, *64* (9), 48–55.

Lippitt, G. L. *Organizational Renewal.* Englewood Cliffs, N.J.: Prentice-Hall, 1969.

McLaughlin, T. A. "Six Keys to Quality." *Quality Progress,* 1985, *18* (11), 77–79.

Musser, S. J. "The Momentum of the Power Redistribution Idea Among Lower Participants in an Organization." *Dissertation Abstracts International,* 1985, *46,* 808A.

Naisbitt, J., and Aburdene, P. *Re-Inventing the Corporation.* New York: Warner Books, 1985.

Nicholas, J. M. "The Comparative Impact of Organization Development Interventions on Hard Criteria Measures." *Academy of Management Review,* 1982, 7 (4), 531–542.

Peters, T. J., and Waterman, R. H., Jr. *In Search of Excellence: Lessons from America's Best-Run Companies.* New York: Harper & Row, 1982.

Pugh, D. S., Hickson, D. J., Hinings, C. R., and Turner, C. "Dimensions of Organization Structure." *Administrative Science Quarterly,* 1968, *13* (1), 65–105.

Ryan, M. P. *Amid the Alien Corn.* St. Charles, Ill.: Jones Wood Press, 1967.

Shepard, H. A. "Changing Interpersonal and Intergroup Relations in Organizations." In J. G. March (ed.), *Handbook of Organizations.* Skokie, Ill.: Rand McNally, 1965.

Silverzweig, S., and Allen, R. F. "Change in Corporate Culture." *Sloan Management Review,* 1976, *17* (3), 33–49.

Toffler, A. *The Third Wave.* New York: Bantam Books, 1981.

Peter Hess
William P. Ferris
Anthony F. Chelte
Russell Fanelli

9

Learning from an Unsuccessful Transformation: A "Perfect Failure"

Nearly ten years ago, Mirvis and Berg (1977) called attention to the inability in our culture to learn from failures in organizations. More recently, the problem was summarized in this way: "In our culture, failure is anathema. We rarely hear about it, we never dwell on it and most of us do our best never to admit it. Especially in organizations, failure is often simply not tolerated and people avoid being associated with failure of any kind. This response makes it almost impossible to learn from the inevitable mistakes and errors that are part of human experience in organizations. And the word 'failure' itself has a great deal of power. Why don't we use 'error' or 'mistake'? Perhaps because they understate the emotions involved in failure" (Berg, 1986, p. 74).

The loss of potential learning is only one consequence of the traditional cultural and organizational response to failure. The other important casualty is the risk taking necessary for innovation. In a punitive environment the experiments that represent anything more than minimal exposure to failure tend to remain orphans. Peters and Waterman (1982) describe the special efforts at Ore-Ida, the frozen-food subsidiary of H. J.

Heinz to ensure that failure does not defeat such risk taking: "[Ore-Ida] has carefully defined what it calls the 'perfect failure,' and has arranged to shoot off a cannon in celebration every time it occurs. The perfect failure concept arises from simple recognition that all research is inherently risky, that the only way to succeed at all is through lots of tries, that management's primary objective should be to induce lots of tries, and that a good try that results in some learning is to be celebrated even when it fails" (p. 69). This chapter attempts to transform into a "perfect failure" an unsuccessful effort to implement an organizationwide employee involvement program. As at Ore-Ida, we focus not on the failure but on what might be learned from it.

The Greymoor Story

Greymoor is a $100 million a year manufacturing firm with production operations at four sites. Its products are considered to be of the highest quality in the industry. Nearly 100 years old, Greymoor is now a subsidiary of a large multinational corporation. The Greymoor division is the most profitable in the organization with a steadily increasing demand for its products.

Like many American firms, Greymoor became more and more concerned about productivity when it began to experience increasing foreign competition in the 1980s. Quality had always been "built in" to Greymoor's manufacturing processes, but over the years adjustments designed to increase output had been made to meet increased demand. As the machines speeded up and output increased, however, quality began to suffer, and the rate of customer complaints, though still relatively low, began to rise significantly. Already committed to the technology of increased rates of production, top management at Greymoor became convinced of the need to take aggressive action to build quality back into the production process.

At the direction of the CEO, the task of recommending a strategy for recapturing quality at Greymoor was undertaken by the vice-president for operations who, after participating in a Deming Institute program on quality and productivity, selected increased employee involvement as a strategy that would work. In the minds of both the CEO and the vice-president, increased employee involvement came to represent the most effective means for systematically returning to the hourly people the responsibility for decisions about their work. Because this responsibility had accrued to the supervisory level over the past decade or so, increased employee involvement also represented the possibility of freeing supervisors for the planning and problem solving that they viewed as the core of their responsibilities. The vice-president envisioned a system in which suggestions for quality improvements would be logged and guaranteed a full and timely response, the four facilities would compete against each other as teams, and quality achievements would be recognized and celebrated.

Greymoor's CEO wholeheartedly and enthusiastically supported the plan. In fact, as an indication of that support, he obtained from corporate headquarters a one-time substantial increase in the capital expenditure budget specifically to ensure management's ability to implement the suggestions anticipated from the involvement effort. Both the CEO and the vice-president agreed, however, that the crucial ingredients for a successful change would be the cooperation and commitment of the manufacturing supervisors.

The first steps in the change process, then, were to meet with the supervisors in groups at each of the four facilities, to gain their support for the employee involvement concept, and to provide each supervisor with extended communications training on an individualized basis. The actual employee involvement program would begin only when it was clear that the supervisors were ready for it.

At each of the four initial site meetings called to introduce the concept of employee involvement, the supervisors' reactions were similar — interest leavened with skepticism, especially among the more senior supervisors. The interest was based on the supervisors' recognition of the benefits of increased employee involvement. The optimists, for example, viewed employee involvement as a return to the way things used to be done at Greymoor when decisions were made closer to the site of the problems and hourly people were responsible for their own work. They saw in employee involvement a strengthening of the supervisor's hand and the possibility of more time for planning and problem solving. The skeptics came in two varieties. The first pointed out that Greymoor had always been very "top-down" in its decision making and that employee involvement appeared to be about 180 degrees from that. The second made reference to Greymoor's apparent tendency to begin programs and never finish them. These supervisors were concerned that employee involvement might be perceived by the hourly people as just one more management brainstorm that would go away in time. In sum, the supervisors indicated support for the concept to the consultants, but questioned whether employee involvement was really what top management wanted and expected.

After being told of the supervisors' reactions and as a demonstration of management's commitment to employee involvement, both the vice-president and the CEO sat in on the next round of meetings at each of the four sites. The CEO had agreed to be present in the role of observer, to take notes on the suggestions of the supervisors, and, as a model of what eventually would be expected of the supervisors, to respond formally to their suggestions at some time in the near future. At one site, where questions about top management's commitment to employee involvement continued to surface, however, the CEO felt that the credibility of the commitment being questioned was his own. He responded calmly but emphatically. As evidence of the corporate commitment to the change, he pointed to the dramatically increased capital expense budget, carefully explaining that the increase actually represented an implementation budget for suggestions generated by employee involvement. He directed the vice-president to provide each supervisor with a list of the initial capital expenditures planned for each facility and asked him to meet with each group "within a week" to make sure that the groups agreed with the priorities for their respective facilities. Finally, he pointed to his own presence at the meetings as evidence of top management's willingness to take the lead in the change process. He did not bother to add that to be present at this round of meetings he had canceled a vacation scheduled months in advance.

Subsequent conversations with the supervisors indicated that even most of the skeptics felt that, based on the CEO's strong showing, employee involvement was "at least worth a shot." Within four months, the communications training for supervisors at all four facilities was complete. Unfortunately, any talk of employee involvement at Greymoor had virtually disappeared.

Reversing Course

Two events in particular marked Greymoor's retreat from employee involvement. The first was the introduction of accountability reports for each supervisor. Midway through the training phase, it was announced that data reflecting the performance for each supervisor's group would be accumulated, summarized, and posted on a weekly basis at each facility. Management viewed these reports as opportunities to identify substandard performance, as motivators, and as a source for documenting trends in group performance.

At the training sessions following the announcement of these reports, however, the supervisors expressed to the vice-president their concern that the reports focused almost entirely on production and provided no reinforcement of the supposed reemphasis on quality as Greymoor's first priority. They also pointed out that at the same time that Greymoor was attempting to increase teamwork and cooperation for problem solving, the accountability reports would encourage one shift on a machine to "make its numbers" by "sticking" the next shift with machine maintenance and changeovers. Management's refusal to consider alternative ways to accumulate the desired information without identifying and embarrassing individual supervisors and their teams was seen as proof of its lack of commitment to true employee involvement.

Furthermore, the accountability reports sent mixed messages. For example, some supervisors whom management expected to do well instead performed poorly. Paradoxically, they had been given more difficult assignments because of management's high expectations of them, but now the sense of self-esteem that had been instilled by those high expectations became threatened by unflattering numerical comparisons that did not reveal the difficulty levels of the assignments. In addition other, newer supervisors did not do as well because they were "outmaneuvered" by more senior supervisors.

The second important issue marking Greymoor's retreat from employee involvement was related to the capital improvements program discussed earlier. Much of the equipment and repairs initially promised in the budget were scheduled for delivery or completion within the first 120 days of the fiscal year. At the end of that period the CEO asked for a progress report. Progress varied from site to site. Some projects were on schedule, but many were not, and some important ones had not even been begun. Nor did it appear that the situation might improve anytime soon. Problems ranged from a lack of availability of needed parts to management indecision about how to proceed; the latter problem was exacerbated by the absence of inter-departmental cooperation regarding the selection, purchase, and installation of equipment. Greymoor simply was not ready to do so much in so little time.

The problems with the accountability reports and the unmet capital improvement schedules further eroded the integrity of the program. Casualties of the resulting turmoil extended right to the vice-president for operations himself, who "resigned" at the request of the CEO. His successor, who moved over from his position as vice-president of marketing, discouraged the CEO from completing the employee involvement program on the public grounds that the supervisory group did not have the skills necessary to supply effective input. Privately, he confided that the state of unreadiness extended from the very top down. That was two years ago. And although some small positive steps have recently been taken by the CEO and the new vice-president, employee involvement at Greymoor is still "on hold."

What We Learned. We came away from our experience at Greymoor with a number of increased appreciations. One of the strongest was of the importance of correctly assessing top management's commitment to a change effort, that is, its actual motivation to do the work required for a plan to succeed. As noted earlier, the supervisors' initial response to the proposed change at Greymoor centered on questions of top management's commitment to employee involvement. While we did not question the sincerity of these concerns, I think we attributed them to a combination of projection on the part of the supervisors and the resistance to such programs that some researchers suggest is typical of this group (Klein, 1984). Nor did we underestimate the importance of top management's commitment to the kind of effort that was being undertaken. But when we balanced the concerns of the supervisors against the initiatives taken by the top management to provide the necessary funds and to be "out front" in the early meetings with the supervisors, we were satisfied that the commitment of top management to employee involvement at Greymoor was real.

Our failure resulted not from underestimating the importance of top management's commitment but from assessing that commitment incorrectly. We neglected to take into account that top management's commitment had yet to be tested by any actual experience with the change process. We failed to adequately comprehend the supervisors' warnings that just because top management said it wanted employee involvement and even initiated the effort to achieve it, this did not necessarily mean that these executives understood what they were saying. And, although we worked hard to alert the CEO to the perils of the individualized accountability reports and to make him aware of how he was distorting employee input by sending messages that suggested what he did and did not expect to hear, perhaps we failed in our attempts to educate him; in other words, we may have failed to provide him with the clear understandings that he needed for employee involvement to succeed. Expectancy theory provides a model for comprehending this link between motivation, on the one hand, and understanding or expectancy, as it is called in the model, on the other.

Expectancy Theory. This theory suggests that the strength of an individual's motivation to perform a task is a function of the expectation (1) that effort can be converted into performance and (2) that performance will result in desired outcomes (Nadler and Lawler, 1983). An analysis of what happened at Greymoor based on this theory suggests that unrealistic or inaccurate expectations relative to effort, performance, and outcomes resulted both in top management's initial commitment to the proposed change and, in a different way, in the eventual withdrawal of that commitment. This suggests that our failing at Greymoor was twofold: in terms of the intervention, we did not provide management with the realistic expectations necessary to sustain their commitment to employee involvement; in terms of assessment, we failed to comprehend top management's motivation for change to the degree necessary in order to provide accurate feedback about the process.

In retrospect, we realize that management's familiarity with the vocabulary of change did not necessarily reflect a full understanding of the requirements of the change process. And it appears that the capital investment and the "out-front" position that management took—which we viewed as evidence of its commitment—were in fact the extent of its commitment, not because it was unwilling to commit more but because it thought that was all it would take.

For us, Greymoor has become a dramatic demonstration of how critical it is (1) to establish in top managers at the outset the kind of complete and realistic expectations that will support their continued commitment to the very difficult task of change, and (2) to assist top managers to accurately assess their motivation and readiness to change. Wanous (1975, 1980, 1983) has described a method to facilitate realistic task expectations in job candidates that may be generalized to the change "task." It is called the *realistic job preview* (RJP).

Realistic Job Preview

In relating organizational entry practices to turnover and dissatisfaction, Wanous describes the consequences of the tendency of organizations and individuals to try to "sell" themselves to each other: "The organizational entry process is a bit like a courtship; i.e., each party tries to appear as attractive as possible to the other. Thus, individual job candidates emphasize their strengths and minimize (or try to conceal) their weaknesses. Similarly, organizations recruit new employees by stressing their most positive characteristics and minimizing negative information. As a result of this, both individuals and organizations present distorted images of themselves, making it difficult for each to make optimal choices of the other" (Wanous, 1983, p. 161). Citing "the accumulated research evidence," Wanous concludes that as a result of this pattern new employees tend to enter organizations with "unrealistically inflated expectations" that result in eventual dissatisfaction and potential turnover.

It seems to us that the process by which top management gains entry to the change task is not unlike that described by Wanous. The pattern of "courtship," the resulting unrealistic expectations, the dissatisfaction, and ultimately the "turnover" seems to us to be a reasonably accurate description of what happened at Greymoor. There can be little doubt of the tendency among consultants to try to "sell" change and their own services to organizations. And in our experience at least, there is a tendency on the part of management, especially in an organization interested in transformation, also to present itself in the best possible light.

Unfortunately, however, this is not the only factor working against the development of realistic expectations relative to organizational change. The very processes by which specific change programs come to the attention of management are also part of the problem. A major impetus for the proposed change at Greymoor, for example, was the success of a similar program at one of Greymoor's corporate sisters. And in our early discussions with top management, it had become clear that the other critical sources of their information about the change process were their involvement at a Deming Institute conference and the book *In Search of Excellence* (Peters and Waterman, 1982). A recent cover article in *Business Week* suggests that this may not be atypical: "Edward E. Lawler III, director of the University of Southern California's Center for Effective Organizations, says that [change programs] are partly a fad. 'In a number of cases we studied,' says Lawler, 'the CEO of the company had seen a TV program or read a magazine article on [the programs] and decided to give them a try" (Byrne, 1986, p. 60).

In response to the question of why, the article offers the following suggestion: "Perhaps it's because many managers are frustrated by their inability to compete in the marketplace. Or perhaps it's because they are under intense pressure from Wall Street to perform short-term miracles. The result is a mad, almost aimless scramble for instant solutions. 'We're all looking for magic,' explains Thomas R. Horton, president of the American Management Association. 'If you tell me I can avoid a cold by taking half a pound of vitamin C, I'll want to believe you even if it only gives me indigestion'" (p. 54).

This is hardly the kind of situation that fosters realistic expectations. In expectancy terms, the promised outcomes of the popular programs are so powerful in their valence to managers that effort-performance and performance-outcome estimates receive only superficial consideration. The resulting inaccurate expectation is further confounded by the understandable tendency of the popular media to focus on the success stories and the benefits of change rather than on the problems inherent in any change process or on questions about the longer-term success or staying power of the change.

For both of these reasons—the desire for "instant" solutions and the media focus on the success aspects of change programs—management's attention, from the beginning, is on the program's benefits, rather than on the costs of the program in terms of effort, time, and changes in their own behavior. There needs to be a clear understanding by top managers that not all costs are financial. For example, will they find it possible to work with those employees that they have already written off as incompetent? Are they ready to publicly accept the failure of some of their own previously favored ideas or programs? Are they committed to adopting, in the case of an employee involvement program, *selected* lower-management and employee suggestions with appropriate symbolic fanfare and regardless of past objections? And finally, are they willing to underwrite whatever financial costs may be required either for start-up or

Figure 9-1. The Potential Impact of Unrealistic Expectations on Management Commitment to Change.

Pressure on management
to perform and compete

↓

Incomplete exposure to change program;
media focus on program benefits and valued outcomes

↓

Tendency to overestimate program benefits and outcomes
and to underestimate program costs in terms of effort,
performance, and nonvalued outcomes

↓

Distorted "cost-benefit" analysis

↓

Initial commitment to change program

↓

Experience with program contrary to expectations

↓

Management dissatisfaction

↓

"Cost-benefit" recalculation
with "cost" factor adjusted

↓

Withdrawal of management commitment;
"turnover" from change program

implementation of various program components? Incidentally, while these questions apply to members of the top management team in general, they have special relevance for the CEO, who is probably the most important ingredient in the success or failure of the change process. At Greymoor, for example, the CEO was finally unwilling to adopt any of the supervisors' or the change agents' suggestions on the accountability report. Too often these other costs of change are either ignored or underestimated by the organization, resulting in distorted perceptions of what the process requires. The potential consequences of these distorted perceptions are shown in Figure 9-1.

This pattern is certainly descriptive of our experience

with Greymoor. To the extent that it generalizes to others' experiences, it indicates the need for systematic intervention to correct management's initial, unrealistic expectations.

In response to unrealistic expectations among job candidates, Wanous (1980) proposed a realistic job preview to "inoculate" individuals against subsequent job dissatisfaction by providing them with a detailed and accurate understanding of the requirements of the job for which they are applying. By analogy, if top management can be considered a kind of candidate for the change program that it is proposing, then perhaps it needs a *realistic change preview* (RCP) to provide a detailed and accurate understanding of just what the change "task" will require of it and the organization that it heads.

Realistic Change Preview

The purpose of the RCP would be to restructure the pattern described in Figure 9-1 by giving a realistic change preview prior to the initial "cost-benefit" analysis to provide a more balanced understanding of the requirements of the proposed change program. It is not that potential failure needs to be focused on; rather, the change agent's role here is to ensure that the client's expectations are in accord with the change agent's informed understanding of what can be expected to happen. Figure 9-2 shows how the restructured sequence might look.

The obvious risk with the RCP is that rather than being "inoculated" against subsequent dissatisfaction with the requirements of the change task, management will be dissuaded from committing itself to the task. Two points might be considered here. First, the client who would be dissuaded merely by a realistic preview of the change process in all probability would not have been successful in achieving the proposed change. Second, and perhaps more reassuring, research on the effects of the RJP suggests that (1) realistic information does not "scare off" job candidates, (2) expectations of job candidates are effectively lowered, (3) the RJP is not potent enough to actually reverse a job candidate's initial organizational choice, and (4) turnover is

Figure 9-2. Anticipated Impact of the Realistic Change Preview.

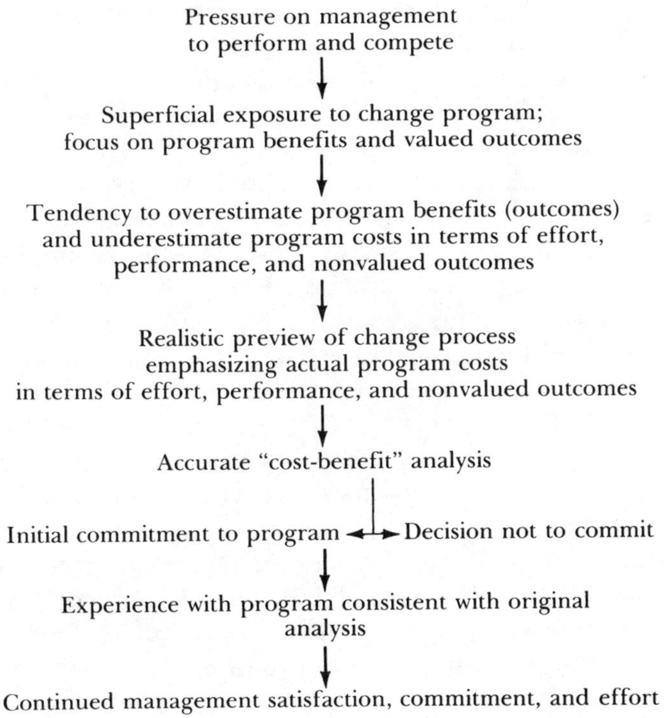

Pressure on management
to perform and compete

↓

Superficial exposure to change program;
focus on program benefits and valued outcomes

↓

Tendency to overestimate program benefits (outcomes)
and underestimate program costs in terms of effort,
performance, and nonvalued outcomes

↓

Realistic preview of change process
emphasizing actual program costs
in terms of effort, performance, and nonvalued outcomes

↓

Accurate "cost-benefit" analysis

Initial commitment to program ◄—►Decision not to commit

↓

Experience with program consistent with original
analysis

↓

Continued management satisfaction, commitment, and effort

significantly lower when the RJP is used (Wanous, 1983). But the question here is, how reasonable is it to expect similar outcomes from the RCP?

Expected Outcomes from the RCP. The following is an attempt to translate these demonstrated impacts of Wanous' RJP directly into potential outcomes from the RCP and then to assess the viability of each.

1. *Realistic information should not necessarily deter change process candidates (clients) from undertaking the change.* Organizations seeking change generally do so because someone in top management has a vision of what could or should be happening in the organization that is significantly different from what is actually happening. Once this vision of what is possible has

begun to be clarified, articulated, and shared with others in top management, there begins to be an investment in it. Combined with the "can do" mentality often found at the executive level, this leads us to expect that top management would not back away easily from its vision of change. If the threat or the opportunity is of sufficient magnitude to motivate the consideration of a genuinely significant change, the RCP in itself will probably not be sufficient to deter at least an initial commitment.

As Lawler (1986) suggests, however, if this vision is simply one of an improvement rather than of a change in the status quo — in Lawler's terms a change on the order of only 10 to 15 percent — then the felt need for that change may not be strong enough to sustain even initial interest in the kind of process required. But as we noted earlier a client who would be dissuaded merely by a realistic preview of the change process probably does not represent a promising candidate for the change task.

2. *The expectations of change process candidates can be effectively lowered.* To accept this statement, it is necessary only to assume that top managers in one organization can learn either from the experience of other organizations that have attempted similar changes or from "sample" experiences of the proposed change. That learning occurs is, we feel, a reasonable assumption. The question here is which strategy or method is likely to be most effective in facilitating the desired learning. Some possible answers to this question are considered in the next section of the chapter.

3. *Realistically previewed management would tend to have a more positive attitude toward the change task.* As the change process unfolds, managers who have undergone the RCP would anticipate the emergence of problems and would not be surprised when there was little or no progress in some areas. As experience confirmed rather than disconfirmed their expectations, we think that these managers would tend to remain satisfied — despite problems and slow progress — that the change process was nevertheless going forward. Consequently, we would expect them to be more likely to allow the process the time necessary for results to begin to emerge.

4. *The change process itself should be more effective as a result of the RCP.* The concern here is that the RCP might engender in top management a negative self-fulfilling prophecy. The question is whether top management's expectation of difficulty with the change process might, through the mechanisms of this prophecy, increase the probability of the occurrence of those difficulties. We think the answer is that it probably would not. Once top management commits itself—despite the negative information provided in the RCP—to a process of change, it is with the now-tested belief that the process will succeed. Once this commitment has been made, we expect that management will work even harder to prove its belief correct, especially since "unexpected problems" have been ruled out as a potential management parachute from the process.

5. *Turnover from the change process should be lower where the RCP is used.* Here, the word *turnover* refers to either management's withdrawal from the change process or the discontinuation of the change agent's services by the client organization. One prominent reason for anticipating a lower rate of turnover, in this sense, is that the atmosphere of increased communication required by the RCP will result in fewer surprises, that is, fewer departures from expectations. Clients will better understand the length of time required for the expected change process to prove effective. And the measure of success may well become more flexible and subject to modification as expectations become fully informed.

More generally, turnover is often suggested to be a correlate of job dissatisfaction. We feel that this is no less true for the change task. When expectations about the change are realistic, when management has a positive attitude toward the process, and when the process itself is carried out effectively, we expect that satisfaction will be enhanced and turnover correspondingly reduced.

The expectations presented here are based not only on this analysis but on our experiences with Greymoor and other (more successful) change experiences. Our conclusion, obviously, is that the RCP can be just as effective relative to the change task as the RJP is for individuals. Earlier we had suggested that for us the crucial question was how the RCP could most effectively be provided. Let us turn then to a discussion of possible responses to this question.

Method of the RCP. Wanous (1983) points out that the method used to present realistic information in the RJP may have an effect on whether turnover is reduced or not. His review of research on the RJP suggests that oral description and audio-visual methods have tended not to result in lowered turnover, while printed materials and work sample approaches have been successful. For the RCP, perhaps a combination of the two more successful methods might be considered.

Printed materials, in this context, might include cases that focus on the difficulties of the change process. Interviews might be included with managers who have direct experience with organizational change similar to that being considered. In the National Steel Corporation case (Chapter Seventeen of this volume) the consultants used material on death and dying to sensitize managers to the idea that a period of mourning will be required as familiar processes, relationships, and policies are supplanted by new ones. And, in the spirit of making failures "perfect," some discussion of unsuccessful change might also be instructive, especially in balancing the success-oriented accounts provided in the popular media.

The second method or technique—a realistic work sample—might actually come about as a by-product of the same activities required to prepare printed materials. For example, based on a review of the literature reporting other organizations' experiences with change, the change agent could identify for the change candidate a set of "sticking points" typically encountered in the change process. These would be junctures at which the appropriate management response was found to have been critical or the commitment of top management appeared to be most severely tested. Top management could be asked to respond to these situations either in a discussion or in an experiential format such as a role play or simulation. Additionally, organizations in which successful changes have been instituted might be visited and studied.

A number of other methods also appear worth considering for the RCP. A limited pilot program—for example, a much scaled-down version of the proposed change—is a closely related alternative to the realistic work sample. In this approach, management would not be responding to hypothetical situations or to events in other organizations but rather to actual events in its own organization. In this alternative, not only could more realistic expectations be achieved, but appropriate management responses could be tested and reinforced.

Still another alternative is what has been termed *envisioning* or *vision-getting*. This is a process by which the incompletely articulated change vision of top management becomes more completely articulated in terms of very specific objectives. The lack of these kinds of specific objectives was clearly a problem for us at Greymoor. There, top management did express a concern for identifying "weak links" at the plant management or supervisory levels—that is, employees who, if they were not capable of adopting to the change, might need to be reassigned or dismissed. When we indicated that this kind of action, if taken prematurely, would undermine his credibility, ours, and that of the entire change process, it was agreed that no such action would be taken until the employee involvement program was fully implemented and operational. The kind of objective definition of "fully implemented and operational" possible through envisioning or vision-getting, however, was never developed at Greymoor. As a result, well before we would have said that we had reached the operational stage, top management was able to institute accountability forms clearly intended to identify "weak links" among the supervisors, without feeling that our agreement had been abridged. The kind of specific objectives articulated through an envisioning process might have permitted us to give more effective feedback earlier in the process.

Finally, we feel that involving top management in a careful review of the organization's previous experience with change would be valuable. Here, management and the change agent would together review previous change efforts in the organization, even those that on the surface might appear to be unrelated to the change under consideration. This review would include an assessment of the degree of success of the attempted changes, with an emphasis on understanding the key reasons for success or failure. Like the pilot program, this approach would complement the work sample by balancing responses to hypo-thetical situations with actual performance data viewed from a historical perspective.

While printed materials and the work sample might serve to set manager's expectations at a more realistic level, the work sample, the pilot program, the envisioning process, and the review of the organization's change experience are of particular usefulness to the change agent in his second responsibility in the change process: assessing the organization's readiness and motivation to change. In this sense the RCP has diagnostic as well as intervention value.

Assessing the "Match." While other factors must be consid-ered, clearly top management is the appropriate focus for as-sessing whether the organization is ready and motivated to change. Figure 9-3 suggests that top management's readiness or motivation for the proposed change must be assessed at two levels—the outcome level and the process level. At the outcome level, the assessment must be of the match between top manage-ment's goals and the outcomes of the various change program alternatives. This is the level where perhaps both top manage-ment and the change agent are most comfortable. The goals are a given, and the task is one of identifying or designing the appropriate program.

The second, or process, level, however, tends to be ne-glected. At this level, the assessment must be of the match between the culture of the organization, on the one hand, and the requirements of the change process, on the other. As we learned at Greymoor, the sustained commitment necessary for success appears to require top management's satisfaction that the change is proceeding as expected. The model suggests that this satisfaction is a product of the match between the organiza-tion's culture and the requirements of the change program.

Management values are, for us, the key component of the organizational culture. At Greymoor, the core management val-

Figure 9-3. Assessing the Match Between the Organization
and the Proposed Change Program.

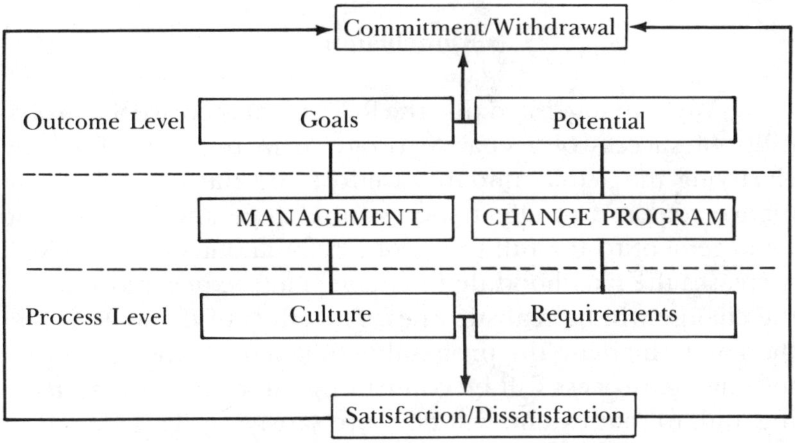

ues were finally mismatched to the requirements of the change attempted there. Top management was clearly autocratic in its decision making, while the change program just as clearly required the potential to encourage, or at least to accept, an increased level of participation in decision making. The result of this mismatch, as we have said, was management dissatisfaction and, as the model predicts, a withdrawal of commitment from the change program.

In many ways, the assessment of this match is an assessment of potential. It could be argued that any significant organizationwide change is to a greater or lesser extent an effort to change the organization's culture and that an assessment based on present patterns ignores the very intent of the proposed change. Nevertheless, as with individuals, it seems reasonable to suggest that some organizations simply possess more change potential than others. It is beyond the scope of this chapter to suggest a system for classifying organizations on this dimension, but we do assert that it is the responsibility of the change agent to assist the organization in the assessment of its change potential. In particular, the simulation and change experience review elements of the RCP should generate considerable data—for both the organization and the change agent—to facilitate this critical assessment.

Conclusion

We have suggested that the RCP might increase the probability of success of a change program in two ways. First, by clarifying the actual amount of effort and the kind of performance required to effect successful change and by exposing management to the full range of potential outcomes, the RCP increases the likelihood that management's expectations about the change will be realistic ones. The effect of the RCP should then be to increase the probability that actual experience with the change process will be confirming rather than disconfirming and, to that extent, will be more satisfying. This should in turn result in sustained commitment to the change process. Second, using the RCP improves the chances that expectations concerning the organization's own readiness to pursue the proposed change are made more realistic. We have suggested that the assessment of this readiness should focus not just on goals and program outcomes but also on the quality of the match between the culture of the organization—especially management values—and the requirements of the change program.

In contrast to the change agent role as more typically enacted, we have asserted that both the intervention into management expectations and the assessment of organizational readiness or potential for change are important responsibilities of the change agent. There appear to be, however, at least three significant barriers to the role redefinition of the change agent required for an effective RCP.

First, and perhaps most importantly, redefining the role of the change agent requires that the potential client also accept a redefined role, in this case that of "candidate" for the proposed change. This redefined client role is certainly contrary to the "take charge" approach typical of the top-level manager, but acceptance or rejection of it might represent at least one test of the organization's readiness for change.

Second, the required client role redefinition is also contrary to the "can do" norm that often pervades the business environment. And certainly the change agent is not immune to this norm. Implicit in the RCP concept, however, is the recognition that there are some things that the change agent cannot do, such as make a change effort successful where there is a poor match between an organization's management culture and the requirements of the change process. Accepting this fact is perhaps as difficult for the change agent as it is for the potential client.

Finally, the change agent can reduce the likelihood that management will withdraw commitment later in the process, but the cost will be increased exposure to this possibility earlier in the process. The first such exposure is at the point when management decides whether or not to submit to the RCP. The second exposure to risk follows the RCP, when management decides whether or not to accept the change task as offered. We have already suggested that, on the basis of the reported effects of the RJP, the risk of withdrawal of management commitment is probably minimal.

Ultimately, the success of the RCP approach rests on the strong conviction, shared by both the change agent and the client organization, that the exchange of complete and accurate information is an essential condition for effective organizational change and that a critical responsibility of the change agent is to assist the organization to assess its motivation realistically.

References

Berg, D. N. "Learning from Failure." In D. M. Hai (ed.), *Organizational Behavior Experiences and Cases*. St. Paul: West, 1986.

Byrne, J. A. "Business Fads: What's in — and out." *Business Week*, Jan. 20, 1986, pp. 52–61.

Klein, J. "Why Supervisors Resist Employee Involvement." *Harvard Business Review*, 1984, *62* (5), 87–95.

Lawler, E. E. "Employee Involvement: A Strategic Advantage." Paper presented at Conference on Organizationwide Transformation, University of Pittsburgh, Oct. 1986.

Mirvis, P. H., and Berg, D. N. (eds.). *Failures in Organization Development and Change.* New York: Wiley-Interscience, 1977.

Nadler, D. A., and Lawler, E. E. "Motivation: A Diagnostic Approach." In J. R. Hackman and others (eds.), *Perspectives on Behavior in Organizations.* New York: McGraw-Hill, 1983.

Peters, T. J., and Waterman, R. H., Jr. *In Search of Excellence: Lessons from America's Best-Run Companies.* New York: Harper & Row, 1982.

Wanous, J. P. "Tell It Like It Is at Realistic Job Previews." *Personnel,* 1975, *52* (4), 50–60.

Wanous, J. P. *Organizational Entry: Recruitment, Selection, and Socialization of Newcomers.* Reading, Mass.: Addison-Wesley, 1980.

Wanous, J. P. "The Entry of Newcomers into Organizations." In J. R. Hackman and others (eds.)., *Perspectives on Behavior in Organizations.* New York: McGraw-Hill, 1983.

David B. Roitman
Jeffrey K. Liker
Ethel Roskies

10

Birthing a Factory
of the Future: When Is
"All at Once" Too Much?

In the decade of the 1980s, American manufacturing entered an era of revolutionary technological change; at least this perception was trumpeted from all our popular business media (see "America Rushes to...," 1983; "Technology in the Workplace," 1985). Yet only a few years later, more cautious articles began appearing, reporting that computer-integrated manufacturing (CIM) was not fulfilling its promise as a panacea for industry's ills (Olson, 1986; Winter, 1986; Zygmont, 1986). Rather, the pioneering manufacturers who had led the way in CIM implementation encountered considerable difficulty in reaping the expected benefits from the new technology. Many who recognized CIM's limitations, however, claimed that they were not primarily technological; instead, they stemmed from organizational obstacles involved in implementing complex technology.

Indeed, the emerging wisdom is that CIM is more than a

We are grateful to Bobbie Turniansky and Bilha Mannheim for their major contributions to the research on which this chapter is based. We are also grateful to William Hetzner, Mitchell Fleischer, and Manoj Sinha for their helpful comments.

technology or set of technologies; instead, it is a "philosophy" requiring fundamental changes in organizational thinking and culture to succeed. In short, it requires changing social as well as technical systems (Ettlie, 1986; Lee, 1986; Majchrzak, 1985; Nadler and Robinson, 1983; "Roundtable Participants Talk About...," 1985; Susman and Chase, 1985; Tornatzky, 1985). The terms *social system* and *technical system* are used in this chapter as they are used by writers in the sociotechnical systems tradition (Pasmore and Sherwood, 1978). Sociotechnical theorists assume that all organizations are comprised of both technical and social systems and that effective organizations "jointly optimize" the functioning of both systems. Useful and commonly accepted definitions of the terms were proposed by Davis (1982) as follows: "A technical system consists of a set of artifacts, tools, machines, facilities, methods, programs, and procedures, which are the means by which the people in the organization transform the inputs [into outputs, i.e. products or services].... The social system consists of both people and structure. It consists of the set of members of the organization acting in their roles. It also consists of the set of roles and their role relationships, the authority structure, communication structure, adaptation mechanisms, learning mechanisms, social system maintenance mechanisms, career structure, and so on" (p. 2.1.7).

This chapter describes the case of one company that attempted such a comprehensive transformation. This manufacturing firm made major changes in its departmental structure, staffing levels, compensation system, job design, and other organizational aspects while implementing a full-blown CIM system. The case study is based on intensive interviews with managers and workers in the midst of this implementation and on follow-up interviews sixteen months later. Three interviewers conducted the initial data collection, each interviewing twenty individuals. Eighteen of the sixty individuals interviewed were managers. Three of the remaining forty-two employees worked in the plant office, while thirty-nine worked on the shop floor. Interviews were open-ended and semistructured and focused on interviewees' perceptions of the changes taking place at the company. Interviews lasted between a half hour to one hour. They were tape recorded and transcribed for purposes of analysis. Thirteen individuals were interviewed for follow-up sixteen months later, including six managers and seven workers. These follow-up interviews focused on the changes that had taken place since the previous interviews. This in-depth approach enabled us to obtain a clear picture of both the vision that top-level managers held of the Factory of the Future, as well as the reality of impacts on the shop floor and in the office as the vision was translated into action. We found the contrast between vision and reality both striking and informative.

Key Questions

This chapter presents the lessons we learned from that experience. These lessons begin to answer three important questions for practicing manufacturing managers, as well as others interested in the implementation of new technology:

1. What can be expected during the transformation of manufacturing plants into Factories of the Future, in terms of the impacts that the technological change will have on the jobs and lives of employees?
2. What actions should be taken to improve the odds for successfully implementing technological change?
3. How rapidly, and in what sequence, should these actions be taken?

But before presenting the lessons from the case, we will first elaborate some key features of the Factory of the Future and explain our use of the term *birthing* in our title.

The Factory of the Future. This term has attained widespread currency as a symbol for the CIM environment (see Kops, 1980). Popularizers of CIM portray an environment in which engineers sit in front of computer-aided design (CAD) terminals, entering product design data. The punched-in designs then result in a series of different products automatically machined, assembled, and transported to a distribution point. Manufacturing is linked to business systems through a shared data base, and marketing forecasts can be translated directly into production planning. Ultimately, all functions may be linked by computer, enabling rapid and flexible coordination among all departments. As Goldhar and Jelinek (1983) observe, this level of integration would revolutionize manufacturing planning and strategy. Previously, a fundamental principle of capacity and production planning required companies to seek the "economies of scale" that result from large-volume runs produced by dedicated, inflexible machines and transfer lines. The ability of CIM technology to change over to production of new parts rapidly and accurately could potentially lead to this principle's inverse. Rather than seeking economies of scale, managers would try to gain "economies of scope" by utilizing flexible manufacturing capabilities to their full advantage, shifting frequently from design to design or product to product and meeting the needs of highly segmented market niches with virtually customized products. However, implicit in this thinking is the assumption that the organization's social, as well as its technical, systems will be able to support flexibility.

Susman and Chase (1985) have recently presented a theoretical sociotechnical analysis of the CIM environment that stresses the greater requirement for interdependence and the greater amount of uncertainty present in this highly flexible Factory of the Future. These writers and others (for example, Nadler and Robinson, 1983) discuss numerous strategies for increasing organizational flexibility by improving human as well as machine integration and for dealing more effectively with organizational uncertainty. For simplicity, these strategies can be clustered under two headings: multi-skilling and organization design. Multi-skilling increases overall flexibility and coordination by having each worker trained in several skills; this enables workers to switch from task to task quickly to meet the rapidly changing needs of the production system. For example, the time spent getting a skilled maintenance worker to the scene of failed equipment may make up a large proportion of equipment downtime. If the individual at the work station can make the necessary repairs, or at least initiate diagnosis of the problem, considerable time can be saved. Furthermore, the nature of computer-based shop-floor equipment requires a range of "attention" skills as opposed to manual skills (Hirschhorn, 1984). Monitoring processes and responding to emergencies are models of work that clearly require multi-skilling. As succinctly put in the title of a recent paper, "flexible manufacturing systems require flexible people" (Graham and Rosenthal, 1985).

Organization design can increase flexibility by improving communication and coordination between different departments, such as design, production, and manufacturing. For example, product design and product manufacture must be tightly coordinated in the CIM facility. Yet the usual communication pattern between these units shows product engineers "throwing the design over the wall" to production managers, who complain bitterly about the "nonmanufacturability" of the design. Modifying organizational structure by having design engineers report to the same individuals as production managers may be one way to improve communication and understanding between the functions. Indeed, the eventual evolution of CIM technology may virtually require some merging of design and production units, since the technology may enable the two functions to be controlled from the same work station. Also, the links from marketing to other functions (chiefly design and production) become highly critical in CIM. As described earlier, quick and accurate response by design and production departments to rapid changes in market demands may be the hallmark of the future factory. By the same token, marketing personnel must have a sophisticated understanding of the capabilities of their firms' process technologies to enable them to take advantage of these capabilities in diversifying to new products or markets. This more flexible marketing will be required to feed the production system with the "scope" of orders required to support the capital investment for the flexible systems. Changes in reporting lines or the judicious use of multifunctional task forces may improve mutual understanding between departments.

Prescriptions for accomplishing changes in social systems

to accompany CIM technology have thus already appeared in print. However, these prescriptions have not been followed by many organizations, and even fewer cases of documenting the consequences of such attempts exist. The specific steps that practicing managers can take to ensure success are therefore difficult to chart.

Birthing. The recently coined term *birthing* has several connotations that make it useful to our examination of CIM implementation. The word is frequently used in connection with birth preparation programs designed to enable women to bear children without the use of drugs to relieve pain. Although childbirth has traditionally been associated with great pain, the preparation techniques are successful because they reduce uncertainty about the birth process, and provide the mother with a set of conditioned responses that enable her to relax during birth and cooperate with, rather than struggle against, her body's natural birth rhythm. The mental and physical preparation techniques are learned systematically and gradually, and women are encouraged to select from a range of techniques, tailoring their own personal approaches. The birthing environment usually consists of a team that includes the father, doctor, nurses and/or midwives, and perhaps even a friend or two, all of whom form a supportive system, enhancing the support of the conditioned relaxation responses.

In short, the reduction of pain through reduction of uncertainty and the systematic and gradual development of support systems tailored to meet specific needs are connotations of the term *birthing* that have implications for advanced manufacturing. We will argue that successful implementation of advanced manufacturing technology requires similar attention to the development of support systems, and "birthing" is a helpful metaphor to remind managers and others concerned with the implementation process of the importance of preparation in reducing the pain that inevitably accompanies organizational transformation.

Lessons Learned: Why Is "All at Once" Too Much?

One of the more popular categorization schemes used to come to grips with organizational change contrasts "radical" with "incremental" innovations (Zaltman, Duncan, and Holbek, 1973; Duchesneau and Dutton, 1977; Hage, 1980). This body of research treats radical versus incremental as a dimension along which various innovations can be scaled. Thus, innovations have been rated on their degree of radicalness, and various organizational strategies or structures have been associated with innovations that seem to be a radical departure from previous practice in contrast to those that represent a more minor departure (for example, Ettlie, Bridges, and O'Keefe, 1984; Ettlie, 1986). Yet this body of work does not directly address the following question: What pace should be utilized when implementing a radical innovation? Should the pace be relatively rapid to ensure that the company can capitalize on the relative advantage offered by the innovation, or should the pace be very gradual to enable it to build support systems for the innovation? What types of middle ground exist between these two approaches, and what criteria can guide the practicing manager in setting the pace for innovation? (For one of the few empirically grounded discussions of implementation "pace" in the literature, see Lawler, 1986.)

The discussion of radical versus incremental change has become especially relevant to CIM, since early experiments have led some pioneers in CIM to conclude that they moved too fast too soon and to advocate a more incremental pace for CIM implementation (Zygmont, 1986). Nonetheless, there remain strong temptations to implement as much and as quickly as possible. In the words of one manager interviewed for the present study, "We see a window of opportunity, but it's closing fast." Thus, the pace of technological change is so rapid that managers are under considerable pressure to install new process technology before their competitors seize market advantage using the same technology.

The case study described in this chapter illustrates in some detail the negative consequences of using an "all at once" approach. The management team in this case possessed a powerful and sophisticated vision of the Factory of the Future and attached considerable importance to developing social system features that would support and complement the integrated technical system they were planning. However, in order to implement a highly complex CIM system within a short time frame, they chose to focus their planning and resources on technical system changes, and they did not develop policies and procedures in sufficient detail nor allocate sufficient resources to support implementation of the social system components. By failing to prepare, and by failing to move at a pace slow enough to accommodate the change in organizational culture that they were attempting, they ultimately failed to bring their vision of the Factory of the Future to life. In short, they did not devote sufficient planning and resources to preparing a social system to match the CIM technical system. This theme runs throughout all the following specific lessons we learned from the case:

1. *Winners and Losers.* When the company's top management first announced the automation program, it conveyed the impression to employees that "we're all part of the same team, and everyone will be a winner in the Factory of the Future." Yet as the program unfolded, it became clear that some jobs were central to the program and others would soon be obsolete. Various management actions accentuated the distinction, resulting in low morale among employees in threatened jobs. But contrary to management expectations, there was evidence that low morale among "losers" contaminated morale among winners, and our follow-up interviews showed that one-fourth of the supposed "winners" had actually quit the company. We conclude that the "all at once" approach tends to focus resources on a select group of employees and to discard the rest. Preparing a select group of employees for the Factory of the Future and ignoring or discarding others will damage morale and may actually impede implementation.

2. *Integrity on the Line.* The statement by the company's CEO that "no one will lose their job due to automation" raised expectations that were later dashed. This one symbolic

event tended to poison much of the effort to build involvement in the automation program. We conclude that under conditions of uncertainty, management integrity is on the line. All messages that deal with uncertainty, and especially those that deal with job security, must be consistent and realistic. Reactions to these messages will permeate all other efforts to foster change. Although trust can be quickly destroyed, it takes time and patience to build it.

3. *Cheerleading and Misleading.* Although the CEO and his top managers seemed to sincerely want to build a culture of commitment, their attempts were hampered by a failure to resolve in their own minds the balance of power between top management decision makers and other employees. Consequently, meetings and task forces intended to build involvement were instead perceived by some as either "cheerleading" efforts or misleading and a waste of time, since the important decisions had already been made by top management. There was little evidence that gains in commitment were achieved; the meetings and task forces seemed to reduce the sense of involvement rather than build it. Whenever managers attempt to use meetings and task forces to encourage involvement and participation, genuine participation in decision making needs to occur; otherwise, the attempts will likely backfire. If building commitment and involvement is a high priority, managers must be willing to provide the additional time required to achieve genuine participation.

4. *Running While Changing.* High-level managers expected the benefits of the new technologies to be gained fairly quickly. In anticipation of these benefits, and in an attempt to start with a "clean slate" of managers who supported the changes, engineering and supervisory staff were cut dramatically. However, we learned that the transition to full functioning of integrated systems may be more labor-intensive than expected, and premature cutbacks in staff in anticipation of productivity gains can actually retard those gains. A staffing plan that allows for gradual, staged cutbacks to allow for adjustment to new technology is preferable.

5. *Building a New Culture.* When describing their vision of the Factory of the Future, the top management group emphasized the importance of "culture change" and the new beliefs and values that would support the integrated, complex technical system. Yet they did not take into account the depth and interconnectedness of these cultural components. Consequently, their efforts to change organizational culture fell far short of expectations. We conclude that organizational culture is much easier to destroy than to build. Creating a new culture is a time-consuming and uncertain process, requiring considerable planning and resources. The social system characteristics of the Factory of the Future need to be viewed as part of the same fabric as its technical system characteristics, and the process of change must weave them together rather than tear them apart.

The remainder of the chapter is organized as follows: First, we will describe the company and its efforts to change its technical and social systems. Our description of social system change efforts will contrast the vision of top management with the policies, procedures, and resources actually used to carry out that vision. After describing the change efforts, we will show how the five lessons listed above were derived from the case, and how these lessons all relate to limitations of the "all at once" approach.

Delta Products: Case Description

The focus of our case is Delta Products, Inc. (Throughout this chapter, all names and all information that could be used to identify the company or its employees are disguised to protect confidentiality.) Delta is a manufacturer of components for material-handling equipment. Its major customers are manufacturers in the automotive, furniture, and agricultural equipment industries. Delta is located in a small midwestern city and has traditionally drawn its work force of less than 250 persons from the city and surrounding countryside. The work force is not unionized, and new employees are often recruited from family members or friends of current employees.

The company was started in the early part of the century, and was a closely held, family-owned and -operated organization until 1981. At that time, an umbrella corporation was established, and several operations were set up as independent subsidiaries. These included an operation to produce a proprietary material-handling product and an international sales operation. Delta, however, continued to be the major manufacturing operation in the corporation. At the time interviews were conducted, the grandson of the company founder was serving as chief executive officer, having replaced his father in that position about ten years ago.

Before the beginning of the current automation effort, the major operations on the shop floor were machining, secondary operations (for example, grinding, deburring, drilling), heat treating, and assembly. Most of the main machinery and equipment dated back to the 1940s. Shop-floor workers were predominantly male except for the assembly operation, which was largely female. Major machining operations ran on three shifts, but the majority of employees worked the day shift. In addition to the shop-floor workers, the company employed personnel for sales, purchasing, engineering, accounting, production control, machine maintenance and repair, data processing, and secretarial functions.

Most of Delta's employees were relatively isolated from the automation planning since a separate corporation, Automation Management, Inc. (AM Inc.) had been formed for that purpose. AM Inc.'s mission was to manage the automation of technologically outmoded manufacturing operations (as a consultant or partial owner). Thus, its organizational purpose extended beyond that of Delta Products, and it intended to use Delta as a "living laboratory" to develop its expertise for managing automation projects and eventually as a showcase for that expertise.

AM Inc. was composed of a close-knit group of three individuals: the CEO of Delta Products (who was also the CEO of AM Inc.), an experienced marketing manager, and a manufacturing engineer. The marketing manager and manufacturing engineer had been selected by the CEO to join him in forming AM Inc. after an attempt to justify the purchase of automation for Delta on the basis of traditional cost justification methods had failed. This justification project, conducted by Delta's controller and other managers, had treated computer numerical control (CNC) machines as stand-alone equipment. The marketing manager and manufacturing engineer then developed a justification model that projected that an integrated automation approach would pay back investment within 2.2 years. According to the manufacturing engineer, "We couldn't keep pulling off this kind of thinking in the plant, the office walls were just too thin, so we had to move out." In short, the CEO and the two creative thinkers he selected had concluded that their vision would be hampered and constrained by the day-to-day realities of the production environment, as well as by the fairly traditional manufacturing management culture that characterized the plant. Consequently, AM Inc. was established shortly before our interviews in an executive office suite twenty miles from the plant.

The formal introduction of the three-year plan for shop-floor and office automation developed by AM Inc. took place in October 1983 when all company employees were invited to a daylong presentation of the new program at a local hotel. Based on interviews with AM Inc. and Delta management in June 1984, we developed the following summary of the main characteristics of the automation program.

Intended Technical System Innovations. The aim was to achieve a totally integrated manufacturing system, including CAD, CNC, distributed numerical control (DNC), manufacturing resources planning (MRP II), automated materials handling, laser inspectors, and automatic tool changing. As a first step in that direction, over twenty-five pieces of standard machining equipment would be replaced by five CNC machining centers to be loaded and unloaded by robots. The transition to these machining centers was intended to replace not only most existing primary machining equipment but also most secondary operations. For example, parts cut on the new machining centers would have a fine finish, eliminating the secondary grinding function. The machinery itself would be operated by former operators of the standard machining equipment, specially trained to program, operate, and maintain the machinery in the new machining centers.

Another major component of the first implementation phase was the planning and start-up of a comprehensive, companywide MRP II system. MRP II is a computerized approach to business planning and production control. Since MRP II requires integration of information systems into one global computerized system, a wide variety of personnel would be using it. Responsibility for implementation and training was given to a task force headed by the plant manager and including managers from data processing, production control, and accounting.

In addition to CAD and MRP II, other office automation would be implemented. All managers and secretarial staff would be affected in that managers would receive personal computers and would be expected to use them to handle most of their own paper work. Sales staff were also impacted by the automation program, since sales would have to be increased and new product lines marketed to pay back the heavy capital investment in CIM and to take advantage of its capability for flexible manufacturing. Also, telecommunications would be used to link large-volume customers to Delta so that some of the work load of the sales staff could be computerized.

In short, AM Inc. expected virtually all functions in the shop and office to be changed in a major way by the automation program.

Intended Social System Innovations. The AM Inc. managers prided themselves on their progressive management approach. They were well versed in popular management literature (for example, Peters and Waterman, 1982), and their marketing brochures highlighted their skills at managing "culture change." They were convinced that in order to successfully operate highly automated facilities, a new kind of worker was required: one who was educated, committed, and prepared to assume considerable responsibility for the general smooth running of the plant, as well as of his or her specific job. In fact, the AM Inc. team frequently referred to this "people change" as the most difficult and uncertain aspect of the change to a CIM system.

During our first visit to the Delta plant, we were handed a list of nineteen programs, many of which were designed to affect education, communications, and other aspects of the plant social system. To simplify the case study, we have organized these programs and other efforts by Delta management to change their plant culture into the following eight areas: (1) education, (2) job displacement, (3) autonomy and job enrichment, (4) compensation, (5) building involvement, (6) communication, (7) restructuring departments, and (8) supplier and customer relations.

Our first interviews with the AM team impressed us with the breadth and sophistication of their vision of the plant's future culture. Yet we also noted the apparent lack of detail in their broad brushstrokes. The plan for completing phase 1 of the automation program called for all five machining centers to be up and running in August 1984, but AM Inc. was much less clear about the timing of the social system changes. Furthermore, the team had not yet operationalized key implementation components at the time of our interviews in July, one month before the planned completion of phase 1. That is, the AM team had not translated their vision into the specific policies, procedures, and resources needed to guide and support the implementation of social system change.

The section that follows contains descriptions of the AM team's vision for each social system program area. Each program description is followed by a description of whatever policies, procedures, and resources had been put in place to support the vision. These descriptions will begin to illustrate the contrast between the AM Inc. vision and the reality of its shop-floor and office implementation.

1. *Education.* The AM team emphasized that an educated work force was one of the keys to the Factory of the Future. When asked about their expectations for the operators in the plant, one of the AM team replied, "We want them to become techni-

cians, we want them walking around with white coats on." When we asked Delta's CEO how he would know that the plant culture had actually changed, he answered, "You know it's there when everybody throws their hammers away. You know it's there when instead of tearing into the problem, the guy stops and thinks it through. What's happening is, it's more of an intellectual problem."

Familiarity with computers would be encouraged by a home computer purchase plan in which the company would pay 50 percent of the price for any employee who wanted to partici-pate. Introductory-level classes were to be offered to all inter-ested employees on various topics related to CIM; these one-day orientations were to be held on Saturdays, off site, and employ-ees would be paid for their time. Employees who would work with the automated machining centers and the CAD and MRP II systems would receive training from equipment and systems vendors. Workers would be encouraged to obtain technical training outside the plant, and the CEO was attempting to develop technical programs related to CIM at a local college.

At the time of our first interviews, over two-thirds of the work force had purchased the home computers. However, our interviews revealed that they were little used by most employees. Only one class had been offered, a general introduction to computers. There had been a good deal of vendor-provided training for those assigned to new computer-based operations; however, most workers we spoke to complained that it was diffi-cult to get much out of the training for machining centers without some background in math and computers. Finally, there was discussion of a reimbursement policy for workers studying technical courses at college, but no actual policy had been worked out.

2. *Job Displacement.* At the October 1983 announcement of the automation program, an important message was delivered by the CEO: "No one will lose their job due to automation." With the new, flexible technology, AM Inc. told us that it expected to generate enough new business to maintain or increase employ-ment levels and internally place people in new jobs if their old jobs were eliminated. In addition, new hires were added only as

part-time employees, so this "temporary" work force could be used to absorb changes in employment levels.

However, the statement that "no one will lose their job due to automation" had been modified by the time of our interviews nine months later. According to Delta's CEO: "The promise that was made . . . was that no one goes to the streets. The concept being just simply that . . . you help people find another job." Although several people had left the plant since the announcement, there was no explicit program for helping displaced employees find work, and we heard differing accounts of the degree to which these employees had been assisted. There was also some sentiment that part-time workers had been hired purely as a means for minimizing costs rather than as part of a policy to retain full-time employees.

3. *Autonomy and Job Enrichment.* A major part of the new culture of Delta would be a transformation of the way people related to their jobs. Jobs would become careers to which employees were deeply committed. Every employee would have a challenging job, considerable responsibility, and autonomy to make most routine decisions. The new machining centers would be operated by "cell managers" with complete responsibility for the functioning of their machines (for example, programming, maintenance, and operation). Eventually this "functional management" approach would extend to all jobs throughout the plant. Every person in the plant would have a clearly delineated function and be the "manager" of that function. Each manager would delegate all that he or she was not uniquely positioned to accomplish to his subordinates. In anticipation of this delegation of responsibility, the number of supervisors had been dramatically reduced and a full layer of management had been eliminated.

The term *functional management* was used frequently by the AM team and by other top-level Delta managers. However, we found that education in the skills required for functional management had not been planned. Although there was some awareness of the term among managers, there was also confusion as to its operational meaning. Since there had been a recent reduction in the number of supervisors and department heads, there did appear to be considerable delegation of authority on day-to-day decisions, although there was some uncertainty about boundaries of responsibility. Regarding job enrichment, there was no management training in methods such as planning or scheduling for the machinists who were to become the new "cell managers." Moreover, during our follow-up visits, we learned that only one cell manager was actually programming the machining centers. This individual had had previous experience in programming, and the other machinists were "too busy" to spend enough time programming in order to master the new skills.

4. *Compensation.* To achieve their vision of a committed work force, the AM team was aware that entirely new forms of compensation would be required. In the words of Delta's CEO: "Isn't it sad that benefits have to be treated the way they are. . . . Wouldn't it be neat if [the benefits] were meaningful, and could become something that everybody was excited about. . . . Why can't this be a motivation device rather than just something that's laid over on the side."

To make compensation "a motivation device," AM Inc. hired a consulting firm to design an entirely new pay and benefits package. These consultants recommended a program that would emphasize "wellness" and prevention of illness. It was also decided to design the program as a cafeteria-style menu of benefits. Other radical changes were the shift to "all on salary" for the work force, a profit-sharing plan to cover all employees, and gifts of Delta shares for all. A task force (including two representatives from the hourly work force, the plant manager, and a member of the AM team) was formed to review the plan. A brochure listing some of the key features was circulated to all employees, and the task force was asked to informally solicit reactions to the new ideas. This effort uncovered some questions and doubts; for example, the all-on-salary plan was viewed by some as a means to get employees to work overtime without paying overtime rates. The AM team decided to postpone the start-up date for the new compensation program.

At the time of our first interviews, Delta employees were anticipating a full-day "fair" designed to celebrate and share information about the new compensation package. The exact date for the fair had not yet been set. Meanwhile, hourly employees with "satisfactory" ratings had received a ten-cent raise following their annual review, a much smaller amount than expected and a sum many perceived as demeaning. Therefore, the profit-sharing plan was viewed by some employees as a "replacement" for the raise that they should have gotten, and they viewed the program as a cost-cutting effort in disguise. When we conducted our follow-up interviews, we learned that the profit-sharing plan and the gifts of shares actually turned out to involve extremely small sums. Also, the "wellness" benefits package was criticized by some employees for taking away as many benefits as it added.

5. *Building Involvement.* The AM team spoke of the need to "build involvement," to develop the commitment that would be a keystone of the new culture. One of Delta's top plant managers had this to say when we asked him what the biggest change at the plant would be: "It would be in the people. What's ahead of us yet is the people as far as the education and involvement. . . . I say give it a year or so, something that looks strange or different right now then will look useful."

One program to encourage involvement was called "Action Needed," a type of employee suggestion program. Employees filled in "action-needed" suggestion forms, and management was required to follow up either through action or an explanation for inaction. Delta managers also told us that multifunctional task forces would be used whenever possible, and we heard the word *teamwork* used frequently. The two examples of task forces at the time of our interviews were the MRP II and the benefits task forces described above.

Yet there was some ambiguity in AM Inc.'s vision concerning the decision-making authority of task forces. The following exchange illustrates this ambiguity:

> *AM Inc. Manager:* We've kicked this around quite a bit, and we're pretty clear that there's no such thing as voluntary automation . . . some

leader always has to force it. People get comfortable in their jobs and don't want to change. We are using participation — for example, in our MRP II task force. It has top management, manufacturing, accounting, and data-processing people. But we've told them several things flat out, like, "Don't try to change the software, we'll change our business systems to fit the software."

Interviewer: Isn't there a contradiction between participation and a belief that automation has to be forced?

AM Inc. Manager: Yes, it's contradicting. We want participation, but you sometimes try to do it right and can't. Try it right first, anyway that works, second. You need both, participation and force . . . you need a balance.

6. *Communication.* Good communication between different levels of management and between managers and workers was viewed as essential to building involvement, and would be a key to effective "functional management" in the new Delta culture. The most visible mechanism to achieve effective communication was a recently started program of periodic meetings (monthly or more frequently) to discuss the changes at the plant. The plant manager and operations manager met with groups of about five to fifteen employees on all shifts for about one hour on company time. In these meetings (labeled "Let's Talk" meetings by Delta management), it was explained to employees that they should be "networking," that is, going directly to the person they needed to talk to to solve any particular problem ("going

right to the source") rather than communicating indirectly through the management hierarchy. Another means for achieving management-subordinate communication was "management by walking around" (Peters and Waterman, 1982). The CEO actively promoted this style of management for the top-level plant managers in several ways. For example, he had begun to personally distribute the paychecks to all employees to encourage informal conversation, and he told plant managers that their performance would be measured on their practice of management by walking around.

At the time of our first interviews, the "Let's Talk" meetings were taking place, but we observed little two-way communication; instead, the meetings appeared to be orchestrated presentations with little dialogue. There were no plans to support networking behavior except for encouragement from top management; and when we questioned employees, we found mostly confusion about the idea. There was an obvious awareness among top-level plant managers that they were now expected to practice a different management style, but again there was some confusion about exactly what this was and how to go about doing it. The CEO recognized this problem when he told us: "We're trying to pick up our communications now on the basis of walking around, and those people who are supposed to be walking around and communicating are also caught with the old job, and they've got one foot in and one foot out."

7. *Restructuring Departments.* Recall that AM Inc. had been formed as a "skunk works" (Peters and Waterman, 1982) to remove creative thinkers from the traditional management atmosphere, an atmosphere that fostered the type of thinking that could not initially justify the automation program. As one AM manager put it: "It's the managers who've resisted the most, not the workers. People get comfortable, they climb from one rut to another. But our managers will have to become rut jumpers in the new high-tech world."

To create a break with the thinking of the past, the AM team engineered a radical restructuring of plant management. First, the entire layer of twelve department heads was eliminated through reassignment and resignation. Three new departments were created: external, internal, and financial. The sales and engineering departments were combined to form the external department. This change was intended to dramatically shorten the turnaround time for new product designs and improve technical communications with customers. Production, production control, and data processing were combined to form the internal department to improve production-oriented information management. Accounting and business services comprised the financial department. The external department was headed by an experienced sales manager with no engineering background. This did not present an immediate problem, since the engineering staff had been recently cut from thirteen to two members in anticipation of the changeover to CAD technology, and these two engineers did not require much supervision. The three new department heads reported directly to Delta's CEO.

Although the new structural arrangements seemed to be in place during our interviews, there had been little in the way of training or orientation to prepare for them. For example, the external manager seemed ill prepared to launch innovative marketing programs and had few ideas about managing the engineering function and its interface with marketing. The changes also had little salience for the work force, who were largely unaware of them; although the size of the work force was fairly small (fewer than 250 employees), many were unable to specify the new job positions of their top plant managers.

8. *Supplier and Customer Relations.* The AM Inc. team was aware of CIM's implications for their relations with suppliers of raw materials and parts and also for their ties to customers. To capitalize on the benefits of flexibility, they would need to respond quickly to market opportunities, and they would have to purchase high-quality materials to be able to produce consistently high-quality products. They also realized that they would need to diversify away from their traditional bread-and-butter market in which they had been recognized as a market share leader for many years. As related to us by one of the AM Inc. team: "We're going to have to start seeing ourselves as makers of round things, not just the specialized round things we're used to making. Sure, our sales and marketing guys are well tied in to

their old buddies, but that's got to change. We're doing a lot to put our energy into new products and new customers; that's what will make us big kids with little cost."

To achieve these goals, Delta planned to take the following steps: First, they would organize their relations with suppliers to segment strategic activity from day-to-day dealing. They would do so by setting up a dedicated "sourcing" function that would explore new methods, part designs, and materials for both existing and new products. The general purchasing function would be handled by another unit. Delta would attempt the same strategic versus day-to-day segmentation for their relationships with customers by dedicating a function within sales to focus on existing customers, leaving the external department manager free to develop new markets and customer relationships. Second, the sourcing manager would use a team-building philosophy with important suppliers; AM Inc. expected that "team" relationships between Delta and its suppliers would help ensure the steady and timely flow of high-quality inputs. Third, the external department manager would develop networks of exclusive, regional distributorships for Delta products. (Previously, Delta had dealt with multiple distributors within regions or directly with original equipment manufacturers who used their product.) The exclusive distributorship approach would serve to "lock in" customers to a price and make forecasting for Delta more predictable.

At the time of our interviews, the dedicated functions had been established, and the sourcing manager was beginning one team-building project. However, he complained to us that "my time is being dragged off so that I can't even get to sourcing." This manager, because of his breadth of experience in general management and consulting, had been enlisted by the internal manager to assist in a variety of activities to support internal plant programs. Regarding distributorships, the external manager referred to the approach as "an item of controversy" and seemed to be resisting a major push in that direction.

Summary: Programs, Visions, and Reality. Table 10-1 summarizes the programs and visions, plus the levels of policy, procedure, and resource implementation we have just reviewed. This table conveys the massive scope of change at Delta; clearly, AM Inc. was attempting to implement a comprehensive set of technological changes while simultaneously mounting a complete transformation of its social systems. But the table also shows what little attention had been paid to planning the transformation of the social system and operationalizing key implementation details. It seems that the AM team assumed that many of these details would work themselves out once the technology was in place, and therefore had devoted many more resources to the hardware and software rather than to the social system elements required to ensure that the technical system would actually work.

Thus far, we have limited our description of "reality" to the status of policies, procedures, and resources employed to support AM Inc.'s vision. The following section will describe in greater detail the actual results of the "all at once" approach and will show how we derived the five lessons from the case.

Delta Products: Case Analysis

Winners and Losers. Our original intent in conducting the case study was to identify barriers to implementation of CIM, and we were predisposed to focus our attention on the potential barriers most widely discussed in the literature, such as problems in staffing and communication (Roitman, Turniansky, and Liker, 1985). However, upon closer examination it became clear that the workers and managers we interviewed had interpreted the changes at Delta primarily in terms of the impacts these changes would have on their own lives rather than in terms of the impacts that they would have on the company. The highly personal and emotional tone characterizing the interviews led to a set of analyses focusing on employees' subjective reactions to the changes.

It was apparent that some of the employees and managers perceived that they would come out of the changes as "winners," while others expected to be "losers." In fact, we were able to reliably sort individuals into three categories:

Table 10-1. Vision Versus Reality.

Programs	Vision	Policies, Procedures, and Resources
1. Education a. Home computer purchase plan b. Introductory classes c. Vendor-provided training d. Reimbursement for technical courses	Work force will have advanced technical skills ("white coats"), problem-solving orientation, and computer literacy.	a. Two-thirds of work force bought computers, but they were little used at home. b. One introductory class held. c. Vendor training provided, but received mixed evaluations. d. No policy in place.
2. Job Displacement a. Outplacement b. Part-time "temporaries"	Work force will have job security since company will be highly profitable. There will be a high level of trust in management.	a. Original announcement "No one will lose their jobs to automation" became "company will help place those who lose their jobs." No explicit program in place, though some help given. b. "Temporaries" employed.
3. Autonomy and Job Enrichment a. "Functional management" b. Enriched jobs (for example, cell manager) c. Fewer supervisors	All employees will manage their own clearly delineated functions. Decision-making authority will be delegated whenever possible. Few if any "physical" jobs will exist. Jobs will be challenging. Work force will be responsible, motivated, and committed to the Delta mission.	a. No training for "functional management," and some confusion about meaning of term. b. No management training for cell managers. At follow-up, only one cell manager doing programming. c. Considerable delegation of authority for day-to-day decisions.
4. Compensation a. Wellness programs	Joint sense of "ownership" in Delta shared by all managers	a.–d. New programs not yet in place. Task force reviewed consultant's proposal. Ten-cent

Program Element	Intended Goal	Current Status
b. Cafeteria-style benefits c. All on salary d. Profit sharing e. Gifts of Delta shares	and workers. Pay and benefits will function as a true motivating device, retaining and attracting skilled people.	raise viewed as demeaning. Profit sharing and share gifts were very small amounts.

5. Building Involvement
  a. "Action-Needed" program
  b. Task forces
	Managers and workers will be involved in and committed to changes at Delta that support its mission.	a. "Action Needed" in place.
		b. Two task forces in place (benefits and MRP II); ambiguity about task force decision-making authority.

6. Communication
  a. "Let's Talk" meetings
  b. Networking
  c. "Management by walking around"
	Information will pass freely as needed between individuals, regardless of relative job positions. Good communication will support involvement and commitment.	a. "Let's Talk" meetings in place, but little dialogue occurred.
		b. No training for networking and confusion about its meaning.
		c. "Management by walking around" practiced by CEO.

7. Restructuring Departments a. External, internal, and financial departments created	Organization structure will facilitate rapid and flexible response to environmental demands and support CIM technology.	a. New departments in place, but no preparation for them.

8. Supplier and Customer Relations
  a. Segmenting strategic activity from day-to-day operations by establishing dedicated functions
  b. Team building with suppliers
  c. Regional distributorships
		a. Dedicated functions were established.
		b. One team-building project begun, but "no time to work on it."
		c. Plans for distributorship program in place, but resisted by external manager.

1. Winners (twenty-one employees) saw the automation program mostly in terms of personal gain. For them, the change brought new challenges and opportunities.
2. Losers (seventeen employees) saw the automation program mostly in terms of personal loss. The automation meant that their old world was being destroyed and a new world was being created in which they had no place.
3. Sideliners (eighteen employees) comprised three sub-categories.* Some were uncertain about whether they would gain or lose from the automation program. Others did not expect their jobs to be affected at all by it. The third subgroup included part-time ("temporary") workers who did not perceive Delta's environment as central to their lives.

After dividing the sample into these three groups, we searched for variables that could discriminate winners, losers, and sideliners. The variables we examined included (1) personal characteristics (age, amount of education, and so on); (2) tenure, identification, and satisfaction with the company; (3) job characteristics (including job level and use of new machines); (4) orientation to change (for example, spontaneous mention of the need to change); and (5) perceptions of future job prospects. The results were quite clear. Losers were remarkably similar to winners; like winners, they identified with the company and felt committed to change. However, losers saw themselves as excluded from the world of CIM, while winners fully expected to find work in the Factory of the Future; all winners felt that the skills they were learning at Delta would assure them a job at Delta or elsewhere, while no losers expressed this sense of assurance (see Roskies, Liker, and Roitman, 1986, for a complete report of these analyses).

The self-perception of winner-loser status corresponded

---

* The numbers sum to fifty-six, instead of the sixty total interviews since (1) we did not include the three AM team members in this analysis, and (2) one of the tapes could not be used for coding. This left us with fifty-six transcripts for analysis.

closely to an objective measure of job prospects within Delta (we are grateful to Rosabeth Moss Kanter for her helpful suggestions on this issue). We called this measure *job fate,* and it reflected whether a worker's or manager's job would be (1) protected or expanded by the automation program, (2) threatened or diminished by automation at Delta, or (3) unaffected. We sorted interviewees into these three categories based on their jobs at the time of the interviews. Seventeen interviewees were considered to have protected or expanded jobs (for example, the cell managers and the CAD operator). Fifteen people were expected to have threatened or diminished jobs (including those employees who worked on machines that would be replaced by the new machining centers and who had not signed up for training). Twenty-one employees were in jobs that were unlikely to be affected by the automation program (these included workers in the heat-treating and tool and die departments). The individual's objective job fate proved to be an excellent predictor of whether he or she felt like a winner, loser, or sideliner. Eleven of the fifteen employees whose jobs were objectively threatened were coded losers, and only one was rated a winner. Of those whose jobs were likely to be protected or expanded, thirteen of seventeen were coded as winners, and only one was coded as a loser.

In another set of analyses, we coded employee evaluations of the impacts on quality of working life of the changes at Delta. Their evaluations proved to be closely related both to their self-perceptions and to the objective assessments of career prospects. Those who saw themselves as losers (and those whose jobs were objectively threatened) spoke negatively and with strong emotions about the lack of job security, deterioration in pay and benefits, lack of top-down communication, and lack of trust in Delta's management. In contrast, those who expected to be winners (and those whose jobs were likely to be protected and expanded) evaluated changes in these same quality of working life dimensions (job security, pay and benefits, communication, and trust) to be positive. Sideliners (and those whose jobs would be unaffected) consistently fell between the two extremes (see

Liker, Roitman, and Roskies, forthcoming, for a complete report of these analyses).

Perhaps it is inevitable that any change of this type will produce some winners and some losers. However, AM Inc.'s actions tended to widen the gap between the two groups. For example, contrary to statements made by AM Inc. that potentially all employees could be involved in the changes and educated in high-technology skills, we found that none of those in threatened jobs were substantially involved in planning and none had received company-sponsored training beyond the orientation session on computers. Another action accentuating the distinction between winners and losers was the "ten-cent raise." Delta's finances were severely strained by the automation program, and the annual raise for hourly employees (announced just before our interviews) was only ten cents an hour for those with "satisfactory" evaluations. However, several employees holding jobs likely to be protected or expanded told us they had received fifty-cent raises. The ten-cent raise was described to us by several employees as a clear sign that Delta's management was more willing to invest in new technology than in its work force.

A third example of management actions that seemed to widen the winner-loser gap was reported to us by several employees during our follow-up interviews. At Delta's annual progress review, attended by all employees, the company had ceremonially honored some of its winners with testimonials and awards, while huge blowups of their faces appeared on a screen in front of the crowd. Both winners and losers were angered. As one loser put it: "What about the rest of us? Don't we count? One of the girls I work with [a winner] said, 'If I had known this is what they were going to do, I'd never let them do it . . . singling out just a few doesn't make for a real team.'" And, from a winner: "A lot of people would have wanted their picture on the screen . . . you're just asking for trouble, with all the natural jealousy."

Although the approach taken by Delta's management clearly widened the gulf between winners and losers, one might still reason that a strategy that focused company resources on likely winners would be the best way of ensuring that these important contributors would stay with the company. This tactic makes apparent sense when one considers the heavy financial burden brought upon the company by its use of the "all at once" approach. When resources are scarce, why waste them on those who would likely be gone from the company within a short period of time? However, when we returned to the plant sixteen months after our first interviews, we did not find a plant popu- lated largely by self-perceived winners or those whose jobs were likely to have been protected. We did find a great deal of up- heaval; 60 percent of the employees that we had originally interviewed had experienced a major job change (that is, they were fired or they quit; they moved from part time to full time status; or they were promoted or demoted). However, neither subjective nor objective measures proved to be good predictors of "real" job fate. Especially important was the finding that although one-fourth of the individuals whose jobs were sup- posedly "protected" by automation received promotions, 12 percent had been fired, 6 percent had been demoted, and 24 percent had quit. Results were similar when we looked at those who had expected to be winners; although only one had been fired, 28 percent had quit. Overall, 34 percent of the previous interviewees were no longer at Delta; 11 percent had been terminated, and 23 percent had quit. In short, not only was there a great deal of upheaval, but many winners were gone, while many losers were still with the company.

We also found anecdotal evidence on our return that the low morale among self-perceived losers had contaminated the morale of the winners. For example, one of the cell managers, who said that he "felt optimistic, although a lot of people don't," also had this to say: "We've lost a lot of machinists because of bad morale . . . nobody was out there talking to them to reassure them that they still had a job with the company. . . . They've lost some of the better people . . . the ones who know maintenance and set-up . . . they've left."

Unfortunately, our follow-up interviews did not obtain evidence concerning the reasons that apparent winners (and those whose jobs had seemed protected) had quit the firm. However, it seems reasonable to surmise that they had gained enough skills in computer-based manufacturing to find good jobs elsewhere and that the work environment at Delta was not sufficiently attractive to hold them. With over one-quarter of its "winners" quitting, Delta could look forward to continued high training costs and to some of the other negative effects on computer-based manufacturing that accompany high turnover. For example, costly production time would be lost while new people learned the cell manager job. And the gains in uptime expected by having individuals trained in programming and maintenance as well as operation would be considerably delayed, perhaps substantially affecting the flexibility of the system. We might also surmise that a work environment that could not hold its own "winners" might have trouble attracting high-quality individuals from outside.

Therefore, we conclude that a strategy that focuses on preparing a select group of employees for participation in the Factory of the Future and either deliberately, or through neglect, discards those who are considered unworthy may prove to be a dangerous one. Although this strategy might seem to be a logical way to maximize the use of scarce resources, the negative consequences in terms of morale, turnover, and company image may outweigh any potential benefits.

Integrity on the Line. Job security is an extremely sensitive issue for employees in any automation program. How was this issue handled at Delta? Perhaps the most striking contrasts between the perceptions of management and those of the hourly work force revolved around this issue. For example, the following excerpts from interviews with employees are illustrative:

> *Employee #1:*   When we started this automation, we were promised we would all have our jobs; and in June, there were three or four women . . . fired. Coincidentally, they were all fired on the same day, and they [Delta management] said they had not been doing their jobs. One of the women had been

	here for fifteen years. I can't understand why they would keep somebody for fifteen years if she wasn't doing her job.
Employee #2:	The four women got fired . . . they were trying to keep it hushed up . . . then we got about three different stories. First of all they were fired, and then they were laid off . . . I mean we just got all kinds of different stories, and then we were told, "Well, if you want to hear what happened, you have to go up there and ask." Then we were told, "It's none of your business." But yet, we are all supposed to be a team.
Employee #3:	I feel that in the winter months of this year they had started to build trust. But I think as we got closer toward summertime . . . when they first started automation, they said we'd all have our jobs. Then probably February they said, "If we have to lay people off, we'll help them find jobs." So I would say right in that period everybody started thinking, "Is this going to happen again?" Because a lot of people just got back from layoffs . . . *so you just don't know whether to believe them or not. . . . I think the big turning point was when they came down and said, "Well, if we can't keep you here, we'll help you find other jobs"* (italics added).

In short, the symbolic importance of this one event in the minds of employees was a consistent theme in the interviews. That is, once having raised doubts by appearing inconsistent on the issue of job security, Delta's top management could do little to reestablish the sense of trust and "family feeling" that had characterized its culture before. Ironically, Delta's CEO claimed to appreciate the importance of consistency. When we asked him his views about what needed to be done to create a culture of trust between management and employees, he replied, "The way you provide it is through absolute consistency. Over and over and over . . . every single time that you do anything."

AM Inc. was following sound management instincts when it originally sought to proclaim a no-layoff policy. This type of policy can enhance productivity through difficult periods (Bolt, 1983), and research has shown that labor productivity drops during times when layoffs are perceived by the work force to be imminent (McKersie and Klein, 1983–1984). However, the perceived inconsistency in policy resulted in effects counter to those intended by AM Inc. Peters and Austin, in their recent book *A Passion for Excellence* (1985), place great emphasis on management integrity; in fact, they claim that without integrity, all their other suggestions for achieving excellence will probably backfire. We observed this quite plainly at Delta, but it remains an exceedingly difficult lesson to learn.

In sum, management integrity is on the line when widespread automation is introduced and job security is perceived to be threatened. Although these may be the most difficult times to maintain consistency in communications, they are also the most important times. Employee reactions to communications about job security will influence their reactions to all other attempts to change the company, and these communications must be consistent and realistic.

Cheerleading and Misleading. Another extremely difficult lesson concerns what it takes to build a committed and involved work force through participation programs. We were fortunate in being able to observe three of the monthly meetings intended to build involvement and improve communication among employees and also to interview four members of Delta's MRP II task force and three members of the benefits task force. These observations and interviews provide excellent evidence concerning the failure of the participation approach at Delta to build involvement, and they also suggest reasons why the approach failed.

The three "Let's Talk" meetings followed a common format: The internal department manager, the plant manager, and one of the automation area managers would spend about twenty minutes describing some of the recent and planned changes in the plant. They would then ask for questions. They were usually met with bored silence. Occasionally, a single skeptical question would surface, or one individual might complain, but we never observed a prolonged discussion involving the entire group.

The managerial style during the meetings was aptly labeled by a Delta employee as "cheerleading." Or, as another employee put it, "They treat us like children. Now, nobody likes to be treated like children. Hell, even little kids don't like to be treated like children." The chasm between the managers' forced enthusiasm and the skepticism and apathy exhibited by the work force was painful to observe. It was apparent that no attempt had been made to prepare Delta managers for the meetings by training them in group participation methods. It was also clear that there had been no attempt to structure the meetings to stimulate involvement and serious worker-manager communication.

Turning to Delta's task force approach, a key event that captured the character of the task forces was succinctly described to us by one of the MRP II task force members: "What happened is we were going to put the system in, [and] the questions came to us whether we were going to modify the software or modify our operations to fit the software. We went under the assumption that we were going to do some modifications to the software to fit our business, when in fact that wasn't what they [AM Inc.] wanted. . . . We were under the assumption we were going to try and fit it into our business where they were going under the assumption that we were just going to put it in and work with it. . . the communication wasn't there."

In short, the task force had been led to believe that it had decision-making authority when, in fact, the decision had already been made. Recall that one of the AM Inc. managers had used this very incident to illustrate the company's position on "voluntary versus forced" automation. And recall that AM Inc. seemed to have deliberately taken an ambiguous position. As one manager there said, "Yes, it's contradicting. We want participation, but you sometimes try to do it right and can't. Try it right first, anyway that works, second."

In summary, Delta failed to provide managers and workers with training in group participation methods; this again illustrated AM Inc.'s attitude that social system change could "take care of itself" as long as the correct philosophy was there. Furthermore, AM Inc. adopted a deliberately ambiguous position with respect to delegation of decision-making authority; task forces could make decisions, as long as they were the right ones. These attitudes had unambiguous results: we found that the reaction most clearly shared by employees whose jobs were protected, employees whose jobs were threatened, and those whose jobs were unaffected by the changes at Delta was their dissatisfaction with their lack of real influence in the changes (Liker, Roitman, and Roskies, forthcoming).

In their analysis of "what's wrong with the human resources approach to management," Nord and Durand (1978) noted that "executives who attempt strategies of power equalization are constantly faced with decisions that they believe . . . must be made at their level" (p. 18). This frequently results in the type of ambiguity we saw at Delta, where participation is encouraged but employees wind up feeling that the decisions have already been made. In these situations, subordinates typically consider their involvement to be "pseudoparticipation," and the increases in motivation expected by their superiors do not occur. In our experience, increased commitment to organizational goals can be achieved through participation only if managers first take the time to think through their own "boundaries" for subordinate decision making (that is, which issues can be left to the discretion of subordinates and which cannot) and then communicate these boundaries clearly. Managers must then have the patience to live with the increased time required for groups to make decisions, and they must adhere to their original boundary statements. Finally, subordinates need training in group decision making and must have access to the information needed to support decision making, in order for participation to succeed.

Training managers and workers in group participation and allowing them to debate issues before arriving at decisions, obviously requires more time than a nonparticipative approach. However, if increased commitment is sought, genuine participation has been shown to be an excellent way to achieve it and may be worth the extra time it takes (Vroom and Yetton, 1973). In short, if participation methods are used in an attempt to build commitment, participation must be genuine and clearly legitimized by top management.

Running While Changing. We have not yet found the right cartoonist to portray one of the vivid images that formed in our minds as we reflected on Delta's experience; but imagine, if you will, a runner trying to wriggle out of his sweat suit while in the midst of the most important race of his career. This notion of "running while changing" captures the feelings of frustration and stress shared with us by many employees, especially supervisors and middle managers. As one harried manager put it: "It's like, how do you know when someone's ready for suicide? You don't realize it until after it happens. Well, I hope we don't get to that point here, but some of us are sure feeling the heat." We heard from this manager, and others, specific examples of the problems resulting from trying to "get the product out the door" after the company had made dramatic cuts in supervisory and engineering staff in anticipation of productivity gains. As an illustration, consider the case of the process plan for a new product sent by engineering to the shop floor missing a key secondary operation in its routing; or the failure of the short-handed sales staff to accurately complete their paper work, resulting in scheduling delays; or moving "the best 15 percent of our machinists" to the automation project, resulting in slower setup and production runs in the soon-to-be-replaced equipment, which in turn caused the loss of some contracts.

Although these types of problems are common in cases of comprehensive and rapid change, they stood out as a major feature of Delta's organizational landscape; more importantly, there seemed to be little in the way of programmatic attempts to deal with the stress and operational failures caused by overworking employees and spreading responsibilities too thinly. Furthermore, by failing to provide adequate staffing, AM Inc. compounded the sense of skepticism, apathy, and diminished credibility we observed in a number of interviews. One manager summarized these feelings by saying, "For a while I assumed that top management knew what was coming. Lately I've started to wonder if even they know. They may be winging it and just playing it from one hit to the next. Hope not. Hope there's a long-range plan, but I've not seen any indication of one."

To make it through the marketplace "window of opportunity" before it closed, AM Inc. had set out to complete phase 1 of the automation program within ten months; instead, it took twenty-three months. In sum, successful implementation of advanced technology requires considerable debugging, not only of software but of organizational features that support the new technology. Staffing levels need to be high enough to support this uncertain and difficult activity, or the organization risks slipping further and further behind its implementation timetable.

Building a New Culture. From our very first meeting with the AM Inc. team, it was clear that their vision of the Factory of the Future genuinely involved major changes in employee beliefs and attitudes as well as changes in the hardware and software of the plant. Table 10-1 summarized these changes, and referred to new beliefs such as "workers should have advanced technical skills," " the work force will be responsible, motivated, and committed to Delta's mission," and "there will be a joint sense of 'ownership' in Delta shared by all managers and workers." Yet our reporting of the case thus far has shown that policies, procedures, and resources to support these beliefs were not put in place, nor in most cases were they planned. Although one might view this situation as simply a case of "bad management," it is important to realize that Delta was a market share leader in its major product line when it began its automation

program, and had been a leader ever since the CEO had assumed control of the company ten years prior to forming AM
Inc. The Delta managers were far from novices and had been
running an excellent manufacturing operation for some time.
However, they were relatively unprepared to deal with the scope
of culture and social system change that their vision of the
Factory of the Future implied. Their backgrounds were entirely
in engineering, marketing, and general management. Although
their vision showed their awareness of key issues involved in
transforming organizational culture, they did not have the nuts
and bolts perspective required to implement the necessary policies and procedures in the right place at the right time. Indeed,
our impression gained from reviewing the literature and from
numerous discussions and interviews with other manufacturing
managers and workers is that concentration on technical system
change and neglect of social system change is the rule rather
than the exception in plant changeovers to computer-based
manufacturing. For example, Liker and Thomas (forthcoming)
reported on the technological renovation of an automotive
engine plant. These authors found that despite the progressive
vision of management, the social system that was actually implemented closely resembled the old, traditional system.

The evidence that we have presented thus far has shown
how AM Inc. made considerable progress in destroying Delta's
traditional organizational culture but failed to make progress in
creating a new culture to support the Factory of the Future. Our
observations suggest three specific criticisms of the way AM Inc.
went about building a new culture. From the luxury of
hindsight, we can turn these criticisms into suggestions for
implementation tactics in any organizational transformation
effort:

First, the time frame for such social system changes as
functional management and networking was impossibly short
and did not allow employees or managers time to learn new
skills — skills that ranged from programming machining centers
to group decision making. Furthermore, although "education"
was an important buzz-word at Delta, there were no plans in
place to prepare people for the demands of these social system

changes. Clearly, social system changes that require learning new skills must allow people time to learn them.

Second, the "cultural" components of AM Inc.'s vision were never arrayed in a systems model so that their interrelationships could be examined and a reasonable sequence for implementation determined. For example, key motivational components (for example, compensation innovations and genuine participation in decision making) should be in place before activities that depend on increased motivation (such as functional management and networking) are promoted. Similarly, a staffing plan and outplacement program should be outlined before making drastic cuts in personnel and announcing expected impacts of new technology. We conclude that the interrelationship between social system components needs to be examined and a logical sequence should be planned before attempting to implement a complex set of social system changes.

Finally, we have already presented examples illustrating how symbolic actions such as the "ten-cent raise" and the change from "no one will lose their jobs" to "no one will hit the streets" lowered morale and trust in management. What should be stressed is the disproportionate destructive power of these symbolic events on the foundation of organizational culture. In short, organizational culture is much easier to destroy than to build. Visionaries who recognize the importance of culture in the Factory of the Future must also attach priority to the policies and procedures needed to prepare for and to support that culture.

Conclusion

In summary, we have examined the case of one company that attempted an ambitious and comprehensive set of radical changes in both its technical and social systems in order to achieve the benefits promised by the Factory of the Future within as short a period of time as possible. When we revisited the plant, we found the following results:

- Phase 1 of the automation project was completed fifteen months behind schedule.
- Delta remained highly dependent on its old machining equipment and was producing over 60 percent of its parts on these machines even though the sale of its old equipment was in the final stage of negotiation.
- Employee turnover was very high (34 percent of the employees we had interviewed were no longer at the plant sixteen months later).
- There was low morale among losers, and there were signs of low morale among winners as well.
- There were few indications of the increases in motivation and commitment that were expected to result from the social system programs.
- There was evidence of financial strain (for instance, inability to pay suppliers on time) and quality problems (due to the use of low-cost, low-quality raw materials as stock for the machining centers).
- Delta had failed to significantly diversify from its traditional product line.

In sum, the results fell far short of AM Inc.'s optimistic expectations. In this chapter, we have attempted to explain some of the reasons why their achievements did not match their expectations. These reasons were summarized in the five specific lessons of the case. All these lessons related to the "all at once" approach used by the company; by attempting to do too much too fast, Delta sacrificed work force morale and the trust of its employees and failed to achieve the benefits it expected from the CIM technology.

In closing, we return to the metaphor of our title: the type of organizational transformation associated with computer-integrated manufacturing requires the same preparation and concentration as the event of "birthing." The story of a relatively pain-free and fulfilling birth experience is not only told from the onset of labor until delivery, but it also embraces the months of preparatory exercises and support-system building that precede the birth itself. Just as this preparation eases the pain of birth by reducing uncertainty, so can the pain of implementing new technology be eased through preparations that lay the groundwork for the new culture required by the Factory of the Future. Without this preparation, the odds of achieving relatively painless implementation are exceedingly slim.

References

"America Rushes to High Technology for Growth." *Business Week*, Mar. 28, 1983, pp. 84–98.

Bolt, J. F. "Job Security: Its Time Has Come." *Harvard Business Review*, 1983, *61* (6), 115–123.

Davis, L. E. "Organizational Design." In G. Salvendy (ed.), *Handbook of Industrial Engineering*. New York: Wiley, 1982.

Duchesneau, T. D., and Dutton, J. E. "Innovation in the Footwear Industry: Characteristics of Decision Making and the Determinants of Adoption." Paper presented at annual meeting of Operations Research Society of America/The Institute of Management Sciences, Atlanta, Nov. 1977.

Ettlie, J. E. "Synchronistic Innovation." Paper presented at annual meeting of Decision Sciences Institute, Honolulu, Nov. 1986.

Ettlie, J. E., Bridges, W. P., and O'Keefe, R. D. "Organization Strategy and Structural Differences for Radical Versus Incremental Innovation." *Management Science*, 1984, *30* (6), 682–695.

Goldhar, J., and Jelinek, M. "Plan for Economies of Scope." *Harvard Business Review*, 1983, *62* (6), 141–148.

Graham, M. B. W., and Rosenthal, S. R. "Flexible Manufacturing Systems Require Flexible People." Paper presented at annual meeting of Operations Research Society of America/The Institute of Management Sciences, Atlanta, Nov. 1985.

Hage, J. *Theories of Organizations*. New York: Wiley, 1980.

Hirschhorn, L. *Beyond Mechanization*. Cambridge, Mass.: MIT Press, 1984.

Kops, L. *Toward the Factory of the Future*. New York: American Society of Mechanical Engineers, 1980.

Lawler, E. E. *High Involvement Management*. San Francisco: Jossey-Bass, 1986.

Lee, D. M. S. "Computer-Integrated Manufacturing: Technological Promises Versus Management Realities." Working Paper, no. MG-86-002. Worcester, Mass.: Department of Management, Worcester Polytechnic Institute, 1986.

Liker, J. K., Roitman, D. B., and Roskies, E. "Changing Everything All at Once: Worklife and Technological Change." *Sloan Management Review*, forthcoming.

Liker, J. K., and Thomas, R. J. "Prospects for Human Resource Development in the Context of Technological Change: Lessons from a Major Technological Renovation." In D. F. Kocaoglu (ed.), *Handbook of Technology Management*. New York: Wiley, forthcoming.

McKersie, R. B., and Klein, J. A. "Productivity: The Industrial Relations Connection." *National Productivity Review*, 1983–1984, *3* (1), 26–35.

Majchrzak, A. "Effects of Computerized Integration on Shop-Floor Human Resources and Structure." Paper presented at Autofact Conference, Society of Manufacturing Engineers, Dearborn, Mich., 1985.

Nadler, G., and Robinson, G. H. "Design of the Automated Factory: More Than Robots." *Annals of the AAPSS*, 1983, *470*, 68–80.

Nord, W. R., and Durand, D. E. "What's Wrong with the Human Resources Approach to Management?" *Organizational Dynamics*, 1978, *6* (3), 18–25.

Olson, L. "Autofact Drives Home Need for Integration." *Detroit News*, Nov. 7, 1986, p. 1E.

Pasmore, W. A., and Sherwood, J. J. *Sociotechnical Systems: A Sourcebook*. La Jolla, Calif.: University Associates, 1978.

Peters, T. J., and Austin, N. K. *A Passion for Excellence: The Leadership Difference*. New York: Random House, 1985.

Peters, T. J., and Waterman, R. H., Jr. *In Search of Excellence: Lessons from America's Best-Run Companies*. New York: Harper & Row, 1982.

Roitman, D. B., Turniansky, B., and Liker, J. K. "Organizational Development: Midwife to the Factory of the Future?" Paper presented at annual conference of Southeastern Industrial/ Organizational Psychological Association, Atlanta, Mar. 1985.

Roskies, E., Liker, J. K., and Roitman, D. B. "Winners and Losers: Employee Perceptions of Their Company's Technological Transformation." Unpublished paper, Department of Psychology, University of Montreal, 1986.

"Roundtable Participants Talk About CIM Myths and Realities, People Aspects, and the Future." *Industrial Engineering*, Jan. 1985, pp. 35–51.

Susman, G. I., and Chase, R. B. *A Sociotechnical Analysis of the Integrated Factory*. University Park: Center for the Management of Technological and Organizational Change, Pennsylvania State University, 1985.

"Technology in the Workplace." *Wall Street Journal*, Sept. 16, 1985.

Tornatzky, L. G. "Technological Change and the Structure of Work." In M. S. Pallak and R. O. Perloff (eds.), *Psychology and Work: Productivity, Change, and Employment*. Washington, D.C.: American Psychological Association, 1985.

Vroom, V. H., and Yetton, P. W. *Leadership and Decision Making*. Pittsburgh: University of Pittsburgh Press, 1973.

Winter, D. "Computer Culture Clash: CIM Dream Is Still There . . . but It's Downsized." *Wards Auto World*, Aug. 1986, pp. 42–44.

Zaltman, G., Duncan, R., and Holbek, J. *Innovations and Organizations*. New York: Wiley, 1973.

Zygmont, J. "Flexible Manufacturing Systems: Curing the Cure-All." *High Technology*, Oct. 1986, pp. 22–27.

Part Three

Strategies and Methods for Corporate Transformation

This section provides background on some of the strategies and methods developed to assist the implementation of corporate transformation. While there are no panaceas, the following chapters describe various methods that have been tested in organizational settings.

Robert R. Blake and Jane Srygley Mouton begin this section with a discussion of several approaches to organizational transformation and their implications for successful transformation. The authors discuss two major barriers to organizational transformation: the misuse of power and authority and the coercive effects of conformity. Their own approach, the Managerial Grid, is discussed and compared to other current popular change technologies. The grid approach uses the power and authority structure of the organization to encourage change while managing conformity and compliance within the organization.

Michael Finney, David E. Bowen, Christine M. Pearson, and Caren Siehl follow Blake and Mouton with a model for managing organizationwide transformation and show how this model was used in assisting the transformation of a data-processing subsidiary of a major bank. The authors suggest that transformation requires changing the systems of meaning within an organization. The transformation described was facilitated by an ongoing process of visioning, reframing, and adaptive experimentation.

The next two chapters describe specific programs that have been developed to assist corporate transformation. In Chapter Thirteen, Ralph H. Kilmann presents his five-track approach to organizational transformation. The organizational culture, management skills, team relations, strategy-structure, and reward system track are all viewed as important components of an effective organizational transformation.

Bill Veltrop and Karin Harrington follow with a discussion of a method that they have utilized in their consulting work and that they believe shows good promise for meeting the challenges of large-system change. The authors build on the work of Herb Stokes, who has developed the program over his twenty-five years of consulting experience. The approach is composed of four technologies for achieving organizationwide transformation: learning how to learn, creating shared visions, organization design, and planning and leading organizational transitions. The authors discuss how this approach has been applied and the results that might be expected from using it.

Katharine Esty describes a structural approach to transformation in Chapter Fifteen. The author defines transformation as developing within the organization the capacity to continually adapt to the changing environment and suggests that group structures are one way to achieve this goal. Esty shows how group structures can be utilized to improve communication and provide feedback to upper management, as well as to identify critical issues and implement various parts of the improvement program. She uses her experience with International Harvester (now Navistar International) to show how this participative group process builds commitment to necessary changes.

Maggie Moore and Paul Gergen conclude the section with the presentation of a technology for dealing with one of the most difficult barriers to effective transformation. The authors focus on the change anxiety and resistance to change experienced by employees, with the goal of turning these negative feelings into productive behaviors to aid the transformation. The method described helps individuals at all levels of the organization better cope with change, and does so by considering both individual and organizational forces that might impede progress. The authors suggest specific ways that change leaders can encourage risk taking throughout the organization.

These discussions of specific strategies and methods of organizationwide transformation will lead to a consideration of actual cases of transformation in the public and private sector in the final section of this volume.

Robert R. Blake

11

Jane Srygley Mouton

Comparing Strategies for Incremental and Transformational Change

There are two main strategies for increasing the likelihood that a given organization will be able to compete successfully in the current world economy. One is control driven; here, change activity is triggered by fear and threats. The other is vision led and relies on the kind of commitment that comes from understanding and insight into behavior as the motivational stimulus to effort. There is, of course, a radical difference between the two strategies.

In the first, executive management acknowledges that corporate survival is at stake and uses various pressure tactics including threats, to get the organization moving. The leader's thinking is: "It's the necessary thing to do. Why not put it on the line and let everybody know what's expected and that they'll be rewarded or punished in accordance with how much they contribute?" Training seminars and group discussions, sometimes led by business school professors, are often used to strengthen the communication of the leader's aspirations as well as to overcome resistance to change by getting managers to look at the consequences of not moving in lockstep. Survival is the stick. The carrots are financial security and advancement for those who buckle under and give their commitment. This was ITT under Geneen (Geneen, 1984). It is General Electric under Welch (Flax, 1984), Gallo Winery under Ernest and Julio Gallo (Fierman, 1986), and Simon & Schuster under Snyder (Flax, 1984).

An alternative strategy originates in radically different thinking. It is based on the assumption that the causes for resistance to change and the failure of managements to understand them explain why the survival of certain sections of American industry is now in doubt. It acknowledges that ways of managing that earn involvement and commitment were the missing elements in previous change efforts. It argues that changes must take place in the behavioral infrastructure before managers will be ready to embrace a vision for remolding the operational superstructure and working for it in a committed way.

There are, however, two major barriers to organizational transformation. One is the misuse of power and authority that either causes conflict to erupt or drives it underground. The other is the coercive effect of conformity that encourages either silence or the saluting of traditional norms that now stand in the way of needed changes.

Any approach for eliciting stronger and more effective participation in change efforts, then, is confronted with these two impediments that may prevent the required involvement and commitment from appearing. But when commitments based on understanding and insight replace fear and threat as motivations, it is possible to evoke the kind of synergistic teamwork that will produce sound, strength-giving answers to the many problems that face organizations. Once leaders at all levels understand and have "live" experiences of the dynamics of change, organizations can take actions that will enhance their chances of survival. These actions will be based on insight, understanding, and agreement, as well as on involvement, shared commitment, and the contribution of members to achieving the organizational mission. This approach to transformation has been taken by Connolly at Connecticut Bank & Trust, Benjamin Edwards III at A. G. Edwards & Sons, Sheppard

Figure 11-1. How Are Boss-Subordinate Conflicts Resolved?

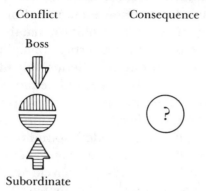

Conflict   Consequence

Boss

Subordinate

at ConAgra, Bice at Lutheran Health Systems, and Addison at the Southern Company.

Several other chapters in this volume illustrate how fear and threat are being used to induce transformation through leverage and pressure. The remainder of this chapter concentrates on the Managerial Grid approach and compares it with four other commitment approaches. The goal of this discussion is to show how power and authority can be used in less abusive ways and how norms and standards adverse to performance can be altered or bypassed in the effort to achieve organizational change.

Sound and Unsound Approaches to Direction and Control

Given that the use of power and authority is at the core of organization performance, it becomes important to dig into the differences between sound and unsound bases for exercising leadership. The questions here are, Who has the power, and how is it used as a means of influencing outcomes?

The key to understanding is provided by the handling of conflict (Blake and Mouton, 1985a). Conflict is always potentially present as a disruptive force; and, if poorly handled, it slows the wheels of progress. An illustration of the variety of unhealthy and healthy ways of handling conflict appears in boss is represented by vertical lines on the arrow pointing downward. A subordinate is represented by horizontal lines on the arrow pointing upward. The solution that the boss wants for dealing with some problem is a vertical one, that is, he thinks that the up-and-down solution is better. But the subordinate thinks that a horizontal solution would be more effective. Both vertical and horizontal solutions cannot be implemented simultaneously. One or the other or some third possibility must prevail, depending upon the leader's sound or unsound use of power and authority. In the case shown here, the boss and subordinate are at loggerheads. The circle at the right, under the word *Consequence,* conveys the notion that whatever happens, whether it is healthy or not, is predictable. But the question mark indicates that the method for resolving the conflict has not yet been worked out.

Figure 11-2. Boss Overwhelms Subordinate.

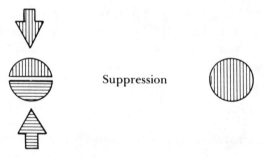

Suppression

Figure 11-3. Boss and Subordinate in Win-Lose Fighting.

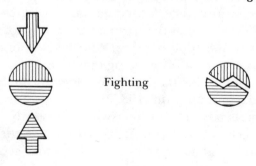

Fighting

Figure 11-4. Boss Backs Off.

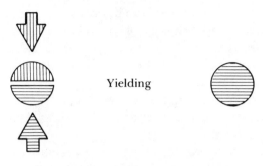

Yielding

Figure 11-5. Boss Remains Uninvolved.

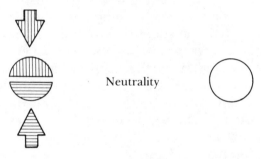

Neutrality

The boss's authority permits him or her to call the shots. When using rank to suppress disagreement (Figure 11-2), the boss in effect tells the subordinate, "I said vertical. You said horizontal. I have the final word. Vertical it is. Do it or else." This is fear and threat motivation.

While the disagreement has been settled, the subordinate is not necessarily convinced that the boss is right just because he or she was overruled. If the subordinate does not buckle under and continues to resist, a fight breaks out as shown in Figure 11-3. Both are 9,1 (win-lose) approaches to conflict, but neither suppression nor fighting is a healthy way of dealing with conflict. One causes opposition to go underground, the other causes it to break out into the open. Both have a destructive effect on the boss-subordinate relationship.

The next abuse of power and authority occurs when the

boss sells out his or her personal convictions by yielding to the subordinate's horizontal solution in order to garner the subordinate's approval and feelings of goodwill (Figure 11-4). This approach destroys effective participation because it teaches arrogant subordinates that they can mistreat the boss with impunity. If the boss does not take an active part in arriving at effective decisions, subordinates are likely to fall to fighting among themselves, which further undermines the boss's ability to exercise leadership.

A fourth solution is for the boss to remain neutral; this is the 1,1 approach (Figure 11-5). But neutrality is an even less effective strategy than yielding to a subordinate's wishes. If a subordinate sees a boss maintaining neutrality when the boss should be involved, the subordinate's reaction may be one of disgust, and he may grasp the initiative without even telling the boss what he is doing. When this happens repeatedly, the subordinate may begin to ask, Why should I go to the boss with a complex problem when neither help nor authorization is likely to be forthcoming? The boss's neutrality becomes an impediment to effective participation because the boss is no longer a link in the hierarchical chain.

Some bosses deal with conflict in a manner calculated to increase their popularity. The "reasonable" or "regular guy" solution involves a compromise; it gives the boss something of what he or she wanted in the beginning and also gives the subordinate something. This mixture of two solutions repre-

Figure 11-6. Boss and Subordinate Split the Difference.

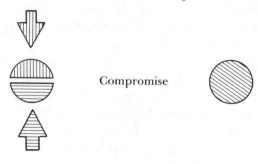

Compromise

Figure 11-7. After Open Discussion, the Subordinate Prevails.

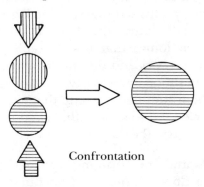

Confrontation

sented by the diagonal lines in Figure 11-6, is likely to fall between the original positions of boss and subordinate. But this 5,5-oriented approach (compromise) is one that can play havoc with effective performance if neither the boss nor the subordinate has the well-being of the organization in mind.

Now we can answer the question, How does a leader use power and authority when the aim of conflict resolution is to achieve a sound result from an organization achievement perspective, one that earns the committed support of both boss and subordinate? When power and authority are exercised in a 9,9-oriented way (win-win), the boss has no desire to prove himself right and put the subordinate in the wrong. That is not the point. The point is to find the best answer to the problem. There are three different possibilities here.

First, in listening to the horizontal point of view, the boss may find that the subordinate is on the right track and that his own thinking was wrong. Then the boss shifts, accepting the subordinate's view of the matter because the boss is convinced that it is the correct one (Figure 11-7). This is not yielding. It is the boss saying, "I am wrong. You are right. Let's go."

Second, the discussion between boss and subordinate may reveal that the horizontal point of view is limited or wrong and that it is the boss's view that should prevail, as shown in Figure 11-8.

As boss and subordinate discuss the matter, however, a

third possibility may become evident—a solution that neither had seen previously. This is represented in Figure 11-9 by a solid circle of substantially larger size than the other circles. A new solution has been found that is preferable to the positions initially held by the boss and the subordinate. Such teamwork between boss and subordinate is a two-way process. The interaction between them stimulated a state that exceeded the contribution of either or the sum of both. When that happens they have achieved synergy; the meaning of excellence in teamwork.

Sound and Unsound Approaches to Cooperation and Coordination

A second main source of resistance to change is conformity, that is, the uniformities of thought, attitudes, and actions

Figure 11-8. After Open Discussion, the Boss Prevails.

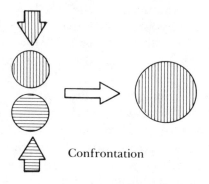

Confrontation

Figure 11-9. After Discussion, a New Solution Emerges.

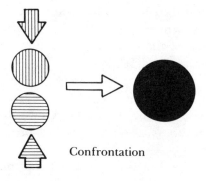

Confrontation

Figure 11-10. An Opinion in a Vacuum Means Nothing.

Figure 11-11. An Opinion That Is Different Stands Out.

that people come to embrace by virtue of membership in a group. These uniformities are referred to as norms or standards. They serve important purposes by enabling people to coordinate their activities, to anticipate and to predict what each is likely to do under given circumstances, and to indicate behavior that is objectionable or unacceptable. Norms and standards, therefore, are neither good nor bad. They are inevitable and necessary for cooperation and coordination to occur (Blake and Mouton, 1982).

How do norms emerge and begin to hold behavior in place? Start with a polka dot and let it represent someone's opinion or attitude. But, as shown in Figure 11-10, a polka dot by itself does not have much meaning. For an individual's opinion to be meaningful, it has to be put in the context of the behavior, attitudes, and thinking of others. In any organization, not only are there polka dots, but there are also solid dots, that is, people who think in another way. When there are solid dots, say four, the polka-dot attitude now takes on meaning because it is different from the solid-dot attitude. It is not a shared attitude or opinion. It stands out conspicuously, as shown in Figure 11-11.

Assume that the four people represented by solid dots think the same way about some issue of organizational life. The distance between the solid dots and the polka dot tends to increase if the polka dot is a member of the team. The solid dots draw closer together, as shown in Figure 11-12, and now feel even more like one another than they did before the polka dot appeared. The four solid dots are likely to feel threatened by the polka dot. The polka dot may represent the soundest position, but that position does not have much chance of being "bought" by the four solid dots. After a while the polka dot gets pressure

Figure 11-12. Team Members Distance Themselves from the Deviant.

Figure 11-13. The Deviant Yields to Pressures by Changing Opinion.

to fall in line and to become a solid dot. When this happens, as shown in Figure 11-13, the polka dot turns into a fifth solid dot and becomes a "reasonable" dot, one of "us."

By contrast, a polka dot that remains a polka dot is likely to be in trouble. The four solid dots begin to wall the polka dot off or squeeze him or her out. The polka dot is no longer party to needed information. He or she is "out"; freedom to participate has been sacrificed. Not pushed out physically, perhaps. The polka dot may still in some sense be a colleague of the solid dots, but the circle of membership has been redrawn as shown in Figure 11-14. The polka dot is no longer an effective, participating member of the group.

Most members of organizations prefer to be inside the circle and would rather swallow disagreements than be squeezed out. Most are ready in varying degrees to make their personal attitudes conform to those that prevail in their membership groups. The negative aspects of norms and standards come about when they produce behavior that is adverse to organizational achievement. As with power and authority, they exist throughout the infrastructure of most organizations, but since members are unlikely to appreciate how they work or where they come from, these norms and standards are under no one's deliberate control. No one is likely to know how to help people shift away from a negative or destructive norm and toward a positive norm that will benefit the organization. This is the second reason why an organizational transformation driven by fear and threats more often than not produces "no change."

Once insight into the dynamics of convergence and conformity has been gained, however, prevailing norms and stan-

Figure 11-14. The Deviant Who Maintains Independence Is Cast Out.

dards can be subjected to deliberate examination and change by those who are their carriers. Then, the hold of the past can be broken, and this powerful source of resistance to change can be replaced by norms and standards that support and reinforce enthusiasm for change.

Incremental and Transformational Change

The past five or so years have seen the emergence or reemergence of five major approaches to organization change. These five approaches share three basic premises about system-wide change. This is true, even though on the surface it appears that uniquely different objectives are being pursued in the drive toward excellence. One approach, for example, concentrates on quality, another on innovation, a third on caring for customers, a fourth on how to give a competitive edge to a company that currently lags behind others in its industry, and a fifth on safety. In each case, then, the approach focuses on some corporatewide issue that is impeding effectiveness. The entry point for change may be different, but each approach shares three underlying premises:

1. Participation throughout the organization needs to be made more effective to strengthen the commitment of organization members to solving whatever problems need to be solved.
2. While effective participation is the key to solving any problem, it cannot be mandated, that is, it cannot be brought into existence simply by demanding that people do more of "it."
3. Effective participation cannot be bought. Giving them more money does not cause organization members to work

harder or better to overcome barriers to effectiveness; something else is required.

The similarities among the five approaches stop there. The "something else" in the various approaches is what makes them distinct. Thus, we are dealing here with two approaches that are transformational in character. One of these involves strengthening theory-based process skills for diagnosing authority- and conformity-based barriers to effectiveness and for participating in problem solving throughout an organization. The other calls for changing organizational structure in a radical way. We also have three incremental approaches; they include the sociological approach, the approach that attempts to strengthen motivation through inspiration, and the approach that emphasizes top-initiated conformity-managed change.

Theory-Based Process Skills Approach. The theory-based process skills approach, rooted in social psychology, characterizes the work of McGregor (1960), Argyris (1962), Blake and Mouton (1968), Likert (1961), and subvarieties of these. This approach can be illustrated by examining a particular set of circumstances found in the cockpit of the modern airliner, which provides a prototype for decision making in the executive suite as well.

Thus, while management in one airline had repeatedly stated its commitment to safety, accident rates had remained constant. At this point in time (1979), the National Aeronautics and Space Administration reported a ten-year research project that led to the conclusion that 80 percent of fatal accidents could not be traced to the following "causes": poor air-to-ground communication, bad weather, crew members' lack of technical competence, insufficient time to discover and implement the correct solution, or equipment failure (Cooper, White, and Lauber, 1980). When these factors were eliminated, the question remained, Why do 80 percent of fatal accidents continue to occur? The further fascinating conclusion from the cockpit project was that crashes occurred even though no one had made a mistake and no one had failed to carry out his assigned activity.

In the hope of improving airline safety by finding additional causes that increased the likelihood of risks, the researchers first turned their attention to the behavioral infrastructure found in the cockpit in the modern jetliner. They began by focusing on the most experienced members of the cockpit, that is, the captains. In interviews captains were asked for their explanation of the safety problem. They reported that two factors in the behavioral infrastructure had to be addressed to decrease risk. First, they felt that "respect for captain authority" had been slowly eroding in the postwar period, particularly in the 1960s and 1970s. Captains, they argued, could no longer act with decisiveness and receive the anticipated compliance that was once characteristic of power and authority systems based on suppression of differences. Second, the captains felt that greater cockpit discipline was needed; that is, flying safety could be increased if the operation of the cockpit was conducted in conformance with the most rigorous norms and standards set forth in operation manuals, checklists, and so on. Both of these suggestions called for increasing the captain's authority through greater decisiveness and better cockpit discipline, which represented a shift in cockpit culture toward obedience norms as the basis of reinforcing the captain's authority.

Was this the correct diagnosis? One of the issues in effective transformation is, of course, valid diagnosis. Change efforts based on a faulty definition of barriers to effectiveness or strategies for removing them do not bring about valid solutions, no matter how much energy and devotion are applied. Therefore, a series of experiments to test whether this diagnosis was correct or whether something different might be involved was conducted.

A sample of thirty captains participated in the experiments. They counted off in threes. The captain whose number was "1" became the designated captain for each experiment, captain "2" was the designated first officer, and captain "3" the designated second officer. They organized themselves into crew formations and were provided certain specifications for the "leg" that they were about to fly, say, from New York to Los Angeles. All this took place in a conference room, and, therefore, the replication is of the human aspects of the situation, not of the high-tech aspects of the cockpit itself.

During the flight, a planned dilemma was created for each crew that it had had no prior opportunity to consider. In this context, a dilemma was a problem to be solved but one for which no standard solution had been established in an operations manual or elsewhere. The upshot of the experiment was that some of the crews landed safely, some limped in, and some crashed along the way.

On the completion of an experiment, members of each crew evaluated how well they had dealt with the dilemma. While some crews were satisfied with their performance, in many cases the first or second officers were resentful of the way that the designated captain had dealt with the dilemma. The designated captain's tendency was to centralize authority in himself and tell the first and second officers what to do, in the authority-obedience, compliance-premised style discussed earlier. The crew complied, but their resentment was revealed in the discussions that followed. When the captain centralized authority, he effectively shut out their input and had left needed information unexamined and elegant solutions unidentified. Time had been available for the exchange of ideas, and crew members were convinced that, had they been brought in, a better solution would have been found with less risk to life and limb.

This important finding was at odds with the interview-based conclusions. The issues were not "respect for captain authority" or "cockpit discipline." Rather, it appeared that the cockpit had to be opened to fuller participation in order to mobilize the resources that other crew members could contribute. An entirely different formulation of the problem came into view, namely, How can cockpit leadership be experienced to bring forth collaborative use of resources in the interest of safe flying? In this approach, the captain would make himself accessible to the potential contributions of colleagues and reinforce the norms of openness and candor (Blake and Mouton, 1985a).

The change that had taken place is depicted in Figure 11-15. Think of the two circles on the left as representing cock-

**Figure 11-15. Learning Experiences Shift Opinions
About Sound Leadership.**

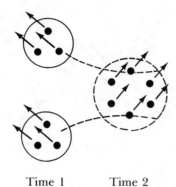

Time 1   Time 2

pits and of the arrows as indicating the way that most crew members were thinking at Time 1, prior to the learning experiments. The direction of the arrows can be referred to as ten o'clock. All captains leaving the learning experiment became committed to taking advantage of the resources of all crew members by practicing greater openness and candor; this is shown at Time 2, where the arrows point to two o'clock.

A fundamental commitment to cockpit transformation had been reached, but now a new problem arose as the captains returned to their real-life cockpits. They sought to implement 9,9 (win-win) leadership according to the conventional approach to bringing about improvement. They "intuitively" selected *modeling* as the way to promote the desired behavior. In effect, each captain said, "The way to get getter cockpit performance is for me to act differently, to open the situation up, and to let crew members experience the benefits of greater participation in cockpit problem diagnosis." What happened when captains had a new view of how to exercise power and authority and the importance of the openness and candor norm, but where first and second officers still did not, is illustrated in what follows.

When the first crisis occurred, a captain might have said, "Look, this is not routine; the instruments are giving contradic-

Figure 11-16. The Learner Returns as a Deviant to the Culture of the Old Cockpit.

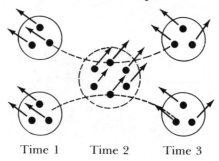

Time 1   Time 2   Time 3

tory readings. What's going on here? What do you think is the problem?" One might think that such openness would have brought forth an immediate and spirited response from other crew members, but no. In effect, crew members said to themselves, "We're in a jam and the captain doesn't know what to do! We're really in trouble!"

The explanation is shown in Figure 11-16. On returning to their cockpits at Time 3, the captains joined two other crew members who had not learned the lessons of the experiment. Ten o'clock continued to be their point of view. When the captain acted in a two o'clock way, they misinterpreted his actions, unable to understand why he was not performing in the typical ten o'clock way.

The captains came to the conclusion that they had learned a "better way" in the experiment but that it was not subject to effective implementation. They returned to greater reliance on their authority and the needed changes in cockpit operations did not occur. Figure 11-17 shows the circumstances at Time 4.

As a popular song of some years ago put it, "It Takes Two to Tango." If the partners do not know the tune and the rhythm and do not have the skills to share in the activity, they will get tangled up—but no tango.

The approach to changing the cockpit norms that was finally taken (and that appears to be successful) required several steps. One was a theory-based process learning in which all

Figure 11-17. Back in the Cockpit, Pressures to Conform
Reduce the Use of Learnings.

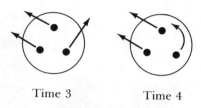

Time 3   Time 4

Figure 11-18. When All Crew Learn, the Cockpit Culture
Can Be Changed.

officers learned the Managerial Grid theory and the skills necessary to operate in a synergistic way. This was the basis for
building a new cockpit culture—not as an incremental modification of the past but as a transformation of the past, as shown in
Figure 11-18. Now all crew have commitment based on understanding and insight.

The second step for further strengthening the value system and the behavioral skills requisite to its use in flying the
Boeing 727, 737, 747, and 767 combined process learning with
team-building experiences, allowing crew members to meet
crises and to critique their skills in effectively mobilizing their
resources under simulator conditions.

Significant decreases in routine flying errors as measured
in proficiency checks have now been confirmed successively
over a three-year period (Jackson, 1983). The number of hours
flown without a hull loss has increased from 1.54, the industry
average in the five years before the intervention, to 4.7 million
hours in the five years afterwards, as shown in Figure 11-19
("Command/Leadership/Resource Management. . .," 1986).

We concentrated on the cockpit because it provides an

Figure 11-19. Cockpit Resource Management (CRM) Training Increases Damage-Free Use of Equipment.

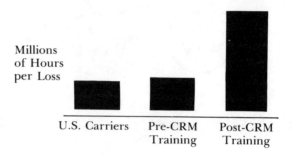

x-ray of what was actually going on in terms of the misuse of power and authority and the negative effects of conformity pressures. These principles are general, but their manifestations in specific situations are concrete and sometimes unique. The same dynamics and the same adverse impact on organization productivity have been amply demonstrated in corporate applications in smokestack and high-tech industries, in petrochemical and energy companies, and in financial institutions of various sorts, including banks, stock brokerage firms, and other financial service systems, as well as throughout the wide range of government organizations.

The learning strategies of the Grid® Seminar generate convictions based on insights into the human and dollar price paid for abuses of power and authority and blind adherence to conformity expectations. Once everyone in the organization has attended the seminar, the basis has been created for shifting the organization's infrastructure. Phase 2 Grid Team Building (Blake, Mouton, and Allen, 1987) and Phase 3 Interface Conflict Resolution (Blake and Mouton, 1984) complete the reformation of the infrastructure and set up the conditions for rebuilding the superstructure, which can now be done through commitment based on understanding and insight. Phase 4 provides a strategy for redesigning the business logic on which the firm has operated. Phases 5 and 6 are concerned with implementation and consolidation of this redesign.

This strategy should be contrasted with the strategies that

rely on fear and threats. Thus, seeking to shift business logic while ignoring the infrastructure brings about a need for leverage and pressure to overcome the resistance to change embedded in the infrastructure. Various chapters in the present volume discuss the long time horizons needed for bringing about change under the fear and threat model; it may be a question of six, eight, even ten years. Given organizations of the same size, we estimate that when the behavioral infrastructure is initially concentrated upon, the time scale for comparable change is two to three years.

Structure Without Hierarchy. This strategy is based on entirely different assumptions about how to bring about transformation, but it too centers on changing the power and authority structure and related norms and standards. It can be illustrated by reference to the Saturn project, General Motors' revolutionary approach to making automobiles (Fisher, 1985). This project was stimulated by the recognition that current manufacturing methods simply do not work effectively in a highly competitive global environment—a recognition that is essential if American companies are to stay in the business of making small or compact automobiles.

General Motors appointed a committee to study the problem and recommend a solution. After a worldwide comparative study, the solutions agreed upon included the following: remove power and authority by removing bosses; put operational decision making in the hands of the working team; create conditions that compel shared cooperation. This solution was designed to create a "new" organization and to populate it in a new way. It involves the elimination of all hierarchies.

An illustration of how the Saturn plant is supposed to perform is provided in Figure 11-20. The larger circles shown at the bottom are two of many work teams. The smaller six circles at the top represent technical specialists, such as marketing, personnel, and engineering specialists. Two arrows connect the work team on the left, one to the first hovering circle and another to the fourth hovering circle. In the middle of the dotted arrows is a small circle that represents liaison personnel who are

Figure 11-20. How Power and Authority Are Removed from a Hierarchy.

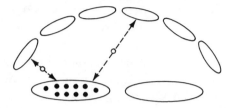

Figure 11-21. How Conformity Affects Team Member Selection.

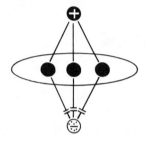

members of neither level and who lack power and authority to compel one level to do what the other level thinks it should be doing. The liaison person's effectiveness is determined primarily by his or her skill in representing one activity level to another and vice versa. This solution connects levels while eliminating hierarchical power and authority as the basis for direction and coordination.

Another characteristic is that teams select, retain, or terminate their own members. This is shown in Figure 11-21, which depicts a three-member work team. The possibility of adding a fourth member to the team is under review by the three current members, who look with favor upon one candidate (the plus in the upper circle) and with disfavor on another (the minus in the bottom circle). The candidates will be accepted or rejected as team members on the basis of a consensus decision by the three current members.

Two aspects become evident when colleague selection is evaluated from the standpoint of norms and standards of conformity. One is that acceptance or rejection of a candidate by existing team members involves the extent to which he or she "speaks their language," that is, seems to be like one of them, as in the case of the solid dot with the (+) embedded within it. In contrast, the potential new member represented by the polka dot at the bottom of the figure is likely to be seen as different from the current team members and as less capable of fitting in. Such a person will probably be looked upon as an undesirable team member.

The Saturn project at General Motors provides a unique illustration of organization transformation. It is not driven by fear and threat. Nor does it rely on leverage and pressure or on understanding and insight. It simply eliminates the power and authority problem under the presumption that involvement, commitment, and teamwork will fill the vacuum created by the absence of hierarchy. It is a structural solution that seeks to redesign the behavioral infrastructure by eliminating the concept of "boss." The solution shifts the character of relationships, but as of now it offers organization members no increased understanding of how to solve conflicts and control norms, which is the prerequisite in the theory-based process approach illustrated earlier.

The Sociological Approach. Most organizations build up hierarchies to handle repetitive activities, with jobs assigned and segmented into authority levels (workers, supervisors, managers, and executives). The sociological solution is to maintain classical hierarchical power and authority and use it for what it is said to do best, but then to create new power and authority structures in order to stimulate creativity and innovation. In other words, structures are added through which out-of-the-ordinary possibilities can be discovered and implemented.

In the sociological approach of Kanter (1983), these arrangements of minimum assigned power and authority are called parallel structures. But they are also known as temporary systems, collateral systems, entrepreneurial teams, "skunk works," and so on. Supporters of this approach include Miles (1964), Zand (1974), Wiesbord, Lamb, and Drexler (1974), Bennis and Slater (1968), and Pinchot (1985).

In the parallel organization the word of the person of highest rank is of no greater importance than anyone else's. Therefore, in this "open" system, people are expected to think freely and do not have to double-guess the boss, play politics, and so on. An example of a parallel organization is the functional cross-category team made up of people from different departments, divisions, or activities. The matrix organization concept may also be brought into use. This use of a parallel system encourages people to come forth with good ideas that they may have been unwilling to voice because of fear of adverse reactions by persons in positions of power and authority or because the ideas challenged existing norms and standards.

As Kanter (1983) describes it, "The idea behind having a second or parallel organization alongside routine operations only makes explicit what is already implicit in an integrative, innovating company: the capacity to work together cooperatively regardless of the field or level, to tackle the unknown, the uncertain. In a formal, explicit, parallel organization, this is not left to happenstance, but is guided—managed—to get the best results from both the company and the people" (p. 359).

But what, according to this model, can be done to stimulate needed innovation beyond adding nonhierarchical parallel structures? The model argues that the place to start is with individuals. Case studies have tracked actual innovations from their inception to implementation. Common behavioral elements present in different innovations were identified and organized in a sequential way so as to clarify all the steps from beginning to end.

Kanter outlines a three-part sequence to escape unrecognized conformity pressures from the inception of an innovation to its eventual acceptance and implementation, starting with problem definition. This process provides individuals with suggestions for how they can become more competent in developing and bringing a new idea into use. The goals are to help people gain appreciation as to where new ideas come from, to test each possibility for its salability, to develop coalitions of support, to stimulate cheerleaders who can bring attention to good ideas, and then to gain support higher in the organization in order to protect, defend, and carry out innovations that have begun to flourish.

The Kanter version of the sociological approach is premised on making incremental changes rather than on transforming the organization from what it was into something different and more viable, as in the theory-based or Saturn approaches. It identifies the abuse of power and authority as one of the problems that prevent organization members from being creative, but it also recognizes the adverse effects of pressures to conform. This approach accepts the behavioral infrastructure as it is and seeks to diminish its harmful effects by creating bypass mechanisms, thus obviating the need for organizational transformation.

Motivational Approach. A different solution relies on appealing for change within the system that currently exists (Peters and Waterman, 1982; Peters and Austin, 1985). The assumption is that "turned off" people are the key problem and that the solution is to motivate them to greater effort. These "new" motivations are more than conventional ways of rewarding performance such as salary increases and promotions. They are different from the individual incentives associated with suggestion boxes and other forms of inviting members to contribute their ideas.

"Passion for excellence" is the code phrase. The term *passion* here refers to a highly motivated state of "being" in behalf of the corporation. It implies far more involvement and commitment than such phrases as "doing your job," "a fair day's work for a fair day's pay," or "keeping your nose clean," which are the conventional conformity norms in most organizations.

As part of the change process, the executive may place his or her "desk" in the middle of the action. Such notions as "management by walking around" are used to break down formal barriers, to increase communication across and between hierarchical levels, and to provide models of conduct and passionate concern for the corporation that others are expected to emulate. The executive is encouraged to pay attention to symbols, drama, and vision, and to coach subordinates as well as to provide strong leadership. Recognition and celebration of success are expected to arouse feelings of acceptance, involvement, and inclusion. These in turn lead to expansion of confidence, heightened self-esteem, increased performance, creativity, and so on.

How is this done? Desired aspects of performance are identified and made the targets for recognition, praise, and celebration. For example, if improved customer service is the goal, people are encouraged to get to know and cherish their customers by advancing the notion that they should be fanatical about providing customer service. Outstanding service contributions are acknowledged by creating heroes at all levels through rewards, plaques, banquets, and cheerleading, as well as through trips to vacation spots where chosen members celebrate and share with one another their common achievements.

Greater creativity is encouraged. Even "cheating," that is, going behind the backs of naysayers in authority to get needed clearances and materials, is condoned. The existence of "skunk works" encourages entrepreneurial activity through aggressive selling of ideas within the organization; talented people are freed from the demands of paper work; and creative "different drummer" types who may have innovative solutions in mind are cultivated.

Peters and Austin reject fear and threats, leverage and pressure as viable solutions for bringing the wanted degree of passion into being, but they also reject the notion that understanding and insight into the dynamics embedded within the behavioral infrastructure are necessary preconditions of change. Thus the problem of diffusion is solved by accepting the "as is" behavioral infrastructure and stimulating those parts of it that are most ready to be "turned on" first. Others in the middle are then expected to model the behavior of the champions, and conformity pressures build to move the rest of the organization toward a more passionate concern for corporate performance.

This diffusion model, shown in Figure 11-22, is read from right to left. On the extreme right are the "crazies," the polka dots who are thoroughgoing nonconformists. They are known as oddballs and cannot be used as models. Next to them, how-

Figure 11-22. One Diffusion Model for Change.

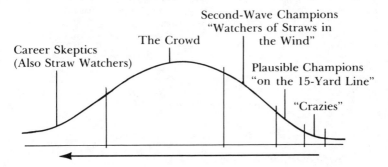

ever, are the "plausible champions," those to whom a nudge is sufficient to cause better performance. When this occurs, it is quickly celebrated both to reinforce the likelihood of continuation and to signal to the rest of the organization that not only is change expected but it will be rewarded. Coming next are those who "watch for straws in the wind." They are followed by "the crowd," those who make up the conformity-driven center. Once they become aware that their conventional behavior is outmoded, they will jump on the bandwagon so as to enjoy their share of success.

This model emphasizes the stimulation of desired behavior and acknowledgment of it when it is successful by the "leaders" or champions of change. Dollars may follow, but what is really needed is executive-level modeling with encouragement, praise, and celebration institutionalized as part and parcel of a process that filters down through the organization and becomes the new corporate culture for those who conform to it.

Top-Initiated, Conformity-Managed Change. The Crosby (1979, 1984) approach is a rational model for bringing about incremental change. The focus is the resolution of quality difficulties that might be impediments to success. "Perfect" quality cannot be brought about by fear or threats nor can it be bought by dollars. Rather, quality will appear only if people become committed to producing it. Change comes by establishing fac-

Figure 11-23. Another Diffusion Model.

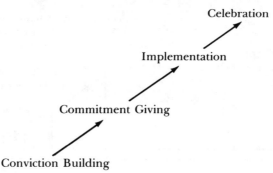

tual evidence of the existence of a solvable problem and developing widespread commitment to implementing the solution with constant follow-up to ensure renewed commitment.

Fourteen steps are required to travel down the quality corridor from error-prone to zero-defect operations. These steps can be consolidated into four phases, as shown in Figure 11-23, starting at the bottom and proceeding to the top. At the bottom of the sequence is conviction building, that is, convincing people that poor quality is a problem that should be solved because of the expense in terms of reduced competitiveness from failure to solve it. Quality is an attitude problem, and therefore the whole organization has to be convinced of the necessity of achieving it.

Conviction building is steered by a quality staff with the point of entry being policy-level executive management. It is top management that has to develop quality-centered convictions and put these convictions on the line, and it may have to be willing to tolerate lowered productivity for the time being. The process starts with a policy statement from the top that says error-free performance or zero defects are the goal for the organization. Once this policy is in place, data are gathered to provide evidence concerning the actual quality situation and the costs associated with poor quality. Skill training is then provided in the use of quality control techniques. Power and authority at the top are used to reinforce an attitude of compliance as the message is pushed down through the organization that inferior quality no longer is acceptable.

The second phase includes energizing people to make the operational effort that can turn conviction into actuality. It is not just the top or the bottom but the entire organization that has to make a commitment to a new quality standard. To do this, the organization may sponsor a "commitment day" when management affirms its support of the change effort and everyone is asked to give his or her public commitment to achieving zero defects. This is a strategy for making explicit a new norm and building conformity pressures to support its acceptance.

The third phase is implementation. Plans for implementation are also developed across the organization but made specific to the character of the distinctive quality problems within each organization component. Identifying and removing the causes of errors come next. Employees describe on a form any problem that prevents them from performing error-free work.

Celebration of success to give people recognition for changed behavior is the fourth phase. Those who are to be recognized for quality achievement are picked by their coworkers. Next comes the actual celebration of the accomplishments of those who have been chosen. This is done by giving awards at companywide events. This step of celebrating quality seals the commitment of those who are recognized to the new quality norm and stimulates others to emulate them.

Quality problems solved by the Crosby approach are not considered solved once and for all. After these four phases have been completed, the sequence starts over again and becomes an annual program of rededication to accomplishment. This approach utilizes the power and authority within the existing structure for focusing attention on a problem to be solved. Conformity dynamics are basic to the approach, as revealed in the public commitment aspect, but no explicit effort is made to aid organization members to understand how conformity dynamics arise, how they become resistant to change, and how they can be shifted as a result of understanding and insight. Crosby's is a prescriptive approach in which key organization members learn how to use authority and pressure tactics to support quality achievement.

Which Way to Go?

These five major approaches to organization change identify interesting possibilities for bringing widespread participation into use as an organization style. The question is, Which one or what combination of these approaches offers the greatest promise of success for any corporation that wishes to strengthen its effectiveness?

Two of the approaches, the structural approach exemplified by the Saturn project and the sociological approach, share much in common but have different goals. The Saturn solution literally wipes out authority as it is normally found in corporations and seeks to replace it with mechanisms that compel the reaching of consensus by those responsible for the design and implementation of work. By comparison, the Kanter version (the sociological approach) seeks to retain power and authority for decision making and implementation of routine work. To encourage innovation, this approach does not attempt to eliminate all authority but rather to diminish reliance on power and authority by adding mechanisms that encourage creative efforts.

Both approaches identify power and authority as the critical factors that have an adverse impact on productivity. The solution to the authority problem in both cases is to manipulate the organization structure in order to skirt the authority problem. Both are "external" solutions to the problem because they do not deal with the behavioral infrastructure on the basis of understanding and insight. They are external because the "natural" but unexamined inclinations of managers to exercise control over others remain intact. No opportunity is provided for managers to gain insight into how their actions limit the participation of others and therefore hamper their involvement, commitment, and readiness to perform and innovate.

The motivational approach found in Peters and Waterman (1982) and Peters and Austin (1985) seeks the same objectives as are central to Crosby's conformity approach and the sociological approach. The existing infrastructure is retained, but direct appeal is made to organization members by pleading the case for excellence and seeking to spread acts of excellence by acknowledging and celebrating them once they occur.

The Crosby approach makes use of power and authority, as well as conformity pressures, to motivate the actions required to solve quality problems. Working with the top first to gain shared convictions puts organizers in a position to lead the quality-solving effort. The mechanics of how to proceed are relatively simple once the effort is organized for implementation.

Shared responsibility brought about by public expression of readiness to eliminate quality problems creates a new pattern of conformity, but now the conformity is in line with organization-centered desires. Because insight is not gained into the way conformity dynamics shape behavior, social pressures are created to get members to do the "right" thing. As with Kanter's and Peters and Waterman's tactics, the Crosby approach is also an external kind that accepts the behavioral infrastructure and seeks to bring about change within its prevailing constraints.

The approach presented in this chapter identifies the existing behavioral infrastructure as the "cause" of operational deficiencies in the business logic superstructure. In order to solve the superstructure problems, whether they be profitability, quality, caring for customers, creativity, innovation, safety, and so on, it is necessary first to eliminate the behavioral infrastructure abuses of power and authority found in the behavioral infrastructure and to become aware of the silent pressures of conformity and compliance. These are learned on a self-convincing basis. Two additional phases are necessary to shift the behavioral infrastructure to a sounder basis. Then further steps can be taken for changing the operational superstructure to strengthen competitive advantages.

The importance of these five approaches is that all of them provide alternatives that avoid the disruptive effects inherent in the use of fear and threat and pressure and leverage to force an organization to perform more competitively. Two do so through transforming the behavioral infrastructure in order to grapple more effectively with the business superstructure. Three take the behavioral infrastructure as given and seek to build upon it.

Fear and threat certainly are important motivators, but understanding and insight are potentially even better ones. In our view, to bypass the dynamics embedded within the behavioral infrastructure is to risk that the changes achieved will not be deep and enduring ones.

References

Argyris, C. *Interpersonal Competence and Organizational Effectiveness.* Homewood, Ill.: Dow Jones-Irwin, 1962.

Bennis, W. G., and Slater, P. E. *The Temporary Society.* New York: Harper & Row, 1968.

Blake, R. R., and Mouton, J. S. *Corporate Excellence Through Grid Organization Development.* Houston: Gulf, 1968.

Blake, R. R., and Mouton, J. S. *Productivity: The Human Side.* New York: American Management Association, 1982.

Blake, R. R., and Mouton, J. S. *Solving Costly Organizational Conflicts: Achieving Intergroup Trust, Cooperation, and Teamwork.* San Francisco: Jossey-Bass, 1984.

Blake, R. R., and Mouton, J. S. "Effective Crisis Management." *New Management,* 1985a, *3* (1), 14–17.

Blake, R. R., and Mouton, J. S. *The Managerial Grid III: The Key to Leadership Excellence.* (3rd ed.) Houston: Gulf, 1985b.

Blake, R. R., Mouton, J. S., and Allen, R. L. *Spectacular Teamwork.* New York: Wiley, 1987.

"Command/Leadership/Resource Management: A Joint Effort." *The Cockpit,* Mar.–Apr. 1986, p. 3.

Cooper, G. E., White, M. D., and Lauber, J. K. (eds.) *Resource Management on the Flight Deck.* Moffett Field, Calif.: National Aeronautics and Space Administration, 1980.

Crosby, P. B. *Quality Is Free: The Art of Making Quality Certain.* New York: McGraw-Hill, 1979.

Crosby, P. B. *Quality Without Tears.* New York: McGraw-Hill, 1984.

Fierman, J. "How Gallo Crushes the Competition." *Fortune*, Sept. 1, 1986, pp. 24–31.

Fisher, A. B. "Beyond the Hype at GM's Saturn." *Fortune*, Nov. 11, 1985, pp. 34–36, 40, 44–46.

Flax, S. "The Ten Toughest Bosses in America." *Fortune*, Aug. 6, 1984, pp. 18–23.

Geneen, H. *Managing*. New York: Doubleday, 1984.

Jackson, D. "United Airlines' Cockpit Resource Management Training." *Proceedings of the 2nd Symposium on Aviation Psychology*. Columbus, Ohio, Apr. 1983.

Kanter, R. M. *The Change Masters: Innovation for Productivity in the American Corporation*. New York: Simon & Schuster, 1983.

Likert, R. *New Patterns of Management*. New York: McGraw-Hill, 1961.

McGregor, D. *The Human Side of Enterprise*. New York: McGraw-Hill, 1960.

Miles, M. B. *Innovation in Education*. New York: Columbia University Press, 1964.

Peters, T. J., and Austin, N. K. *A Passion for Excellence: The Leadership Difference*. New York: Random House, 1985.

Peters, T. J., and Waterman, R. H., Jr. *In Search of Excellence: Lessons from America's Best-Run Companies*. New York: Harper & Row, 1982.

Pinchot, G. III. *Intrapreneuring*. New York: Harper & Row, 1985.

Weisbord, M. R., Lamb, H., and Drexler, A. *Improving Police Department Management Through Problem-Solving Task Forces: A Case Study in Organization Development*. Reading, Mass.: Addison-Wesley, 1974.

Zand, D. E. "Collateral Organization: A New Change Strategy." *Journal of Applied Behavioral Science*, 1974, *10* (1), 63–89.

Michael Finney
David E. Bowen
Christine M. Pearson
Caren Siehl

12

Designing Blueprints for Organizationwide Transformation

Michael Brougham recently described an in-progress organizationwide transformation to the 400 employees of the Electronic Technology Center of First National Services Company, of which he is president and CEO as follows: "Can you imagine repairing an engine in a 747, 30,000 feet off the ground, moving at 700 miles per hour? Well, the change we're undertaking is not a whole lot different. While we're adjusting the nuts and bolts of our operation, we must meet our customers' needs uninterrupted—our company must stay in the air." (Electronic Technology Center and First National Services Company are pseudonyms.) The transformation project and the model used for organizing the transformation are the focuses of this chapter. The model proposes that the organization of the change effort should be a working blueprint of how the organization itself will appear following its transformation. That is, design choices about which constituencies are to be empowered during the transformation effort and what kind of internal and external structures are to support those choices should model the organizational dynamics that are expected to be in place after the transformation. Further, it is proposed that enduring transformation occurs only when a change effort succeeds in changing a company's systems of meaning.

Enacting Transformation Through the Change of Meaning

There can be no denying the difficulty of organization-wide transformation (Kilmann, 1984; Tichy, 1983). As adjustments and alterations are made to various parts of the organization, day-to-day operations and performance must be maintained with minimal interruption. To further complicate the change process, it is not enough to alter the way things are done or the structure under which they are accomplished. To achieve long-term, sustained change, the meaning or beliefs held within the organization must also be changed.

The patterns of meaning that develop within an organization perpetuate behavior within that system; conversely, organizational meaning or belief is reinforced by interactive relations or behaviors carried on throughout the system. In order to bring about enduring organizationwide change, therefore, meaning must be transformed throughout the system. As meaning affects practice, so in turn practice affects meaning. A change in one will in some way transform the other.

In Figure 12-1, we offer a model for enacting organizationwide transformation. It identifies the mission, diagnostic and prescriptive strategies, and structures necessary to support organizationwide transformation. The model embodies the two principal assumptions that we hold regarding such transformations. First, organizationwide transformation requires changing the systems of meaning within a company through an ongoing process of visioning, reframing, and adaptive experimentation; and, second, the structures used to guide the change effort strongly shape the meanings and practices that emerge later in the effort. These structures can represent the organization's first attempts at "practicing" the meanings that, it is hoped, will endure in the organization. Decisions made about which constituencies are really "in or out" as empowered players in the change effort and the organization of these players reinforce the desired meaning changes.

Figure 12-1. Transformation Model.

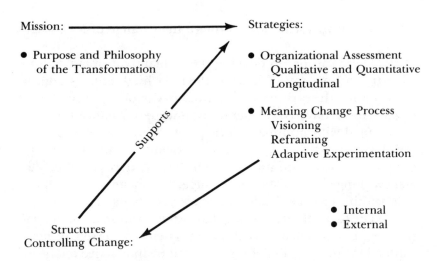

The model in Figure 12-1 presents a view of organization-wide transformation as a set of mission-driven strategies supported by enacting structures. The mission of the transformation effort reported here is to change the values guiding the way work is done in the transforming organization.

The strategies designed to accomplish the mission involve an assessment process that identifies the present belief systems of employees and the impact (positive and negative) of these systems on the way work is done in the company. A second strategic thrust centers on a three-stage meaning change process. The initial stage, visioning, is concerned with identifying the ideal characteristics and values that the company wants to espouse *and* enact in the future. The second stage, reframing, focuses on identifying the best means of changing meaning from that assessed as "present" to that identified as "ideal." Finally, adaptive experimentation is concerned with the implementation, monitoring, evaluation, and (where necessary) redesign of reframing activity.

The strategies described above are enacted jointly by internal structures—here, management and employee groups—and by external temporary structure—the consulting/research team. The multiple structures controlling the transformation process presented here offer an alternative to single-structure change models such as top-down or bottom-up models. The express purpose of the multiple structures is to *control and direct* change.

In what follows, we will describe the application of each section of this model to an actual case of organizationwide transformation.

The Electronic Technology Center (ETC)

First National Services Company (FNSC) is a sophisticated data-processing subsidiary of a major American bank. ETC, where the organizationwide transformation described in this chapter is taking place, is the largest of the eight geographically dispersed centers that constitute FNSC. Whereas FNSC could be described as the nervous system that provides on-line computer support to regional banks, ETC could be termed the high-tech "brains" of that nervous system. It is the central repository of technical knowledge, services design, hardware, and software for FNSC. ETC has approximately 400 employees, the majority of whom are young computer technology professionals; it is located in southern California.

Although ETC performance exceeded corporate requirements at the initiation of the project, the personal, social, and professional cost of performance within the ETC environment was of great concern to Brougham and to Don Schmidt (executive vice-president in charge of ETC). These organizational leaders shared the philosophy that employees were the most valuable resource of any business, and they felt that employees at ETC were beginning to show signs of stress, resentment, and occupational burnout.

An exploratory investigation at ETC validated the concerns of Brougham and Schmidt. Three underlying belief systems that seemed to be contributing to employee dissatisfaction were identified: the emphasis on information hoarding, inter-departmental favoritism, and "pure magic" as the means of task accomplishment. Regarding the first belief, although ETC is the information node for the FNSC network, the standard practice within ETC was to withhold information from those who were outside one's own departmental boundary. Possession of exclusive information was believed to be a valuable resource and, consequently, a source of power for the holder. Divulgence of that information to the wrong source or at the wrong time could turn it, in the words of one ETC employee, into a "club" with which the one who gave out the information could later be "beaten up."

In reference to the second belief, there was a strong sentiment among ETC employees that several departments received preferential treatment. The members of these departments were seen as receiving more than their fair share of resources and "strokes," often when their supposed accomplishments had been in fact furthered and supported by members of other departments. Employees at ETC begrudgingly referred to these groups as the "prima donnas" of the company. In addition, employees in each of the departments believed that their group was "better than" groups in other departments. This attitude led to negative evaluative statements about the quality of work done in other departments. This evaluation behavior was designed to make "us" look good and "them" look bad. The result was considerable defensiveness in interactions and communication between departments.

The third belief system that permeated the ETC organization was task accomplishment by "pure magic." Data collected during the exploratory investigation indicated that employees believed that work was getting done in spite of management and organizational policies and practices; in their words, it was almost as if the company's high performance levels were reached by legerdemain. Employees believed that their efforts and achievements received little or no structural support. Morale was low, and many employees expressed general dissatisfaction with the environment at ETC.

Given this initial feedback about the meaning systems at

ETC, Brougham and Schmidt decided to initiate an organizationwide change effort. But first they had to consider the mission for organizationwide transformation.

In our model, the change effort mission deals with why change is believed to be necessary and the overarching philosophy that should drive the change. At the outset of the effort, Schmidt stated that the mission of the change effort should be to improve the working environment at ETC or, in employees' terms, to "make ETC a better place to work." Schmidt later in the effort expressed this mission rather eloquently in a newsletter to ETC employees: "Our concern in this change effort is not with *what* we accomplish but rather *how* we accomplish it. In terms of what we accomplish, conventional measures such as profitability and growth indicate we are succeeding admirably. However, we can still improve a great deal on *how* we get there . . . how we deal with one another, how we exhibit certain values that we would like to have define our company."

Schmidt was defining a broad mission for the change effort, but he was clear about his intentions. In essence, we, as members of the consulting team, were being asked to assist the organization in instituting what has been called *normative-reeducative* change (Chin and Benne, 1976). This type of change centers on the normative structures and role definitions that comprise the culture of a given setting. The emphasis is on reeducating members, with the goal of collaboratively enhancing knowledge and changing accepted norms.

Schmidt and ETC were not interested in a quick fix; they were interested in fundamental changes in "how we do things around here." It was a situation that offered the consultants the rarest of opportunities—a setting in which to try to achieve organizationwide transformation, through meaning change, with the express support of the company's CEO.

Assessing the Organization

Innovative strategies for diagnosis are required for organizationwide transformation of meaning. Given the complexity and subtleties of shared organizational meaning, it must be

Figure 12-2. Assessment Process.

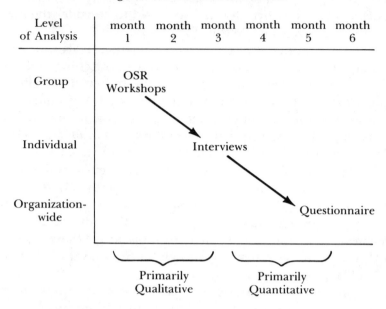

assessed by using multiple sources and methods at multiple points in time. For purposes of diagnosis, the consulting team designed an assessment model (Figure 12-2) that used qualitative and quantitative methods to gather information over time. They deliberately selected this approach rather than an intensive short-term data-gathering technique. Because the team collected data over the longer term, the themes about the systems of meaning that gradually emerged could more accurately serve as a basis for transformation activities (Kirk and Miller, 1985). The longer data-gathering period also made it possible to create a state of "readiness" for change throughout the organization. That is, the prolonged period of assessment helped raise organizational awareness that a change effort was underway. Data collection spanned a six-month period, as represented in Figure 12-2.

During the first two months of the assessment phase, data about meaning systems were collected from the representative groups of employees by using the organizational self-reflection workshop methodology (Finney, 1985; Finney and Mitroff, 1986). Organizational self-reflection workshops (OSRs) are designed to unearth consensually held belief systems. In using the term *consensual*, we mean that there is a reasonable amount of implicit agreement among organizational members as to the meaning of the information or events. OSRs are assumption-surfacing exercises that help groups identify the consensual belief systems guiding their behavior in their respective company environments.

Assumptions here are explicit and implicit beliefs about stakeholder groups (that is, "management" generically, employees, middle managers, customers, and so on). Assumptions are also held about the way work should be done. These guide the "way things are done around here" and serve as blueprints for practice—they are the meanings that drive practice in the organization and should be the focus of change efforts.

The OSRs provide an arena in which organization members "self-reflect" on the way they work as well as on why they work that way. The process involves the identification of stakeholder assumptions, behaviors guided by the assumptions, and an opportunity to test the usefulness and validity of the surfaced assumptions (Finney and Mitroff, 1986). For example, top management at FNSC considered itself a significant organizational stakeholder. During their OSR workshop, these executives brought to the surface consensual assumptions that they held about themselves. They believed that they would be rewarded on the basis of individual performance rather than on that of unified group performance. They considered themselves competent individuals who were competing for scarce rewards (praise from the CEO, raises, promotions). They also held the assumption that each of them individually had their own "fires to fight" and did not have the time or motivation to help others with their fires. This set of interacting assumptions proved to be counterproductive in that trust, respect, and unity (espoused values) were next to impossible to practice. This competitive spirit and individual fire fighting by top managers were modeled by each hierarchy of management down through the company.

The OSR workshops were conducted with the top management group of ETC, a representative mid-level group that consisted of professional employees and middle managers, and two groups of front-line employees. The total sample size represented approximately 10 percent of the ETC population. The results of the workshops were content analyzed to identify belief systems common across all groups. The belief systems that emerged then provided the framework for follow-up interviews.

Individual interviews were conducted by members of the consultant team with fifty employees. These employees represented more than 10 percent of the population of ETC. The interview sample was representative across hierarchies and functions. The agenda of questions consisted of items related to the belief systems that emerged during the OSR workshops. The interviews were semistructured to facilitate further exploration of identified beliefs while at the same time allowing for considerable flexibility of discussion topics. Interview data were then compiled and content analyzed. The issues and belief systems thus identified were next addressed by a questionnaire administered to the entire organization.

The questionnaire measured employee perceptions regarding the work environment, managerial competencies, the attitudes and approaches to the provision of customer service, and the usefulness of structural control mechanisms such as regulations and procedures. In addition, respondents were asked to evaluate the reward system and to assess whether or not a managerially advocated value set was actually practiced by various hierarchical groups. The questionnaire was composed both of closed-end questions (organized as Likert scales) and of sections that allowed for open-ended comments about each topic area. Eighty-nine percent of the total ETC population responded to the closed-end questions; the response rate for the open-ended sections was nearly 45 percent.

Analysis of the data from the organizational self-reflection workshops, the individual interviews, and the questionnaire revealed that several sets of beliefs dominate the work environment at ETC. First, a lack of respect and trust between management and employees was revealed. Management had a bad reputation and low credibility among ETC employees. Conversely, managerial patterns of behavior did not involve much sharing of responsibility with subordinates or any other indications of a high level of trust for employees. Managers tended to overcontrol work activity out of a fear of failure. It was believed that survival in the organization was dependent on managing an image, and this meant that managers hoarded the glory for the successes of their respective work groups and shared the blame — loudly — for their work groups' failures. Such attitudes and behavior contributed to a belief system based on a lack of respect and trust between employees and management.

The second set of beliefs that emerged centered on political behavior. Employees believed that the formal system was very weak and that the informal system was extremely strong. They thought that tasks could best be accomplished and problems solved by working informally with their peers. At the same time, they expended considerable effort circumventing formal structures and policies, which they believed only made the problems worse.

Employees did not believe that the formal hierarchical system of authority held significant meaning. Entrenched patterns for resisting managerial decisions existed. One subtle form of sabotage that employees used to thwart management decisions and activities involved *doing nothing*. Employees would simply delay or not act, and then blame employees in other functional areas for the ensuing rush to meet deadlines and for project failures. High management turnover and a poorly operationalized performance appraisal system helped create a system of beliefs that made this form of sabotage a fairly safe activity. One of the common sayings in the organization was, "If you don't like who you're working for now, just wait six months and you'll have a new boss."

Finally, a set of beliefs had evolved around the firefighting, "fix-it" mentality at ETC. For example, employees believed that they would not be rewarded for providing good customer service initially and thus preventing service delivery problems from arising, but rather for *fixing* problems that they had previously caused. In other words, doing your job right the first time was not as highly valued as doing it wrong and then being able to fix the resultant problems.

A second example of this same mentality involves the beliefs of middle managers about their work environment. Middle managers reported that they worked under high-pressure conditions most of the time. They believed that their jobs were "on the line" daily. The way they talked about their jobs was particularly revealing. The use of combat metaphors was pervasive. Middle managers described being issued "bulletproof vests" during their orientation; they described the importance of "dodging bullets" and the necessity of being a "fast healer if you took a direct hit." The metaphor created by one group of middle managers described the overall environment at ETC as that of "a rudderless battleship with a hole in one side."

In sum, the assessment process helped to uncover the meanings and beliefs that guided practice at ETC as well as the practices that reinforced the systems of belief. The assessment process helped define "how things are done around here." The meaning and belief systems present a picture of an organization characterized by low managerial credibility, weak formal control systems, a powerful political system, and established patterns for resisting managerial decisions.

Structures for Managing Organizationwide Transformation

As discussed above, the control structures used to guide a change effort must be designed to support and enact the strategies indicated in our transformational model. These structures can come to represent the organization's first attempts at practicing the meaning changes that will, it is hoped, endure in the organization. Decisions about what constituencies are "in or out" as empowered players in the change effort are critical. Most importantly, the control structures strongly shape, model, and mirror the meanings and practices that are the core products of the transformation process.

The two most popular change models involve either a top-down or a bottom-up change in control structure. In top-down change efforts the top managers of the firm design the change strategy and then encourage or force middle managers to implement the strategy. In contrast, bottom-up change efforts encourage lower-level employees to act in a democratic fashion and attempt to force change up through the hierarchy. In many organizations neither of these change structures is appropriate because both require a high level of trust for the change of meaning to occur. In other words, neither top-down nor bottom-up change structures will accomplish an organizationwide transformation unless most members of the organization believe that a high level of trust and credibility exists among them. A paradox arises when the purpose of an organizationwide transformation is to improve the level of trust among members of an organization, and yet traditional change structures are based implicitly on an assumption of an existing level of trust. Where this paradox exists, the transformation effort will most probably fail in the long term if traditional structures are used to effect the change.

Having identified the systems of meaning and beliefs at ETC during the assessment process, we concluded that neither of the two generic change structures would have much chance of success. A top-down change structure was inappropriate because of the low managerial credibility at ETC. Also, established patterns for resisting managerial decisions were firmly in place. A bottom-up change structure was inappropriate because of managerial needs for control and because of the need of managers to be "right" and to make employees look "wrong."

The situation necessitated an innovative way of integrating the dual internal structures. These dual structures jointly guide the change of meaning during the transformation process (with the assistance of the consulting group that serves as a temporary external structure). One internal structure consists of the top management team, the other of an employee team. The eight-member employee team includes representatives from front-line, supervisory, and professional levels across all functions at ETC. This group elected to call themselves the "ETC team." They closely resemble what Alderfer and Smith (1982) refer to as a microcosm group. Microcosm groups mirror the organization on a reduced scale. These teams constitute the

Figure 12-3. Multiple Structures Controlling Change.

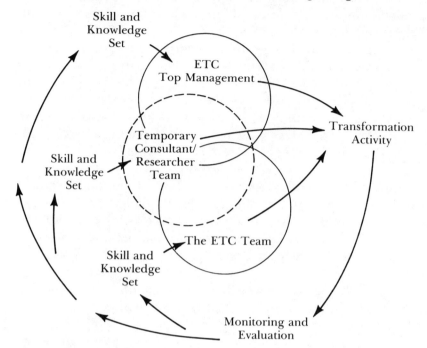

multiple structures controlling change, as depicted in Figure 12-3.

The ETC team was charged with providing input during all phases of the transformation process and facilitating employee involvement. The group quickly established itself as the front-runner for the transformation process. The assessment process revealed that employees were much more likely to trust other employees than to trust managers. In many cases, the ETC team members were believed to be more trustworthy than the members of the top management team.

The Meaning Change Process

We began by describing the mission of organizationwide transformation as it relates to the change of meaning. We then presented an assessment process that aided in the diagnosis of current systems of meaning and practice. Finally, we defined the change structures that need to work together if the change of meaning is to occur. We will now describe the three phases of meaning change.

Visioning. This initial stage of the meaning change process entails identifying the ideal characteristics and values that organization members want to guide the way work gets done in their company. Our visioning process integrates stakeholder analysis methodologies (Mason and Mitroff, 1981); organizational self-reflection workshops (Finney and Mitroff, 1986), and values visioning as proposed by Ackoff (1979). Groups within the organization—both managerial and employee—generate an integrated, exhaustive "wish list" that describes how they would like to work together, communicate with one another, structure the organization, and so on. At ETC groups of top and middle managers worked to identify the values that they hoped would guide the way work was accomplished. They "visioned" trust, respect, and unity, among others. These values served as the basis for the mission of the transformation effort.

Reframing. Reframing involves the planning of meaning change. Visioning presents the ideal, while the assessment process details the present reality. The control structures—internal and external interacting groups—are supplied with information focused on "this is how we are" and "this is the way we want to be.". . . So, how do we get there? The very pondering of meaning change facilitates its occurrence. The reframing stage not only brings about decisions that help organizational members get from "here" to "there," it initiates the movement by involving increasing numbers of members. The sharing of power in design and decision making related to the transformation process is an expression of trust, respect, and unity. The internal structures model the meaning changes for other participating groups. The external structure—the consulting group—designs activities that facilitate the interactions of the top management and employee structures. The consulting group helps managers and employees discover what trust, respect, and unity feel and look like and then helps the group members communicate and model the new meanings and practices to the larger organizational community.

Adaptive Experimentation. This stage of the meaning change process involves the implementation, monitoring, evaluation, and any necessary redesign of actions planned in the reframing stage. Espousing and designing change do not always result in enacted change. Adaptive experimentation, as described by Lundberg and Finney (1986), is action research enacted (Lewin, 1951; Lawler, 1977). It assumes the weaknesses of both theory and the practice of others and fosters carefully grounded, individualized transformation activities based upon ongoing assessment-based processes.

Adaptive experimentation presents an opportunity to act, react, and redesign during the transformation process. If unforeseen consequences of change activities call for redesign, adaptive experimentation provides the flexibility necessary to keep the process moving. The alternative, and the bane of most change efforts, is to stop the process simply because something did not work as intended. This "stopping" becomes a change effort failure. The only failure possible in adaptive experimentation is that associated with *not* redesigning, reimplementing, and reevaluating.

Each stage of the meaning change process brings about different levels of control exercised by the various structures. The three groups — top management, ETC team, and consulting group — vary in their degree of influence and in the contributions that they make during the three-stage process. This movement of influence and control among the groups is graphically presented in Figure 12-4. The expertise, experience, and knowledge, as well as the formal and informal power of each of the controlling structures determines "who's in" and "who's out" at each stage of the meaning change process.

Signs of Change

The organizationwide transformation process is working at ETC. While it is too early to evaluate the long-term success of

Figure 12-4. Strategic Involvement of Principal Change Agent Groups.

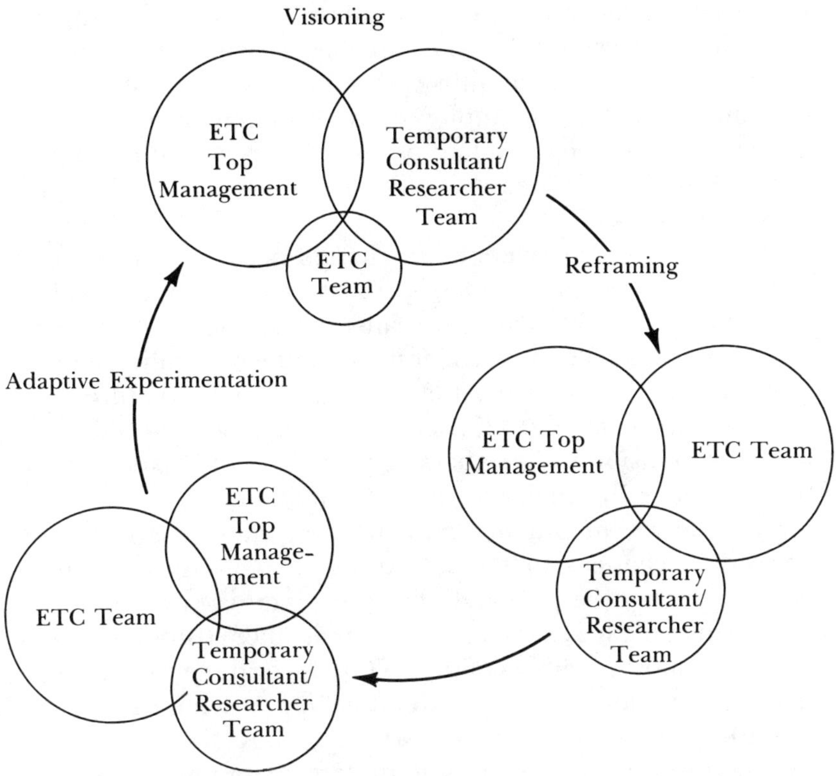

Visioning

ETC
Top
Management

Temporary
Consultant/
Researcher
Team

ETC
Team

Reframing

Adaptive Experimentation

ETC Top
Management

ETC Team

ETC
Top
Manage-
ment

ETC Team

Temporary
Consultant/
Researcher
Team

Temporary
Consultant/
Researcher
Team

the application of the model, meaning and practice are changing at ETC. Employees acknowledge that ETC is becoming "a
better place to work." The evidence of transformation of meaning was first noted by the ETC team approximately six months
after its formation. During an evaluative OSR session, team
members suddenly found it difficult to voice assumptions about
the same stakeholder groups that they had found easy to characterize during an OSR workshop six months earlier. After several
moments of silence, the team acknowledged that beliefs were
indeed beginning to change at ETC. Because beliefs were in
transition, it was difficult for the group to attribute clear-cut
meaning to certain stakeholder groups.

A momentous demonstration of the movement of belief

and practice occurred during an action-planning meeting held by the top management group to address the issue of raising the commitment level of the middle management at ETC. Although this issue would three months earlier have been considered far outside the purview of employees, the top management group brought the meeting to a halt because it was unwilling to proceed until the ETC team could participate in the decision-making process.

There is also evidence of change occurring in the employee view of management. Approximately seven months after initiation of the ETC team, the team members formally came to recognize their role as one of enhancing the credibility of management and empowering the existing formal structure. The outcome of the change effort was no longer seen as "management's responsibility"; if setbacks occurred, the ETC team members would realize their own hand in the failure.

Changes in practice and meaning have also been evidenced in changes in the structures controlling the change effort. For example, although the consultant/research team was held in high regard by the very top management (Brougham and Schmidt), most members of the ETC team and the top management group viewed them as "vendors" upon whom they were resentfully dependent for support services. As the change process has progressed, the status of the consultant/researcher team has also grown. The team is treated as an equal, if temporary, partner in the change process. The group has been allocated private office space at ETC, as well as full access to staff assistance; it is the only vendor interacting anywhere in the entire system that has been issued security badges for total system access.

Concluding Thoughts

We have described a model of organizationwide transformation that is intended to reframe systems of meaning within a company. Early indications point to the model's success. However, there have also been indications of rough spots in the model's application that require attention to enhance the model's future effectiveness.

The consulting team needs to be adept at balancing the advantages and disadvantages of being essentially an organizational insider. Advantages included access to key players and information and the client's inability to ignore us. Unfortunately, however, senior management also tried to set our on-site work schedules and insisted on a given amount of "management by walking around" time from the consultant/researcher team. Also, this closeness brought with it a certain amount of emotional baggage. For example, consultants, ETC team members, and senior management began talking about "being hurt" or "misunderstood" by one another. This is a very different dynamic and language from what usually typifies the consultant-as-vendor role. Indeed, this issue involves the very definition of the relationship between consultant and client. Should it be "us plus them" or "we"? If "we," how can consultants follow this definition and operationalize it as a partnership rather than as cooptation?

The consulting team needs to balance the pluses of extending a voice to "many" in the change effort with the increased demands and naysaying that may result. Strategies also need to be developed for dealing with individuals who are using the process to advance their own personal goals or inhibit the change effort because it threatens their personal vested interests.

A final issue may be both the most difficult and the most important one. The structures participating in the change effort must be committed to a dynamic enactment of the change model in Figure 12-1. This portrayal of the model needs to be viewed not as a snapshot, but as a motion picture. Emergent systems of meaning need to be continually assessed against the change effort's mission and guiding structures for an enduring approach to visioning, reframing, and adaptive experimentation. This is the path to both creating *and* sustaining organizationwide transformation.

In sum, this chapter has presented an overview of organizationwide transformation currently underway and entering its second year of activity at the Electronic Technology Center of First National Services Company. The description of the model reveals a complex process designed to facilitate the change of meaning. Although this chapter precedes completion of the transformation effort, implementation of the model has succeeded in bringing about change within the ETC system. It is the shared belief of top management, the ETC team, and the consultant team that the model will serve as a blueprint for ongoing organizationwide learning and transformation.

References

Ackoff, R. L. "Obstructions to Corporate Development." In C. A. Bromlette, Jr., and M. Mescou (eds.), *The Individual and the Future of Organizations.* Vol. 8. Atlanta: Georgia State University Press, 1979.

Alderfer, C., and Smith, K. "Studying Intergroup Relations Embedded in Organizations." *Administrative Science Quarterly,* 1982, *27,* 35–65.

Chin, R., and Benne, K. D. "General Strategies for Effecting Changes in Human Systems." In W. Bennis, K. D. Benne, R. Chin, and K. Corey (eds.), *The Planning of Change.* New York: Holt, Rinehart & Winston, 1976.

Finney, M. L. "The Organizational Self-Reflection Method." Working paper, Department of Management and Organization, School of Business, University of Southern California, 1985.

Finney, M. L., and Mitroff, I. "Strategic Plan Failures: The Organization as Its Own Worst Enemy." In H. P. Sims, Jr., and D. A. Gioia (eds.), *The Thinking Organization: Dynamics of Organizational Social Cognition.* San Francisco: Jossey-Bass, 1986.

Kilmann, R. H. *Beyond the Quick Fix: Managing Five Tracks to Organizational Success.* San Francisco: Jossey-Bass, 1984.

Kirk, J., and Miller, M. L. *Reliability and Validity in Qualitative Research.* Beverly Hills, Calif.: Sage, 1985.

Lawler, E. E. III. "Adaptive Experiments: An Approach to Organizational Behavior Research." *Academy of Management Review,* 1977, *2,* 576–585.

Lewin, K. *Field Theory in Social Science*. New York: Harper & Row, 1951.

Lundberg, C. C., and Finney, M. L. "Emerging Models of Consultancy." In *Handbook for Management Consultants*. Englewood Cliffs, N.J.: Prentice-Hall, 1986.

Mason, R. O., and Mitroff, I. I. *Challenging Strategic Planning Assumptions*. New York: Wiley, 1981.

Tichy, N. M. *Managing Strategic Change: Technical, Political, and Cultural Dynamics*. New York: Wiley, 1983.

13

Ralph H. Kilmann

❦ ❦ ❦ ❦ ❦ ❦ ❦ ❦

Toward a Complete Program for Corporate Transformation

The field of organization development, as it first emerged in the 1950s, was envisioned as providing methods for systemwide planned change that would significantly improve the functioning of entire organizations. For the most part, however, this majestic vision has been lost and forgotten.

During the 1960s and 1970s, efforts at improving organizations became more and more specialized and, eventually, fragmented, primarily because they focused on the narrow use of specific techniques, such as team building, survey feedback, and performance appraisal. Academics, following traditional guidelines for rigorous research, tended to study improvement methods primarily suited for tightly controlled, isolated parts of the organization, thereby ignoring systemwide perspectives. Executives found this research approach to be consistent with their own traditional prerogatives, since it did not require them to question either the corporate culture or the power structure of their organizations. Until now, there has been little incentive for either academics or practitioners to pursue improvement efforts on an organizationwide basis.

Special acknowledgment is given to Teresa Joyce Covin and Ines Martin for their helpful ideas and suggestions for this chapter.

In the 1980s, however, as many organizations are coming to realize that "future shock" is upon them, the need for thoroughgoing changes is being voiced more and more frequently. Now entire organizations must be transformed into market-driven, innovative, and adaptive systems if they are to survive and prosper in the highly competitive, global environment of the next decades. Given this situation, there is a dire need to rejuvenate the vision and methods of organization development.

A Program of Planned Change

A large-scale change program that is designed to bring about corporate transformation must specify: (1) "all" controllable variables that affect organizational success and (2) "all" action steps by which managers and consultants can adjust these controllable variables for organizational success (Kilmann, 1984). *Organizational success* is a matter of creating and maintaining high performance and morale for all or most stakeholders over an extended period of time.

Regarding the first ingredient, a large-scale change program must integrate a variety of approaches — ranging from those that recognize the intrapsychic conflicts of individuals to those that act on the systemwide properties of organizations. This enables managers and consultants to control "all" leverage points in the organization — not just one or two. I organize these leverage points into five categories of *tracks:* (1) the culture track, (2) the management skills track, (3) the team-building track, (4) the strategy-structure track, and (5) the reward system track.

Regarding the second ingredient, it is not enough to indicate *what* must be changed; a large-scale change program must outline *how* change can be effectively managed in any organization. While a quick-fix approach blindly implements one remedy after another, a more complete program recognizes the intricacy of introducing and managing change, including the need for top management support, the importance of defining problems before solutions are chosen, and the necessity to be flexible while implementing change in a living, breathing organization. Specifically, the five stages of planned change are: (1) initiating the program, (2) diagnosing the problems, (3) scheduling the tracks, (4) implementing the tracks, and (5) evaluating the results. During these five stages, the full range of action levers are addressed by means of the five tracks.

Figure 13-1 shows the five stages of planned change in the form of a model. To be successful, all programs for improving organizations must devote sufficient time and effort to complete each stage. Movement from one stage to the next, shown by the single arrows, should not take place until all the criteria for the earlier stages are satisfied. Otherwise, any glossed-over stages will come back to haunt the organization. Also, continual recycling through all five stages, without success, will eventually wear down the organization. It is desirable, therefore, to halt the entire change program until a particular stage can be conducted properly; or, if it seems that the necessary commitment and learning are unlikely to develop, the entire program should be terminated. There is simply no reason for an organization to go through a long and difficult change process if success is not possible.

The five stages of planned change should be approached as a collaborative effort among managers, members, and internal and external consultants; this is the best way I know to guarantee the success of the whole program. While some top managers may prefer to manage the five stages on their own, I do caution them not to conduct single-handedly those aspects of the program that are clearly beyond their skills and experiences. It is to be hoped that managers will recognize their limitations.

At any rate, it helps to have external consultants for collecting sensitive information about management and organizational problems, surfacing cultural norms, exposing outdated assumptions, confronting the organization's troublemakers, and helping managers receive honest feedback about the functioning of their teams. Therefore, the diagnostic stage — and major portions of the culture, management skills, and team-building tracks — should be guided by external consultants. Implementing the strategy-structure and the reward system tracks can be done primarily by the managers, although even here

Figure 13-1. The Five Stages of Planned Change.

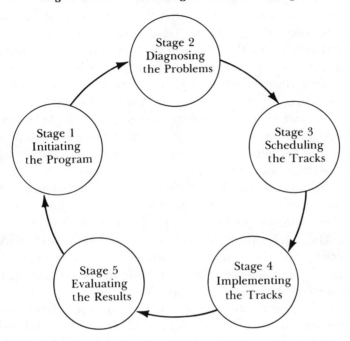

external consultants can help foster a more participative approach than managers by themselves tend to utilize.

Initiating the Program

The search for a way of initiating corporate transformation is often undertaken in a rather informal manner by a few key executives of the firm. Several times now I have witnessed a pattern that begins when one enlightened executive or manager is thrilled to learn that at least one other person also sees the growing problems that face the organization. Following several informal discussions, they search out other executives who either share their perceptions or can be influenced to see things in the same way. Eventually, when enough informal support of this kind has been mobilized, the executives find a way to put the topic of transformation (or whatever they choose to call it) on a formal meeting agenda. A discussion then ensues during which additional executives learn about the issues and are given a chance to voice their opinions. If the necessary commitment has not been developed, the item will be dropped from the formal agenda and will once again become a topic for informal discussion among disgruntled executives. However, if the informal mobilization of commitment *has* been successful, a task force or committee will be formed to explore the question of change in much greater depth. Following a formal presentation of the committee's deliberations, one or more executives are charged with contacting external consultants.

The consultants who are contacted should first determine if the organization is ready for change. While managers may voice their commitment to change, the real test is subsequent action. Thus, the consultants attempt to infer from several indicators the existence of true commitment. For example, do the managers openly acknowledge their role in the creation of the problem? Are they willing to consider alternative perspectives and approaches? Do they seem receptive to a full diagnosis of the problem by the consultants? Do they realize the extensive and involving nature of the program? Or do they hope to find another quick fix? If the consultants do not believe that sufficient commitment exists for a large-scale program of change or that it is likely to be generated, I recommend that they share this conclusion with the top management group as the primary reason for terminating the project.

If there appears to be sufficient basis for continuing, however, the consultants meet with more managers (including the top management group) to share objectives and expectations more widely. Much as in the formation of an interpersonal relationship, the outside consultants and the organization try to determine if there is a good fit between them. If this rapport does not develop, it may be due to personal quirks or to a true difference in style. Regardless, I have not heard or read of a successful case of change in which the client and consultant did not first "hit it off." A difficult process of change must be rooted in a firm foundation of trust, liking, and mutual respect.

It is important to recognize, however, that some organizations seem to have the capacity to *anticipate* problems before a crisis or critical juncture is reached. This is the case when a number of senior executives recognize that it might be easier to conduct transformation while the organization is in a relatively healthy state. Members might be more willing to participate in various programs to improve performance and morale when their jobs are not on the line and there are high expectations of long-term success.

I have found it useful to think of a window of opportunity for transformation. This window opens somewhere between the point where an organization does not quite recognize that certain problems will only become worse if they are not addressed in the near future and the point of crisis when members do not believe that the organization has the time and capacity to alter its gloomy prospects (see Beer, 1980). It seems that in most cases, however, a change program is initiated amidst a crisis or during a time of great uncertainty. Too infrequently do consultants and managers come into partnership under anticipatory conditions. Most often it seems that the organization has to be *hurting* for some significant period of time before the call for a new approach will be sounded and accepted.

Diagnosing the Problems

This stage is very much guided by the external consultants, who have to be sure that the diagnosis is based on their assessments independently of the initial reasons that brought them into the organization. The consultants, with the aid of the managers, develop a plan to identify any and all problems across the entire organization. The objective is to sample each level in the hierarchy—and each division and department—so that a representative view of the organization is obtained. I always insist on interviewing all persons in the top management group simply because their views, and especially their commitment to change, are so critical to the program.

It is essential to explicate the paradigm, model, or selective filters that are used to ask questions and record responses during the interviews (see Tichy, 1983). If the interviewers see organizations only as interpersonal relationships, they will only ask questions and record responses with regard to interpersonal problems and experiences. The same holds true for seeing organizations as document-producing systems (strategies, organization charts, or job descriptions), as cultural phenomena, or in terms of their management styles. Instead, corporate transformation must be seen as a complex holographic image—a three-dimensional image created by reflecting beams of light at different angles—including the multitude of views about how organizations function and why. Any perceptual filters that limit the search for a full understanding of the organization's problems will necessarily limit the variety of action levers for change that are considered, and this will automatically prevent corporate transformation from occurring.

Figure 13-2 shows organizational life as a holographic image. This image or model is used for discovering the full range of problems that stand in the way of an organization's success—what we might call its *barriers* to *success*. The model consists of five broad categories representing the at-the-surface aspects of an organization, plus, at center stage, three below-the-surface aspects that add the dimension of depth. The five broad categories are (1) the setting, (2) the organization, (3) the manager, (4) the group, and (5) the results. The three holographic aspects are (1) culture, (2) assumptions, and (3) psyches. The double arrows surrounding the "holographic diamond" signify the strong reciprocal influence between the three below-the-surface aspects and the other categories. Similarly, the single arrows show the primary (but not exclusive) impact that one category has on another and particularly how several categories combine to determine decision making and action taking, as well as morale and performance.

At the top of the Barriers to Success model is the broadest category of all. It includes every possible event and force that can affect the success of the organization. Even if many of these possible events are generally irrelevant, they can become significant factors for the organization to consider at any time. The term *dynamic complexity* summarizes the two qualities that are having increasing impact on all organizations: rapid change

Figure 13-2. The Complex Hologram.

Barriers to Success

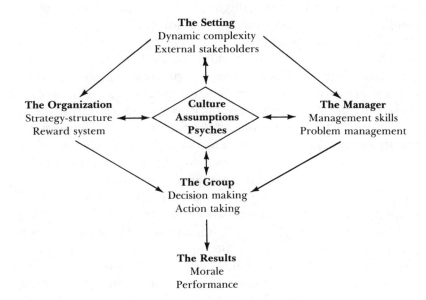

and interdependence in a global marketplace. External stakeholders are any individual, group, other organization, or community that has some stake in what the focal organization does—making dynamic complexity both unique and operational for any organization. Not only do the stakeholders vary tremendously depending on the organization being studied, but new stakeholders can enter into the organization's setting at any time—for example, new competitors with improved products, new government agencies with new regulations, new research groups developing new production methods, and new consumers with different tastes. The setting provides the context by which the organization's internal properties and dynamics are understood, interpreted and, subsequently, aligned.

On the left-hand side of the Barriers to Success model, the formal organization can be diagnosed according to strategy, structure, and reward systems. Strategy refers to all the documents that signify direction: statements of vision, mission, purpose, goals, and objectives. Structure refers to the way resources are organized in order to move the organization in the designated direction; methods might include organization charts, policy statements, job descriptions, formal rules and regulations. The reward system includes all documented methods to attract and retain employees and, in particular, to motivate them to high levels of performance — given the established strategy and structure of the firm. The essential issue is whether all these documented systems are barriers or channels to success.

On the right-hand side of the Barriers to Success model, the styles and skills of the managers can be diagnosed for how well these fit with the types of people and problems in the organization. Until recently, managers have been thought of primarily as decision makers — persons who must choose among a set of given alternatives to arrive at an optimal or satisfactory solution. This is all well and good if the alternatives are already determined and the rules for choosing among the alternatives are clear-cut. Under conditions of dynamic complexity, however, it may not even be clear what the essential problem is, let alone what the alternative choices are. Today's managers have to be problem managers, who sense and define problems, even more than decision makers, who select and implement solutions.

At the center of the Barriers to Success model, the uniquely holographic, below-the-surface aspects of the organization can be diagnosed: culture, assumptions, and psyches. Each of these aspects functions at a different level of depth.

Just below the surface, and thus easiest of the three to manage, is culture. This is the invisible force behind the tangibles and observables in any organization, the social energy that moves the membership into action. Culture is defined as *shared* values, beliefs, expectations, and norms. Norms are easiest to define: they are the unwritten rules of the game. For example, some norms are: Don't disagree with your boss; don't rock the boat; don't share information with other groups. These norms are seldom written down or discussed. Often, work groups pressure their members to follow such dysfunctional norms out of habit; the consequence of this is that culture — as manifested in norms of behavior—greatly affects how formal statements get interpreted and provides what written documents leave out. Of special concern is how culture often steers behavior in the opposite direction from what is "requested" by job descriptions and work procedures or "dictated" by supervisors and higher-level managers.

The second of the holographic aspects of organizations is found at the level of depth after culture. Simply put, assumptions are those beliefs whose truth has been taken for granted but that may turn out to be false under closer analysis. Underlying any decision or action is a large set of generally unstated and untested assumptions. For example, managers may well assume that the following unstated beliefs are unquestionably true: No new competitors will enter the industry; the economy will steadily improve; the government will continue to restrict foreign imports for the industry; the consumer will buy whatever the firm produces; the availability of capital will remain the same; employees will continue to accept the same compensation package and benefits plan; yesterday's structures are best for solving today's problems. In short, all previous decisions and actions may have been based more on fantasy and habit than on reality and choice.

The third of the holographic aspects of organizations is also the deepest: the innermost qualities of the human mind and spirit. While psyches cannot be changed in a short period of time, if at all, an accurate understanding of human nature is essential in order to design strategy, structure, reward systems, cultures, and the implementation of business decisions. In essence, the assumptions members make concerning human nature—what people want, fear, resist, support, and defend—underlie the eventual success or failure of all these systems and decisions.

The lower part of the model portrays the decisions and actions that follow from group efforts. While individuals do make decisions and take actions on their own, today's organization requires multiple inputs from members of one or more groups in order to manage complex problems. Some groups are merely nominal, and there is little discussion or sharing of information among their members. Worse yet, in some groups information is kept secret— this is often the case with powerful cliques. Alternatively, groups can be teams—highly interactive, cohesive sets of individuals all working toward the same objectives. Generally, it is the team approach that will provide the most comprehensive source of expertise and information to solve complex problems; here, synergism enables the team to contribute more than the sum of its members. Such team efforts will result in high-quality decisions *and* member commitment to implement these decisions effectively: this is the ideal model for organizational success under conditions of dynamic complexity and shifting stakeholders.

The holographic model illustrates why the team approach will fail in most organizations in which the previous barriers to success are still in place. If a manager does not have the proper styles and skills to manage complex problems, group decisions will be made by majority rule or by the dictates of the manager himself. If the culture pressures members to withhold information so that each member can protect his or her own territory, the quality of decisions will again be adversely affected. If the strategy of the organization is rooted in false assumptions about the consumer and the firm's competitors, any group decision will be moving the organization in the wrong direction. If the structure of the organization makes it difficult for members in various departments to join together on decisions that affect them all, the expertise and information needed to make such high-quality decisions will simply not be present in the group. Furthermore, if the reward system encourages individual efforts instead of team efforts, members will not be motivated to commit themselves to the group decision-making process in the first place. Indeed, only if an organization is composed of well-functioning teams with minimal barriers to success in every category will it have a chance to be a truly breakaway company in our competitive, global marketplace.

These interrelated dynamics, as captured by the Barriers to Success model, illustrate the variety of issues that arise again and again while diagnosing organizations. Naturally, there are differences from one organization to another; there always are some unique circumstances or histories that moderate the extent and variety of these basic issues. However, I wish to emphasize the almost uncanny pattern that has emerged in all the research and consulting that I have done in organizations. Very rarely do I find the formal organization *alone* needs readjustment for organizational success. Rarely do I find that managers' learning of new skills about complex problems will *by itself* solve the organization's performance and morale problems. I have never encountered a case in which only the culture had lagged behind and there was an effective formal organization already in place, with managers applying up-to-date skills. The culture problem *always* has been associated with problems in the organization, the group, and the manager as well.

These general findings are really not that surprising. Seeing the organization as a holographic image reveals an interrelated set of above-the-surface and below-the-surface dynamics and properties. Given such a filter, what is the likelihood that today's organizations can cope with dynamic complexity and shifting external stakeholders by adjusting only one category in the Barriers to Success model? It is very unlikely indeed. But what about adjusting most but not all the categories shown in Figure 13-2? That is just as unlikely to be successful, sorry to say. Rather, it seems that *all* categories have to be considered and acted upon in all cases. This is the new rule of corporate transformation, not the exception. Management development, organizational design, and culture change, all undertaken with an enlightened view of the world and its various stakeholders, are necessary to revitalize our organizations. Otherwise, the extent and variety of complex problems will continue to impose troublesome barriers to organizational success and will continue to prevent corporate transformation from occurring.

When the top managers accept the general diagnosis provided by the consultants, as summarized by the Barriers to Success model, it then becomes desirable to share these findings with the entire membership. Naturally, it takes conviction for the top managers to be willing to share the diagnosis with others. But this willingness is critical for demonstrating commitment to the membership. The act of top managers acknowledging problems to themselves and to others, while painful, is an important event in the life of an organization.

Scheduling the Tracks

The Barriers to Success model, which guides the full diagnosis of the organization's problems and opportunities, contains two categories that are uncontrollable, at least in the short run. The setting, the most macro category, is more powerful than the organization itself while the psyche, the most micro category, is too deep-seated to change. But five categories that fall between these macro and micro aspects of the model are directly controllable by managers and consultants: culture, management skills, teams, strategy-structure, and reward systems. These action levers constitute the five-track program.

This stage of planned change involves: (1) selecting the first unit to participate in the program and planning the spread of change to the remaining organizational units, (2) selecting the techniques (methods for bringing about change) that will make up each of the five tracks in each unit—to address the specific problems identified during the diagnostic stage, and (3) scheduling the five tracks into a timed sequence of activity in order to promote effective learning and change in each organizational unit. Once a plan for action has been formalized in this stage, managers, members, and consultants will work together to implement it in the following stage.

Scheduling the five tracks first requires a decision as to which unit of the organization should begin the program (see Beckhard and Harris, 1987). Sometimes an autonomous business unit is chosen for a pilot project. Following an evaluation of the results (to be described in the last stage of transformation), other business units one by one implement the program of planned change. This sequence proceeds until all business units desiring or requiring change have implemented some version of the five tracks. Alternatively, corporate headquarters might be the first unit to be scheduled for the program, followed in turn by the remaining units.

My experience in scheduling units in the organization for transformation suggests that the first unit scheduled should be a *primary* business unit. The criterion for such a choice is that of credibility: Which unit, if it undergoes the change program and is successful, would serve as the best example to the other units that such change is important, necessary, and possible? In most cases, however, I have found that business units chosen are ones that are isolated and removed from the core business of the organization. Perhaps this represents a safe strategy: If the program is not successful, the whole organization is hardly affected. However, if the program is successful, the other business units will not see the pilot project as a relevant example of what they should be doing. If the intent is to spread change throughout the organization, units should be chosen that are critical to the success of the whole enterprise, which necessarily involves greater risk: an unsuccessful program will be damaging to the whole company. This greater risk in picking the core business units to implement the program should be reason enough for the senior executives to do whatever it takes to make the program a success (see Beer, 1980).

A plan is then developed that specifies the ways in which the spread of change throughout the organization can be facilitated. This plan specifies not only the order in which the remaining units will be scheduled for the change program but also the supporting mechanisms and procedures that will be employed. For example, once the pilot project is underway (and as other units begin the process as well), regular communications can be provided to the rest of the organization indicating what is taking place and why. Some managers or members from the pilot project might be temporarily transferred to the next unit to help facilitate the change process. In addition, various organizational rewards and perquisites might be offered to those units as they participate in the program in order to convey the special nature of the project and the importance of successful results (see Walton, 1975).

While the choice of the pilot project to begin the program and the sequence and methods by which other business units participate certainly vary from company to company, what makes each application of a change program different are the particular techniques used in each of the five tracks. Just as the diagnosis varies for each organizational unit, so does the choice of technique to address each identified problem. For example, in some cases the management skills track will include material on leadership styles, conflict-handling modes, and ways for minimizing defensive communication. In other cases in which the managers have already acquired these skills, management training moves directly to teaching methods for managing complex problems. Clearly, the consultants and managers should be aware of the diversity of techniques that exist so that they can choose the ones that best fit the problems in each organizational unit (Huse, 1980).

The one thing that most distinguishes the change program from the quick fix is the integrated nature of the five tracks. These tracks and their host of techniques are not scheduled in a random order, nor is a "shotgun" approach used (in which all tracks are implemented haphazardly or indiscriminately). The guiding principles in organizing and sequencing the five tracks include the capacity of the organization and its members to change, which changes are easiest and best to accomplish early, and which changes should be left to occur later. Specifically, the first three tracks concentrate on the informal organization, while the last two tracks address the formal documents. My experience with corporate transformation has shown repeatedly that if the informal organization is not properly prepared for change, modifications in the documents will be ignored.

Table 13-1 provides a brief summary of the primary objectives of the five tracks: culture, management skills, team building, strategy-structure, and reward system.

The culture track is the ideal place to start the program for several reasons. It is enlightening to openly discuss what previously was seldom written down or mentioned in conversations. Members enjoy—even laugh at—the revelations that occur as the dysfunctional norms—the unwritten rules of the game—are brought to everyone's attention. It is also much easier to blame norms than to blame oneself or other people. As long

Table 13-1. The Five Tracks.

1. *The Culture Track*. Establishing trust, information sharing, and adaptiveness; being receptive to change and improvement.
2. *The Management Skills Track*. Augmenting skills to cope with complexity; exposing and updating assumptions.
3. *The Team-Building Track*. Infusing new cultural norms and assumptions into each work unit; fostering cooperative efforts.
4. *The Strategy-Structure Track*. Aligning all work units and resources with new strategic directions.
5. *The Reward System Track*. Establishing a performance-based reward system; sustaining the whole improvement effort.

as members take responsibility for change, it does not really matter if using norms as a scapegoat takes some of the pressure off their egos. Without an initial culture change, however, it is highly unlikely that the other four tracks can be successful. The members must believe that this program has the backing of management and that it is entirely unlike all the other short-term programs that have not been successful in the past. The culture track consists of a five-step process: (1) bringing actual norms to the surface, (2) articulating what is needed for success today, (3) establishing new norms, (4) identifying differences between actual and ideal norms (culture gaps), and (5) closing culture gaps. Thus, the culture track first exposes the old culture and then, if necessary, creates a new *adaptive* culture.

Once the culture track is in place, the next order of business is to implement the management skills track. In most cases, the managers have contributed substantially, if unintentionally, to the organization's problems. The managers usually have not kept up with the changing environment and the new kinds of problems that it presents. Traditionally, managers pick the first available solution without even bothering to define the root causes of the problem and then, to top it all off, they implement it in a mechanistic manner; not surprisingly, the problem never gets resolved. However, once managers become receptive to change—through the culture track—they can be taught the full set of skills needed to conduct a five-step process for effective problem management: (1) sensing problems,

(2) defining problems, (3) deriving solutions, (4) implementing solutions, and (5) evaluating outcomes.

The management skills track also offers a systematic method for uncovering the underlying assumptions that drive all decisions into action. If these assumptions have remained unstated and therefore untested, managers may have continually made the wrong decisions. However, given a new culture that encourages trust and openness, members now will be able to analyze their previously unstated assumptions before any critical decisions are made. No longer will the membership be held back by its own faulty assumptions.

As the culture track and the management skills track begin to provide some early successes (even if these tracks are conducted primarily in a classroom setting away from the job), the next effort lies in directly transferring what has been learned into the mainstream of organizational life. Specifically, the team-building track does three things: (1) it keeps the troublemakers in check so that they will not disrupt cooperative efforts; (2) it brings the new cultural norms and management skills into the day-to-day activities of each work group; and (3) it enables cooperative decisions to be made across group boundaries, as in multiple-team efforts. In this way, all available expertise and information will be marshaled to manage the complex technical and business problems that arise within and between work groups. As the culture begins to open up people's minds as well as their hearts, work groups can examine, maybe for the first time, the particular barriers that have held them back in the past. Through various kinds of feedback sessions, old warring cliques can become effective teams.

Eventually it becomes time for the membership to take on one of the most difficult problems facing any organization in a dynamic environment: aligning its formally documented systems. One might think that the mission of the firm and its corresponding strategic choices should have been the first topics addressed. Why should the organization proceed with changes in culture, management skills, and team efforts before the new directions are formalized? Is it not logical to first know the directions in which the organization wants to go before the rest of the system is put in place? Yes, that is logical. But there are other things operating in a complex organization besides logic. If we understand human nature and organizational culture, we recognize that it makes little sense to plan the future directions of the firm if members do not trust one another and refuse to share important information with one another, expose their tried and true assumptions, or commit themselves to the new directions because the culture will not allow it. If the prior tracks have not accomplished their purposes, the strategy-structure problem will be addressed through political maneuvering by vested interests, not through an open exchange of ideas and a cooperative effort to achieve organizational success.

The strategy-structure track is conducted in an eight-step process: (1) making strategic choices, (2) listing objectives to be achieved and tasks to be performed, (3) analyzing objective/task relationships, (4) calculating inefficiencies that stem from an out-of-date structure, (5) diagnosing structural problems, (6) designing a new structure, (7) implementing the new structure, and (8) evaluating the new structure. As a result of this process, the members remove bureaucratic red tape that moves the organization in the wrong direction. In its place is a structure aligned with the firm's strategy.

Once the organization is moving in the right direction with the needed structure and resources, the reward system track completes the change program by paying for performance. A seven-step process is used in setting up a performance-based reward system: (1) designing special task forces to study the problem, (2) reviewing the types of reward systems available, (3) establishing several alternative reward systems, (4) debating the assumptions behind the different reward systems, (5) designing the new reward system, (6) implementing the new reward system, and (7) evaluating the new reward system. Only if the earlier tracks have accomplished their objectives will members believe that the reward system is genuine and that rewards will vary with performance. Such a reward system motivates excellence.

In order to help members improve their performance from one work cycle to the next, the reward system also takes into account how performance results and reward decisions will be communicated to each member of the organization during face-to-face meetings with a superior. Two different types of meetings are established: (1) a performance review to provide information for evaluative purposes and (2) a counseling session to provide feedback for learning purposes. With a well-functioning reward system in place, all improvements derived from the change program will be implanted in the everyday life of the organization.

The reward system track is futile if all the other tracks have not been managed properly. Without a supportive culture, members will not believe that rewards are tied to performance — regardless of what the formal documents state; instead, they will believe that it is useless to work hard since they see rewards as being based on favoritism and politics. Similarly, if managers do not have the skills needed to conduct performance appraisals, any well-intentioned reward system will be thwarted; a poor appraisal will cause defensiveness, which will inhibit each member's motivation to improve his performance. Without effective teams, managers and members will not be comfortable in openly sharing information about the results of performance reviews and the distribution of rewards; in the absence of such information, imaginations will run wild since nobody will know for sure whether high performers receive significantly more rewards than low performers. Furthermore, if the strategy and structures are not designed properly, the reward system cannot measure performance objectively; only if each group is autonomous can its output be assessed as a separate quantity as close to the individual level as possible — a necessary condition to make the pay-for-performance link a reality in everyone's eyes.

But what if individuals disregard the formal reward system and strive to excel for the sake of intrinsic rewards, such as personal satisfaction for a job well done? If the other tracks have not been managed properly, even the most dedicated efforts by the members will not lead to high performance for the organization. Instead, members' efforts will be blocked by all the barriers to success that are still in force: dysfunctional cultures, outdated management skills, poorly functioning work groups, unrealistic strategic choices, and misaligned structures. Alternatively, whatever improvements were realized as a result of the earlier tracks will not be sustained if the membership is not ultimately rewarded for high performance: the old dysfunctional cultures, assumptions, and behaviors will creep back into the workplace. Thus, the reward system is the last major barrier that must be transformed into a channel for success, the bottom line for the membership.

Figure 13-3 illustrates the scheduling of the five tracks for a major industrial organization. The horizontal line for each track signifies an ongoing cycle of off-site meetings (in a workshop setting *with* consultants present) and informal meetings (organized at the workplace *without* consultants present) in order to pursue the topic in question (for example, cultural change). Also, as the figure shows, each track does not have to be completed before the next track is initiated. The guiding principle is that the earlier track should have established the necessary conditions in order for the next track to be successful. For example, after the culture track has established a basic foundation of trust with regard to the change program, managers will now be receptive to learning new styles and skills; thus, the management skills workshops can begin. After the managers have learned some new skills, the team-building track can begin to encourage managers to use these new skills on the job. It is not as if the entire culture change must be in place and all new skills learned before the membership can make use of the new culture and skills in their various business and technical decisions. Similarly, the individuals who will be involved throughout the strategy-structure and reward system tracks can begin their discussions on this topic before every manager and team has completed the whole program.

If the planned change program is scheduled over too long a period of time, the membership will gradually lose interest and be disillusioned because the promised benefits (such as the new reward system) are not forthcoming. Alternatively, if the program is scheduled for too short a time period, it will be impossible to lay the foundation for the successful completion of each track, and the membership will experience some

Figure 13-3. Scheduling the Five Tracks.

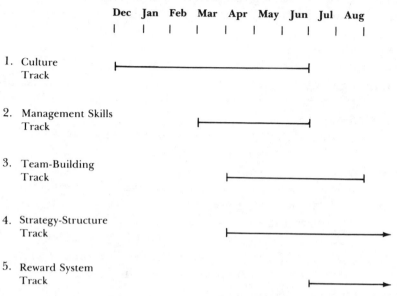

amount of disappointment or even failure with the results of each track. Thus, careful orchestration of corporate transformation requires an understanding of human nature and the capacity of organizations to undergo massive change.

Implementing the Tracks

A "shadow" track (running parallel to and continuous with all the five tracks) has been developed to facilitate implementation of the large-scale change program; this track places primary responsibility for the program on the shoulders of one group (the shadow group). This group of approximately ten to fifteen members, representing every level and division in the organization, meets regularly to monitor the program and to discover ways to improve the whole process of implementation. For example, this group might monitor every written document distributed by the executive office to ensure that a consistent message (signal) is being given. If the content or tone of a memorandum on a new policy about to be sent to the membership seems deficient or out of key, the shadow group would review it and suggest how the memorandum could be reworded to be more consistent with the intentions behind the program of planned change in general and the culture change in particular.

The shadow track also seeks to increase member involvement in the program by having the outside consultants work with any available inside consultants (for example, human resource professionals or organization development practitioners). This collaborative effort might include the training of the inside consultants by the outside consultants or entail some sort of pairing method (for instance, an outside consultant might conduct each track with the aid of one or more inside consultants). In these ways, the organization not only utilizes its internal resources as a partial substitute for excessive reliance on outside experts but also builds its own base of expertise to implement change in the future.

In whatever way the shadow track is designed and conducted, it is one thing to schedule the five tracks but it is quite another to adjust and modify the schedule as it is being implemented. Needless to say, the plan *never* takes place exactly as intended. There are always surprises. Being what they are, human nature and human systems do not lend themselves to a predictable path. Besides, if people feel they are being programmed in any way, it is not unlike them to purposely do something illogical, irrational, or unexpected just to show how free and independent they really are.

The key issue during implementation, therefore, is flexibility. It is important not to get tightly locked into any plan; doing so makes it very difficult to back off and change to a new one. The schedule of five tracks is helpful as a starting point since without it there would be confusion and misguided efforts. As the schedule is implemented, however, the consultants must look for cues, take suggestions and, in short, adapt the initial plan.

Special requests will be made for counseling sessions, feedback sessions for staff meetings, additional culture sessions, more management skills training, and so forth. In each case, the consultants and the managers must consider the request and respond according to their objectives and their sense of what will work. Sometimes requests may be turned down, but the reasons should always be presented and discussed. At other times, the requests may be acted upon — but in a fashion different from that first suggested. Often, it is the consultants themselves who initiate additional activity, adjusting to what they perceive is needed — to nudge this person or that group or to support some effort that turned out to be more difficult than first thought.

A shared expectation, which should develop as the program is initiated, is that the consultants will have the freedom to schedule whatever activities are necessary to move the change effort forward. I have come across a number of organizations that at first failed to appreciate the importance of this option. I remember a few cases in which the managers expected the consultants to know exactly what activities would take place and when. However, since the needs and demands of the members are constantly changing, frequent adjustment is essential to any improvement effort.

The most enjoyable part of the implementation stage is seeing changes and improvements take hold. Initially, everyone is a little leery of what to expect and unsure of whether the organization has the ability to change. As early successes are won, however, confidence develops, and this inspires an even greater effort at improvement. This is not to suggest that the road will be smooth and without obstacles; on a week-by-week basis, some things will get a lot worse before they get better. In some cases, the organization expects the change to develop quickly and with little pain, regardless of what the managers or consultants have told them. When an event takes place that seems to reinforce the old ways or attitudes of the past, it is easy to be discouraged and feel that nothing has changed. But if instead of examining week-by-week fluctuations one looks at month-by-month trends, the process will probably show a more definite pattern of improvement.

These fluctuations in perceived accomplishments and moods illustrate the importance of setting realistic expectations in the beginning and making sure that impatience for change does not raise member expectations to unattainable levels. Disappointment and frustration result when these expectations are out of line with reality, which subsequently affects both the individual's and the organization's confidence to continue the change effort. Managers and consultants have to nurture expectations very carefully during implementation.

After a number of months go by, it will become more and more apparent that the membership has internalized the overt behaviors that have been observed. Each person does not have to apply new skills and enact new cultural norms in a conscious and deliberate manner; rather, the new ways are enacted quite automatically and the new skills and behaviors become more natural and easier to put into practice. At a certain point (and this is very difficult to specify in advance), the "hump" is crossed and the old gives way to the new. The best way I can describe this transition is to say that the members and the managers could not return to the old ways even if they tried to because the new ways are so obviously better and contribute more to their personal satisfaction and to accomplishing the organization's mission. The past is really put aside in their behaviors, attitudes, and memories.

The implementation stage is complete when the external consultants and managers both believe that the organization can manage its problems on its own. During the last few months of implementation, the outside consultants become less involved in scheduling and implementing activities; the managers and the inside consultants now decide on their own what team-building or skills training is needed and then proceed to fill the gap—sometimes with outside help, sometimes not. The organization thus moves into a state of "independence." The membership has solved, and can continue to solve, the problems for which the program was initiated in the beginning.

Regarding how long the whole change program will take, only some rough guidelines can be suggested. These guidelines consider the size and age of the organization, the number of organizational units involved, the complexity of the problems that were uncovered in each unit, the severity of the problems, the time available for conducting the five tracks, and the desire on the part of both managers and other members to learn and change. Since the organization cannot shut down its operations just to engage in a change program, the five tracks have to be conducted as other work gets done—even during crises and peak seasons.

In general, one can expect most large-scale change efforts to take anywhere from one to five years. A period of less than one year might work for a small division in which the formally documented systems need only a fine tuning. However, a program taking more than five years might be necessary for a large, older organization that had to break with its past in practically every way. If the program were to take more than ten years, I would assume that there was insufficient commitment over this time period, which prevented the momentum for change to prevail.

Evaluating the Results

There are essentially three purposes for evaluating the results of the program: (1) collecting information from the pilot project (or any earlier application) in order to improve the implementation process for the remaining organizational units, (2) collecting information from any unit that implemented the program to learn what barriers to success still remain in that unit so that additional activities can be conducted to remove these barriers, and (3) determining the impact of the whole program of transformation on organizational success.

The first purpose for evaluation recognizes that something is learned every time that the program of five tracks is implemented. A most important task is monitoring the pilot project to learn what to modify as other units begin the program. It is recommended that the shadow track or some independent group keep a close watch on the process so that any new insights or methods can be utilized as one unit after another embarks on the journey of planned change.

The second purpose for evaluation recognizes that transformation is never complete—it is ongoing and forever. Thus,

evaluating the results of any one unit is done to uncover problems (barriers) that still need attention in that unit. For example,
an evaluation might reveal the need for additional work to close
the culture gaps in a few of the more troublesome work groups.
Or, if new managers enter the organizational unit after most of
the program has been implemented, additional skills-training
sessions can be conducted to bring the new managers up to
speed with the rest of the membership. Typically, running
through the five stages a second or third time entails fine tuning
(incremental change) rather than corporate transformation
(revolutionary change).

Both the first and second purposes for evaluation (collecting information in one unit in order to benefit other organizational units and collecting information to enhance the change
process for the focal unit in continuing cycles of planned
change) can be approached by engaging in another round of
interviews. If diagnostic interviews were the most effective way
to learn about the organization's barriers at the start, this same
methodology can be applied again to assess (1) what could have
been done differently and (2) what still needs to be done in
order to remove any additional barriers to success. I find it
useful to have the internal consultants conduct these interviews
at the evaluation stage rather than the external consultants who
conducted the first round of interviews during the diagnostic
stage. I have found that the internal consultants are often more
objective at this point in the process, than the external ones.
Alternatively, a number of trained professionals acting independently of the other external and internal consultants might be
the best solution to maintaining objectivity.

The third purpose for evaluation is to determine whether
the program has improved organizational success. From the
point of view of stakeholders—such as consumers, stockholders,
suppliers, federal agencies, and the community—one usually
can suggest some "hard" outcome measures: return on investment, earnings per share, profit, sales, number of clients served,
market share, budget increases, number of patents and new
products, new contracts and orders, productivity gains, and so
on. Making a before-and-after comparison on any of these mea-

sures (before and after the change program) should provide a solid basis for assessing the impact of the program. If the change effort was successful, the differences in these measures should be evident—or so the argument goes.

While these hard, bottom-line measures certainly can be convincing, one has to recognize their limitations. Improvements in the quality of decisions and actions, for instance, do not translate into one-for-one increments in performance and morale. Normally, a whole series of decisions and actions must be combined in complicated ways before their effects are noticed.

One should also not forget the time lag between decisions and actions on the one hand and performance on the other. Some of the bottom-line measures would not be affected until months or years after a key decision has been made. For instance, improved decision making that results in new approaches to product development will not be felt in the organization's setting for years. If the before-and-after comparisons are made right after the change program has concluded, one cannot expect outside stakeholders to take note of any observable differences in outcomes. Ironically, if such before-and-after comparisons were to suggest significant improvements (or declines), they probably would be spurious or artificial. Only if the bottom-line measurements are made over a long enough period of time—a period in which true effects can be expected—can one take the results of such an evaluation seriously.

Conclusion

While the five stages of planned change are certainly complex, so are the problems that this program is designed to resolve. Quick fixes cannot solve complex problems; it is time that both managers and consultants accepted this fact of organizational life. Any serious improvement effort must be able to affect every controllable variable in the organization, not just one or two. At the same time, if the whole program is not initiated properly with top management support and if the problems of the organization are not diagnosed correctly, the complete program cannot provide its potential benefits. More-over, the program must be implemented in an integrated man-ner, with flexibility and adaptability. Attempting to quick fix any program for large-system change would do the field of organiza-tional studies—and the organization in question—a great disservice.

References

Beckhard, R., and Harris, R. T. *Organizational Transitions: Manag-ing Complex Change.* (2nd ed.) Reading, Mass.: Addison-Wesley, 1987.

Beer, M. *Organization Change and Development: A Systems View.* Glenview, Ill.: Scott, Foresman, 1980.

Huse, E. F. *Organization Development and Change.* (2nd ed.) St. Paul: West, 1980.

Kilmann, R. H. *Beyond the Quick Fix: Managing Five Tracks to Organizational Success.* San Francisco: Jossey-Bass, 1984.

Tichy, N. M. *Managing Strategic Change: Technical, Political, and Cultural Dynamics.* New York: Wiley, 1983.

Walton, R. E. "The Diffusion of New Work Structures: Explaining Why Success Didn't Take." *Organizational Dynamics,* 1975, *3* (3), 3–22.

Bill Veltrop

Karin Harrington

14

Proven Technologies for Transformation

This chapter is written for organization leaders and resource people who want to make a significant and lasting difference in the organizations they serve—for those individuals who are interested in breaking through to new territories in organization performance and flexibility. This chapter:

1. contrasts "new paradigm" organizations with the traditional forms so ill suited for today's changing world.
2. identifies five major challenges to organizationwide transformation.
3. describes a four-technology approach that has proven useful in addressing those challenges.
4. suggests that equipping organizational leadership with the capabilities to transform their systems can represent a bold and timely strategic initiative.

In today's world, it seems that the only constant is change. In *The Turning Point*, Capra (1982) shows how the revolution in modern physics is merely the first wave of a revolution in all the sciences and the precursor of a global transformation of our world view and values. Toffler (1981) has provided us with abundant evidence that the world is changing at an ever increasing

330

rate and that many of our traditional structures and ways of thinking simply are not working for us any more. In their book, *Re-Inventing the Corporation*, Naisbitt and Aburdene (1985) make a compelling case that the time has come to transform our organizations.

We agree with these people. We believe that the time to break through the barriers of our outmoded and constraining beliefs about people and organizations is now. Many organizations are showing increasing readiness for organizational transformation—for a true metamorphosis in beliefs, values, and structures. The more visionary of our corporate leaders are reaching the conclusion that the thriving organizations of the 1990s and beyond will be fundamentally different from the kinds of organizations we now have. The more inquisitive of these leaders have visited one or more of the dozens of new innovative plants now found throughout the United States. They are asking themselves some very pertinent questions:

> "If these innovative new plants consistently demonstrate dramatic advantages over comparably equipped traditional plants, what would it take to achieve the same results in existing plants?"
>
> "If designing an organization in a way that frees up the potential of people and creates a culture of commitment, caring, and excellence makes sense in manufacturing, why not in other functions?"
>
> "Why not in headquarters? What if our approach to our work and to shaping our mission, strategies, policies, and culture was as well designed and executed as the approach of these technician teams to their work?"

For these visionary leaders and practitioners, we offer our vision of the art of the possible, along with a very practical road map for getting there.

New Paradigm Organizations—A Beginning Vision

As a society, our lenses for "seeing" organizations have been ground and polished by bureaucracies: schools, churches,

**Figure 14-1. From Traditional to New Paradigm Organizations —
A Fundamental Shift in Thinking, Values, and Design.**

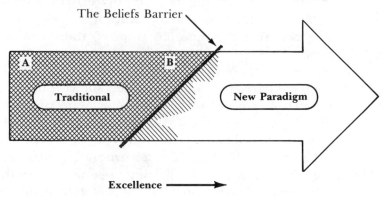

Traditional	*New Paradigm*
• Marginal to excellent results	• Extraordinary results
• Power and role orientation	• Task and people orientation
• "Control over"	• High commitment
• Machine and parts	• Open living system
• Stockholder focus	• Ecological view
• Design a "given"	• Ongoing self-design
• Individual-focused	• Team-focused
• Employees as costs/liabilities	• Members most valued assets
	• Learning highly valued

Source: Veltrop and Harrington, 1986.

the military, governments, and corporations. Our ability to envision what is possible in organizations is clouded by archaic concepts such as the need for hierarchies, chains of command, spans of control, superiors, subordinates, and so on. Before we can bring about organizationwide transformation, we need to try on a new set of lenses, one that will allow us to see new possibilities.

In Figure 14-1 we contrast traditional and new paradigm organizations. A number of the comparisons reflect the fundamentally different ways of looking at and thinking about organizations found in these paradigms.

The new paradigm characteristics are derived mainly from new manufacturing plants established by large corporations such as Procter & Gamble, General Motors, General Electric, Ford Motor, AT&T, Digital Equipment, Sherwin-Williams, Alcoa, Rohm & Haas, PepsiCo, and Exxon. The dramatic results achieved by these new innovative organizations have also begun to be achieved by redesigning existing manufacturing plants and other functions. The potential payouts for redesigning whole organizations and bringing them into the new paradigm territory have only begun to be tapped.

There are many technologies available for moving a large corporation from point A to point B; the rub is that most of these technologies are rooted in and shaped by the traditional belief system and cannot move an organization beyond the "beliefs barrier." Breaking through the "beliefs barrier" from the traditional side is not easy. Our beliefs are as natural to us as water is to a fish, and as limiting. If I had lived only under water, I would be unable to conceive of walking on land. If I had experienced only traditional organizations, the new paradigm organizations would seem impossibly idealistic to me.

The differences between the new and the traditional are embedded in the paradigms of members and stakeholders, that is, in their patterns of thinking about and visualizing their organizations. While traditional change strategies can improve an organization's effectiveness without changing its basic form, organizationwide transformation must, of necessity, begin by shifting members' and stakeholders' paradigms and giving them new lenses for seeing the possibilities. Breaking through this barrier is rarely just a cognitive process. Visiting an innovative plant is one very effective way to allow organizational members to see how new ideas work in practice and to experience life in a "transformed" organization.

The above vision may seem idealistic and impractical to those who have experienced only traditional systems. However, those who have crossed over from traditional systems and have experienced this vision see organizations through very different lenses. To them, it is the traditional, top-down control organization that begins to feel strange and unnatural. When they look back they can clearly see how traditional beliefs and organizing forms are a continual drain on an organization's vitality and resources.

But bringing this vision to life in a new, innovative plant is not easy. Transforming an existing plant is even more difficult, and organizationwide transformation represents a still larger challenge. In this section, we identify five challenges that seem inescapable in such efforts:

1. *Complexity of organization design—how to manage all the critical variables without oversimplification.* Organization design involves hundreds of choices that do not begin to be represented by the organization chart. Organization design serves as the skeleton that gives a culture much of its form and defines its possibilities for movement and performance. If an outmoded design does not support high commitment and cannot respond to our rapidly changing environment, then the option is ours to create more appropriate forms. The possibilities are unlimited. The challenge here is to deal effectively with all the critical design variables without oversimplifying them or becoming overwhelmed by them.

2. *Diffusion—how to create a hospitable environment for spreading success.* Most innovative design work to date has been done in new manufacturing plants. No matter how dramatic their successes, diffusion has generally been a slow and difficult process (Walton, 1975). Problems of understanding and communication between the innovative plant and both its parent organization and sibling plants have tended to be the rule rather than the exception. It seems to be the nature of social systems that all their parts unconsciously collude in holding the current state in place. No matter where a new paradigm is introduced, there will be a natural tendency for the rest of the system to want to reject it.

A related issue is that of what to diffuse. Attempts to transplant a solution (that is, an organization design or elements of the design) optimized for one system to a different system are rarely successful. What *can* be diffused, and how to best diffuse it, are critical issues to address.

3. *Leadership development—how to achieve leadership align-*

ment. Traditional hierarchies tend to foster a form of "bureausis" that we call "upward focus"; this gives a higher priority to image than to action. It makes it impossible to focus on a shared vision. Organization members will not align themselves with an organization's vision unless that same alignment is demonstrated consistently by those above them in the hierarchy. The challenge is to create a compelling corporate vision and then to empower the leadership to orchestrate a shift from the traditional upward focus to a focus on purpose and vision.

4. *Culture change — how to rebuild the iceberg.* An organization's culture, like an iceberg, is mostly invisible, quite deep, and not easily accessible. What shows above the surface — the behavioral norms or the "rules of the game" — represents that aspect of culture most easily identified and managed. Organizationwide transformation implies a significant shift in the culture of the organization. An effective transformation strategy needs to find a way to adjust, supplant, or reprogram those invisible assumptions and beliefs that are holding the counterproductive aspects of the existing culture in place.

5. *Ever increasing rate of change — how to maintain the best fit with a moving target.* Assuming that organizationwide transformation is effected, how do we sustain its benefits in an increasingly complex and changing world? In this highly volatile environment, no fixed organizing form will remain optimal for very long. Indeed, with technical and social change progressing more and more rapidly, the life span of any optimal fit is steadily decreasing. The challenge is to equip organizations with the capacity to be self-adapting to these changes and to maintain a good fit with the constantly moving target.

The above list, though by no means exhaustive, does cover some of the challenges in transformation efforts, and sets the stage for a look at some of the more powerful and unique features of the four-technology approach.

Four-Technology Approach to Organizationwide Transformation

We have chosen to focus on a four-technology approach in this chapter for a variety of reasons, all of which can be summarized in two words: it works. Why and how it works, and what makes it unique, are worth considering briefly before we get into a detailed description of exactly what "it" is.

The approach we are describing actually comprises a broad range of technologies; we identify and highlight four primary technology clusters because they represent useful ways to label and think about the approach. The four technologies are:

1. Learning how to learn
2. Creating shared visions
3. Organization design
4. Planning and leading organization transitions

The four technologies used in this approach derive from the work of many of the seminal thinkers and practitioners in the field of organization design and development. The process draws on a variety of disciplines, including open systems theory, sociotechnical systems analysis, adult learning theory, visioning, transition planning, and group and interpersonal dynamics. The man most responsible for synthesizing these technologies into one cohesive approach to organization design and renewal is Herb Stokes, a pioneer practitioner with a twenty-five-year track record of successes, both in Procter & Gamble and as an external consultant.

This broad theoretical base means that the four-technology approach is an extremely comprehensive approach, one that looks at all possible levels of a system, from intrapersonal beliefs and assumptions to systemwide integration and interaction with the external environment. The process eventually involves people at all levels of the system, from top management to the work force. The biggest single factor contributing to the effectiveness of the approach is the delivery vehicle — a series of five to ten workshops, each spanning two to five days, presented over a period of six to eighteen months, and involving the leaders and resource people of the organization in question. These workshops are:

1. *organic* — they easily adapt to differing and evolving needs within any project; while the workshop process is supplied by the consultant, the content and products of the workshop are determined by the participants.
2. *generic* — they apply equally well either to the redesign/renewal of an existing system or to the design and startup of a new plant; they are equally applicable to manufacturing and nonmanufacturing functions, at all levels and in all systems.
3. *holistic* — they constitute a pilot model of the ideal future organization. Participants become a high-performing learning/doing organization engaged in the task of creating a high-performing learning/doing organization.
4. *highly leveraged* — the workshops are geared to give participants the ability to diffuse what they have learned throughout their organization on their own. Participants frequently develop and present their own workshops to a larger population within the organization while still in the early stages of the process.
5. *pragmatic* — they provide a "learning by doing" environment for creating the visions, designs, and plans needed to support the organization's revitalization. Each workshop results in immediately useful products for the organization.
6. *developmental* — they provide an organization's leadership with a framework for evolving and testing their beliefs and values as they engage in this most important work of leadership. By doing the work of transformation, the participants transform themselves as well as their organization.

When applied in a plant setting, the design/redesign work typically includes the top managers of the facility, functional representatives from headquarters, and key resource people. Managers from sister organizations may also be included to (1) begin their preparation for the application of the process in their own organization, (2) make use of their knowledge and experience in the design/redesign work, and (3) create a broader base of support for and ownership in the new organization.

The result of such a workshop series will be a high-performance leadership team. The participation of the organization's leadership (including key stakeholders) means that the workshop products will be well supported. The timing and overall duration of the workshop series are designed to permit appropriate interaction with and involvement of the rest of the organization during this phase.

The best way to appreciate the four-technology process itself is to see it unfold. Piecewise examination of the models and methods used does not do justice to the synergy between the many parts. In this section, we will take the reader on a guided tour of the four technologies as they are applied in a workshop series.

Learning How to Learn. "There is nothing more practical than a good theory, nothing more dangerous than a bad one" (Stokes, personal correspondence, April 1986). Relying on textbook theories of organizational change tends to result in change strategies that are imperfectly understood and not fully "owned" by the people in charge of applying them; consequently, they simply do not work. Conversely, people are very committed to theories born of their own experiences and beliefs; it is important that these theories be complete and workable. Utilizing theoretical readings as well as their own experience, participants develop their own working theories and, as a group, reach consensus on the working theories and norms that they want to use both in their workshops and in their new organization. These theories are refined as the participants' experience grows.

The participants also learn how to learn—from each other, from their environment, from their own experience. The so-called corkscrew model (Figure 14-2) is a tool for learning from experience that is used each step of the way in the workshops; ideally, this process becomes a way of life for the organization's members. (The iterative nature of the process, in which new learnings build on prior ones, led to the name "corkscrew.")

The participants are also introduced to a new set of lenses for seeing organizations—the four-box systems model. This model is used both as a diagnostic tool and as a planning guide for design/redesign. The model assumes that the primary objec-

Figure 14-2. Corkscrew Model.

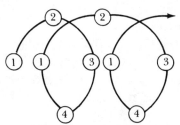

1. Before you act, clarify your working theories and predict the outcome.
2. Take action.
3. Observe what happens—all the outcomes.
4. Analyze why it happened.
1. Note learnings and generalizations and create new working theories.

Source: Veltrop and Harrington, 1986.

tive of organizational planning and development efforts is to achieve a high degree of coherence or "fit" between each of the various organizational design elements, the organization's vision and objectives, and the organization's external environment. It is generally true that any given outcome will have multiple causes and that any given design change will have more than one outcome. This means that if a given design change does not fit with the other design elements, with the external environment, or with the work culture, you can count on some unintended outcomes.

In our basic model, the environmental factors are those aspects of the organization's environment that are important to its survival. They include: (1) environmental demands and opportunities, including the expectations from the parent company, customers, the community, and competitors, as well as potential business opportunities; (2) conditioning factors, such as the prevailing culture of the parent company or society, past events and practices in the company or industry, and technological developments or economic conditions; and (3) resource inputs in the form of people, money, materials, and information required for carrying out organizational purposes and achieving organizational objectives.

The design elements are those structures and systems that define "what's intended" in the organization. As the following list indicates, they are the result of the design choices an organization makes to achieve a "best fit" with its environment and a "best fit" internally among its various elements:

- The organization's vision, which reflects the underlying values and beliefs of the organization and the objectives and strategies that flow from that vision
- The organization's tasks and technologies—the work that it does and the methods it employs for doing it
- The structure of the organization—the way the tasks are divided and assigned to individuals or groups, as well as how subunits are linked to one another
- The organization's information flow and decision-making processes
- The people systems within the organization—the means by which it selects, assimilates, and develops its human resources
- The organization's reward systems, including intrinsic as well as extrinsic rewards
- The organization's renewal systems—the mechanisms used for detecting lack of internal or external fit and for designing and implementing adjustments to the design elements as needed

Organizational qualities describe "what's happening" in an organization, and include (1) the organization's culture—its personality, norms, values, beliefs, and assumptions; (2) its climate (for example, members' attitudes and feelings); and (3) how the leadership behaves and is seen.

The organizational outcomes include (1) business results such as profit and product quality; (2) the need satisfaction and growth of members that occurs as a result of their participation in the organization's activities; (3) environmental relations, including organizational image and reputation and the organization's handling of its interactions with its environment; and (4) organization development, that is, the growth in the organization's capacity to add value in its social, economic, and physical environment.

The four-box model serves as a generic reference map throughout the workshops. It is equally useful for diagnosis, design, and planning. Its frequent application reinforces a systems view of the organization and provides a sound overview context when the focus is on specific issues.

Creating Shared Visions. This is perhaps the most "magical" and exciting of the four technologies. In a world of constant change, both internal and external, a commonly held vision can be the unchanging ideal toward which the organization is always moving and around which it builds or reshapes its culture. As the environment shifts, the organization's form and structure may change, but its vision will be relatively enduring.

Alignment around a common goal, mission, or quest has always been a powerful motivating force — much more powerful than the traditional carrot and stick approach, even much more powerful than rational planning. The vision challenges the organization's members to seek out the best in themselves and the best possible common future. It is a powerful first step in freeing the spirit and energy in the organization (Richards and Engel, 1986).

It is important to note the fundamental difference between a vision-focused change strategy and a problem-focused intervention. The problem-focused intervention, which emphasizes what is wrong and how can it be fixed, is fraught with energy-consuming and mind-limiting traps for the organization. In contrast, the emphasis on the ideal vision, that is, on our highest goals and how we can achieve them, opens the participants to a broad view of the possibilities for the organization. It draws attention away from the defensiveness and "blaming" associated with a problem focus, while allowing for the development of creative ways to minimize problems in the future. As Tice (1980) explains it, the vision "programs" our subconscious minds to selectively perceive that which we need in order to achieve our purposes. In the workshops, the motto is, "If you can dream it, you can do it."

Organization Design. A "whole-to-parts" approach to organization design is the keystone of the process. The initial focus is on the ideal design for the organization in the future. Having created an organizational vision, the participants are then pressed to design an ideal organization aligned with that vision. Again we see the emphasis on possibilities, not problems, in the four-technology approach. The concept is deceptively simple: Create your vision of an ideal future and design an organization consistent with that vision—without considering feasibility, cost, or any other limiting realities. The creativity begins to flow and multiply. As the ideal future design takes shape, the participants become more and more aware of the possibilities open to them. They begin to develop a good sense of how everything can fit together in more synergistic ways. Once they have worked long enough in the ideal future, it becomes alive and real for them.

The design work begins with technical analysis. This is a close-up look at the core work of the organization—at the actual steps involved in producing the organization's products or services, from the incoming raw materials to the delivery of the finished product. The work is analyzed to identify the variances, namely, those points in the process where things can deviate from specifications. The variances that have the greatest impact on the rest of the core operating process are the key variances. The ideal is to design the organization to either eliminate the variances or to control them at their source.

Using the technical analysis, the vision, the working theories, and the design criteria developed in previous workshops, the participants turn their attention to the design of the core operating system. The intention is to design an operating system that is efficient, flexible, and rewarding for its members and that has the tools, resources, and information it needs to be accountable for its outcomes. The team becomes the basic organizing unit. Many tasks typically relegated to separate departments, such as maintenance, sanitation, and quality control, are made a part of the core operating system and shared by team members. A minimum of work is "exported" to other systems. The design proceeds from the operating system through the support, managing, and strategic subsystems as shown in Figure 14-3.

The support subsystem includes activities that cut across teams—for example, payroll, engineering, and security. The managing subsystem is that portion of the organization put in

Figure 14-3. Design of the Operating System.

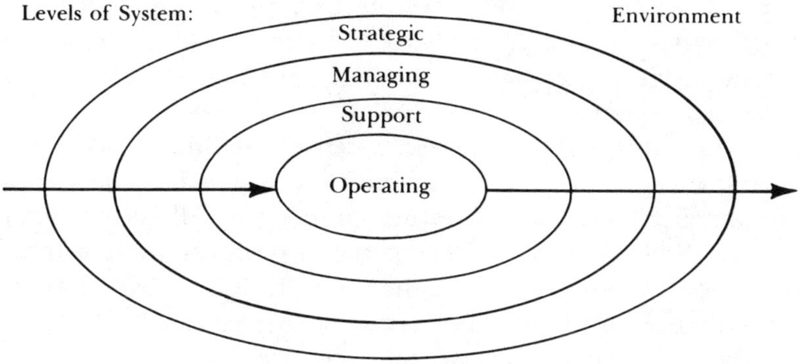

Levels of System: Environment

Strategic

Managing

Support

Operating

Source: Veltrop and Harrington, 1986.

place to ensure alignment within the organization and alignment with the vision. It is there to serve the operating system,
rather than the other way around. The strategic subsystem will
handle boundary management between the organization and its
external environment, maintaining alignment with the outside
world. The strategic subsystem also provides for the routine
gathering and processing of data on demands, needs, changes,
trends, and so on in the external world that could have an
impact on the health and vitality of the organization. It will then
direct whatever organizational renewal or redesign seems
appropriate.

Information and decision-making systems are designed
in parallel with each of the above levels of the system. In the
design of these systems, priority is given to identifying what
decisions need to be made at each level and what information is
needed at that level in order for those decisions to be made. The
ideal is to have decisions made at the point where the impact of
those decisions will be felt.

As each of these subsystems is designed, it is checked for
fit with the vision, with the guidelines, and with the work already
done. If there are misfits, one or all parts may be adjusted as
necessary.

People systems include the processes for the selection,

training, and development of organization membership and help ensure a fit between people and the organization—its vision, purpose, design and work to be done. Once the people system design is sketched in, the designers turn their attention to reward systems.

The problem with reward systems is that they work. If you want teamwork and high commitment but you reward individual achievement and "looking good," you will get what you reward. When you use money to try to motivate people to do what they already like to do, they tend to like it less. We have found that people like to learn, they like to make things happen, and they like to excel. The secret to reward systems is to design the rest of the systems so that most of the members' intrinsic needs are met. The primary goal of an extrinsic reward system is to meet those needs that cannot be met intrinsically.

Renewal systems are unique to the new paradigm organization. In sharp contrast with the rigid designs of traditional organizations, this four-technology approach assumes that change is the only certainty. When leaders and resources are equipped with these four technologies, they can redesign their organization as needed. They become aligned with and attuned to the environment, rather than being at its mercy. We see designing for self-renewal as a key to sustaining high performance in a changing environment. The recurring theme in this exercise is "fit"—fit with the vision, fit with the design guidelines, and fit between all parts and levels of the system. The iterative nature of the process provides the participants with the opportunity to refine the design as they address progressively more detailed levels and begin to involve other organization members.

Planning and Leading Organization Transitions. Here again the four-technology approach departs from conventional wisdom. By now, workshop participants have spent considerable time living in an "ideal future state." As they have iterated through their ideal future designs, those designs have become increasingly detailed, increasingly real, and increasingly doable. At this point, those elements of that future state design that can be implemented immediately are implemented. No energy is wasted looking at the problems of the current state.

In parallel with implementing these immediately doable elements, the participants look at the gap between the new "current state" and their ideal future, and then plan the transition. They look at ways of gaining needed commitment, ways of evaluating progress and stabilizing change, ways of identifying and acquiring needed resources. Particular attention needs to be paid to the information flow and decision-making systems, as well as the reward systems that will be supporting the transition.

The implementation process is generally designed to demonstrate the activities of the workshops, bringing them to life in very concrete ways. By this time, organization members will have internalized their vision and principles, and will be sufficiently experienced in the application of the workshop process to be able to complete their renewal/redesign efforts with little or no outside help. And that is the ultimate intention of the process: to give an organization the ability to continue to analyze the needs of the environment and design the most appropriate organizational systems in response to or, better yet, in anticipation of those needs.

Five Major Challenges

With the forgoing description as background, we can now review the challenges described earlier and see how they are addressed by the four-technology approach.

Complexity. Much of the difficulty in dealing with the true complexity of organizations is the result of inadequate and fragmented models. With the consistent use of a good reference map of the territory, and an experienced and knowledgeable guide, the participants are led through a generic sequence of steps that become increasingly tailored to their own organization as they assume more and more ownership of the work.

The process strikes a balance between the overwhelming complexity of an organization and the ability of our minds to focus on only a limited amount of information at any instant. At each step of the way, the concept of "minimal critical specification" is employed. This means that the workshop participants work only to the level of detail required to finish one step and move on to the next. Workshop leaders encourage participants to move through the steps of the process with deliberate speed and as often as necessary.

This strategy to emphasize and maintain focus on designing the ideal future state organization reduces both confusion and complexity. By iterating through the various design elements in a short time with this focus on the ideal, the participants develop a holistic view of their organization; that is, they internalize a good understanding of the parts, of the whole, and of how the parts fit together. This then serves as a shared background picture that remains constant as the group focuses on specific design issues.

Diffusion. In the four-technology approach, leadership development, organization transformation, and diffusion all occur simultaneously and all use the same process. For instance, by involving top management at headquarters in the same experience as local leaders, the usual problems of understanding and communication are greatly relieved. Further, when managers assist in the design of a sister organization, diffusion of what they have learned to their own organization becomes a very natural process.

This approach emphasizes the development, improvement, and diffusion of processes rather than of specific solutions. These processes are tailored to the needs of each organization as they are implemented. Each organizational unit is designed by its own members in accordance with their unique situation, within the corporate vision and guidelines. Although subsequent projects will learn from prototype efforts, their plans and designs are not imported as is.

Leadership Development. Since the designers of an organization include the managers and key leaders of that organization, leadership development is intrinsic to the design and planning process. By transferring their learnings to the rest of the organization, managers reinforce their own understanding of the technologies. They become role models to the organization membership and provide proof of the commitment of the top leadership to the ideals and objectives of the transformation. Their role in disseminating the new vision, principles, and ideals is an important factor in fostering organizationwide alignment.

Culture. We see leadership behavior and organization design as the two most powerful determinants of organization culture; in fact, they are the warp and woof of the fabric of that culture. Attempting to change one without a corresponding change in the other will not produce the desired results. A major strength in this approach is that it simultaneously addresses both leadership behavior and organization design with an effectiveness and efficiency that would not be possible if they were addressed separately. The culture clashes that seem to accompany any innovative design effort are greatly reduced by the inclusion of a broad circle of leaders and resource people at each stage of the process.

Ever Increasing Rate of Change. The four-technology approach equips organization leadership with the knowledge and skills to scan their environment and to diagnose, redesign, and renew their organizations; it also results in responsive and flexible designs that explicitly provide for those kinds of activity at appropriate intervals.

Conclusion

The time has come to approach the revitalization of our organizations with a new level of boldness and collaboration. It is time to shift our collective focus toward organizationwide strategies and away from partial approaches; to concentrate on vision-focused projects rather than problem-driven interventions; and to equip ourselves to provide the technologies, support, and confidence that encourage corporations to step beyond bureaucratic organizing forms and assumptions.

The size of the opportunities for organizationwide transformation is almost beyond comprehension. We are just beginning to scratch the surface. Corporate readiness is accelerating. The technologies for supporting this work are available, but not yet widely shared. As practitioners, we need to come up with strategies for developing ourselves that match the size of the opportunity, that synthesize the best expertise available, and that demonstrate our ideal of collaboration. As corporate leaders, we need to expand the definition of our roles to include those of visionary, organizational architect, and champion of transformation.

The consequences of reinventing the corporation go beyond the corporate bottom line, beyond the well-being of the corporate membership, and even beyond the direct effects on corporate environments. Corporations have been and will continue to be in the best position to pioneer the processes of organizationwide transformation. Their successes can significantly influence the public sectors as well.

In this chapter we have shared our beginning vision of the new paradigm organization. We have described some of the challenges facing practitioners and leaders who want to implement organizationwide transformations, and we have described one workable approach for managing those challenges while accomplishing that transformation. We are aware of other approaches and encourage an open exchange and synthesis of those technologies that work. We believe we are living in the best of all possible times for making a significant and lasting difference in organizations. We are committed to collaboration in pursuit of that vision.

References

Capra, F. *The Turning Point*. New York: Simon & Schuster, 1982.

Harrison, R. "Strategies for a New Age." *Human Resource Management*, 1983, *22*, 209–235.

Naisbitt, J., and Aburdene, P. *Re-Inventing the Corporation*. New York: Warner Books, 1985.

Richards, R., and Engel, S. "After the Vision: Suggestions to

Corporate Visionaries and Vision Champions." In J. Adams (ed.), *Transforming Leadership*. Norfolk, Va.: Miles River Press, 1986.

Tice, L. *New Age Thinking for Achieving Your Potential*. Seattle: Pacific Institute, 1980.

Toffler, A. *The Third Wave*. New York: Bantam Books, 1981.

Veltrop, B., and Harrington, K. "Vision/Action." *Journal of the Bay Area Organization Development Network*, 1986, *6* (2), 4–7.

Walton, R. E. "The Diffusion of New Work Structures: Explaining Why Success Didn't Take." *Organizational Dynamics*, 1975, *3* (3), 3–22.

15

Katharine Esty

Group Methods for Transformation

To survive and prosper in the years ahead, organizations will have to develop an ongoing ability to adapt to rapidly changing environments. While group methods have been used as vehicles for personal change for many years, their use to transform entire organizations is relatively new. In this chapter, a *structural approach* to organizationwide transformation using groups is first presented. This is followed by a description of how the approach worked in the Information System Services (ISS) at International Harvester (now Navistar International) where a series of group structures became the cornerstones of the organizational change effort.

The need to transform organizations is more critical today than ever before. Some industries, such as airlines and banking are being deregulated while others—health care, for example—face new regulations that are turning their work practices upside down. Advances in technology are shortening the life span of many products from trucks to soap. How we work on the plant floor and how we work in the office have been revolutionized by technological advances. Competition from Europe, Japan, and, more recently, Korea has permanently disabled some of our industries, such as the steel and textile industries, and is seriously threatening many others, including the automotive and electronic industries. At the same time, the demographics of the work force are changing as the percentage of women and foreign-born workers increases steadily. To add to the complexity of the situation, these changes are happening simultaneously and interacting with each other in unexpected ways.

Adapting to this turbulent atmosphere is absolutely necessary if a company is to survive, but it is not sufficient. It is not a question of playing catch-up—modifying the corporation and then entering a period of stabilization. Rather, adapting to change must be conceptualized as a continuous process because the environment is relentlessly changing and, indeed, it is changing at an ever increasing rate. Organizational transformation in this context is best defined as an attempt to develop within the organization the capacity to continually adapt to the changing environment. What characterizes this kind of organizational change is not only the magnitude of the changes required and the breadth of the arenas transformed, but, most importantly, the ongoing nature of the change process.

In the past, many organization development practitioners concentrated their efforts on changing the attitudes and behaviors of employees. In this "person" approach to change, the hearts and minds of individuals are the targets of change. Practitioners have usually made executive education programs, management development programs, and other types of training the centerpieces of organizational change efforts.

In the 1970s, as organizations sought to modify their cultures, there was a proliferation of team-building sessions, male-female awareness programs, and black-white encounter groups. More recently, as organizations have tried to become more productive, they have sponsored programs to encourage employee involvement and participative management. At Exxon Shipping, for example, when top managers wanted to create a more flexible organizational culture, a majority of its employees—both officers and nonsupervisors—were asked to attend a five-day training program designed to encourage teamwork and promote innovation.

The Structural Approach

The structural approach using group methods is an alter-native and broader means for bringing about change in organizations. In this approach, the target of the change effort includes the systems, practices, and procedures of the organization as well as the attitudes of employees. It is assumed that attitudinal and behavior change follows naturally in the wake of organizational changes and that these organizational changes therefore must be the first priority.

This approach builds upon the work of Kanter (1977), who asserts that the job makes the person. When employees are underachieving, passive, and unmotivated, this is frequently a consequence of the way their jobs are structured rather than of their individual character traits. At any rate, since it is notori-ously difficult to change character traits, it makes sense to focus first on the organizational structures. Modifying the organizational systems, policies, practices, and procedures leads more quickly and more directly to the objective of changed behavior. In particular, according to Kanter, designing more opportu-nity and more power into jobs will result in more effective employees.

Beckhard and Harris, in their book *Organizational Transition: Managing Complex Change* (1977), suggest that organizations should designate special structures to do the work of managing the change during a "transition state." The CEO, a project manager, or a task force can take on this function, but they believe that change efforts are best facilitated by creating a management system that is separate and different from the present management system.

The Parallel Organization. Stein and Kanter (1980) develop the ideas of Beckhard and Harris somewhat further. During an organizational transition period, they suggest, the organization should create a "parallel organization" that consists of a steering committee and flexible, temporary problem-solving groups to supplement the work of the more hierarchical and bureaucratic management structure. The two organizations exist side by side, and the parallel organization is not intended in any way to replace the management system. Parallel organizations can be both reactive (dealing with those changes necessitated by changes in the environment) and proactive (implementing changes in anticipation of future developments).

Group Methods. In the structural approach to organizationwide transformation being presented here, various kinds of group structures become the parallel organization. Groups are developed to improve communication and to provide top management with feedback. Other groups are created to identify the critical issues before the organization and to develop projects that address these issues. Finally, there are groups whose purpose is to implement the change projects. Some of the groups involve all the employees, some involve natural work groups of peers, and others consist of a diagonal slice of the organization, with a membership that represents every level, function, and location of the organization.

Not only do these groups carry out and coordinate the change effort, but they perform a number of other functions. First, they build commitment to the new corporate direction by providing the opportunity for large numbers of employees to become directly involved in the change process. Second, these groups serve as channels for information about the progress of the change effort. They provide top management with a good forum for sharing its vision of the new organization. Employees gradually come to understand the meaning of the changes as they listen to top management discuss them again and again and as they talk about them with their co-workers in a variety of settings. Morale is typically raised by the interaction with management at the meetings, as well as by the chance to express a wide range of feelings and reactions to the change effort. Getting feelings out in the open accelerates the process of working through the inevitable losses that all change entails. Lastly, productivity improves as groups of employees engage in the tasks of identifying the critical issues of the organization and of actually implementing action steps that will improve the effectiveness of the organization.

This is the basic blueprint of the structural approach to organizational change using group methods. How well does it actually work? How are these group structures initially launched? How is commitment gained? What are the drawbacks and the pitfalls of this approach? What is the actual impact of these structures on the organization and its employees? Case material from the Information System Services (ISS) at International Harvester illustrates the application of this approach at one organization and also provides some preliminary answers to these questions.

ISS at International Harvester

In November of 1984, International Harvester announced that it was selling its agricultural equipment business to Tenneco. The ISS organization needed to designate about 100 of its 640 employees to "migrate" from Harvester to J. I. Case in Racine, Wisconsin, the Tenneco subsidiary that was actually acquiring the business, and it also had to lay off approximately 100 other employees. Although International Harvester had a history of selling off parts of its businesses and had laid off a number of employees in the preceding five years, the divestiture of the "ag" business was a traumatic experience for many employees. Not only was the company selling a very large part of its remaining business (40 percent) but it was also giving up the rights to the Harvester name. (It was awkward for a company that produced trucks and engines to be named International Harvester, in any case.)

On the day of the announcement, the corporate vice-president, Mike Clayton, telephoned Goodmeasure and asked for some assistance in managing the organizational transition. Three days later when my partner, Ralph Loftin, and I arrived on the scene, Clayton and his staff vice-president, John Bowyer, summarized the situation this way: Morale was at an all-time low and cynicism about the company was at an all-time high. ISS had been charged with the seemingly impossible task of keeping all of Harvester's computer systems up and running while the "ag" systems were being moved to Racine.

Clayton and Bowyer felt pressure to make immediate decisions on the triage question: Who would be laid off, who would be assigned to Case, and who would remain at ISS? They had major concerns that employees whom they wanted and needed to keep in ISS would quit because of Harvester's uncertain future and because ISS's technically trained employees were highly mobile. Even in good times, the ISS organization had experienced a fairly high level of turnover.

But Clayton also saw an opportunity in the crisis that lay ahead at ISS to fundamentally transform the organization. The ISS employees described International Harvester as "hierarchical," "bureaucratic," "unimaginative," and "stuck in the past." They described themselves (the employees in ISS) as "dedicated" and "hardworking," and they believed their work to be of "very high quality." But many of their users saw it somewhat differently. They described ISS as slow moving, unresponsive, and expensive.

Clayton realized that if the company was to survive, ISS, as well as the rest of International Harvester, had to make organizational effectiveness a top priority. He believed that in order for ISS to become more productive, trust must be reestablished, communication improved, and more participative ways of working developed. In the months that followed, the ISS managers, with the assistance of Goodmeasure, developed a number of group structures to move the organization toward these desired changes.

All-Employee Meeting. During the first weeks after the announcement, employees were anxious, angry, confused, and depressed. Gallows humor flourished. Someone placed a note on a central bulletin board saying, "Will the last group sold please turn out the lights?" Several months before the divestiture, a large number of posters saying, "The commitment is forever," had appeared throughout the organization. The day after the divestiture announcement, one of these posters had been altered to read, "The commitment is forever or until next Tuesday, whichever comes first."

Managers were deluged with questions about the divestiture, and the rumor mill was turning fast. It was obvious that the usual channels of communication were not adequate to handle the situation, so Clayton and Bowyer decided to hold a briefing for all ISS employees. Getting ISS employees together in one spot was difficult to arrange since they were scattered over three states and six or seven work sites. This all-employee meeting was the first group structure created to manage the organizational transformation.

The meeting was held just ten days after the divestiture announcement. The two vice-presidents, their senior managers, and a corporate human resources representative sat on a platform facing a sea of scared and sullen faces. Clayton and Bowyer presented the facts about Harvester's situation and how ISS would probably be affected. They responded to all the questions from the floor, although many of their answers were "We just don't know yet."

At a second all-employee meeting that was held two weeks later, the collective mood was somewhat less depressed. As at the first meeting, questions poured in. Many were about benefits and compensation, and a few were openly hostile, such as, "When will you start treating people like people?" and "Do you believe in the mushroom theory—in keeping us all in the dark?" The managers were able to remain calm and did not become defensive; they kept on answering questions as long as they came. And at the end of this two-and-a-half-hour meeting, unlike the first one, there was even a small ripple of applause.

During the next year and a half, ISS top managers sponsored five more of these all-employee meetings. In the beginning, these meetings served primarily to provide information about the divestiture. As time passed, however, the meetings changed in character. A top corporate manager was invited to speak, and several ISS managers reported on progress in various arenas. Over time, too, the meetings became a place for Clayton and Bowyer to present their interpretation of what was happening.

Research informs us that it is not change itself that troubles employees, but the meaning that employees give to that change (Esty, 1984). Here was a forum in which top-level managers could share their vision of organizational events and express their cautious optimism about the company's future. By September of 1986, it was clear that the ISS all-employee meetings had become a cornerstone of the new ISS.

Feedback Sessions. The second cornerstone of the ISS change effort was a system of "feedback sessions" whose purpose was to further develop bottom-up communications. At these forty-six small-group meetings, eight to twelve employees meet together with one of their co-workers in the leadership role. Confidentiality is assured, and the opportunity to "vent"—to react to the organizational events that are taking place—is provided. More importantly, these sessions provide every employee the chance to give feedback to ISS senior managers and to influence their thinking. During the meetings, which last from one to two hours, the group leader records the questions, concerns, and comments of the group on "feedback sheets" that are then sent on to top management. At the initial sessions, ISS managers promised to read every comment and to respond in writing to all questions.

Before this first set of feedback sessions, some of those who reported directly to Bowyer were dubious about whether this kind of meeting would be useful. The human resource department expressed strong reservations about trying to train the leaders of the group in a single training session of an hour or two. These leaders had been appointed from the rank and file, and it was not clear that they were interested in leading a group. Others warned that "these sessions will open up a can of worms" and that "they are going to deteriorate into gripe sessions." In spite of these concerns, the manager in charge finally decided that since "we don't have much to lose, let's give it a try."

The first set of sessions was scheduled between the first and second all-employee meetings, in mid December of 1984. The vast majority of ISS employees chose to attend. Pages and pages of feedback were collected and passed on to top management. Responding in writing to each and every question turned out to be an incredibly time-consuming task. By the third round of feedback sessions in the spring of 1985, top management

merely promised to read and seriously consider all the comments. The concerns and questions that were raised by many
groups would then become major topics at the next all-employee
meeting.

There were other problems with the feedback sessions.
Initially, some employees found themselves in a group with their
supervisor and did not feel comfortable talking openly. Others
were left off the lists of participants. The reactions on the whole,
however, were strongly positive. Employee after employee expressed enthusiasm about the process and about being given the
opportunity to make his or her concerns known to the senior
managers.

The pattern of alternating all-employee meetings with
feedback sessions continued. Many pages of comments were
generated from each set of feedback sessions, and the shifting
emphases of the comments demonstrate the changing organizational concerns. For example, in January of 1986, the feedback
sessions were used to capture employees' reactions to the new
corporate name (Navistar International) and to the multimedia
event where the new name was announced. But if a majority of
employees have found these sessions effective, a minority continues to feel uneasy about them. Managers wonder if the sessions are degenerating into "bitching sessions," or if they have
outlived their usefulness. And the rank and file sometimes
complain that "we have given our feedback over and over and
nothing much has changed."

Attendance at feedback sessions by mid 1986 was somewhat down compared to the 1984 and early 1985 sessions. This
probably reflects the growing stability of the corporation. In a
survey taken in May 1986, employees evaluated these sessions as
"very useful" and indicated that they wanted to see them
continued.

By April of 1985, it was clear that ISS had moved beyond
the crisis set in motion by the divestiture. Neither of the vice-
presidents, however, was satisfied with progress toward the "new
ISS" that would be more innovative, effective, participative, and
responsive. "We're dead in the water" is how Bowyer described
the situation to us. He went on to explain, "Everything still takes

much longer to do than it should. I give out an assignment and weeks later I am told that they are still gathering information. Deadlines are missed and decisions frequently get postponed." Exactly what made it so difficult to get things done was somewhat puzzling. We proposed that the time was ripe for a major organizational assessment — and Bowyer agreed.

During the next six weeks, my consulting partner and I interviewed over 140 employees within ISS and over 40 people in their key user organizations. In semistructured interviews we asked them what was working well? What was not? What were the critical issues before the organization and what were the opportunities for improving ISS effectiveness? In keeping with our emphasis on group structures, many of these interviews were small-group interviews. It soon became clear to us that employees displayed far greater candor in these group interviews than in the individual interviews that we conducted.

The interviews were themselves an important step in the change effort. A quarter of the organizational members were asked in some depth for their views on how the organization was functioning. We learned that the fact that outside consultants had been hired signaled to the organization that ISS management was serious about the change effort. Expectations that something would happen were raised, although at the same time there was widespread concern that nothing would change.

Council for the Future. During May of 1985, at the same time that the audit was taking place, we formed a steering committee called the Council for the Future to manage the process of organizational change within ISS. This was the third cornerstone, the third group structure, of the organizational transformation.

The council was composed of a group of twenty-four ISS employees that included the top six managers (the two vice-presidents and their direct reports) and representatives from each level, function, and major site. The purpose of the council was to identify the critical issues of the organization and to oversee the implementation of action projects that would at least partially resolve the identified problems. Except for the senior managers, council members are selected by lot and rotate off the council after a term of about a year.

In July of 1985, at a two-day off-site meeting, the results of our interviews were presented to the council. Each council member received a "data book" listing the twenty-two issues that had emerged as the most critical ones for the organization. We had written a summary sentence for each issue, and we presented a number of direct quotations from the interview material on each issue. The quotations had been selected to illustrate the various facets of the issue and to suggest the range of opinions within the organization.

As we walked through the data that first time, most of the council members sat in silence. They told us later that they were shocked at the openly critical nature of many of the comments. They were very skeptical that any good could come about from airing "dirty linen." But other members felt enormous relief to hear their concerns about the organization stated publicly.

As outside consultants to ISS, we had observed that the general issues of organizational effectiveness were often ignored. Each project team was working in its own corner and usually could not see far beyond it. Individual managers, when they were aware of the larger issues, were often paralyzed by the enormity of the issues and by their own inability to resolve the problems.

We had come to understand from the interviews that, on the whole, the ISS employees lacked implementation skills. At every level of the organization, employees needed to learn how to divide up a large problem into smaller, more workable pieces. Delegation was problematic. Often, when managers were given an assignment, they lacked clarity about their personal responsibility. As they put it, they were never quite sure if the baton had been passed to them or not. Tracking systems to provide accountability and note progress were underdeveloped. Finally, there was a widespread fear of making a mistake, and there were few incentives to implement proposals quickly.

During the off-site meeting the council members mulled over the data and then selected the eight issues that they felt deserved the highest priority, including these five:

1. *Opportunity.* Professional development is haphazard and inadequate; many people feel stuck in their jobs.
2. *Intergroup Cooperation.* A number of intergroup conflicts exist within ISS.
3. *Supervision.* Although the quality of supervision varies widely, most typically it is characterized by little feedback, benign neglect, and unclear expectations.
4. *Priorities.* There is no system to establish or modify priorities with users and within ISS.
5. *Client Relations.* There are serious problems and strained relations with a number of ISS users.

The next step was for the council to develop "tasks" or action projects to address an aspect of these larger, even global issues. Criteria for these projects were spelled out. They should (1) be doable in three to six months or less; (2) not be expected to fully resolve the issue; (3) have clearly defined end products; and (4) provide leverage — a great deal of improvement in effectiveness for the least amount of effort. Each small group that developed a task also named an appropriate person or group to implement the task, proposed a timetable, and suggested what resources would probably be required.

After discussion and modification of the tasks by the council, the next step was for the top management team to approve or reject the task. Once the go-ahead was given, it was emphasized that the implementers had no need to return again to the council or to line managers for further approvals. This decision process highlights the fact that the council supplements rather than undermines the usual authority lines. It is also meant to encourage a "bias for action."

What kinds of projects were actually developed? For example, to address the issue of Opportunity, the task suggested was to develop a bimonthly organizational chart supplement. This informed ISS employees which positions were open within ISS — information that previously had not been available to them. To improve Intergroup Cooperation, the implementer started up a series of monthly luncheon meetings for project leaders from all the various ISS sites to talk about their work and to share concerns. As a first step in addressing the Client Relations issues, a series of visits to ISS users (that is, other Harvester sites and facilities) was arranged for those ISS employees who were working on their systems but had never actually met any of the users.

At the council meetings that are held every six weeks, reports on the status of each of the tasks are given. As a task is finished, it is added to the roll of completed tasks, and the implementer is formally recognized at a council meeting and presented with a T-shirt as a "thank-you." By the June 1986 meeting, all the original eight tasks had been completed. Each time a project is finished another one is launched, so that there are always eight tasks in process.

By its second cycle, the honeymoon of the council was over. Top management rejected several of the tasks that were recommended to it by the council, announcing that it did not think the projects were workable. This was a blow to the small groups that had designed these tasks. It was an important step, however, in keeping the top managers committed to the council process. They needed visible proof that they could veto projects that they believed were trivial or ill advised.

At this point, the roadblocks that made implementation so difficult in the organization became more and more evident. Corporate policies, ISS work practices, and the emergence of new "hot" projects all were preventing the implementers from actually finishing their projects. It took a great deal of energy and hands-on support from the consultants to keep the tasks moving ahead.

Although in the early months of the council the consultants played a key role in making the process work, efforts to transfer the leadership of the council to council members had been initiated early on. By October of 1985, ISS employees had become the co-chairpersons of the council, and by June of 1986, Goodmeasure had stepped completely aside.

The results of the council's work are impressive. In the first year, over fifteen projects were actually implemented — each of them addressing an aspect of a critical organizational issue. In addition, ISS council members had learned one model for organization change and had gained considerable practice in using that model. They had experienced first hand the processes of breaking larger issues into smaller tasks, setting shorter rather than longer time frames, looking for leverage points, tracking change projects once they had been assigned, deciding when a task was "done," and then recognizing the implementers of completed projects.

The spirit of the council has spread to other parts of the organization. Council language such as "bias for action," "deliverables," and "leverage" has worked its way into the ISS vernacular, and there is a new emphasis on delegating assignments as many levels down the organization as possible.

Results

When we assessed the state of the organization a year and a half after the divestiture announcement, we believed that it was not an exaggeration to call what had happened in ISS an organizationwide transformation. Fifteen projects had been designed and implemented. Morale in ISS was universally high according to all reports and every indicator. Turnover, which had soared to the frighteningly high rate of 40 percent in the winter months following the divestiture, had dwindled to less than 2 percent — and was still at that unusually low level in November of 1986.

In May of 1986, a minisurvey was administered to the ISS organization. Employees reported that they felt there had been considerable improvement on twenty-one of the original twenty-two critical issues. The greatest improvement, they felt, had come in the areas of innovation in ISS and receptivity to new ideas. Users, too, reported increased satisfaction with ISS performance, and the top corporate executives of Navistar have cited the ISS organizational effectiveness program as a model for the whole organization. At the same time, some managers outside of ISS complain that ISS is too far ahead of the rest of the organization!

By mid 1986, the three group structures that were the primary vehicles for change, that is, the all-employee meeting, the feedback sessions, and the Council for the Future, had all been made a part of the way that ISS does its work. ISS has the capacity to continue to bring its critical issues to the surface and to deal with them without outside assistance. The organization has successfully institutionalized structures that allow it to respond flexibly to a changing and uncertain environment.

Learnings. The preeminent learning that emerged from this project was the power of groups as a vehicle of organizational change. Morale at ISS, the trust level, and the turnover rate improved dramatically during the months that followed the divestiture. Moreover, most of the parties involved agree that these three group structures acted as important catalysts in the change process.

Resistance to group methods is to be expected since most managers tend to be quite wary of meetings and groups. We learned that with a little experience in handling small groups and with a few successes, the resistance shrinks rather quickly. The difficult task is getting the initial "buy-in." In our case, most of those who reported directly to the vice-presidents were never more than lukewarm about these group structures, but, once in place, they accepted them as "the way we work around here." Managers saw the council as the most threatening of the new structures because of its perceived power, and our greatest concern was that its basic structure would be undermined when we were no longer present at ISS on a regular basis.

We also learned that this approach requires consultants who are well trained in group process and who are comfortable playing an active role in the early stages of these groups. Throughout the consultation our primary focus was on the development of these group structures. While we did a good deal of individual coaching, this was almost always in support of the council or the other group structures.

We learned — once again — how difficult it is to implement change. The work of some consultants ends when they make their reports and give their recommendations. In this kind of approach, the major focus is on working with a number of different managers in the organization to design, introduce, and nurture the group structures. Although this approach is fraught with hazards, we believe the benefits make the work worthwhile.

Helping and Hindering Factors. The fact that Harvester was in a period of crisis was clearly an important factor in the success of the change effort. The divestiture created a period of "unfreezing" during which the ISS managers felt open to trying some new approaches. But the window of opportunity is time limited, and it is important to move quickly. We feel that the fact that we began work three days after the announcement of the divestiture was critical. This quick start-up was possible because Goodmeasure already had an established relationship with the client.

Another factor that was critical for the project's success was having champions of the effort. Without Clayton's and Bowyer's support, there were dozens of points where the change effort could easily have been derailed. At several of these junctures, Clayton spoke to the council to assure it that nothing was more important than its work. The positive impact of this ongoing public commitment by the top manager cannot be overestimated.

Yet another factor that helped our work was our focus on the future. People were ready to stop looking backward and mourning the past. The very name of the Council for the Future highlighted our forward-looking orientation. Also contributing to a positive outcome was our ability to find a middle ground between top management initiatives and grass-roots involvement. Tension between these two is inevitable, and it is a demanding challenge to keep both power sources engaged in a change effort. In more concrete terms, it meant that we, as consultants to the change effort, needed to do a good deal of day-to-day follow-up work with many levels of the organization.

The pitfalls of this structural approach to change became all too clear to us during our eighteen months at ISS. To design and start up these group structures required a great deal of time, energy, and attention from top management as well as from us. When a new crisis emerged or there was a shift in the organizational climate, it was difficult to keep up the momentum. Even though our highest priority was the institutionalization of these group structures, their precarious position was a constant concern to us.

Widespread skepticism about using outside consultants was still another obstacle to our work. Many people blamed Harvester's financial difficulties on management consultants. ISS, as well, had had some bad experiences with consulting firms. We believe that it was not until we had set a specific date to leave ISS that our credibility with some managers was finally established. Still another factor that made our work difficult was the hardiness of the Harvester culture. International Harvester was an old company, and some of the managers we worked with were third-generation Harvester employees. The authoritarian norms of yesteryear were slow to die, and many times employees would revert to their old ways of operating.

Generalizability. How generalizable is our experience? We are convinced that this approach is applicable to practically any organization in the midst of a crisis. It will probably also work well in organizations that are downsizing. It is less clear that a similar program could be successfully launched in a growing, relatively pain-free organization. However, the acceleration of change in the external environment now places many, if not most, organizations in what could be called a crisis mode. Thus, we believe that a broad range of organizations would be good candidates for this approach. Alan Kay, one of Apple Computer's chief scientists, has said, "The best way to predict the future is to invent it." The group method approach to organizationwide transformation not only provides organizations with the structures and processes to continually invent their future but also, in itself, appears to be a technology of the future.

References

Beckhard, R., and Harris, R. *Organizational Transition: Managing Complex Change.* Reading, Mass.: Addison-Wesley, 1977.

Esty, K. C. *Job Distress in Contracting Organizations: When Smaller Is*

Not Beautiful. Unpublished doctoral dissertation, Department of Social Psychology, Boston University, 1984.

Kanter, R. M. *Men and Women of the Corporation.* New York: Basic Books, 1977.

Kanter, R. M. *The Change Masters: Innovation for Productivity in the American Corporation.* New York: Simon & Schuster, 1983.

Loftin, R. D., and Moosbruker, J. M. "Organizational Development Methods in the Management of the Information Systems Function." *MIS Quarterly,* Sept. 1982, pp. 15–28.

Stein, B. A., and Kanter, R. M. "Building the Parallel Organization: Creating Mechanisms for Permanent Quality of Work Life." *Journal of Applied Behavioral Science,* 1980, *16,* 371–388.

Maggie Moore

Paul Gergen

16

Turning the Pain of Change into Creativity and Structure for the New Order

Whether the transformation of an organization ultimately succeeds depends on the people who take part in it. This chapter describes a process for helping employees throughout an organization become what Kanter (1983) has termed *change masters*, that is, people who develop skills that enable them to manage change personally and to help co-workers manage change. This approach is based on two perspectives: (1) the evolutionary and revolutionary nature of organizational transformation and (2) our understanding of change and human behavior. Together, these perspectives suggest a way to manage the complexities of organizational transformation by supporting the people involved and enabling them to competently contribute to the future organization.

Everywhere we go in our professional travels, we hear our colleagues tell story after heart-wrenching story of the pain being suffered by people at all levels of organizations as leaders, managers, and employees struggle to cope with massive changes driven by the environment and technology. We see the management of change-induced pain as critical to the success of any transformation process. In our work we have seen that when

368

pain is eased, a new, innovative culture develops that uses the knowledge and expertise of the organization's work force in establishing the best ways to move into the future. When the new order has been established, the innovative culture will foster new products and services, thus taking the organization even further into the future.

In the pages that follow, we discuss transformation from the organization's and the individual's points of view. We discuss the nuts and bolts of our approach to transformation and our experiences with how the process has worked in client organizations. Finally, we share our observations on some knotty organization resource issues that often plague leaders and managers as they strive to build cultures that will produce change masters.

Change and the Organization

Kilmann and Covin's definition of transformation in Chapter One emphasizes that transformation is a major evolutionary and revolutionary shift in what Beckhard (Chapter Five) calls the shape, structure, or nature of the organization. Nadler (Chapter Four) offers the further insight that transformation is difficult because of (1) the uncertainty of future states (visions are often incomplete or at least fuzzy), (2) multiple transitions are occurring at the same time, (3) some transitions are incomplete (possibly becoming obsolete before fruition), and (4) transformation is so sweeping that the process can take five to ten years and, in fact, may never be concluded.

Our view is that most corporations will find themselves undergoing anywhere from five to twenty years of serial transition as our economy adjusts to a new world order. This macroshift is driven by both new technology and foreign competition. It appears to us to be of a magnitude on the order of the industrial revolution of the last century. We believe that stability will return, but only after a series of changes, modifications, and reorientations as the pieces of the worldwide economic shift settle into place. What we will experience for the foreseeable future, then, is change and more change. As a result, there must be a commensurate shift in the work of managers from managing stability to managing change. This is foreign to many CEOs and managers who are finding that tried and true ways are not working, that they are working too slowly, or that making them work is proving very costly. This becomes apparent to them when their companies begin to experience lost productivity, low morale, or diminished public images.

In Table 16-1, we outline the necessary shifts in focus relative to the roles and tasks of management. The keys to moving in these new directions are: (1) developing the skills of top managers as "visionary changemasters," (2) reconceptualiz-ing resistance to change as an opportunity to better understand what change means to the organization and its people, and (3) using the opportunity to nurture changemasters throughout the organization. For many organizations, survival may well be found in *causing* instability or change, but not without this concurrent shift in management focus.

There is wide agreement among the contributors to this book that the transformation process begins with a vision, that energy to achieve the new vision must be mobilized, and that there can be no turning back once change begins. There is also wide agreement that this effort means massive loss and upheaval for the work force, whether white or blue collar.

We commonly hear that organizations must become in-novative and competitive and get down to their fighting weight. But this requires a change in core values and methods. The implicit challenge in this is to help our work forces enthusi-astically embrace new core values at a time when their custom-ary methods are being questioned, their jobs are in jeopardy, and they are being asked to perform in new ways that they feel may be beyond their capabilities. The critical questions from the organization's point of view are: How do we manage the work force, the great infrastructure of the organization that is the key to whether the transformation will succeed or fail? How do we convert shock and resistance into creativity and commitment to the new order? To answer these questions, we find it helpful to move beyond the huge task of conceptualizing the transforma-tion and to focus instead on the individuals who will make it

Table 16-1. Shifts in Roles and Tasks of Managers.

Organizations Then (Fifty years of stability)	Organizations Now (Five to twenty years of serial change and transformation)
Top Management Roles and Tasks:	
Managers of stability	Managers of change: highly skilled, visionary, and flexible
Strategic planning	Shorter, flexible planning cycles that can respond to environmental shifts
Longer-range planning cycles	Anticipating future opportunities and constraints, developing ways to meet opportunities, evaluating progress, learning from new experiences, and midcourse corrections
	Innovation in management methods, work methods, products
Conservative application of resources to maintain the status quo	Allocate resources to support transformation and innovation
Implications for Managing the Work Force:	
Management decides what will happen and gets workers to go along	Management guides change
Management solely determines how resources will be allocated	Management solicits ideas from workers
Management sees resistance to change as an obstacle to go over, around, or through	Management sees resistance to change as an opportunity to learn what will facilitate change and make it easier next time

work. This gives us a manageable point of intervention because we know quite a bit about how people respond to change.

All change, of course, is risky because we never know for sure how things will turn out—and they may turn out in ways that we do not like or that cause us pain. As change occurs, people act in predictable ways. For example, when they are threatened, people seek safety. Most people want to do a good job for their organization, but when caught up in a painful change process, it is difficult to tell what a good job is. Pain is highly motivating. The more we hurt, the greater our determination to stop hurting. It follows that if we have a work force in pain, we have a motivated work force. The challenge is to direct this motivation toward confronting and building the future rather than trying desperately to hold onto the past.

We have found the technology presented here to be highly successful in transforming anxiety and resistance into commitment and creativity, while concurrently transforming the corporate culture in the direction of responsible risk taking and innovation. The approach empowers people with a process for implementing change that is responsive to the human givens in environments of high risk, high ambiguity, and high uncertainty. Transformation is like leaving shore to look for new lands — not knowing exactly where we are going, how far the journey is, or what opportunities and perils lie in our path. However, vessels, provisions, and navigation aids for this journey are attainable if we pay attention to and learn from what is happening around us.

Risk Taking and Organization Change

Our work with organizations undergoing transition and transformation has produced a conceptual framework and methodology that uses risk taking as a central theme. The underlying premise is that all change is risky. We have found that using a process that attends to what is at stake for those affected by the change enables employees to move quickly from resisting change to becoming partners in helping it succeed. This movement occurs because the perception of risk changes. The employee now becomes aware of the potential gains and organizational supports available to him or her rather than focusing only on potential loss. Our process also provides information that helps managers determine how to (1) support the change effort and (2) shift organizational culture in the direction of fostering the kind of innovation necessary to create the systems that will support the new order.

Our work has verified the commonsense truth that people differ in their comfort levels with and readiness for taking risks. Our theory states that readiness is based on two factors: (1) a personal tendency toward risk taking and (2) perception of the degree to which the organization supports risk taking. The elements of these two factors are diagrammed in Figure 16-1.

Individual tendency factors are based on (1) a general inclination (or disinclination) to take risks; (2) past experience with risk taking, particularly in the employee's current organization; and (3) decision-making skills, which allow people to analyze and make educated guesses about the level of risk involved and their abilities to cope with unplanned events. *Structural/cultural factors* that influence individual risk takers in organizations are (1) the degree to which the organization "says" it values and wants employees to take risks (organization expectations), (2) the ways in which risk taking is rewarded (or punished), (3) support systems, and (4) the amount and kind of resources available to the risk taker.

The lower the individual tendency toward risk taking, the higher the *perceived* organizational supports must be for the risk-taking behavior to occur and vice versa. Perception is a key variable. Our research (Moore and Gergen, 1985) shows that often support exists but is not perceived. In the case of individual risk-taking behavior, perception is reality. We hypothesize that an organization tends to attract and keep employees whose individual tendencies for risk taking match the organization's cultural norms around risk taking. Organizations with low support for risk taking tend to attract and keep lower-level risk takers. Organizations with higher expectations and support attract and keep higher-level risk takers. Consequently, one stumbling block for organizations that have been conservative and now want to become innovative is a work force that was developed to maintain the status quo.

In change projects there are often employees who favor the change (higher-level risk takers), others who are opposed to it (lower-level risk takers), and still others who are ambivalent about it (moderate risk takers). When employees perceive organization supports to be lower than their ideal for risk taking, they tend to become immobilized and "resist" taking action. They fear that there is more at stake than they want to risk in

Figure 16-1. Organizational Risk Taking: Contributing Factors.

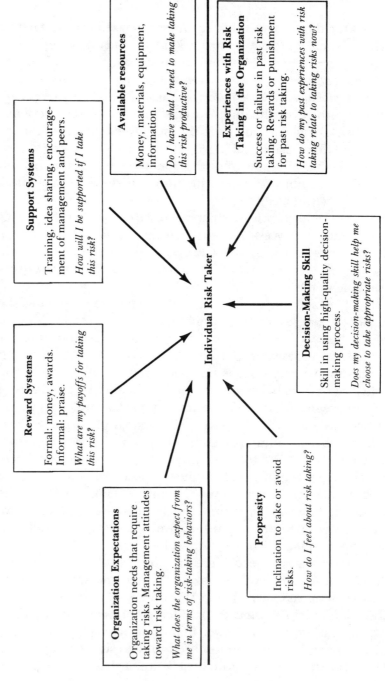

Organization Structural/Cultural Factors

Reward Systems

Formal: money, awards.
Informal: praise.

What are my payoffs for taking this risk?

Support Systems

Training, idea sharing, encouragement of management and peers.

How will I be supported if I take this risk?

Available resources

Money, materials, equipment, information.

Do I have what I need to make taking this risk productive?

Experiences with Risk Taking in the Organization

Success or failure in past risk taking. Rewards or punishment for past risk taking.

How do my past experiences with risk taking relate to taking risks now?

Individual Risk Taker

Organization Expectations

Organization needs that require taking risks. Management attitudes toward risk taking.

What does the organization expect from me in terms of risk-taking behaviors?

Propensity

Inclination to take or avoid risks.

How do I feel about risk taking?

Decision-Making Skill

Skill in using high-quality decision-making process.

Does my decision-making skill help me choose to take appropriate risks?

Individual Tendency Factors

Source: Moore, 1983.

terms of self-esteem, perceived competence, or status. We believe this to be the underlying reason for what has been called
resistance to change. By focusing on the risk taking required
and how the organization supports risk taking as a critical
element in the change process, we are focusing on resistance in a
positive way, presenting a problem that employees become involved in solving.

Dealing with Resistance

One way to help people understand their responses to
change is to consider the "stages of transition" suggested by
Fink, Beak, and Taddeo (1971). We have made some additions to
this formulation to emphasize the relationship of risk taking to
change. Our version of "Change: Stages of Transition" appears
in Table 16-2. It is our observation that most people experience
change in this manner, although people who are relatively comfortable with change may move very quickly through stages 1
(Shock) and 2 (Defensive Retreat). Thinking in terms of the four
stages of transition allows us to clear up some events that can be
confusing for managers when they are working at managing
change. We have also found it helps employees understand their
own reactions to change. They begin to realize that their discomfort may not really be based on factual matters but on their
emotional reactions. This leads very nicely into the solution:
making the environment safe enough for people to take necessary risks.

There are at least three different categories of risk taking:
(1) economic risks (high risk: gambling; low risk: passbook savings), (2) physical risks (high: sky diving; low: tennis), and (3) self-
esteem risks (high: running for public office; low: stating an
opinion among friends). The risks faced by people involved in
organization change are risks to self-esteem — loss of face, appearing incompetent, being unable to learn, even being unable
to change. The best way to protect oneself from such ego as-
saults is to stay with the tried and true. This effort to stay on safe
ground is what has been called resistance. The way to help
people to move through the resistance stages, Shock and Defen-

Table 16-2. Change: Stages of Transition.

Stage 1: Shock

People experience impending change as threat. They shut down thinking and as many systems as possible (just as in physiological shock). People need warm blankets and rest, that is, time to recover, emotional support, information, and an opportunity to gather with others. Productivity is low. People cannot think and do not remember.

What to do: Help people look for common ground in shock, build support network, and give information again and again. Managers should give visible support. Do not involve people in planning. Provide safety, that is, clear organization expectations, reward systems, support systems, and available resources.

Stage 2: Defensive Retreat

Holding on, attempting to maintain old ways. A great deal of anger, refusal to let go of past. People and organizations can get stuck here or recycle back to Stage 1 as each element of change is introduced.

What to do: Help people identify what they are holding on to, and then how to maintain it in the new situation or how to let it go. Identify areas of stability: things that are not changing. Give information continually and consistently. Ask "what is risky" and provide safety in response to discomfort with risk taking.

Stage 3: Acknowledgment

Sense of grief and sadness over loss. Letting go, beginning to see the value of what is coming, and looking for ways to make it work by considering the pros and cons. Ability to take risks begins here. It takes the form of risk taking and exploring new ways to look at things and to do things. Can lead to high energy if managed well.

What to do: Involve people in exploring options and planning through use of careful decision-making process as a structure/support. Overtly encourage and support risk taking by pointing out ways that the organization will support it. Emphasize that everyone is learning.

Stage 4: Adaptation and Change

What is coming has arrived. Ready to establish new routines and to help others. Risk taking comes into full bloom at this stage relative to changing methods, products, whatever is called for.

What to do: Implement plans. Encourage and support risk taking using the supports and structures developed in stage 3. Establish feedback loops so that information travels in all directions, new learning occurs, and midcourse corrections can be made when necessary.

---

sive Retreat, and to the creativity stages, Acknowledgment and Adaptation/Change, is to provide a bridge of safety. Employees can be encouraged to take risks by increasing their feelings of safety regarding abilities, opportunities, competence, and freedom to fail. How is this done? Through acknowledging and accepting the reality of the perceived threat and increasing structural/cultural supports for risk taking (presented in Figure 16-1).

A leader can provide safety by clarifying his or her expectations, clarifying and/or developing reward systems that are meaningful to employees, emphasizing and developing support systems, and making needed resources available. This is done informally all the time. Visionary change masters can, more formally and consciously, adopt "providing safety" as a way of thinking and as a tool when working with people involved in organization change. When the leadership of an organization provides the safety needed by its work force through these four organizational constructs, the work force will be able to apply its skills, expertise, intellect, and sense of adventure to developing the new order.

Our discussions on "providing safety" may sound as though we are trying to eliminate the element of risk. In fact, we cannot eliminate or minimize the actual risk involved, but we can help people achieve the level of confidence they need in order to act in situations where they *perceive* risk. The value is in the outcome, not in the risk taking. We want to enable people to become partners in creating the new organization. Using the "stages of transition" to diagnose difficulties that people have with change provides managers with a way to make sense out of the following situations:

First, managers can reconceptualize resistance to change and think of people who are resisting as people who are stuck in the stages of Shock and Defensive Retreat. Doing so gives managers a way to handle them: provide safety. This has the effect of opening them up to new experiences and moving them to Acknowledgment and Adaptation/Change.

Second, it is not unusual to find that people who were once on board and ready to move suddenly balk and become unwilling to participate in a change effort. If an individual was not aware of (1) the degree of risk taking that would be required for implementation, (2) the amount of disruption the change would cause, or (3) the lack of support from the organization that would ensue, he may experience panic at the moment of realization and Shock may set in.

Third, it is important to involve employees in planning, but not until they are able to do a good job of it, that is, when they reach stage 3, Acknowledgment. If required to plan when they are stuck in the Shock and Defensive Retreat stages, they will instead hold onto the past, letting themselves and the manager down. So it is important to buy time until employees are able to make a valuable contribution to the change effort. If time is scarce, another strategy to consider is identifying the people who have achieved Acknowledgment and ask them for help in planning. They may also be instrumental in helping other employees move into the Acknowledgment stage.

Fourth, it is likely that, at any given time, managers are managing people, including themselves, who represent all four stages of transition. Figure 16-2 shows the manager and employee C in Acknowledgment, looking for ways to make the change work. Employee A is in Adaptation and Change, ready to move and probably impatient with the others who are lagging behind. Employees B and D still need to be provided with safety. The manager, then, must (1) manage the risk taking of employee A, (2) listen to and work with employee C who is still exploring, (3) provide safety to employees B and D, and (4) understand and act on his own reactions to the change at hand. Only by recognizing the behaviors characteristic of each of the four stages will a manager be able to continually sort out where employees are in this process, what they need from him, and what he needs for himself.

Fifth, people who are stuck in Shock and Defensive Retreat will probably not be aware of it. They may well think they are giving a rational response to the situation. So, it would be easy to interpret this as resistance to change. If these people are managed in the right way, however, they can move to Acknowledgment and become partners in making the change successful.

Figure 16-2. Change.

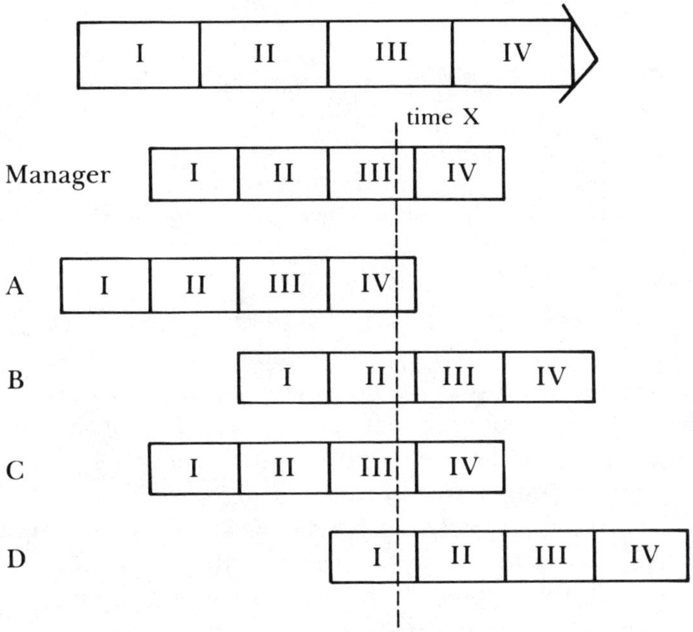

All forms of human change are complex. There are a number of situations above that could be interpreted as resistance to change and call forth a management response that would be counterproductive. For instance, involving people in planning for change will not be helpful if they are not ready to make a worthwhile contribution to the change. Many managers have made attempts to involve employees that backfired, which discouraged the use of employee involvement.

It is critical, then, that in addition to analyzing the *technical* impacts of change, managers understand the *human response* to change and learn how to manage the pain that comes with organizational transformation. Appreciating both aspects could mean the difference between success or failure on a project. The skilled management of change is an expectation leaders can set forth that will have substantial and immediate effects on how the organization comes to terms with transformation.

Providing Safety in Organization Change

We have developed and tested a process for helping groups move through organization transformation using the risk-taking theory described above. It involves the following steps:

Envisioning the Transformation. The challenge here is sharing the vision as explicitly as possible and at the same time encouraging employees to find a place for themselves in the new order. It is important for management to state those aspects of the vision that are not negotiable. Usually there are parts of the vision that are negotiable or not yet fully worked out. An invitation to employees to help management round out the vision may encourage them to try to visualize what the new order will look like and what their place in it might be. The more people who are involved with filling in the vision, or completing it, the more people who will understand it and will be able to help communicate it. Communicating the vision to those who will be responsible for implementing the new order is a step that cannot be overlooked and whose importance should not be underestimated. Messages will have to be clear, consistent, and frequent to put the vision across to those who need to hear it.

We often encounter managers who are put off or frightened by the need to develop a vision. They usually think that they lack "the answers" and that their ideas about the future are therefore not good ones. In response, we talk about the need to involve others in the development of the vision—that no one will have all the answers and perspectives that must be considered in projecting a future for the organization. Above all, we emphasize that in transformational change *everyone* is a learner. Everyone is flying with hampered visibility.

It occurs to us that the very process of formulating the vision gives transformational leaders a certain amount of safety. Being engaged in working out the future direction may provide all the safety that such leaders need to take decisive action. Perhaps involving others in the development of the vision will provide safety for them as well.

Impact of the Change. Figure 16-3 is a picture we have used to help people discuss the technical and human impacts of change. The picture suggests that all organizational subsystems are inter-connected as in a net or web. When one subsystem is hit by change, others are also affected. Just as important, this picture brings into focus the magnitude of change being considered, which is an emotional as well as a technical issue. As employees see and discuss this model, they actually come to realize how large an undertaking transformation is. To minimize the number of surprises in the course of the transformation, we ask change designers to give the best answers they can to the follow-ing questions:

- Where will the change project have primary impact? With what force (on a scale from 1 to 10)?
- Where will secondary impacts be?
- List as many potential impacts — changes, disruptions — as you can for each subsystem that will experience an impact.

This information enables us to anticipate impacts and plan for ways to manage them to the degree that this is possible in trans-formational change. We recognize that the shape and anchor points in the web will change throughout transformation. This exercise allows the change designers to feel that they have thought through impacts carefully; this not only provides them with safety but positions them to learn from events as they unfold.

Work Force Analysis. This analysis is undertaken during a one-day meeting with designers and implementers of change to elicit employee responses to change. Its purposes are several:

- To give the designers of change feedback from implemen-ters on their understanding of the change, as well as an opportunity to clarify elements of the design

Figure 16-3. Impact of Change.

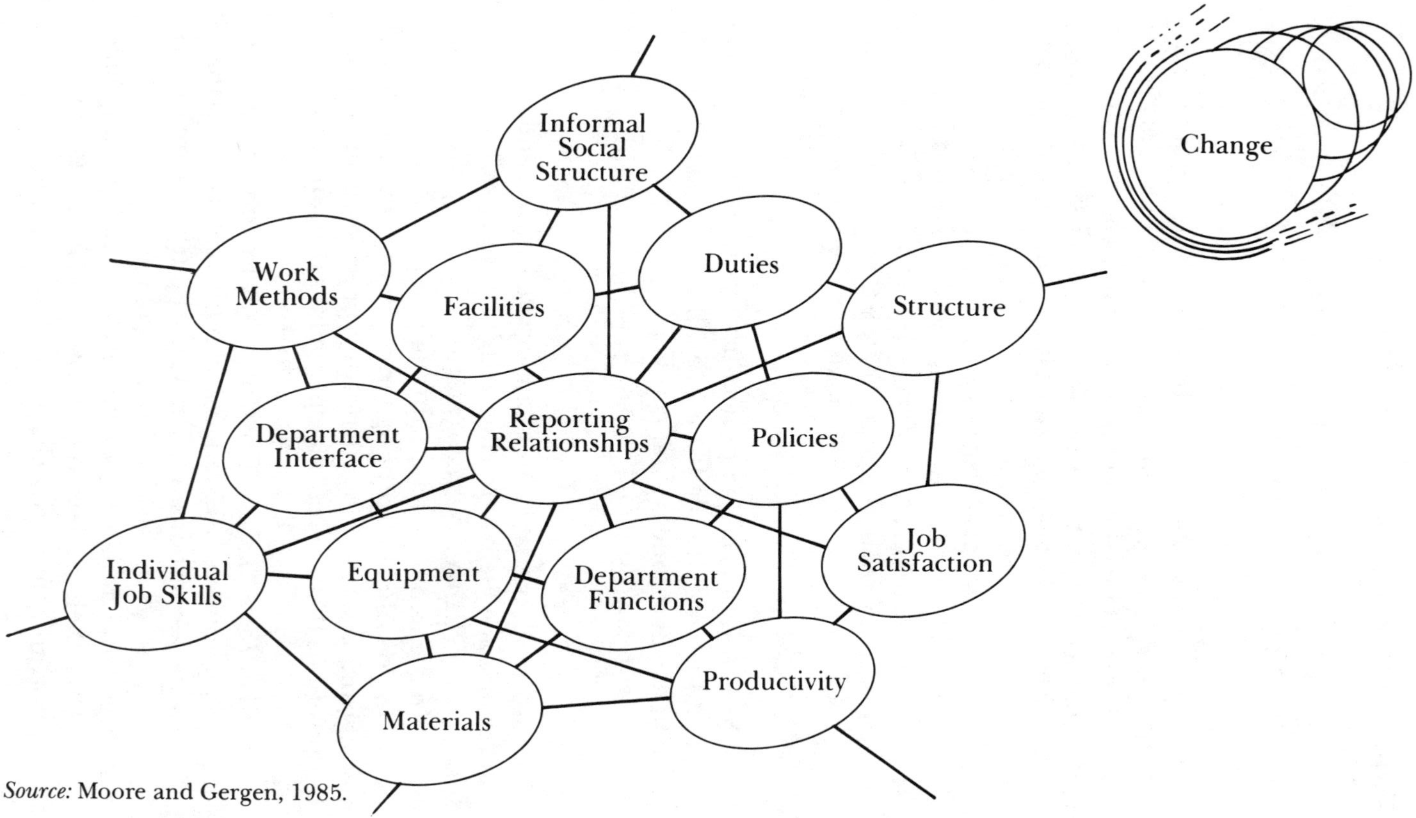

Source: Moore and Gergen, 1985.

- To give implementers an opportunity to consider the impact of change from their various perspectives
- To give all the participants an understanding of the change process at the organizational, managerial, and employee levels
- To assess participants' perceptions of what risks are created by the transformation at the organizational, managerial, and employee levels
- To assess individual risk-taking tendencies of the participants by means of a questionnaire
- To assess perceptions of the degree to which the organization currently supports risk taking by means of a questionnaire
- To get suggestions on what actions the organization can take to enhance its support of risk taking
- To determine ways to help individuals through the four stages of transition

Action Planning. Planning undertaken with managers focuses on weaving the development of supports for risk taking into the transformation plan. The supports generally fall into three categories: (1) those that have no cost and are within the authority of the group's manager to implement; (2) those within the authority of the group's manager and that require additional resources; and (3) those requiring additional resources and not within the unilateral authority of the manager to grant. It is important for managers to commit their energies to improvements that they can make and to attempt to gain additional supports outside their areas of authority. This demonstrates their commitment to supporting employees and thus sends a strong safety message. Implementation steps for safety mechanisms are mapped out after the one-day meeting and then shared with participants of that meeting.

Follow-Through. This involves meeting commitments to enhance risk-taking supports and keeping all stakeholders informed of progress. In the process of following through, a manager may discover that issues raised during the one-day meeting with employees are no longer issues—somewhere along the line they were resolved or became less important. Often the need of employees is to have an opportunity to say what they think in a supportive environment, which this approach provides. This suggests that a manager may want to go back to those who raised issues to verify that more work needs to be done to resolve them.

Progress of the transformation can be tracked by watching to see if the safety mechanisms are serving to help managers and employees over the rough spots. More safety mechanisms may be needed, in which case managers can revisit the question "What's risky?" to learn what kinds of mechanisms would make a difference. Gradually, the safety mechanisms become normative and encourage employees to contribute to creating the new order. As employees see their ideas valued and used, they become more and more comfortable with suggesting new ways to approach their work. This is evidence that a new, innovative culture is emerging.

Application of the Theory

We use the theory we have described in three ways. We use it diagnostically to show why and in what areas people at all levels of the organization will have difficulty with change. We teach the theory to managers and employees so that they will have tools with which they can analyze their own and others' responses to change and begin to manage change productively or, in other words, to become change masters. We help managers use the theories strategically as they design systems and procedures that will support the future organization.

Looking at the transformations in which we have used the theory, we observe that its application seems to be particularly important in the first year. This is the time to establish new norms, to invest in helping people become capable of change and to enlist their aid in the new order. We see the use of the theory paying off at a certain point, six to twelve months after the initiation of the transformation effort. Prior to this, the transformation process has been surrounded by ambiguity, but this is reduced over time as the various changes are implemented. Our experience is that at a certain point, which we call the "point of capability to produce structure," people who have been working with the transformation are suddenly able to create many structures that support the new organization, when previous to that they have been unable to see clearly enough what those structures should look like. However, a distinction is necessary here between bureaucratic structures and those that support people by reducing ambiguity and clarifying expectations and roles. While bureaucratic structures often limit creativity, supportive structures provide direction and offer latitude within which people can take initiatives.

Prior to the point of capability to produce structure, safety is provided primarily by messages sent by leaders. The messages concern the processes that will be used to discover how the new organization should be built and the four organization elements from the risk-taking model: organization expectations, rewards, supports, and available resources. Let us look at an example of each:

Processes for Discovery. "We do not know exactly what structures and procedures we need to establish to support the new organization, but we are going to find out by studying what resources we have and how best to configure them. Task forces will be looking at each area of emphasis. We expect them to take three months before they make suggestions on how to proceed."

Organization Expectations. "Change is here—it is not negotiable. We are all learning how to make this work. There is no magic formula that we can use. We will be trying lots of different things to see what works. We will probably make mistakes. When we make mistakes we will learn from them. We may have to backtrack for midcourse correction. We need to hear your feedback in order to make good choices. Ask for what you need—we want to build it into the new organization."

Rewards. "Rewards are long term, and we need to develop them. In the short term the rewards are in the learning and in being valued as a contributor."

Supports. "We recognize that change is hard. You are not a bad employee just because you are having a hard time. We want to learn to help one another get through Shock and Defensive Retreat to Acknowlegment and Change. We want to help you with painful decisions."

Available Resources. "We must take the *time* to do this well. We will give you as much *information* as we can, as soon as we can. If the messages you receive seem inconsistent, please ask for clarification from your *managers.*"

After the point of capability to produce structure has been reached, safety can be provided through structures that articulate organization expectations, rewards, supports, and available resources. The point of capability seems to occur because of readiness in two areas: (1) a critical mass of people have achieved Adaptation and Change, and (2) the environmental pressures that the new organization must respond to have been studied adequately. People know enough about what they must do, and they are ready to act on that knowledge.

Since organizations are traditionally managed by means of structures, there is a collective sigh of relief when the point of capability is reached. The employees who have, in the face of upheaval, believed that things would get better and easier are pleased with themselves and their leaders for holding onto the vision and coming through. The leaders who promised that things would get better are pleased with themselves for living up to their promises and proud of their employees for the faith and determination that they have demonstrated. The new norms are thereby reinforced and strengthened. Various kinds of structures can provide safety. For example, new work groups can be created to which people and tasks are assigned; sales plans or start-up plans can be formulated; job competencies can be defined; support systems—for example, training programs—can be developed; and policies and procedures can be established. People now find that they are able to describe what their work "looks like" in very specific terms.

Forces That Prevent Leaders from Encouraging Innovation

As much sense as this theory seems to make to those who learn and use it, we find that there are a number of managerial "tugs" that get in the way of consistent application of the theory. Inherent in our approach is the suggestion that organizations involved with change must be managed differently than they were when change was not an issue. In particular, we are concerned with supporting people in transformation by (1) growing a culture that will foster responsible change, (2) establishing norms that encourage entrepreneurial behaviors around making change work, and (3) allocating the organization's resources accordingly.

Stevenson and Gumpert (1985) discuss the pressures on managers to be promoters of innovation, on the one hand, and trustees or administrators of organizational resources, on the other: "At one extreme is what we might call the promoter type of manager, who feels confident of his or her ability to seize opportunity. This manager expects surprises and expects not only to adjust to change but also to capitalize on it and make things happen. At the other extreme is the trustee type, who feels threatened by change and the unknown and whose inclination is to rely on the status quo. To the trustee type, predictability fosters effective management of existing resources while unpredictability endangers them" (p. 86). Most managers lie somewhere in between. The need to change and be innovative and the need to effectively manage the organization's resources are often at odds with one another. Waste, after all, is not acceptable. The two opposite poles represent the constant tension that managers feel between being responsible for the organization's resources and doing whatever it takes to survive and prosper in today's economy. This dilemma goes with the territory.

Stevenson and Gumpert say that most of the risk in the management of change and innovation lies in the effort to pursue opportunity with inappropriate resources — either too few or too many. They support a gradual commitment of resources to a new venture or transformation. For many managers, this represents learning a set of new skills. We suggest using the

Table 16-3. Structured Decision-Making Process.

Making the Preliminary Decision

Target: What do I want/need that I do not now have?

Action plan: How do I get what I need?

Costs: What are the costs of getting what I need?

Supports: What will support me if I choose to go after what I need?

Scenarios: Best case, worst case, most probable case scenarios. Can I live with the worst case if it should materialize?

Certainty: How certain am I that taking the risk will get the results I want? What level of certainty do I need to take the risk?

Preliminary go or no-go decision: Does the risk appear to be worth taking? How quickly/easily can I get out of a risk if it turns sour?

Analyzing the Risks Involved

What is risky? If I choose to go after what I want, what am I risking?

Outcomes: What are the possible outcomes, positive and negative?

Data collection: What can I do or plan for to increase my chances of achieving the outcomes I want?

Confidence: How much confidence do I have that I will be able to manage thing that could go wrong?

Final decision: Am I comfortable enough with the answers to these questions to proceed with taking the risk?

Planning: What plans should I make to avoid the potential pitfalls?

Evaluation and Midcourse Correction

Test actual outcomes: What results have been produced? Is the quality of the results acceptable? Are the costs of the results acceptable?

Feedback: What feedback do the people involved in implementing the plan have about how it worked, what can be improved?

New learnings: What learning has occurred that can be used in the future?

Correction: What corrections should be made, can be made?

---

structured process outlined in Table 16-3 for making decisions about taking risks and allocating resources in risky situations. The process focuses on three major activities: (1) making the preliminary decision, (2) analyzing the risks involved, and (3) evaluating the outcomes of the decision. This provides support for both managers and employees and allows leaders to accomplish several objectives in the following ways:

First, this is a structure that is useful both before and after reaching the point of capability to produce structure. It ensures that risk takers will have done their homework before committing organization resources. Consequently, they are more likely to succeed or at least learn something valuable for the next try. It also makes clear to the risk taker what supports, rewards, and resources are available and enables him or her to earn credibility as an effective risk taker or change master.

Second, it enables managers to responsibly control organization resources. Before resources are committed, the risk taker provides an analysis of the pros, cons, possible outcomes, and plans to overcome potential problems. By following this process, the risk taker creates a support structure for everyone involved in approving the action and implementing the change.

Third, it requires professional development of a kind that will be used by the organization time and time again and works toward establishing a norm relative to what is expected when organization resources are at risk. It is a process that conveys the organization's needs and expectations clearly and explicitly. Everyone who participates in the process is a conveyor of the message.

Fourth, it ensures that progress is evaluated, that new information is used as input in the development of the project, and that risks to both human and capital resources are minimized.

It is important, however, to remember that in spite of the best intentions to manage change in the course of transformation, managers will experience the tug to protect organization resources, and this will often work against the risk taking and innovation that successful transformation requires. Carefully thinking through this problem when it appears is a leadership responsibility.

In our work with top managers, we have come across several examples of difficult resource issues:

First, resources may be acquired faster than they can be managed. Some organizations undergoing transformation are able to allocate blocks of time, money, and personnel to new departments or projects. However, there must also be a structure through which the resources can be managed to keep them from resulting in less than optimal payoff. Yet, it may be impossible at this point to know precisely what kind of structure would best support and manage the department or project. One manager we know uses ad hoc schemes or structures to manage for the short term. This provides adequate means by which to manage the resources, but it is an ambiguous situation for the people on the project, providing them with little structure, that is, support. Therefore, providing safety in any other way possible should be a high priority. When the appropriate long-term structure becomes apparent, it must be established as soon as possible.

Second, a manager may have to turn down resources if they would cause one part of the project to move way out in front when the other parts are not ready. Managing change in the whole organization requires a sense of how fast things can move together and a focus on the whole. The premise here is that the sum of the parts is greater than the whole. To achieve this kind of synergism, the parts have to be "grown" at a careful pace; that is, there should be a gradual commitment of resources.

Third, development of the vision takes time. In a period of change, everyone is learning. As we have said, it takes a while to envision the structure, personnel, and resources that will make a change work for the organization and the people in it. The resources committed have to be consistent with the vision as it develops. Sometimes the only thing that can be offered to support people is the process that will be used to discover the best course of action. That process will serve as a support structure if it is well articulated. The approach we have described will encourage discussion of the process, enhance development of the vision, and shorten the time it takes to implement change.

Fourth, there is the problem of husbanding the organization's human resources. A client told us about his struggle with experienced employees: "Just as you describe, some got ready to change only to move back. We found on inspection that they realized their knowledge of the job would be destroyed or at least seriously damaged. They faced the risk of learning the new job right along with the new employees. They would actually lose their edge of experience. They would be only brand-new 'old' employees. As the manager, one resource you are entrusted with is the experienced employee. With change you turn the whole place into a bunch of rookies. And without experienced people to carry the heavy load you will be understaffed. Yesterday you had enough people—today you don't. Good grief—what have you done?"

Fifth, there are situations in which management has to move quickly in order to take advantage of an opportunity, and the time necessary to use the tools we have described is simply not there. One manager told us, "The needs for decisions are coming and going quickly. The choice for action or process time (the time it takes for people to work through the change) is high risk. You can't always take the time to process, but if you don't, your people may not be there to back you up on the action you take." When it is necessary to take immediate action, it is important to recognize that some people will have difficulty understanding the change, what it requires of them, and how to make it work for themselves. When there is time to go back and pick up loose ends, care must be taken to listen to the needs of people and provide safety.

Finally, the established procedures in an organization often tend to work against risk taking and transformation. They were, after all, established to protect and conserve the organization's resources. The challenge of being an innovator in a conservative system has been described to us as working "just outside the system where there are no established procedures." But this practice or approach comes too close to turning one into an organizational outlaw. Change and innovation must be "normalized" in organization cultures. The need to operate outside of the system means that there will be little, if any, support from the four organizational elements (expectations, rewards, supports, and available resources) of our risk-taking model. Because only high risk takers can operate this way, lack of clear, articulated organizational support will mean that most employees will not be able to participate in, or support and implement, innovation.

Summary

Change is hard—because it is risky, because it is ambiguous, and because organizational resources are at stake. Managers thus sometimes allow themselves to be distracted from the leadership of change by administrative duties. They begin to concentrate on controlling resources and may even start to return to the proven methods of the past. One of our clients describes this occurrence as follows: "When the task looms so large that I don't even know where to begin, I revert to reworking what I've done before—go back to something I know." To overcome this tendency, Drucker says that we "must encourage habits of flexibility, of continuous learning, and of acceptance of change as normal and as opportunity—for institutions as well as individuals" (1985, p. 260). We would add that managers must become visionary change masters and teach their new skills to others. They will need the same supports we have described as necessary for employees if they are to develop these new habits, meet the challenges that we have described, and successfully manage transformation.

References

Drucker, P. *Innovation and Entrepreneurship*. New York: Harper & Row, 1985.

Fink, S. D., Beak, J., and Taddeo, K. "Organizational Crisis and Change." *Journal of Applied Behavioral Science*, 1971, 7, 15–37.

Kanter, R. M. *The Change Masters: Innovation for Productivity in the American Corporation*. New York: Simon & Schuster, 1983.

Moore, M. "Risk Taking in Organizations." Unpublished master's thesis, International College, Los Angeles, 1983.

Moore, M., and Gergen, P. "Risk Taking and Organization Change." *Training and Development Journal*, 1985, *39* (6), 15–37.

Peters, T. J., and Waterman, R. H., Jr. *In Search of Excellence: Lessons from America's Best-Run Companies*. New York: Harper & Row, 1982.

Stevenson, H. H., and Gumpert, D. E. "The Heart of Entrepreneurship." *Harvard Business Review*, 1985, *63* (2), 85–94.

Part Four

Case Studies of
Corporate Transformation

This section contains case studies of actual corporate transformation from the vantage point of top executives, consultants, and researchers who have been directly involved in the change process. The authors discuss why major changes were necessary, how they were accomplished, and what was learned from the experience.

In Chapter Seventeen, Howard M. Love, A. Lee Barrett, Jr., and Lee M. Ozley discuss the transformation of National Steel Corporation. This chapter is a collaboration between the chairman and chief executive officer of the company (Love) and two of the consultants involved in the massive change effort. The authors chronicle the events leading up to and composing the change effort and detail the roles of the CEO and outside consultants in creating a climate for change. They also discuss some of the financial decisions that were major turning points in the change effort. This case shows how a company managed to shape its destiny in the face of increasing environmental uncertainty.

Next, Michael O. Bice describes the case of Lutheran Health Systems. As president and CEO of an organization in the rapidly changing health care field, Bice describes his role in transforming his company, the use of outside experts and internal resources to move the change along, the problems encountered, and the methods used to overcome them. The reader will notice a contrast between this chapter and the descriptions of bottom-up change discussed in earlier chapters. This chapter provides a progress report on the change effort in the fourth year of a seven-year effort.

Creating a Quality Culture at Westinghouse is the focus of the chapter by Thomas J. Murrin. As the president of the Energy and Advanced Technology Group, he describes the fundamental role that the concept of quality played in helping the company better deal with increasing competition. Murrin discusses how his organization developed a Quality Culture and the factors that contributed to and detracted from the emergence of this culture.

While major change efforts in the private sector are clearly difficult, such efforts within the bureaucracy of a government organization provide many additional obstacles. In Chapter Twenty, David O. Renz reports on the case of the Department of Labor and Industry in the state of Minnesota. Renz describes the methods and models used to guide the transformation of this government agency into a more adaptive, responsive organization. The case is presented from the perspective of key organizational managers who have had the task of managing the change process. The author suggests that the dynamics and challenges of governmental change are increasingly applicable to all large-scale complex bureaucracies, both public and private.

In the following chapter, Anthony F. Buono, James L. Bowditch, and John W. Lewis III provide a view of a transformation resulting from the merger of two banks. The authors present an extended case study of the two savings banks prior to, during, and after the merger, and explore the consequences of managerial actions over the course of the merger. The problems associated with bringing together organizations with two very different cultures are highlighted, and the authors propose several suggestions for making this type of transition as painless and effective as possible.

Finally, Ralph H. Kilmann and Teresa Joyce Covin discuss some future directions for researchers and practitioners interested in corporate transformation. The authors believe that managers must learn to view transformation as a long-term commitment — as a new way of managing for the future — rather than as a program for "fixing" specific organizational problems. They suggest that revitalizing management education systems, developing and using new technologies, and improving union-management relations will become increasingly important issues for consideration.

Howard M. Love
A. Lee Barrett, Jr.
Lee M. Ozley

17

The Transformation of National Steel Corporation

In the early 1980s, National Steel Corporation faced many of the problems typical of smokestack industries. National Steel's markets were deteriorating, the cost of capital was increasing, and profits were under extreme pressure. While people within National were aware of these financial conditions, many felt that there was no particular cause for alarm, since the company was doing as well as or better than others in the steel industry.

H. M. (Pete) Love, who took over as chairman and CEO of National Steel in 1981, believed, however, that this was not just another storm to be weathered. There were underlying factors in both the company and the economy that could not be ignored or wished away. To Love it was clear that without significant change, the company was likely to collapse. To avert this financial crisis, Love saw that he must find a way to carry out a major organizational transformation—a change significant enough to save National from oblivion.

The problems that Love and National Steel faced in 1981 are familiar to many managers in mature industries. The organization had grown and matured over a period of decades. However, the environment in which it operated had changed significantly. The very methods that had produced success in the past were now inhibiting the organization's effectiveness. National

Steel faced the challenge of changing from a corporation that could function effectively in the 1960s and 1970s to one that could succeed in the 1980s and 1990s. This chapter will focus on how this transformation was conceived and carried out and the impacts it has had on the company and its people in its first five years.

Background and Setting

The difficulties that Love faced at National Steel were largely rooted in the history of the corporation and the nature of the steel industry. National Steel Corporation was formed in 1929 by the merger of Weirton Steel Company, the Great Lakes Steel Corporation, and certain interests of the M. A. Hanna Company. The men who ran these businesses felt that they could work more effectively as an integrated entity than as separate businesses. The three organizations continued to operate relatively autonomously, and the arrangement proved generally beneficial to all. As years passed, additional units were added for strategic business reasons, and the general pattern of coordinated but relatively independent organizations continued to develop.

By 1980, National had evolved into an integrated steel producer with additional businesses in aluminum, fabricated metal products, energy resources, and financial services. Steel and steel products were the company's core business (over 85 percent of gross revenues), and at that time it was operating four relatively modern and efficient steel mills. The company was self-sufficient in its key raw materials — iron ore, coal, and limestone — and had operations in twenty-five states; it employed over 33,000 people. In 1979, National Steel had revenues of $4.3 billion and profits of $126 million. The corporation was still being managed as a group of essentially independent entities whose activities were coordinated by the CEO and corporate staff.

The economic downturn of the steel industry in the early 1980s caused major problems for National. High inflation, slow economic growth in the United States, and competition from foreign producers in a variety of markets began to severely affect the steel business by 1980. The decline in domestic car sales and the general market shift away from tin cans were particularly troublesome for National. The company managed to stay competitive in these and other market areas, but its revenues declined 9 percent and its profits 33 percent in 1980. Shipments were off 20 percent that year, and overall employment had declined by nearly 5,000 people.

In addition, the company's own operating style and policies were impeding its progress. The focus of management had traditionally been on high-volume, low-cost production, with little attention paid to changing customer needs. Few new products or markets were being sought. The historical autonomy granted to operating units allowed them to maximize their own profitability at the expense of corporate earnings. National, like other steel companies, had also become a victim of its own labor relations policies over the past twenty-five years. These policies had resulted in high labor costs, low productivity, and adversarial relationships.

In short, National Steel, like other companies in the industry, was locked in a downward spiral. Severe internal and external cost pressures, foreign competition, and weak markets had resulted in a weak strategic position, which in turn had led to declining profits and insufficient cash to invest in the changes needed to reverse the trend.

Creating a Climate for Change

The initial problem facing Love was to create a climate that would enable change to occur. National Steel, like many mature organizations, had developed a relatively stable culture that did not promote adaptation and change. People in the organization understood its methods of working, its structure of authority, and its position in the marketplace. They understood their own jobs and objectives as well as those of others. Generally, each individual did his job, guarded his territory, expected to be rewarded when he performed well, and otherwise minded his own business. Open conflict was generally avoided. As the economic environment became more turbulent, however, this lone-wolf method of operation became more problematic.

Moving an organization's culture to one that is more open to information, more willing to change and innovate, and more diffuse in its allocation of responsibility requires that large numbers of its people begin to change the way they think about the organization's purpose, about their roles and jobs, about the risks they are willing to take, and about the way they deal with other employees. Such changes cannot come about until sufficiently large numbers of people understand the need for change and become willing to make that change happen. Love saw that he had to convince large numbers of people to change their view of the purpose of National Steel as a corporation, the way it should work to accomplish this purpose, and the role they should play in making the corporation successful. If this could be done, then the attention of all employees could be turned to the problem of coping with a depressed and changing economic situation.

One of Love's first actions after taking over as chairman was to change the reporting relations at the top of the corporation. Historically, the four steel division presidents reported directly to the chairman, who personally had to intervene in disagreements. To push responsibility for coordination and cooperation downward in the organization, Love created the position of executive vice-president of the steel group, to whom all four steel division presidents would report. Jim Haas, formerly vice-president for steel distribution, was chosen to fill this new job. At the same time, Love began to talk about changing the culture of the corporation, beginning with the senior management. He felt that people needed to set and accomplish more aggressive financial goals, that the corporation had to become more innovative in its approach to business planning and technological improvement, and that the management style of the corporation had to become more participative, with higher commitment and improved quality of work life throughout.

The senior managers felt that these changes would be difficult to accomplish, and not all of them were convinced that the changes were necessary. Everyone recognized that the company was in trouble, but not everyone agreed on the way to respond to its problems.

In the summer of 1981, as a means of further stimulating change at the senior management level, Love asked an outside consulting firm to diagnose problems within the leadership group and to help its members work on their internal relationships. Interviews were conducted with each of the twelve managers reporting to Love. The following perceptions emerged from the interviews:

1. Operating units' autonomy had been extended to the point that they competed with each other for customers, products, and employees.
2. The role of the corporate staff had been minimal and often not welcomed in the operating units when authority was exercised.
3. There had been little coordinated group interaction among senior management officials. Such coordination as did exist was usually instigated by the chairman through individual conversations with subordinate managers.
4. Conflicts between and among executives had been addressed indirectly, if at all.
5. Communications between operating units, organization levels, and senior management had been sketchy and sporadic.
6. The recent creation of the Steel Group required managers to cooperate with and assist each other much more than in the past, and many managers were uncomfortable with this change.
7. There was major concern on the wisdom of introducing participative management in the company at the same time that drastic measures were needed to reduce costs and improve financial performance.

Love and the consultants held a meeting with the interviewees to review the findings and consider possible courses of action. The group decided to begin by developing a joint strategic focus for the corporations and a statement of what they would like National's human resource philosophies and practices to be in the future. This course of action was chosen both to accomplish the specific and necessary task of agreeing on National's strategy and to provide an opportunity for group members to examine and improve the way they worked together.

The managers agreed to begin meeting in a series of half-day sessions. At the first meeting, held in October 1981, the group examined its understanding of current management practices and strategies in eight areas: marketing, innovation and creativity, human organization, financial resources, physical resources, productivity, social responsibility, and profit requirements. A sampling of comments from the meetings demonstrates the divergence of views. For instance, National's marketing philosophy at that time was described by one senior manager as "to maintain market share in the sale of the same products to the same customers year by year." But the comment of another manager was that "the company is currently in a major transition phase from a volume and production orientation to a product and customer mix and a quality and service focus with a wide variation in acceptance of this change."

National's support for creativity and innovation was described by one interviewee as "a corporate management style which discourages creativity and innovation. Top management is defensive of the status quo and threatened by new ideas and approaches." In contrast, another said, "National is and has been above average in innovation [for the steel industry]. Innovation is still low compared with many manufacturers."

In the area of human organization, comments were quite diverse: National is "moving toward a more open, participative style, but groping, somewhat, to get there"; "staff personnel has increased far too much and has stifled operating personnel incentive"; and "National's employees, particularly its management, are under severe strain as the 'new faces' at the top attempt to focus attention on profit and quality versus volume while industry conditions continue to deteriorate."

In its second meeting, the group discussed what the corporation's goals should be for the next decade in each of the eight areas. Again, opinions and points of view varied widely. In marketing, for instance, some felt that National should concentrate on high-margin products and markets, others that it should become a customer-oriented company dedicated to solving problems, and still others that it should simply continue present trends of marketing. In other areas, such as financial and physical resources, goals were often stated in vague terms related to supporting marketing plans supporting corporate strategies.

Defining a Common Direction

As the meetings progressed, the group soon recognized that it must develop a more fundamental basis of understanding if its differences were to be resolved. Members ultimately agreed that the creation of an overall statement of the company's direction or mission might serve as such a basis.

After several more half-day meetings failed to produce agreement on a mission statement, the group decided that it needed a longer period of concentrated effort and agreed to hold a three-day off-site meeting of all thirteen senior managers. The first day and a half of this meeting were spent on obtaining agreement on what the elements of the mission statement should include and on drafting the statements for each of the elements. After a final review of each element of the statement on the third morning, the group spent considerable time discussing what this mission statement really meant to the organization and to each member of senior management. Several people underscored the importance of commitment, both by each individual and by the group as a whole, if the mission statement was to be meaningful.

This meeting also provided an important opportunity for the leader of the change effort to model the new behaviors desired for the organization as a whole. Love had previously indicated his intention to use a participative decision-making style for the entire change effort. Part of the meeting included a structured exercise to demonstrate the value of effective group problem solving to executives whose entire careers and success within those careers had been based on individual performance and individual problem solving. As the task was assigned, one of the members of the group commented, jokingly, "Pete, why don't you just give us your answers so we can all save a lot of time." Love responded very emphatically that he would no longer make all decisions on his own or through one-on-one negotiations. He went on to say that if his presence was going to inhibit the group's effectiveness, he would withdraw from the group. Although the issue of leadership style arose again on other occasions, this event served to underscore Love's commitment to a new style of management for the company as a whole.

The most recent version of the NSC mission is summarized below. It is substantially the same as the mission developed by the senior managers in this meeting, although it does reflect some changes that were made later as a result of questions and critiques by other managers in the corporation.

Summary of National Steel's Mission Statement

Mission: To provide a superior and consistent financial return to stockholders. This mission will be carried out in the framework of and supported by the following key elements:

A.   Financial goals
　　1.   Consistent growth in earnings, with a 20 percent minimum return on investment.
　　2.   Include both businesses that generate cash and those with growth prospects.
　　3.   Upgrade our business portfolio by investment, acquisition, and divestiture to achieve a 15 percent return on equity and a balance sheet to support these goals.
B.   Marketing. Provide products and services of the highest performance and value through:
　　1.   Quality leadership: This is the responsibility of all employees from research and development through manufacturing and distribution.
　　2.   Price leadership: Attain the low-cost position through productivity and capital investment.

     3.   Market leadership: Establish product and service differentiation in markets of focus.

C. Human organization

     1.   A participative management style; a lean, high-quality group of employees; continuous training and development.

     2.   Clearly understood criteria for all jobs.

     3.   Clean and safe work areas.

     4.   Open communications to all employees.

     5.   An atmosphere that enhances employees' pride in their jobs and the corporation.

     6.   Superior compensation for superior performance.

     7.   Nondiscriminatory opportunity for all employees.

D. Creativity and innovation. Encourage and reward creativity, innovation, and entrepreneurial management.

E. Productivity. The goal for all employees is for productivity increases that exceed increases in employment costs.

F. Social responsibility. Maintain an improved environment, uphold the highest ethical standards, and encourage employee participation in serving the needs of their communities.

    A number of aspects of this mission represented substantial departures from the past practice of National Steel:

    1. The return on investment objectives were subtantially higher than anyone expected could be accomplished if National kept the business configuration it currently held. In order to accomplish these objectives, the corporation could not remain primarily a basic steel producer.

    2. The focus on innovation, customer-driven marketing, and low-cost, high-quality production represented significant departures from past definitions of purpose at National. It represented a new approach to defining what businesses the corporation should be in and what objectives managers of these businesses should try to accomplish.

    3. The focus on participative management represented new principles for how people in the organization would deal with each other. In the past, managers had used whatever styles

they had been comfortable with, and many of these styles had not been particularly participative. Making participative management a part of the mission represented a new expectation that would require many managers to change their operating styles.

Taken together, these objectives represented a definition of significant business and cultural change for the organization. To make the mission a reality would require changes in the things people within the corporation did, the criteria for evaluating how well they did them, and the methods that they used for doing them. The members of the senior management group recognized that it would be difficult to get these changes accepted and implemented throughout the organization. A number of the senior managers were themselves not sure they agreed with all aspects of the new direction, and so, although they were committed to support it, they were unsure how well the mission would be accepted.

Broadening Acceptance and Support

To generate wider acceptance for the new mission and begin its implementation, the senior managers developed a three-step communications plan. The first step was to hold a meeting with the people who reported directly to the senior managers. This meeting was to cover the economic conditions facing the company, its mission, and plans for further communications. It was to allow sufficient time for discussion and critique, much of which was to be done in small groups. This meeting was to be followed a month later by a meeting of the top 250 managers in National Steel, where the process would be repeated and plans would be developed for communicating the mission to all employees of the organization. The final step was for each organizational unit to communicate the mission within its own boundaries and start developing plans for implementation.

One of the discussions that occurred as the senior managers thought through these steps demonstrated the beginnings of change within this group. The question was raised, "How much involvement and input do we want or will we accept from our subordinates on *our* draft of the mission statement?" Prior to this set of meetings a question of this kind would not have been asked. The group concluded that their direct reports (approximately forty-nine executives) should have substantial input into the content of the mission statement with less and less input into content at each subsequently lower level of the organization. Discussion of this question enabled these senior executives to gain new insights into the impact of different management styles and different levels of involvement in decision making. In addition, the discussion itself provided a model of effective group decision making.

In preparation for these communications meetings a group of twenty-five middle-level employees were selected to assist in facilitating the small-group discussions that were planned. Criteria for selection included:

- Individuals identified as high-potential employees
- People who were reasonably articulate and at ease with groups
- People from both line and staff functions
- Representation from all parts of the organizations
- People *below* the level of potential participants of the forthcoming meetings (so that they would not be expected to contribute to the content of the discussions and could focus on the process of facilitation).

This group was given training in meeting facilitation by the external consultants. The group's input also was sought in the design of the meetings. As one can imagine, these individuals were initially quite apprehensive about the entire process. Not only was there the question of how sincere senior management really was about this effort, but there were concerns regarding their ability to be effective in their roles, since they would be facilitating groups comprised of individuals two to five levels above them.

The training and design activities provided for the group were designed to help them become more comfortable with their role and allay their misgivings. Part of this work included planning sessions between these internal resources, the external consultants, and the thirteen senior executives. These sessions provided the opportunity to agree in advance on roles and to discuss what behaviors on the part of the senior executives would and would not be helpful to the process.

The first of the communication meetings was held in Pittsburgh in February 1982. It involved the thirteen senior managers who had been instrumental in preparing the mission and the forty-nine managers who reported to them directly. The presentation and discussion produced both a reasonable understanding of the mission by the managers who had not seen it before and some legitimate criticisms that resulted in useful changes to the mission statement. In addition, the groups began a process of identifying the major barriers to mission achievement as they perceived them.

Facilitation of this first meeting was provided solely by the external consultants, who used the design that had been jointly developed with the internal facilitator group. This was done because the senior executives felt comfortable with the external consultants and needed their coaching to ensure that they would behave in "a participative way" with their subordinates.

The meeting proved to be an effective communications vehicle for the new level of management. It was also a significant event in the development of the thirteen senior managers. In the process of explaining, clarifying, and defending the mission to others, the senior managers' own understanding of and commitment to the mission increased. They had to speak as a team with a unified voice, and they tried to model participative, nondirective behavior with subordinates. These behaviors provided some concrete evidence that senior management was serious about the new mission.

In April 1982, the second communications meeting, this time including the top three levels of management—some 250 people—was convened in Pittsburgh. The new invitees were aware of the financial difficulties facing the company, but a meeting of this size to discuss the company's direction was an event unique in National's history. Many of the participants arrived puzzled and somewhat apprehensive.

The meeting structure was similar to that of the February conference. It began with a general session in which Love described the current financial situation, discussed the necessity for a new direction for the corporation, and distributed the mission statement to all participants. Discussion and reaction occurred in small-group meetings made up of a cross-sectional mixture of managers. The sixty-two executives who attended the February meeting were spread among the small groups to explain, discuss, answer questions, and serve as resources to the groups in a participative and nondirective manner. Later in the meeting, groups from the same division or location met to begin preparing plans for communicating and implementing the mission at their locations. In many cases these plans included developing their own mission statement in support of the corporate mission.

The conference concluded on the second day with Love urging participants to recognize this as the first step in a lengthy process of making National a different kind of corporation. He also reminded them that they now had the job of continuing to move the company in the direction that had been spelled out. This job included helping the 99 percent of the company's employees not at the meeting to begin moving in that same direction.

The meeting produced a variety of responses. For some managers the effect was depressing. The information about the economic situation confirmed the bleak picture they had received from other sources. For others, however, the meeting was a hopeful sign because it signaled that substantial changes were going to be made and that they would be involved in making these changes. Naturally, many of the managers in the steel business began to question their own future because they could not see how their business could meet the return on investment objectives in the mission. A few managers in nonsteel businesses felt that the main focus of the mission was on steel and did not apply to them directly. Probably the most typical reaction, how-

ever, was one of skepticism. Many managers felt that the espoused direction was sensible, but they did not believe that the
senior managers were serious enough about change to make it
happen. In spite of this skepticism, the meeting did generate a
lot of interest and anticipation of change.

Structures and Mechanisms for
Generating Further Momentum

Out of the two Pittsburgh meetings the next phase of the
overall change process emerged. This included the following
four parallel sets of activities, each of which will be discussed in
turn: (1) structures and processes to address corporatewide
issues and to integrate the activities of others were established;
(2) training and development of the internal facilitator resource
group continued; (3) individual business units and staff functions communicated the corporate mission to their organizations and began development of their own unit/function mission; and (4) training and development of senior management
continued.

Structures and Processes. To provide energy to and focus for
the changes that would be needed to move the corporations
forward, the senior managers agreed that some form of parallel
organization was required. Such a parallel structure also would
provide visible reinforcement to one of the primary values
articulated in the mission statement: increased participation on
the part of all employees. Central to this parallel process was the
formation of what became known as the National Action Planning (NAP) Coordinating Committee. This group, made up of
seven of the thirteen senior managers, was to create and oversee
the various ad hoc groups and activities needed to address
corporatewide barriers to mission accomplishment.

Additional external consultants and experts were retained within the corporation to provide assistance and bring a
fresh perspective to such functions as strategic planning, market
analysis, and information systems development. Integrating the
activities of these external resources with the overall change

process was also a part of the NAP Coordinating Committee's role.

Task forces were established to work on major issues identified at previous meetings. These included transfer pricing policy, corporatewide human resource policy, line and staff responsibilities and roles, and strategic planning goals and processes. One such group was the policies and procedures task force. This group began by sending a questionnaire to all 250 participants in the April meeting, asking where they felt changes in policies, procedures, or practices were needed. By far the most frequently mentioned item was transfer pricing between business units. The group recommended that a set of teams representing each transfer price issue (for example, purchase of coal by the steel group) be set up to work out an agreement that would be acceptable to each business unit involved. This process was designed to ensure high levels of participation and push decision making to the lowest level practical.

In response to concerns by field managers that severe cost-reduction measures had been instituted at the plant level but that no similar belt-tightening efforts had been undertaken within the corporate office, Love asked for volunteers to serve on a task force to look into ways that the corporate office could cut back on costs. An impressively large number of people volunteered, and a group of twenty was selected, representing a cross section of headquarters employees from vice-presidents to secretaries. The group examined opportunities to save money in over a dozen categories that had been identified through a questionnaire sent to all headquarters employees. Both an oral and a written report were made to members of the senior management group, including Love. The activities of this group were similar to actions that were taking place throughout the organization, and provided evidence that the upward flow of information in the organization was improving and that responsiveness at the top was beginning to increase.

Internal Resource Development. Immediately following the second Pittsburgh meeting, the middle-level employees who had served as facilitators met with the consultants to review their performance and discuss what their future role in the change process might be. By and large they were satisfied with their accomplishments so far and were increasingly committed to doing something further to assist in carrying out the mission. The group developed a recommendation to the NAP Coordinating Committee to designate itself as a continuing source of facilitators who would assist managers in creating desired changes.

One of their first tasks was to identify their additional learning needs. A series of in-depth training and development programs were held on an evolutionary basis. The external consultants trained an initial group in these skills, and they, in turn, transferred these learnings to others within the organization. The initial group of 25 provided the nucleus for the evolution of a group of internal facilitators and consultants that later numbered close to 125 people. This group has provided a wide range of facilitation and change consulting services to various business and staff groups within National. In collaboration with the external consultants, its members also developed a series of training and development programs that enabled line and staff managers to gain operational understanding of participative management and cultural change within a context applicable to each part of a large and complex organization.

Individually and collectively these people served as a primary energy source for change throughout National. While skills and interests within the group varied and their assimilation into the organization sometimes created discomfort, their involvement and actions were critical to the overall change. They became, as Beer (1980) has termed it, the internal guerrillas for change.

Business Unit/Staff Mission Statements. Each operating unit and staff function took on the task of developing its own mission statement in support of the corporate mission. The process of developing individual unit mission statements actually began with the communication of the corporate mission statement throughout the units. Communications sessions were held in every operating and staff unit up to and including participation by hourly employees and their union representatives.

Participation in the development of unit mission statements was modeled on that used by the senior managers and was a positive and energizing force. This process also helped provide a needed sense of direction during a time of severe economic pressure. As each unit or function completed its respective mission statement, it was reviewed by the NAP Coordinating Committee for consistency, completeness, and congruence with the corporate mission statement.

Senior Management Training and Development. Throughout this period, sessions were held with the senior managers in which they continued to address their respective roles in the organization as well as their actions and behaviors in carrying out these roles. Considerable team building occurred as a natural outgrowth of this interaction. While some resistance to "learning for learning's sake" was evident, the group began to learn and change as a consequence of doing "real work." National was no exception to the phenomenon that organizational change and culture evolution activities are often not seen as "real work," at least initially, by members of the organization. By focusing these sessions on tasks that the group saw as meaningful, while using external resources skilled at group development, the managers achieved satisfaction in doing "real work" and learned new skills and behaviors in the process.

Eventually the group came to recognize the value of periodic, dedicated learning sessions and passed along the responsibility for providing these opportunities to the NAP Coordinating Committee. The first of these meetings focused on gaining increased clarity on roles, responsibilities, and interaction relationships among the office of the chairman, business unit presidents, and corporate staff. Other sessions included lectures by experts in the field of organizational change such as Russell Ackoff from Wharton and Michael Beer from Harvard. In addition, they evolved into true learning sessions with active participation in role plays, case studies, and other such activities.

As another aspect of development, the external consultants held periodic meetings with individual senior managers. These meetings not only continued the development of teamwork and improved communications among these individuals, they also fostered continuous strategic thinking and evolution of their vision of National in the future. Finally, they provided introspective discussions that focused on "keeping each other honest" in day-to-day actions, decisions, and behaviors.

Emerging Issues and Responses

During these early stages of the change process several important issues emerged. The leadership's response to these issues had significant impact on the change effort.

Weirton Divestiture. While the new mission was being developed and communicated, financial conditions in the steel business continued to deteriorate. One of the facilities hardest hit was National's steel plant in Weirton, West Virginia. Long regarded as the company flagship, the plant had been forced to shut down all but two of its blast furnaces for several months during 1980 and had laid off more than 3,000 employees. Its major product, tinplate, was competing in a declining tin can market. Upgrading facilities and shifting production to other steel markets would create a cash drain that the company could not afford. After exploring numerous alternatives, Love and Haas decided that the company could no longer afford to continue operating this plant.

In searching for a solution to this problem that would be consistent with the human and social responsibility goals of the mission, as well as with its financial performance goals, National decided to offer the plant to its employees under an employee stock ownership plan (ESOP). This announcement, which occurred in March 1982, just prior to the mission discussion meeting of the 250 top managers, sent shock waves throughout the corporation. People were stunned by the drastic and sudden nature of the action. The decision was significant in two ways. First, it underscored in dramatic terms top management's commitment to change, and, second, it reinforced the mission as being important in its totality—that is, financial and human considerations were equally important.

Changes in Organization Structure. A second set of issues centered on the corporation's structure. As the various task forces and business groups tried to figure out how to implement the mission statement, they increasingly ran into problems with this structure. Managers had difficulty determining what they could do, often disagreed about the best solutions to problems, and were reluctant to initiate action without a clear definition of responsibility.

The senior management group soon recognized that it needed to deal with these organizational issues. A first step was to elaborate on the mission statement by noting that the company would become a "diversified operating company" with comparatively autonomous business units. This statement emphasized that business autonomy would still be encouraged, but, the corporate staff would not operate as passively as under a holding-company concept.

By the summer of 1982, Love realized that further change was needed. He wanted to create a structure in which teamwork would be easier to achieve, individual operating units would be clearly defined, and participative management would be modeled and encouraged. As a result, an entirely new structure for the company was developed.

A four-person group called the Office of the Chairman was created. This group consisted of Love as chairman and CEO, two vice-chairmen, and Haas as the president and COO. Five operating units were designated (steel, aluminum, distribution, diversified manufacturing, and energy), each with its own group president and profit requirements. These business groups were to operate with their own staff offices, augmented and supported, where required, by the corporate staff. The Senior Management Group, made up of those people now reporting to members of the Office of the Chairman, was maintained in the new organization. Its purpose was to ensure that information was shared across business groups and staff functions.

The Office of the Chairman was seen as spending the

majority of its effort on issues of strategic direction. While each member of this office had specifically designated responsibilities, the group was designed to function as a team, and individual members were given wide latitude to make decisions, provide guidance, and speak for the company. Whenever possible, decisions were to be made in a collaborative manner involving both the Office of the Chairman and the Senior Management Group.

This concept was received enthusiastically by some senior managers but skeptically by others. It was a further sign that old ways of interacting with decision makers were no longer appropriate. Rather than dealing directly with the CEO of the company—and negotiating the best deal one could—managers must now operate within a consensus decision-making framework where decisions were tested against the overall needs of the corporation and its mission.

It was also a further signal that the implementation of the mission was occurring in a visible and significant manner. It provided a structure that encouraged business unit heads to get together on issues that they had been unable to resolve in the past. By putting new faces into new positions, the reorganization also underscored the notion that implementing the mission would require new skills and new ways of doing things. Furthermore, by creating a team concept of management at the top of the corporation, the reorganization emphasized that managers had the responsibility for working collaboratively with others in the corporation, not just for managing their own work.

Testing Credibility and Commitment. Both the overall change process and the new organizational concept faced a major test in late 1982. In the face of unusual circumstances, the Office of the Chairman decided on an across-the-board salary reduction that was not only very unpopular among the business unit and functional heads but was made in a unilateral way. This was regarded as a clear "violation" of an implied agreement between the Office of the Chairman and the balance of the Senior Management Group.

To confront this situation directly, the members of the

Office of the Chairman sat down with the entire Senior Management Group in a meeting facilitated by external consultants. While the decision was not changed (external circumstances would not allow it), the open and candid discussion — at times very heated — itself became a clear demonstration of the new values of the corporation. Such a meeting would not have occurred prior to the change process. Mechanisms were agreed upon to prevent this type of unilateral decision — except when absolutely essential — from being made in the future.

Revising the Mechanisms for Change Integration. In the initial stages of the change process the NAP Coordinating Committee served as the integrating mechanism for the overall change effort. The creation of the Office of the Chairman in 1982 and a related change in 1983 that resulted in the creation of National Intergroup, Inc., as the "parent" corporate body overseeing the various business groups, resulted in the decentralization of many actions and functions to the business group level. Because the focus of change implementation had moved to business units, the NAP Coordinating Committee was dissolved. Any overall coordination that was needed during this period was provided by the Senior Management Group as a whole, supported by an informal partnership between the vice-president of Human Resources and the external consultants.

By September 1983, it had become obvious to both the corporate staff and the businesses that a more formal coordination process was again needed. Such a process would provide a mechanism whereby decisions made and actions taken throughout the organization could be tested for congruency with the mission itself, with the corporate image evolving from the various merger activities, and with the business planning mechanisms that were being installed under the guidance of Haas and the corporate planning staff. Thus, strategic change process planning was introduced. This planning method was designed by a subgroup of the senior managers from both line and staff functions with the assistance of external consultants. Its function was to weave together the strands of the change process with the complexities inherent in the emerging activities for strategic business planning. The process was used to identify, track the status of, and, where necessary, integrate the key activities underway to implement the mission, both at the corporate level and within business groups. Descriptors of intermediate stages of the change efforts underway (for example, change goals for one year into the future) were developed to provide guideposts of progress toward mission implementation. One of the most difficult dimensions of this task was to allow for continuous iterations of the planning process to ensure the flexibility that such a fluid process as cultural change requires. While this process proved effective for some time, its use was discontinued during the 1984–1985 retrenchment period.

U.S. Steel and Nippon Kokan. In February 1984, about two years after the Weirton ESOP decision was announced, the steel divisions were shaken by another major surprise. National Intergroup announced that it had agreed to sell its entire steel business to U.S. Steel (since renamed USX). This was a totally unexpected announcement. While the steel business employees knew they would have to struggle to meet the financial goals of the corporate mission, they thought they would be given several years to prove their ability to do so. The first reaction of many was that Love, who had come from the steel business before becoming chairman, had broken trust with his former colleagues in steel.

After the initial shock had passed, however, the senior management of the steel company decided to take responsibility for managing this transition into its own hands. It formed a Transition Committee made up of volunteers who had been actively involved in the mission implementation efforts. This group was to serve as a support staff to plan and monitor the key transition activities and to serve as a communications network for the organization as a whole. It provided tangible evidence that the steel business could help create its own destiny, even in times of crisis.

Within six weeks after the sale to U.S. Steel was announced, the deal was cancelled due to antitrust concerns expressed by the U.S. Department of Justice. Less than a month later, National Intergroup announced that it had reached agreement to sell a 50 percent ownership of its steel business to Nippon Kokan, the second largest steel company in Japan. This announcement was received much more positively. The negotiations with U.S. Steel had made it clear to those in the steel business that it could be sold at any time. To become a part of such a large and highly regarded steel company as Nippon Kokan was seen as a definite step forward.

The Transition Committee had continued to function even after the U.S. Steel sale was canceled. Communications surrounding the Nippon Kokan sale were handled superbly. Information was communicated rapidly and accurately to all divisions. Ongoing methods of maintaining improved communications were also developed in the divisions, including hot lines and newsletters. After the sale was announced, Love and Haas visited each division of the steel company to explain the decision, discuss what they saw happening, and answer questions. This further clarified the situation and began to heal the wounds created by the earlier announcement.

Signs of Progress

Despite—perhaps also because of—the many significant issues that had been dealt with since the change effort was initiated, by the fall of 1984 a definite sense of progress could be felt throughout the organization. The company had transformed itself from a steel company to a diversified operating company to a holding company that takes an active role in managing its investments through planning processes, financial controls, and the dissemination of a clear set of corporate values.

There had also been significant change in the relationships between the corporate staff and the business groups. The business-planning and change-planning processes discussed earlier resulted in the exercise of greater control by corporate staff over some groups that had been highly autonomous while pushing key decisions further downward in others. In other areas, such as compensation policy, considerably more autonomy was given to the business groups. This change in relationships created new challenges for senior managers. For instance, in the case of corporate staff, the realignment of responsibilities meant a need for fewer corporate staff people. The challenge was to reduce the staff size in a manner consistent with expressed humanistic values.

Changes in relationships had occurred in other areas as well. People now expected to have more say in what was going on and were more vocal when they had a chance to participate. They had also become significantly more vocal when they were *not* given the chance to participate. Challenges to management decisions that seem inconsistent with the vision had become common. As one senior manager put it, "We told them we wanted their input and now, damn it, they want to participate." Managers sometimes had to remind themselves that they were getting what they asked for. If at times it seemed as though a "monster" had been unleashed, it was the managers who had agreed to create it.

Not coincidentally, the senior management experienced considerable turnover during the three years of change. Not everyone was comfortable with the new philosophy, and those who had been most successful with previous management styles sometimes felt least comfortable with the new ways. Of the thirteen senior managers who first worked on the new mission, six had left the company, and only two of those remaining were in the same jobs they had when the change process began.

There were other signs that significant change was occurring. National was the only major steel company to post an operating profit in 1983, and 1984 was looking even more profitable. The company's stock price had more than doubled in the three-year period. The joint venture with Nippon Kokan was seen as a marriage of two partners, not a desperation maneuver by National. A subsequent decision by the steel company to withdraw from industrywide labor bargaining was seen as an important step toward forging a new and positive relationship with the union.

In a late 1984 review of the first three years of the transformation, Haas, National Intergroup's president, noted that "we have demonstrated more innovative management thinking in the past three years than we had in the previous fifty. We have gone from a steel company to a diversified company, from an operating company to a holding company. We have a vision, a direction, and a philosophy of how we want to get there. To accomplish all this will be a challenge. We must continue to work with our people to understand and share our vision and to enlist their support and participation in making it a reality."

Haas also saw how his own management style and ways of thinking had been impacted: "Opening communication channels has helped me feel less isolated and allowed me to get better input for higher-quality decisions. I handle people more honestly now, and this has been better for both me and them. I am more effective and have more time for longer-range issues. In short, my job has become more fun, and I have more energy and enthusiasm for work."

Setbacks and Shifts in Focus of Attention

Few major changes in large organizations proceed without setbacks or periods of significant frustration. Several theorists (including Simmons, 1986) have noted that change often proceeds in cycles where periods of forward movement and progress are followed by times of retrenchment and disappointment. The National transformation was no exception.

In October of 1984, plans were announced for a merger with Bergen Brunswig, a major pharmaceutical distributor wtih an outstanding history of earnings and growth. Shortly after this, Leucadia National, a company with a reputation for "greenmail" (buying large shares of a company's stock, threatening an unfriendly takeover, and demanding that the stock be bought back at a premium) began to purchase large blocks of National Intergroup's stock. Soon, letters to stockholders and major newspaper ads began to appear advising NII shareholders not to approve the Bergen Brunswig merger. Determined not to give in to this threat, Love launched an aggressive counterattack that created a major drain on senior management time. National Intergroup took out its own ads and sent letters to stockholders countering Leucadia's charges. Scores of managers throughout the company manned phones urging stockholders to vote in favor of the merger.

While National managed to win stockholder approval of the Bergen Brunswig merger in early 1985, the business economy took a sudden downturn, resulting in major operating losses in National Intergroup's steel businesses. At this same time, the corporation discovered that its aluminum subsidiary had failed to recognize substantial losses on previous trading contracts and purchase commitments. The negative publicity surrounding these trading losses, coupled with National Intergroup's poor financial performance for the first quarter of 1985, caused Bergen Brunswig to cancel the merger at the last minute. Leucadia used this unexpected event to again challenge National by waging a battle for control of its board of directors.

Not only had National Intergroup's economic fortunes been reversed, but the energy and attention needed to fight these battles had left precious little time for the leadership to devote to the other aspects of the overall change effort or to provide the needed coordination and integration of activities already underway. By mid 1985, many people were of the opinion that the transformation process had failed and that NII had become a company under siege with a lost sense of direction.

Regaining Momentum and Direction

By July of 1985, the need to reduce the confusion and uncertainty that the events of the past eight months had created was clear. Love's first step, with the assistance of the external consultants, was to reclarify the roles and responsibilities of the leadership of the corporation and to ensure that his group of senior managers understood how each was expected to support the other.

This was done initially through a series of externally facilitated one-on-one meetings where perceptions of each other's role were shared and descriptions of support requirements were discussed. These meetings were followed by two off-site meetings of the senior managers. The first, held in August

1985, included Love, Haas, and the six staff support managers at National Intergroup.

In preparation for the meeting, Love wrote a brief description of the direction of National Intergroup as he saw it. He realized that, in this time of uncertainty, as CEO and the key figure in initiating the change process four years ago, he personally had to create a sense of direction and leadership for momentum and confidence to be regained. The statement that he prepared and distributed at the meeting said, in part:

> Certainty is a word that has not been used recently regarding National Intergroup. We all would like some structure and definition to enable us to plan more effectively for the future. From the time we first began to define our mission, we have been attempting to add some degree of stability to our efforts. For a variety of reasons, not always within our control, we have not been successful.
>
> Our proposed merger with Bergen was to be the final statement of our future direction. Since the merger's collapse, we have been attempting to redefine our strategic direction. Enough pieces have been put in place that I can, with reasonable certainty, define the strategic direction of National Intergroup for you. National Intergroup will be a $8 to $10 billion holding company comprised of stand-alone units in distribution, services, and specialty manufacturing businesses. It will provide a return to our shareholders that will justify their continued investment in the corporation.
>
> We have not achieved our objective but have begun to build the foundation. We at corporate staff will add value by providing the organization framework in which the various businesses can operate most effectively.

Love also prepared a new organization chart that clarified reporting relationships. One important change was that corporate financial and human resources functions would report to Love directly, enabling Haas to focus more attention on managing the business units.

The frame of mind of the other participants in the August meeting can be seen from the following examples of concerns that they submitted anonymously when they arrived:

- The "true" strategy will never be disclosed.
- People will be afraid to tell the truth at this meeting.
- Nothing will happen as a result of the meeting.
- We will not be open and candid with each other.
- We will place more value on personal "turf" than on collective corporate goal setting.

Participants also raised some searching questions:

- What kind of a company do we want to become?
- How do we get there?
- How will we operate in the future?
- Do we really want to survive and become a new company?

Despite the initial skepticism, the meeting did assist in clarifying some of these issues. The statement of direction prepared by Love provided an anchor that people could use to put aside the recent setbacks and refocus attention on the future. A common understanding of the roles of Love and Haas in particular and the corporate staff generically was reestablished. The group also generated a set of "desired descriptors" of what they collectively "wanted National Intergroup to be good at doing."

Participants agreed on the next set of steps, which culminated in another senior management retreat in October 1985. Those invited included both the eight managers who attended the August meeting and the six line managers in charge of NII's business units. This meeting was an effective next step in beginning to regain momentum and commitment to a common direction. In addition to the discussions regarding line-staff relations and future direction, the group also subjectively rated the corporation's current effectiveness in the descriptors of "what we want to be good at doing" developed in the August meeting. These ratings provided benchmarks that indicated that there was still a long way to go in operationalizing many of those desired norms.

As a next step in the organizationwide communications process, Love wrote a letter to all employees in much the style and tone found in his statement in the August retreat. It outlined the new organizational relationships and the philosophy behind them. The letter concluded as follows:

> Determination, creativity, experimentation, a commitment to excellence and quality—all these are the components of our vision. In essence, we are a company that desires to be very good at enhancing shareholder value, at selecting and buying new businesses, at having well-managed, well-performing businesses, at having strong financial management, at creating imaginative and effective partnerships, and at having an adaptive organizational culture. If all our people can feel they are contributing to this vision on a full partnership basis, National Intergroup, Inc., will have a group of companies each of which will meet the test. We will continually evaluate ourselves to see if we are achieving this vision.
>
> National Intergroup does have a purpose and a direction and a management group that is confident of its ability to create a great company in every respect. We cannot achieve our objectives alone and we trust that all employees will respond to this new definition with renewed confidence and dedication.

Other signs of regained momentum were also apparent. The second proxy fight with Leucadia was won in the summer of 1985. Shortly thereafter, National Intergroup announced the acquisition of the Permian Corporation, a large oil distribution firm. In December, National Intergroup's investment in First

Nationwide Financial Corporation was sold for $400 million, thus providing additional cash to invest in a new core business in support of the defined strategic direction. In early 1986, this objective was realized with the announcement of NII's intention to acquire FoxMeyer Corporation, the third largest pharmaceutical wholesaler in the United States. In addition, National Intergroup's information systems unit was set up as a separate business (and given the name GENIX), thus creating a further opportunity for growth in the service sector of the economy.

In the spring of 1986, the sale of the corporation's steel distribution unit to an outside firm was announced. This action offered benefits for both parties. From National Intergroup's perspective, it was a further step in moving the corporation in its desired direction. From the perspective of the distribution group employees, it was an opportunity to become part of an organization that was committed to steel distribution as a long-term business strategy. Also in early 1986, the steel business announced the signing of a highly innovative contract with its steelworkers' union. Called "precedent breaking" and "a model for survival" by the *Wall Street Journal* and the *Washington Post,* the contract committed both the union and the company to developing cooperative work relationships right down to the shop floor. It included provisions for profit sharing, guaranteed no layoffs, and eliminated many restrictive and inefficient work rules. The leadership of both the union and the company saw this as a major step toward forging a fundamentally different, mutually supportive long-term relationship.

Current Status and Major Accomplishments

In looking back over the first five years of the transformation, the changes and accomplishments have been significant. The company has virtually restructured all its businesses and redeployed most of its assets from cyclical, low-return investments to more profitable businesses in growth markets, while at the same time creating a focus and a new but clearly identifiable corporate image. From a steel company with investments in a

Figure 17-1. National Intergroup's Changing Business Mix.

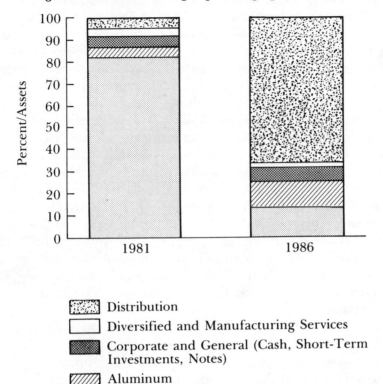

Distribution

Diversified and Manufacturing Services

Corporate and General (Cash, Short-Term Investments, Notes)

Aluminum

Steel

few other businesses, National has become a distribution and services company with some investments in metals. This change in mix of business is shown in Figure 17-1.

The cultural changes that were seen as signs of progress in 1984 have continued in many units. Effectiveness in managing participatively, openness of communications, and cooperation in solving problems for mutual gain have become common work norms in many sections of those businesses involved in the change process from the outset. Attitudes about change, understanding of the need for change, and abilities in managing change effectively have also continued to evolve. Mission statements continue to be used to drive business plans and decisions. At the corporate level, major setbacks have been encountered but are beginning to be overcome. Multiple structural reorganizations have been executed as required by changing internal and external circumstances. People have learned of the need to manage and adapt organizational structures rather than letting the structures manage them. The company's steel division has responded to its relationship with its Japanese partner by setting its sights on becoming a world-class steel producer and by forging a new cooperative partnership with its union.

Another important aspect of the transformation is that it has been accomplished largely by people who were with the company before the changes began. Of the fourteen senior executives who attended the latest planning retreat in October 1985, all but two were with the company at the time Love became chairman in 1981. While there have been numerous, significant changes in management with many key people leaving, the vast majority of the replacements have come from inside the organization.

The internal group of middle managers, first assembled to help facilitate the mission communications meetings and later expanded to provide broad consulting support to the change process, has become an important source of candidates for filling key job openings. These people, many of whom are now in very influential positions, have also remained an informal communications and resource network in support of the emerging corporate culture.

Challenges Ahead

During the past two years much of the attention of the senior managers, Love and Haas in particular, has been devoted to acquisitions and divestitures and external power struggles. During this time, then, little attention has been paid at the corporate level to furthering other aspects of the mission or to overseeing and integrating the change effort as a whole. Now that the business redeployment needed to meet financial goals has largely been accomplished, leaders need to shift their attention to other aspects of the change process. Just as a clear sense of strategic direction was needed in 1985, a renewed sense of the importance of and commitment to other elements of the mission must be high on National Intergroup's list of leadership priorities for the near future.

Another near-term challenge is to integrate the new acquisitions, Permian and FoxMeyer, into an emerging corporate culture. These organizations bring their own management styles and norms of behavior that, while seen as compatible when the merger decisions were being made, must be folded into National Intergroup. A new, participatively developed description of the corporation's culture that all understand and feel committed to is needed. A similar challenge exists in continuing to integrate the style, culture, philosophies, and approach of Nippon Kokan, the Japanese partner, with the existing culture of the steel business.

Implementing the new steel labor agreement is another major challenge for the future. The contract's language and expectations are seen by many employees as requiring a total reversal in the adversarial relationships formed over many decades. In many ways the transformation in attitudes, behaviors, and working relationships required to implement this contract will be as difficult and far-reaching as any of the other aspects of National Intergroup's transformation. At the same time, failure to achieve these changes could be a crippling blow to the economic viability of the steel company.

The role of National Intergroup's corporate staff will need to be examined once again. The support and assistance it will provide to the new businesses must be clarified to the satisfaction of all parties. Its role in rekindling commitment to the human goals and other aspects of the mission must be agreed upon, as must its role in providing integration to the overall change process.

Finally there remains the challenge of continually assessing progress in all aspects of the change effort, monitoring internal and external factors affecting progress, and modifying plans and priorities accordingly. This is a challenge that will never go away. Summarizing the status of the transformation in mid 1986, Love noted that "we haven't executed yet really; we haven't proven yet that these are the right plans. I think it's going to take another three years before we really begin to realize the fruits of our efforts."

Learnings and Implications

We have examined the processes and outcomes to date of the transformation at National. A number of lessons can be drawn from this case. We do not claim that all these lessons are necessarily transferable to other forms of organizational transformation; however, some of them seem to have elements that can be generalized. It is these that we will try to highlight.

1. The first learning is that no single model or approach can by itself be sufficient for planning and executing a large-scale transformation. The melding of multiple models, concepts, and approaches, along with the modification of these to meet the specific requirements of the moment, is essential. Such a "mixed model" is necessary to meet the unique and continually shifting requirements of a "real-world" transformation effort.

2. Change planning must be an iterative process. The change activities described in this chapter illustrate the emergent nature of transformation planning. At each stage, the results of preceding activities and random events influence what will and should happen next. External events—for example, a severe economic recession—can never be fully anticipated, and the consequences of activities such as the communication of the organizational mission can never be completely predicted. As a result, transformation planning should always be thought of as an iterative and evolutionary process in which each new activity is based on the results of the last one.

3. Maximum involvement of all people potentially impacted by the change, in both defining the direction of the change and implementing changes applicable to them, is essential for generating rapid understanding, commitment, and support. The first step in any change process must be the creation of a felt need for change if such a need does not already exist. More importantly, however, the need for change must be felt by the

people whose energy is required for change to happen. This is particularly a problem in mature, stable organizations where people have become accustomed to well-defined limits on their roles and responsibilities. If large numbers of the people affected by a major organizational transformation are not directly involved in and responsible for the changes to be made, the transformation is likely to occur much more slowly and much less uniformly.

4. The development of a standard that indicates the direction of the change, the areas where change is needed, and the values underlying the change is important to the success of the change effort. Simply understanding that change is necessary is not sufficient. Individuals also must know where to direct their efforts in making changes, and they thus need a set of standards that they can use to determine the areas in which they need to do things differently. The mission developed by the senior managers at National Intergroup was such a model. This mission provided guidelines that individuals could use to determine areas where changes were necessary and the direction that such changes should take. Later the strategic direction statement and the description of "the things National Intergroup wants to be good at doing" provided a further standard.

5. Transition structures are an important tool in the change process. The Senior Management Group at National became a useful tool in building a powerful coalition that could communicate the need for change throughout the organization. The creation of the NAP Coordinating Committee provided a mechanism to focus the energy of key top managers on the change process. It helped them monitor the results of the mission communication within the organization, ensure that there was adequate information sharing about problems and successes, and provide resources for change activities to groups that needed them. The various task forces provided structures for examining areas where changes might be needed and for ensuring that barriers to change were identified and dealt with by the appropriate people. The creation of the internal facilitator group provided a structure for training a group of middle-level people in the skills of facilitating change and also provided a

communication channel — between people within the organization and those at the top — that was outside the normal chain of command.

The transition structures used in this change effort also demonstrate that such mechanisms can themselves create problems. The managers who were a part of them generally experienced tension between the demands of the change effort and the demands of their regular jobs. Frustrations also arose because these managers were being asked to operate outside of the basic authority structures that they were used to. For temporary structures to be a useful part of any change effort, managers who are not experienced in working in them require help in understanding their roles and support in carrying them out.

6. In times of transition, the symbolic interpretation of actions has critical impact on furthering or hindering the change process. It is a general phenomenon of leader-follower relations that leaders' actions are significant both for the direct result achieved and for the symbolic messages they send to the organization. The impact of such symbolism is particularly significant during periods of major change when people want to know the meaning behind the words being used to describe the desired new direction and to ascertain the degree to which leaders are committed to the change (do the leaders' actions match their words). The decision to sell the Weirton plant was one such example of a decision that had both real and symbolic impact. This action provided a clear signal that the people at the top of the organization recognized the seriousness of the situation and the need for drastic action. Similarly, the reorganizations and resultant personnel shifts demonstrated that changes were necessary in the way people managed and interacted.

7. The integration and coordination of change processes with other plans and activities within the context of the organization as a total system are important and ongoing challenges. The very nature of change within a large system is so complex and evolutionary that each action taken can — and usually does — impact each other action taken by the organization. The NAP Coordinating Committee and strategic change process

planning were two such systemwide integration efforts used by National Intergroup.

8. At the same time, while integration is a desirable objective, many of the actions initiated in a large-scale systems change cannot be foreseen, planned, or controlled by those leading the change. Managers and change agents can only set the process in motion and create structures to guide it. The changes will occur as a consequence of the interaction of people and events with the programs and activities designed to create change. This can happen effectively only if there are people *throughout* the organization with the skills and knowledge to monitor events and invent change plans that are appropriate to given conditions. A key element of systems change is developing a critical mass of people who understand the changes that are desired, who have the skills to create and manage them, and who can continually invent new programs and structures to reinforce and accelerate the process of changing.

9. A corollary to this is that effective change management must include attention to individuals and individual change as well as to the organization. The behavior of people within an organization is influenced by both the organization's structures and systems and the beliefs and skills that individuals have developed over time. If systems and structures change, but individuals do not develop a new understanding of their purpose and new skills for making them work, their behavior may be affected but will not be qualitatively different from what it was before the change. In the case of National Intergroup, if the responsibilities of new organizational structures had been installed but no attention had been given to creating a new image of how the company was going to function, the effect of the reorganizations would probably have been negligible.

10. Support for change must be provided throughout the process and requires a strong, trusting, mutual relationship between internal and external resources. The process of change and transformation is difficult, painful, and stressful for all involved in it or impacted by it. People within such a transforming organization need support and understanding as they un-

dergo change. Support for change requires the establishment of sufficient resources within the organization to sustain that transformation over time. In the early stages, a major source for the energy, support, and modeling for change may have to come from external resources. From the outset, however, processes should be put in place to nurture and develop that internal resource base within the organization. Creation of this internal resource component requires a strong partnership between external and internal resources for change. In addition, as roles, skills, and needs change over time, an ongoing process of recontracting and role clarification is needed. The development and use of the internal resource group, involvement of the external resources in the change process planning sessions, and one-on-one discussions with internal resources are three examples of the internal-external linkages developed within National.

11. A final learning is that changes of such a complex nature will occur unevenly, with spurts of progress and success followed by unanticipated setbacks and disappointments. From time to time, attention may be focused—intentionally or inadvertently—on only a few elements of the change effort or may be diverted completely to other activities. When this happens, it is important that setbacks be worked through and attention be refocused so that the change effort does not become permanently sidetracked or stalled. Mutual responsibility exists with both internal and external resources to ensure that such energy, support, and leadership are provided during these times of crisis.

References

Beer, M. *Organization Change and Development: A Systems View.* Glenview, Ill.: Scott, Foresman, 1980.

Simmons, J. "Leading Participation: The Role of the CEO." In *Organization Development Network Conference Proceedings.* New York: Organization Development Network, 1986.

18 *Michael O. Bice*

The Transformation of Lutheran Health Systems

Lutheran Health Systems is one of the nation's oldest and largest health care management companies. Founded in 1938, it manages hospitals, nursing homes, chemical dependency programs, physician clinics, congregate housing units, and a school for the multiply handicapped. Most of its seventy-five units are in small or rural communities in a thirteen-state area west of the Mississippi. While the bulk of its activities are nonprofit, it does operate a for-profit subsidiary called Concord Health Services, Inc. This subsidiary presently owns a durable medical equipment company.

The organization is in the midst of a significant transition from a provider-driven company to one driven by the unmet needs in local health care marketplaces. This chapter will attempt to share background on this transition and provide some insights into how it is being managed. We have been engaged in large-scale cultural change and are now (1987) in the fourth year of a seven-year program. We are not seeking surface changes but rather substantive behavioral change in our employees and the system as a whole. Our intention is to *transform* the company so that it will remain a relevant and viable social instrument.

Lutheran Health Systems has many of the components of a long-term player in health care—geographical dispersion,

vertical as well as horizontal integration, a commitment to research and development, and an increasingly positive national
image. What it lacks is a more balanced infrastructure, long-
term financial strength, and, most importantly, market focus.
This orientation is necessary for our survival. We must complete
this organizational transformation in order to legitimately plan
for the system's role in health care in the next century.

Initial Steps

The notion of organizational transformation can be
traced to the summer of 1982. At the time, I was the COO of
Lutheran Health Services and had arrived at several conclusions
about the organization. First, I believed that it had very significant potential but that it did not have either the will or the
resources to be an effective provider of health care over the long
term. It had an organizational structure that had not changed
much in thirty years. Moreover, it had a strong historical culture
that served primarily as a barrier to change. It was a "society of
administrators" with a major norm of conformity. Finally, it was
slow to react to environmental changes and thus was not seen as
being in the mainstream of health care.

I was an outsider in the organization, having spent most of
my career in academic health centers on the East Coast. I was
recruited by the board to eventually succeed the incumbent
president and to provide long-term leadership and direction for
the company. Once I had completed an analysis of the system, I
then began to look for a program that would enable me to
change the direction of the organization. At the time, I was a
Kellogg National Fellow and had decided to study corporate
cultures. It dawned on me that this study had more than academic ramifications; in fact, I saw that it could become the
centerpiece of my plan of organizational revival.

At the time, however, there were few members of the
organization who were willing to openly admit the need for
organizational transformation. The incumbent president remained in a power position. The process of organizational
transformation would significantly alter the so-called old boy

network and would result in new values, heroes, rituals, cere-
monies, and stories. In essence, there would be new rules of the
game and a new order. Most of the players had significant vested
interests in the old order. Thus, I began the program in January
of 1983 largely as an individual effort.

I carefully sought out support from the young future
leaders of the organization, many of whom were disgruntled
with the old order. I recruited new senior managers from outside the organization who were at least open to the idea of
organizational change. Consultants — external auditors, attor-
neys, and strategic planners — were used judiciously in an effort
to lay the groundwork and present a case for large-scale cultural
change. The old guard was not ignored. Rather, I sought out
long-time employees who, while loyal to the organization, also
were frankly concerned about where it was heading.

With this rather inauspicious beginning, I then spent
most of the next eighteen months building my knowledge base
of corporate culture change and also selling the concept to our
board of directors, corporate officers, field managers, and department heads. During this period, I made approximately
twenty-five presentations on my assessment of the culture of
Lutheran Health Systems. Although support for organizational
change grew, this put me in an increasingly combative posture
relative to the incumbent president. The matter came to a head
in June of 1984, when I was promoted to the position of president and CEO. Those in the field generally supported this
change but still had no clear understanding of the implications
of my program of organizational transformation.

Soon after becoming president, I presented my vision for
the organization. I saw it as capable of becoming a leading-edge
health services company, characterized by commitment, credibility, innovation, and market orientation. In an attempt to
appeal to the old guard as well as the emerging new order, my
presidential theme was, "Our methods must change to meet
changing circumstances, but our values will remain the same."
These values were clearly stated at the outset: Christian compas-
sion, people matter more than technology, community partnership, service above self, and self-renewal. My dream was to

create a value-driven business enterprise in which values would clearly come first. The vision, theme, and values were placed in writing and have been consistently presented to the field ever since. Annual meetings and annual reports, as well as our quarterly publications and video newsletters, embody and market both the vision and the values that underlie it.

Mobilizing Commitment and Resources

Early in 1983, I formed a Management Development Committee comprised of the future leadership of Lutheran Health Systems. Although it was *not* stated, the group's primary task was to provide leadership and to gain support for organizational transformation. The group made improvements in our recruitment and management orientation program, and provided significant leadership for efforts in continuing education. They developed the organization's first statement of management philosophy, namely, "local leadership supported by corporate expertise." This suggested a decentralized process of decision making, which would be augmented by corporate services. As support for organizational transformation spread, the committee increasingly began to address the need for corporate culture change. In fact, moving the cultural change process from the corporate office to the field is the single highest priority of this committee today.

In 1985, I formed a Corporate Culture Steering Committee comprised of myself, the senior vice-president for corporate strategy, and the director of human resources, and staffed by a newly appointed coordinator of corporate culture change. I had written a paper on our cultural change efforts in which I explicitly outlined the ten interventions that we were using to alter our culture. This paper was distributed throughout the organization and has been discussed openly and widely.

Lutheran Health Systems also has its share of internal politics. One has to constantly struggle to capture and retain management control. In early 1983, the center of this political organization was more devoted to the old order than to the new. Today, the center of the organization is, on balance, more devoted to the new order. The change has occurred over a four-year period, and while the direction is toward the new order, it is still an effort to maintain the momentum in that direction. Thus, one must seek leverage to move the organization forward.

In a rapidly changing health care environment, this leverage was not hard to find. In 1984, the introduction of a new Medicare payment system accelerated the decline in usage of many of our rural facilities, and we ended the year in poor financial shape. Eight facilities were earmarked for divestiture. The impact of changes in the farming and energy sectors have caused severe economic distress in many of our communities. Thus, changes in federal health care payments, together with economic decline, have been used to convince field managers that they must change their methods and approaches if they are to survive, and a market rather than an operational orientation has been stressed as the pathway to the future.

The question of financial resources to ensure the organizational transformation has not been openly discussed. Increasingly though, specific dollar allocations in the corporate budget are being made to further organizational transformation. A complete accounting has not been made, but intuition suggests that our expenses are in line with Deal and Kennedy's (1982) estimate of what an organizational transformation might cost, that is, approximately five to ten percent of payroll expenses.

With the passage of time, top management has been increasingly supportive of the organizational transformation effort. Ownership of the program has begun to pass from the president through the senior management to the field administrators. In fact, the next three years of the program will be devoted to this part of the transition. Clear signals of the president's support for the program have been sent since June of 1984. I think that every corporate officer or field administrator is convinced that I am determined to make this corporation market sensitive. However, I know that the president's position has to be communicated again and again, that support has to be constantly sought, and that presidential deeds speak louder than words.

In mid 1986, there was a change in leadership on the board of directors. The new chairman was given the mandate to serve as the guardian of the mission and values of the organization. The CEO, it was thought, should not be the only one to bear this responsibility. Joint ownership of the task of protecting and promoting organizational values was perceived as a necessary ingredient in organizational development. It could now be said that the board, as well as the management, was spearheading the effort in organizational transformation.

Key Interventions

It should be noted that the program was not clearly delineated when it began in January of 1983, and it took until mid 1985 for our program format to be spelled out. Ten interventions were selected as methods of altering the historical culture. These interventions represent practical management initiatives except that, in our case, each has a specific focus on organizational transformation.

The first intervention is *recruitment*. Our objectives in management recruitment are to attract individuals to Lutheran Health Systems who are actual or potential leaders, who are committed to multiunit systems, as well as to small and rural communities, and who are open to change. We tried to promote from within wherever possible, but also engaged in a national search for leaders. We provide summer externships and administrative fellowships, and for the past two years have been engaged in a fellowship program with Concordia College in Moorhead, Minnesota.

The second intervention is *management orientation*. We want to prepare and socialize an individual for service in our organization, so as to enhance the likelihood of strong performance and long-term retention. In essence, we are trying to "sell the system" to the incoming manager. We have an administrative residency program and many of our field administrators serve as mentors for young managers. We provide orientation to nursing service administrators, business office managers, and a variety of other individuals. Recently, we have become involved in a

Governing Board Mentor Program with five of our communities participating.

The third intervention is *continuing education*. Our objectives here are to foster lifelong learning and to assist managers in understanding and better utilizing contemporary management tools. Additionally, we want to broaden an individual's perspective beyond health care, since institutions and doctors are not the only factors that improve an individual's health and welfare. Self-analysis and a self-directed educational plan are encouraged. We have provided supervisory education for approximately 1800 of our managers. Sabbaticals, loaned executive programs (allowing executives to take time off to work in a different capacity in other organizations), and attendance at American Management Association courses are encouraged. Many of our managers are participants in the University of Minnesota's Independent Study Program, while others have been involved in the Ohio State University's Executive Finance Series. Finally, a systemwide guest relations program, directed at all employees, is underway.

The fourth intervention is *incentive compensation*. The primary objective of this program is to reward managers who are sensitive to the needs of their local marketplaces and who are moving their organizations away from a reliance on acute-care revenues. We are seeking better financial performance, the retention of good managers, and improved performance measures. We are working closely with Hay Associates to develop a pilot compensation program for implementation in 1987, and we provided a year-end bonus for the first time in 1986.

The fifth intervention — *reorganization* — has both corporate and field components. From the corporate perspective its objectives are to better channel and direct diversification efforts and to guide the company's shift to other than acute-care revenues. We intend to provide upward mobility and expanded duties for management personnel and also want to assist our board with its new roles. A parent holding company was established in October of 1984, and our for-profit arm was incorporated in 1985.

The objectives for field reorganization, like those for corporate reorganization, include assisting in the transition toward a greater reliance on outpatient revenues. In addition, we want to provide the tools and incentives that will enable rank-and-file employees to change, as well as educate local boards and medical staffs as to their role in the transformation process. We feel very strongly that corporate and field reorganization should be mutually supportive. We have adopted a new strategy that will move us away from managing a number of isolated rural institutions and toward the oversight of ten regional networks. Each of our owned facilities has been encouraged to develop local foundations. Over the past two years approximately thirty home health agencies have been started. Grant moneys from the Kellogg Foundation and the Robert Wood Johnson Foundation have been useful with respect to community development studies.

The sixth intervention is an *innovation audit*. The objectives of this audit are to identify where we promoted as well as where we stifled innovative behavior. An innovation index was established and will be remeasured shortly. We have been able to compare our innovative performance to that of firms not in the health care field. Finally, we intend to promote and reward innovative activities throughout Lutheran Health Systems. The audit was completed in January of 1984, and a systemwide innovation steering committee was formed shortly thereafter. This committee, which has been working for two years, has developed and implemented a program called Ideas Create Excellence (ICE). An innovation catalogue has recently been published, and a president's grant program has been in place for three years. We have also developed the Innovation-Communication and Action Planning System (I-CAPS), and this will soon be implemented throughout the organization.

The seventh intervention deals with *corporate communications*. Our communication strategy is to promote a sense of common purpose and to keep our various stakeholders informed about our activities. We want our brand name to become better known, and we want to be considered by our colleague systems and potential customers as a solid, resourceful organization. We have a contract with the Hospital Satellite Network, and

Table 18-1. Overview of Traditional and Target Norms.

Traditional Norms (Provider or Operations Driven)	Target Norms (Market Driven)
Conformity	Accept and encourage diversity
Centralized authority	Decentralized decision making
Reactionary	Proactive
Conflict avoidance	Confront conflict
Information withheld	Information sharing
Job security	Pay linked to performance
Old boy network	"What works" network
Rewards taken for granted	Constant effort at recognition
Faith — one expression	Faith — many expressions

seven of our largest facilities are connected via this network. Legislative teleconferences involving managers from ten states are held monthly in an effort to keep track of various federal and state health initiatives. Video newsletters are distributed twice annually to all our facilities and have been well received. A song was composed to accompany the video newsletters; its lyrics focus on the themes of love and change.

The eighth intervention is *personnel policy administration.* We want our personnel policies to reflect due process, open communications, and ample opportunities for individual growth. Upward mobility should be encouraged, and fair and equitable administration of policies should be pursued. Finally we intend to provide competitive salaries and benefits. The human resources function has been strengthened at the corporate level as well as in the field. Performance appraisal mechanisms are constantly being updated, and we participate in annual national salary and benefit surveys.

The ninth intervention is *norm management.* The objectives of this program are to make unwritten rules explicit and to develop and encourage more desirable norms. Utilizing the work of Kilmann (1984), we have identified many of our traditional unwritten rules, as well as the norms that would be supportive of a market-driven organization. The results of this endeavor are found in Table 18-1.

The tenth and final intervention is *value management.* The

object of this program is to discover and, where appropriate, to enhance the basic value set of our system. We intend to integrate our values into all facets of our work. It is terribly important to identify and reduce gaps that might exist between stated values and actual behavior. Finally, we want to assure our employees that their basic values will be both protected and promoted. We recently completed a video presentation on our five basic values. It is a powerful program, and one cannot watch it without being moved. It makes clear that our values have first priority, that we are different because of our values, and that we will persevere because of them.

Managing and Evaluating the Transformation

As noted, our program of change was initiated and developed at the corporate level. Three years were spent in this endeavor. The fourth year—1986—was a transition year between the home office and the field. Full implementation in the field is planned for 1987 through 1989. From the outset, this was planned as a large-scale change in the company's culture. A model unit strategy was not pursued for several reasons. First, since we are such a diversified organization, it would have been difficult to select a model unit. Second, the impact of the change process was to substantially erode the power and influence of the old order. Subtle, rather than open, change was the order of the day. Finally, we were learning as we went along. We know more today than we did in 1983, and presumably our learning processes will continue.

Overall direction for transformation process has been provided by the Management Executive Committee, a group of senior corporate officers chaired by the president. I recently combined the offices of CEO and COO because I felt that bureaucratic layering would compromise leadership for the transformation process. It is clear that from this point forward, the field can make or break the effort. No amount of cajoling or negative incentives will lead to the widespread acceptance of this transformation. Rather, I believe that the field managers need to perceive that this program is in their best interests as well as in those of the corporations. In fact, they should see it as representing an appropriate response to a rapidly changing environment. Fortunately, many do. The remainder will come on board, given time and a continuing commitment to the program by the senior management of the company.

As I indicated previously, the Management Executive Committee assesses the success of the tranformation process on a continuing basis. The Corporate Culture Steering Committee, as well as the field's Management Development Committee, evaluate the program on a quarterly basis. The measurement process is becoming more systematic. The quarterly review of the transformation program looks at each of the ten interventions carefully. The various tactics are evaluated, and objective measurements are used wherever possible.

We are constantly on the lookout for signals that would suggest either the success or failure of the effort. We look to see whether key opinion leaders from the field are acknowledging the importance of the program and using the terms of culture and cultural change in their everyday speech. We seek out observations from outsiders, particularly our consultants, to get their sense of how well things are going. Finally, we must rely on our own gut sense of whether it is working. The bottom line is that the present method of assessing our effort is not highly refined, nor is it particularly objective. I believe that we are more than halfway to the point of a full transformation of Lutheran Health Systems. I *believe* the program is bearing fruit, that it is the correct one for the organization, and that it is adding value to the field. I can honestly say that if I had the sense that the program was not working, I would scrap the effort.

Looking to the Future

In general, the next three years will be spent in implementing the program throughout the field. Of the interventions previously noted, emphasis will be placed on incentive compensation, innovation, norm management, and reorganization. One of the key elements of incentive compensation is to reward managers who are market sensitive. More pointedly, we want to reward managers who embody the attributes of the new order. Our innovation programming is off to a successful start but needs to prove its worth throughout the corporation. We are at the very early stages of understanding the unwritten rules that govern our behavior. Finally, we have followed a deliberate pattern of reorganization. We need to consider organizing by product lines as distinct from state lines. Our old geographical method of organization may not be responsive to today's environmental pressures.

The key obstacles that stand in the way of our transformation process include first of all, matters that are outside our direct control. For example, federal reimbursement policies dramatically impact our smaller institutions and nursing homes. Again, continued economic downturns in energy and farming could wreak havoc in some of the regions that we serve. The change process would also be hurt by the unanticipated loss of key senior managers or if a major intervention, say our innovation program, went sour and lost credibility. Next, an obvious obstacle would be the acquisition of our organization by another firm. A different management orientation or approach could scuttle the transformation process. Finally, I am reminded that corporate culture is both organizational glue and a barrier to change. Even our target culture could inhibit us from responding effectively to the environment some day. Hence, I argue that we need a flexible rather than a strong culture.

The obstacles noted above are probably recurring obstacles from previous efforts at organizational change. The more disquieting kinds of changes are the unanticipated ones that result from our rapidly changing environment. Our method for overcoming obstacles will simply be to stay the course, but not in a blind way. We will continue to evaluate the interventions and make whatever midcourse corrections are required. Candidly, there is no real assurance that the obstacles can be overcome. Rather, I believe that they can be managed. One must analyze the organization and the environment constantly, and react accordingly. One also has to have faith in the transformation process, in oneself, and in the key people in the organization.

Lessons Learned

At this point, I would like to summarize what I believe are the major principles for managing organizationwide transformation. First, the CEO must make a multiple-year commitment to the effort. His continuing, personal, hands-on involvement is essential. Enormous amounts of time and travel are involved, and, to the extent possible, he should embody the desirable attributes of the new culture. Second, he needs strong leverage—be it an environmental or internal "crisis"—to get and keep people's attention on the need for organizational transformation. Third, as an organization acquires new communities, it also acquires new subcultures, and this makes the transformation more difficult. In essence, the CEO is dealing with a moving target. The local units' subcultures are extremely important and cannot be totally subservient to the corporate culture. Indeed, I sense that there must be a blend between the corporate culture and the community culture. Fourth, the leader must become and remain a student of organizational behavior. Being involved in organizational transformation requires constant learning. The CEO must be open, candid, and do his homework! The fifth principle is to set modest goals. Large-scale cultural change is an imposing undertaking, and any substantive change will not come about overnight. The sixth principle is to recognize and accept that organizational transformation will be an ongoing management task in the health care field during the balance of the 1980s and 1990s. The final principle is to be both patient and persistent. Affected managers need to hear a clear and consistent message of strong CEO support for the transformation process.

From our experience, we have learned that there are certain conditions and events that support the transformation process and others that hamper the process (Table 18-2).

With this list should come the warning that large-scale cultural change is not for everyone. Without the CEO's continuing involvement and endorsement and without a clear and

Table 18-2. Conditions for Successful Transformation.

Supports Transformation	Hampers Transformation
CEO leadership	Leadership of process by person other than CEO
Need to get and keep people's attention (leverage)	Perception that organization is doing well ("if it ain't broke, don't fix it")
Knowledge of the undertaking	
Preselling	
Transformation that protects and promotes basic values	Surface understanding of transformation process
	Initiating interventions without gaining support for them
	Ongoing strength of traditional culture
	Transformation that erodes or compromises basic values

substantive understanding of the magnitude of the task, any attempt at transformation is bound to fail.

If I were starting the process now, rather than being at the midpoint, there are several things I would do differently. First, I would be more systematic about the ten interventions. I would try to identify them clearly and to specifically allocate resources to each of the interventions. A steering committee and a cultural change coordinator would probably have been useful from day one, and certainly would have been helpful in tracking the progress of each intervention. Next, I wish that I had had more appreciation for the complexity of the three levels of culture (artifacts and creations, values, and basic assumptions) that Schein (1985) describes. I do not think I would have been discouraged from proceeding, but I would have started the transformation with a clearer understanding of the difficulty of the tasks that lay ahead. Next, I wish that I had known that cultural change typically creates significant individual and collective loss and hence produces a need for transition rituals (Deal, 1985). I do not think we have provided enough of these transition rituals for our employees, and thus we have probably caused some pain and suffering as we have moved to the new order. Next, I have a clearer sense now that the top and middle management of an organization may be more of a barrier to transformation than the rank-and-file employee. Over the last several years, I have observed that most employees are looking for leadership and want to be sensitive to patient needs. In a way, they may be more market oriented than their supervisors. Finally, it is clear that management cannot undertake such a sweeping program without the full understanding and support of the board of directors. On a deeper level, it is also important to acknowledge that the board, just like management, must undergo a process of change. It goes without saying that this change process must be carefully managed by the CEO.

Conclusion

Lutheran Health Systems is an *organization in transition*. It is moving away from the management of community health resources to the management of regional networks. Its financial resources will come less from cost-based payments and more from capitation programs in which individuals pay a fixed rate that entitles them to a range of services rather than paying on a service-by-service basis. It will treat physicians as partners and not as competitors. Its managers will move from the oversight of one product line — acute-care services — to the oversight of a comprehensive array of health care products. Encompassing all these changes is the need to move away from a company driven by its operations to one driven by the needs of its local marketplaces. In essence, Lutheran Health Systems must be transformed. This transformation, to be accepted, must blend the best of the old order with the requirements of a new and rapidly changing environment. We want to remain a viable social instrument. Through the process of organizational transformation, we seek profound and meaningful changes in the lives of our employees, and in Lutheran Health Systems as a whole.

References

Deal, T. E. "Cultural Change: Opportunity, Silent Killer, or Metamorphosis." In R. H. Kilmann, M. J. Saxton, R. Serpa, and

Associates, *Gaining Control of the Corporate Culture*. San Francisco: Jossey-Bass, 1985.

Deal, T. E., and Kennedy, A. A. *Corporate Cultures: Rites and Rituals of Corporate Life*. Reading, Mass.: Addison-Wesley, 1982.

Kilmann, R. H. *Beyond the Quick Fix: Managing Five Tracks to Organizational Success*. San Francisco: Jossey-Bass, 1984.

Schein, E. H. "How Culture Forms, Develops, and Changes." In R. H. Kilmann, M. J. Saxton, R. Serpa, and Associates, *Gaining Control of the Corporate Culture*. San Francisco: Jossey-Bass, 1985.

19

Thomas J. Murrin

Building a
Quality Culture
at Westinghouse

Changing a large organization is like turning a large ship — the captain charts a new course, the pilot turns the wheel, but it takes a long time to see the results. About seven years ago, management began to turn the wheel at Westinghouse, but it is only now that results are becoming apparent. The new course charted for Westinghouse involved a fundamental shift in the role that quality plays in all its businesses. Prior to this shift, the company tended to think of quality as just another production variable it could monitor and control — like direct labor cost, material cost, and overhead. But Westinghouse slowly became convinced that quality plays a much greater role than it has in the past. In fact, it now sees quality as the key driving force in the success of the business.

Substantial time, money, and energy have been poured into improving quality at Westinghouse. Some managers may feel that it would have been better for the corporation to forgo quality and its corresponding productivity improvement efforts and let other American corporations blaze the trail — to learn from others and then follow their path. But, from the early days of our efforts in 1979, I have believed that the goals of quality and productivity improvement were vital to the future success of the corporation and more than worth the level of commitment we were to make. This chapter summarizes the first seven years of the effort to build a Quality Culture and make quality a driving force for Westinghouse.

Early Heritage

To understand the nature of the task facing Westinghouse in recent years, it is necessary to know something about this century-old company. The Westinghouse Electric Company was founded in 1886 by George Westinghouse, one of the great inventors and engineers of the nineteenth century. By age forty, he already had invented the air brake for trains, electric signals for railroads, and a series of devices for the first practical transmission of natural gas.

He then turned his attention to the problem of transmitting electrical energy over long distances. Up to that time, a power plant had to be located every mile or so if the direct current electricity was to be used over any significant distance. With the help of such brilliant young engineers as Nikola Tesla, the Serbian electrical genius, Westinghouse developed the alternating current system to solve this problem. In so doing, he came into direct and strenuous competition with Thomas Edison, who favored and had considerable investment in the direct current system. Westinghouse had to overcome the "high voltage is too dangerous" arguments of his opponents.

Bidding against Edison, Westinghouse won the contract to light the 1893 Columbian Exposition in Chicago. This first large-scale demonstration of the capability of alternating current proved to be a decisive factor in the ultimate adoption of alternating current as the prevailing system for transmitting and distributing electricity worldwide. It made possible a highly productive, high-quality, and safe system for harnessing electric power.

In the decades that followed, the Westinghouse company grew as the electrification of America grew. A primary supplier of electric generation, transmission, and distribution equipment to electric utilities, the company soon expanded its product line. It began making products that used electricity in industry and the home—motors, lamps, appliances, heating and cooling equipment, and others.

In 1920, Westinghouse pioneered radio broadcasting—its first move toward the diversity that now characterizes the company. The broadcast of the Harding-Cox election returns in 1920 from KDKA's first location atop the East Pittsburgh plant marked the first scheduled commercial radio broadcast. This was the beginning of the Westinghouse Broadcasting Company whose Group W is today a leader in the commercial broadcasting business. With the advent of television—in which Westinghouse played a developmental role—the corporation also became the first to sponsor network television coverage of a national political convention, namely, the Republican convention in 1952 that nominated Dwight D. Eisenhower for the presidency.

The 1950s saw acceleration of the trend toward diversification for Westinghouse. Many of these new efforts were departures from the original core business—electrical apparatus. New businesses included jet aircraft engines, over-the-road truck refrigeration, community land development, medical x-ray equipment, and nuclear power for both naval ship propulsion and commercial use. Launched in 1954, the USS *Nautilus* was the first atomic-powered submarine. It was driven by a nuclear propulsion plant that Westinghouse had designed and built. This was the beginning of the nuclear navy. America's commercial nuclear power industry started with the Shippingport nuclear power plant of Duquesne Light Company. Its reactor also was built by Westinghouse, for the U.S. Atomic Energy Commission.

In 1985, Westinghouse had about $11 billion in sales with approximately 125,000 employees in some 200 major locations around the world. Its business today covers five principal markets: electronics for both defense and industry, electric power equipment and service for utilities and industry, a wide variety of products and services for the construction industry, television and radio broadcasting, and finance through the Westinghouse Credit Corporation.

The Basis for a Quality Culture

It is one thing to recognize the need for quality and generally strive to achieve it. It is another to give it first priority in everything that a company does. For decades, Westinghouse has manufactured products and systems whose high levels of quality were achieved by superior engineering and manufacturing expertise. And the corporation has always recognized this need for quality. Its slogan: "You can be sure . . . if it's Westinghouse" was born of this recognition in 1948.

For example, in the commercial area, our steam turbines and generators have very demanding duty cycles. They must run for years in harsh environments of high-temperature and high-speed rotation. Their performance requires high levels of quality in mechanical, electrical, and metallurgical engineering, as well as in manufacturing technology. Utility customers put considerable value on quality. Failure of a turbine or generator can result in removal of an entire generating station from service. Replacement power costs in a 1,000 megawatt station can be $10,000 an hour. Nuclear steam supply systems and nuclear fuel both are high-tech, high-demand-cycle products with similarly grave economic consequences if they malfunction. Another category of commercial products requiring high quality is transportation systems—elevators, escalators, propulsion and control systems for subways, and so on. Quality is also an important buying influence for the largest single Westinghouse customer—the U.S. government. Products and services purchased by the armed services, such as radar systems for military aircraft and civilian air traffic control, are subject to very stringent specifications.

All this is to point out that Westinghouse's attention to quality is not something new. The corporation has a long history of solving complex technical problems, operating at the state of the art in engineering, materials, and manufacturing and providing customers with the finest products, systems, and services. But shifting gears from this historical attention to quality to building a real Quality Culture was to bring about a major change—a major corporatewide transformation.

Beginning Steps

What, however, do we mean when we speak of a *Quality Culture*? It is an attitude and a commitment by all the company's employees that the most important priority in their jobs is to provide quality in whatever they do. It is a determination by everyone in the company to make Westinghouse the firm that provides the highest quality available in its goods and services. In past years, although quality was the objective, we were too inclined to "inspect quality" into the product, using a group of quality control specialists. But we came to realize that achieving quality is a process that must include the entire organization. It starts with marketing and goes on to include design, manufacture, service, administration, and every other function. If we are successful in involving the entire organization in the search for quality—and we believe we have made substantial progress toward that goal—we will have established a true Quality Culture in the corporation.

How Westinghouse came to recognize this need for a Quality Culture is rather interesting, because it started with the need to compete more effectively in the world market. There were really two factors here. The first was internal. At that time— the late 1970s—a lot of emphasis was put on improving the financial performance of the corporation. The focus was on how to improve operating profit, and thus earnings per share for the stockholder. The assignment was given to our senior financial officer and his staff to reconcile the sought-after improvements in financial performance with the then-current realities of the profit and loss statement and balance sheet. The second factor was external. Overseas travel by Westinghouse executives, particularly to Japan, plus the evidence of increasingly strong foreign competition, led to a closer scrutiny of our overseas competitors. That closer study brought clues—later verified—that the improved performance of competitors was derived from their significant progress in increasing productivity and quality.

The conclusion was that Westinghouse had to "do more with less," and that translated into the need for *productivity improvement*, a term that was later changed to *productivity and quality improvement*. These were the two factors—improvement needed in financial performance and the need to counter strong foreign competition—that led us to zero in on quality and productivity. And, as I will point out shortly, we have since come to the conclusion that quality drives productivity, not the other way around.

But our vigorous effort to transform the corporation really began with the study of productivity. The Westinghouse Management Council meeting in May 1979 was the launch pad. Presentations and discussions at that meeting focused on the need to give top priority to productivity improvement. This commitment was soon given substance in the form of a corporate Productivity Committee that I was appointed to chair.

Subsequently, a dozen subcommittees were formed. The Productivity Committee was backed by a $20 million seed fund designed to encourage managers to implement new tools and techniques. It was to fund projects that would not necessarily qualify for funding under the prevailing guidelines—often because the rate of return on investment was too low. After months of committee work within Westinghouse, along with studies of worldwide competition that included American, European, and Asian corporations, the committee reported on its insights and accomplishments and proposed an outline of action plans to senior management.

The first part of the report said that the newly initiated productivity improvement program was yielding results. Eighty-four productivity improvement projects had been started with the seed fund. Through this fund, many Westinghouse divisions got their first experience with robots. It enabled Westinghouse to join with Carnegie-Mellon University in starting an advanced technology and robotics program that is yielding good results for both organizations. Another project expanded with seed fund money was the CAD program whereby Westinghouse learned the advantages of using computers to improve and speed engineering design work. Today there are some 900 CAD terminals in use by the company's design engineers, and they have proved to be a tremendous aid to productivity and quality.

This "anti-inertia" program, which is what the seed fund amounted to, was continued for five years, and about $60 million was invested to get productivity projects started. It may have been the best money Westinghouse ever spent to promote productivity and quality improvement.

The Productivity Committee's initial report also revealed that more than 600 quality circles already were actively working to find ways to improve productivity in all areas of the company. A quality circle is a group of from ten to fifteen employees who work in the same general area and meet regularly to discuss how their jobs can be done better. The quality circle program began at the Westinghouse Defense and Electronics Center in 1978–1979 after some of the center's executives observed how well that idea was working in Japan. It then was taken up by the Productivity and Quality Center and expanded into a highly successful corporatewide program. The number of circles grew to 2,000 as the idea spread.

The committee report also told how value analysis techniques were substantially reducing costs in a number of target areas. Value analysis is a technique for systematically examining an operation or function to see if it can be either eliminated, simplified, or carried out at lower cost without negative effect on quality. In many cases, this technique improves quality in the course of also lowering costs.

So much for the positive side of this first committee report. But the other part of the report was less optimistic. It noted that a number of competitors, including General Electric, also were making very substantial gains in productivity, using CAD, robotics, microelectronics, and advances in new materials. It further noted that Japan was a source of increasing competition and that its firms were making rather spectacular improvement in the quality of their products and the productivity of their operations. Typically, in the United States, productivity improvement at that time was running 2 to 3 percent a year. In many Japanese companies, it was averaging 10 percent a year.

The committee report cited some specific examples of Japanese productivity. In 1980, Toyota was producing 2,700 cars a day, using about 1.6 workdays of assembly labor. In the United States, the time needed to produce the same number of cars was 3.8 workdays—more than double the Japanese labor content. In addition, the Japanese were using innovative systems to keep their inventories at the lowest possible level by tight management of component flow. This effectively reduced their work in process by 85 percent and increased their ability to respond quickly to customer volume and mix requirements. Nor were these results coming from some magic ingredient in the Japanese work force. When Matsushita took over a failing Motorola television receiver plant in Chicago, it doubled the production rate from 1,000 sets a day to 2,000—with the same direct labor work force, minus 50 percent of the white-collar staff. At the same time, the in-plant rejection rate dropped from 60 percent to about 4 percent.

So the findings of the Productivity Committee showed that we had a substantial challenge ahead of us. We then suggested a corporatewide action plan for productivity improvement. The first item in the action plan was to raise the productivity improvement goals substantially—to a corporate average of at least 6 percent a year. At this sustained rate, a business can nearly double its output every ten years without any increase in the number of employees or factory space. The second item in the plan was to stress quality as a method for building profitable businesses. We cited convincing data showing the higher profitability of businesses offering higher-quality products. Lastly, we proposed developing a Westinghouse productivity improvement plan around the three components that are the secret of Japanese success—improved quality, employee involvement, and enhanced technology. Enhanced technology includes value analysis and closer liaison between engineering, manufacturing, and marketing.

In late 1980, Westinghouse created the position of corporate vice-president of productivity—the first such position in

American industry. The next year it opened the Productivity and Quality Center, staffed with approximately 300 people organized to work in the areas of quality improvement, manufacturing technology, value analysis, and computer systems.

Emergence of Quality as the Driving Force

These early efforts focused primarily on improving productivity, which seemed to be the most direct way to impact a number of our businesses that were experiencing declines in market and increased competition both at home and abroad. However, as we studied the Japanese experience, it became clear that the programs that improved their productivity were, in fact, really aimed at improving quality. This insight resulted in a corresponding shift in thinking. The Productivity Committee began to appreciate that productivity improvement would be difficult, if not impossible, to achieve without a corresponding effort to improve quality. Quality began to emerge as the driving force for a business.

But how does quality drive a business? To help convince our own people that it does, we showed how three business factors are affected by quality — profitability, inventory levels, and customer satisfaction.

To consider profitability first: The Strategic Planning Institute has developed an extensive data base called PIMS, which stands for "profit impact of marketing strategies," to analyze the impact that business strategies have on the bottom line. PIMS analysis provided the committee with insights into the financial ramifications of quality. They showed that return on investment, market share, and net profit as a percentage of sales all are directly dependent on quality.

The PIMS data on several hundred companies clearly showed that companies providing high-quality products or services have about three times the return on investment as those with lower-quality offerings. This seems to hold true regardless of market share. PIMS data also indicate that high quality can consistently command a higher price. The Maytag Company is a good example. The reliability of its products has allowed the company to get about a $150 premium for its washers and maintain an annual 25 percent return on equity over the past ten years.

In the Westinghouse electronics circuit board manufacturing operations, there was clear evidence of the impact of quality on productivity and profitability. It costs $5 to find a bad part at incoming inspection, $50 to find it on a board, $500 to find it in a completed assembly, and $1,500 to find it in a total system. That is just to *find* it, not fix it.

Now look at how quality impacts inventory levels. You can think of inventory as though it were the water in a river. When you lower the water level, you can see the rocks, which here represent quality problems. Only then can you work to remove the rocks. But if you do not remove the rocks, you have to keep the water high enough to safely pass over them. The Japanese are dedicated to continually lowering the water level and removing the rocks. They use just-in-time inventory not only to reduce cost and cycle time but, more importantly, to uncover quality problems. It is not unusual for a Japanese plant to operate with only 10 to 20 percent of the inventory required in comparable American and European plants.

How does quality drive customer satisfaction? Yankelovitch (1983) and other surveys have highlighted the changed value system of the typical American buyer who, for the first time, now puts quality ahead of price, appearance, and availability as the most important factor in selecting a product or service.

Implementing the Quality Culture Effort

The effort to build a Quality Culture has been going on now for seven years. How is it being done and what has been the employee response? Which factors have helped and which have hindered progress? First, let us examine the implementation process. To get such a program rolling requires four areas of effort: communications, top management support, comparison with other companies, and training. We have communicated with our employees on productivity and quality improvement in every way possible. In addition to the quality circles, which are wholly devoted to this cause, Westinghouse plants and divisions have made it the theme of continuing local activities such as quality recognition programs. There have been companywide videotape presentations. The corporate "You can be sure . . ." advertising slogan gave birth to the internal poster "We're making sure. . . ."

The participation of Westinghouse's top management has been intense. Quality and productivity have been the lead items on the agenda at each corporate top management review and planning meeting for the past six years. Of the seven imperatives that the corporate Management Committee has adopted to guide the corporation, quality has the highest priority. Westinghouse chairman and chief executive officer Douglas D. Danforth has made his support most visible. In 1986, for example, he was named chairman of the nationally recognized Quality Month, which is sponsored by the American Society for Quality Control. Whenever possible, speeches delivered by members of Westinghouse top management hit hard on the need for quality and productivity improvement, not only in Westinghouse but throughout American industry.

Comparing ourselves with other companies was the major purpose of the many trips made by Westinghouse people to Japan and elsewhere. Often we took along groups of Westinghouse union leaders so they could see for themselves what was happening in other countries. Comparison has been a strong element of the program. The importance of training also cannot be overstated, whether it is training people in statistical methods and quality control techniques or training them in robotics and CAD. This is a continuous process. The Japanese do a massive training job.

Employee response has surprised us. While it would be expected that Westinghouse managers and supervisors would get solidly behind a program so strongly pushed by top management, the reaction from the rank-and-file employees was not as predictable. It was gratifying, therefore, to find most employees not only welcoming the drive for quality but welcoming it almost with relief. "It's about time" was not an uncommon reaction. People had been so bombarded by cost reduction efforts as industry geared to meet the intense competition of recent years that they wondered if we were going to remember the importance of making high-quality products.

The emphasis on quality appealed to the pride of workmanship that was traditional with our veteran employees. It appealed just as much to our marketing people and their customers. Both were pleased to find management giving highest priority to something they considered of paramount importance in the products they sold and bought. It is much more satisfying to the salesman to sell quality than to sell price. And it makes his job easier. In years past, of course, management thought that higher quality meant higher cost. But that is not so. Higher quality actually can lower costs by eliminating rework, waste of time and materials, and customer dissatisfaction.

Among the other factors that have aided in building a Quality Culture have been business conditions in important Westinghouse markets. Electric utility growth has been very slow in the past decade, severely affecting this important market. To better position Westinghouse to compete for the available business, major quality improvement programs have been instituted by the Energy Systems business units that build and service utility equipment. So these units had no difficulty in recognizing the need to give quality improvement high priority in their business.

Another factor has been the demanding applications of many of the products, systems, and services that the company sells. In buying equipment, for example, the U.S. Department of Defense has very strict specifications as to quality. A number of products and systems also have critical safety requirements that are subject to government oversight and regulation. Examples include nuclear reactors, airborne radar systems, transit systems, elevators, and escalators.

A third factor reinforcing the need for a corporate Quality Culture is the purchasing methods of most Westinghouse customers. Their purchasing is done by professionals with substantial experience in evaluating and buying technical equipment and services.

There are, of course, factors that have worked *counter* to

building a Quality Culture. Perhaps the most significant is the fact that we have been on the leading edge of quality and productivity improvement since the inception of the program in the late 1970s. Thus, we found few domestic examples of corporate quality and productivity programs from which to learn, and there was little case-study material on American companies in the literature. We often felt very lonely on the steep slope of the learning curve.

Another negative factor is that Westinghouse is a very large and diverse corporation. The firm is in a number of fundamentally different businesses, ranging from electric power equipment to soft drink bottling. And it has operations in many different countries and cultures. If Westinghouse were only in the radar business, or only in broadcasting, the procedures that are developed to implement the Quality Culture could be applied more easily throughout the entire corporation. Techniques that worked well in location A could be used with confidence in location B. But since the company operates very diverse businesses, implementation must adapt to different markets, different customers, and different sets of values. While the Quality Culture theme and commitment can always be used, its implementation has to be tailored to meet the needs of the individual business units.

For example, the very sophisticated mathematics that would be used to optimize quality in a nuclear fuel plant simply have no relevancy to KDKA's quality problems in broadcasting. In the same way, the alternative techniques that the television and radio people have been developing to enhance their Quality Culture cannot be applied at the Nuclear Fuel Division. This situation is further complicated by the fact that the corporation is continually moving toward greater decentralization to give division and business unit managers more autonomy in running their operations. Such decentralization, while it has benefits of its own, tends to slow down attempts to spread a Quality Culture throughout the corporation.

The problems of technology transfer in a large organization also affect the building of a Quality Culture. Quality problems are imbedded in the day-to-day operations of divisions and their departments and sections. Implementation of quality improvement opportunities is dependent to a degree on the motivation and actions of people at the local level. But once a solution has been implemented, transfer of that knowledge is complicated by the corporation's size, diversity, and decentralized structure.

Human nature also presents problems. Although the great majority of Westinghouse people have shown great interest in and acceptance of the quality and productivity ideas being used in Japan, some people still refuse to accept the Japanese as models. There is not only the "not invented here" factor, but there remains, in some cases, a residual animosity from the Second World War.

Still another negative factor is what might be called the "program of the month" syndrome. Many improvements over the years have been made through programs on new business techniques. But there have been so many such programs that each new one inevitably generates a certain degree of cynicism: "Look what corporate headquarters has for us this month." In its early stages, the quality and productivity improvement efforts at Westinghouse suffered from this tendency to view them as just management fads. But that attitude has yielded to the sustained impact of the program. When something goes on for seven years, it can hardly be labeled another "program of the month." People are convinced that we mean it.

While much has been accomplished in the past seven years, much remains to be done. Fortunately, however, the corporation's electronic assembly plant at College Station, Texas, is already pointing the way to the future. The College Station plant is one of the newest of the Energy and Advanced Technology Group. It assembles advanced circuit boards for Westinghouse systems, such as the radar for the F-16 fighter aircraft and the B-1B bomber.

This plant was designed from a clean sheet of paper. It was envisioned as a synthesis of our thinking about technology, quality, and people. The plant has about $20 million worth of computers, robots, and specialized automation equipment, and it also features innovations in the work force. Each of the approximately 500 employees is on salary. Raises are based on building and demonstrating new skills, and this has resulted in a flexible, multiskilled work force. The employees, who are known as associates, work in teams of eight to twelve. Teams measure daily how each person's performance compares with that of other members and how the team's performance compares with the whole plant's.

At this electronic assembly plant, manufacturing costs are about half of what they are in traditional plants; turnover is lower and productivity substantially higher. This is not just a new plant. It is a prototype for how to run a business. We gained several insights here. We confirmed the importance of integrating technology and people, the importance of employee selection and training, and the effectiveness of motivation and teamwork. And we have reaffirmed the close linkage between quality and productivity.

Insights We Gained

In the past seven years, Westinghouse has learned more than a few lessons about the process of building a Quality Culture—insights and lessons that may help other organizations. Thus, if we were to begin the effort again, knowing what we now know, we would considerably expand the communications program with employees. We have found videotape to be a very effective communications medium. For several years, the Public Systems Company used a four-times-a-year video program that was seen by all company employees. It featured activities that would contribute to quality and productivity improvement. A continuing, two-way employee communications program is a critical part of building a Quality Culture. Presenting credible case studies can do much to create momentum and break down resistance to new ideas.

We would also sponsor more study trips to Japan for employees. Seeing the factories there was a real eye-opener for most. Our senior manufacturing people came back with substantially changed perceptions of what is possible in a factory. They were impressed by the high levels of housekeeping, the low levels of work-in-process inventory, the short time cycles, and the commitment to quality by workers and managers. Unfortunately, when the visitors returned from Japan and described what they had seen, some listeners did not quite believe them. The differences between some of the manufacturing practices they saw and those in the United States were so great as to create a credibility gap.

Another thrust would be to allocate even more seed money to encourage business unit and general managers to install new tools and techniques. The seed fund broke down inhibitions against trying new ideas by removing the most frequent objection—"not enough money in the budget." The mechanism for applying to get seed money was simple. Applicants simply submitted a one-page form with a description of the improvement to the Productivity Committee. A healthy competition for available seed money developed among the business units and divisions. This competition helped build awareness of the issues of quality and productivity improvement and of the goals of the corporation.

Over the past seven years, we have come to appreciate even more how valuable highly motivated employees can be to quality and productivity improvement, and we have also learned that recognition of employee job performance is an important part of building a Quality Culture. The Energy and Advanced Technology Group is beginning its fourth year of an employee quality recognition program. It is open to all 44,000 group employees and the response has been very encouraging. In the first year, there were more than 4,000 entries. Last year there were over 8,000.

Employees enter the program by describing a quality-related project that they accomplished during the year. One recent winner (an hourly employee) suggested changes that saved over $1 million in scrap and rework. But the benefits go beyond the accomplishments of the winners. The real value of the program is that each entrant made the linkage between a rather abstract idea—quality improvement—and what he or she does every day. Here, as elsewhere, the goal is to build recognition of quality performance into the fabric of Westinghouse culture.

We have also come to realize how important training can be. For example, employees in many areas are being oriented and trained in the use of statistical methods. To promote this use, a third annual groupwide statistical methods symposium is being planned. In addition, we have found that cost data can make quality problems more visible. The Energy and Advanced Technology Group now monitors quality costs for all operations on a monthly basis. One division in Florida, for example, gathers monthly data on more than fifty quality cost items. These include traditional costs, such as scrap, rework, and warranty, but also items such as interest on uncollected receivables and travel by engineers to customer locations to fix problems. Quality cost monitoring provides a focus for quality efforts because it highlights areas where quality problems result in cost increases. Each department of the Operations Division singles out eight to ten items on its list of fifty quality cost factors to work on in a particular quarter.

One of the more recent efforts to improve quality and productivity deals with organization structure. In many companies, Westinghouse included, there has been an organizational wall between the design engineering function and the manufacturing function. Even though each works on the same projects, there often has been a tradition of poor communication, differing sets of priorities, and even animosity.

This situation is being remedied through efforts to integrate engineering and manufacturing. For example, at the Defense Center we have changed the structure of engineering and manufacturing activities to promote a better transition from design to production. The two functions are now integrated. Design and manufacturing engineers work as a team from making preliminary sketches to working out production details on the manufacturing floor. The results are shorter cycle times for design and production engineering and products that are easier to make. At the corporate level, two advisory committees—one in engineering and the other in manufacturing—

have been integrated to focus attention and resources on the corporatewide integration of the two disciplines.

We have also found that promoting closer, in-depth liaisons with customers helps build a Quality Culture. The comments of customers tend to have great credibility with everyone, from top management to the shop floor. When a customer praises or criticizes, these comments are noted and acted upon. Customers help us define quality, and building closer relationships with those customers helps that process.

Conclusion

I find myself even more committed to quality and productivity improvement than when we began the program in 1979. We have not seen any evidence that would change our commitment to quality. We have spoken frequently to industry, government, and academic groups about Westinghouse efforts to improve quality—and the importance of quality improvement to this country. If American businesses are to successfully meet and beat global competition, they must make quality the driving force.

We now recognize that quality improvement drives productivity improvement. The national rate of productivity improvement has a substantial impact, over the long term, on the standard of living. If the United States fails to keep pace with other nations in productivity improvement, its standard of living will fall. Great Britain is a sobering example of a country, and an economy, that now is experiencing the consequences of decades of very low rates of productivity improvement.

Furthermore, there is a link between national productivity and national security. If the economy were to deteriorate, this country would be hard pressed to commit the necessary resources to maintain the global balance with its political adversaries, and specifically with the Soviet Union. So rather than being just a profit or loss issue for business managers and corporate stockholders, quality and productivity improvement—and consequently American competitiveness—are issues of vital importance to national prosperity and security.

The concluding words of the report by the President's Commission on Industrial Competitiveness, on which I was privileged to serve as a member and subcommittee co-chairperson, say it well:

"The goal is clear and within our reach: We must perform up to our potential. Americans enjoy tackling a new problem. One lies before us now. To meet the challenge of competitiveness, we require only a new vision and a new resolve.

"We must acknowledge the reality of a new global economy—an economic era that has come quickly and without fanfare. And just as we explored a vast and unknown American frontier, we must chart a course into this new territory and claim it for generations to come."

References

Yankelovitch, D. *Putting the Work Ethic to Work*. New York: Public Agenda Foundation, 1983.

20

David O. Renz

❦ ❦ ❦ ❦ ❦ ❦ ❦ ❦

The Transformation of
a Public Sector Bureaucracy

Managing the transformation of any large, complex organization is a significant challenge. Managing the transformation of a governmental bureaucracy might seem to be impossible. In 1983, however, the Minnesota Department of Labor and Industry began a major effort to transform its staid and entrenched bureaucracy into a more responsive and effective organization. The effort has involved a systems process to transform the agency in a very short period of time, with the goal of ensuring that it will be able to meet the current and future needs of its stakeholders. This chapter documents the transformation strategies and goals, the process by which the transformation has been managed, and the issues and problems that have emerged from this change effort.

Before turning specifically to the Department of Labor and Industry, we should note that one characteristic is common to almost all governmental organizations, namely, a spirit of conservatism. Through design and evolution, these organizations become the standard bearers that reflect the midrange values and perspectives of society. They act to reinforce the conventional wisdom of the status quo as they guide, regulate, and stabilize the behaviors of individuals and organizations. They tend to be quite impervious to the demands and pressures of their external environment in carrying the specific roles that they were created to fulfill. Some observers suggest that this is appropriate and that government organizations need not adapt to the outside world. On the contrary, it is these organizations that set the standards to which others must adapt.

An increasingly common alternative perspective is that the government organization, guided by its mission and program goals, must be responsive to and reflective of the environment in which it functions; otherwise, it will be of little value to any of its stakeholders. Worst of all, this condition may undermine the organization's ability to fulfill its mission in even a minimal way.

But change in government is supposed to be slow, gradual, and evolutionary. This is the conventional wisdom about the culture of this kind of organization, and it is reinforced and validated by extensive bureaucratic systems that slow the impact of external actions and changes. This is not the setting, it would seem, for a "transformation." It is the setting for incremental "development" over a period of years. Any talk of transformation suggests levels of complexity, of control and interference, and of direction and purpose that many governmental employees perceive as a threat. At Labor and Industry, change managers often heard statements such as, "Oh, great. This is just what I need now!" Or, "See me later when I have more time, more people, more energy." In essence, the agency's managers either demanded or pleaded that no one else bring them any of the "new academic management stuff." They wanted "real help." And they were not being critical, they were being honest.

In such a setting, the transformation of the Department of Labor and Industry was planned, is being implemented, and will be evaluated and refined. The setting of government is unique in some regards, and this chapter will discuss the transformation effort from the perspective of those key organizational managers who have the task of managing the change process. The change process continues on at the time of this writing. This chapter will discuss what was planned, how it has been implemented, and the results realized in the agency to date.

Beginning the Change Process at Labor and Industry

The Department of Labor and Industry is a regulatory agency of the Minnesota state government. It is the tenth largest of Minnesota's state departments, and its mission is to protect the livelihood, safety, and health of Minnesota workers. A key agency function is the regulation of benefits and compensation for injured workers. The agency employs about 400 people and operates on an annual budget of about $13 million. Most employees, except field inspection staff, are located in a single office facility. Almost all state government employees in Minnesota are unionized, and three separate unions represent the agency's employees.

Labor and Industry was once considered by many in and around state government to be an insignificant agency. But as workplace injuries became more costly to business and the insurance industry, its visibility grew. Multiple legislative first-aid packages had resulted in a complex and internally inconsistent administrative system. Every new adjustment caused confusion among all stakeholders, including the agency's own staff. The agency's style and the quality of its work were often perceived as biased and ineffective. By 1983, the consensus among political leaders and other external stakeholders was that the system was "broken." Within the agency some believed there were serious problems, although others thought that operations were going well enough. "What do they expect of us, anyway?" many employees asked. "There's little more that can be done." But the changes they could not foresee were coming fast.

In mid 1983, the legislature enacted a sweeping reform law in workers' compensation. This reform of the compensation system was pivotal to the transformation of the entire agency, for several reasons. This was the vehicle by which the agency secured many additional resources necessary to transform it within a relatively short time span: more and diverse staff, additional funds for training, new equipment, redesigned facilities, and information management technology. It also legitimated top management's orientation to change and the new emphasis on the values of performance and effectiveness. To the extent that change was perceived as necessary, it was in the context of workers' compensation — certainly not in terms of the overall management of the agency.

Culture change was a significant element in this transformation process, though beyond the awareness of most staff members or managers. The reform law enacted a new activist style of agency administration, in great contrast to its previous reactive ("enforcer") role. New roles and perspectives, due both to the changing character of the work force and to the influx of new organization members, came into place. The agency's central office workforce nearly doubled in size over a period of eight months.

The plan for this transformation of the workers' compensation reform program required extensive redesign of most of the organization for it to succeed. This transformation process interacted with some ongoing agency efforts to make incremental improvements in overall organizational management. Both were greatly motivated and interest energized by the commissioner of Labor and Industry's interest in improving the effectiveness of agency management (especially human resource management) and service to clients. He expected to increase productivity, effectiveness, and the image and credibility of department performance among key stakeholders.

The commissioner and his management team agreed upon several results to be realized through the organizational change process. In addition to the previously mentioned workers' compensation reforms, the following objectives were established:

- Work would be organized and managed against goals and plans, and organization design would be based on work functions.
- Decisions would be made as close as possible to the "front lines," and communications would flow freely among levels.
- Internal systems would be developed to measure, encourage, and reward both short-term and long-run performance and success.
- The organization would become more communicative, re-

sponsive, and interactive, both with the external environment and internal stakeholders.
- Opportunities for individual employee growth, development, and promotion would be maximized as these new
  functions and reforms were implemented.

One other element of the transformation (and a cultural value to
achieve) was to minimize the win-lose conflict orientation of the
organization and stakeholders through effective problem-
solving techniques and effective conflict management.

The achievement of these goals was recognized as a considerable challenge by top management. The goals called for
organizationwide acceptance and cooperation based on a significantly different set of values from those of the existing organization. Since no goal-oriented evaluation system existed, it was
difficult to assess the quality of management. Day-to-day behaviors suggested that little actual management or supervision went
on and that there was little interest in results and effectiveness.
The organization's members preferred to act as a family, with
paternalistic leadership and all the dynamics that accompany it.
The change process goals required very different behaviors. But
at the outset, few people perceived that these changes would
require a systematic transformation of the department.

An Evolving Model for Change

The general model for change in Labor and Industry has
been an amalgam of various theories and perspectives, and it
evolved over the period of transformation. The change managers brought to the organization the general perspective that
organizations are open systems that evolve and interact with
their environments. The open systems theory of Katz and Kahn
(1966), the contingency and design theories of Lawrence and
Lorsch (1967) and Galbraith (1973), the theories of adult learning and development of Knowles (1978) and Argyris (1976), and
current theories on organizational adaptiveness all contributed
to the perspective applied in this transformation process. More
recent discussions of organizational change and excellence

(Kanter, 1983; O'Toole, 1985), organizational culture (Deal and Kennedy, 1982; and especially Schein, 1985), and strategic planning (Steiner, 1979) also contributed to and reinforced the approaches being implemented in the agency.

The concepts and theory behind the actual process of change were similarly developed as an amalgam of several models. The models of Beckhard and Harris (1977), Nadler and Tushman (1986), and Nadler (1981) were particularly useful in designing the transition management, and the work of Tichy (1983) further helped to systematically evaluate and monitor the transformation of the agency. This transformation, as managed by the key change agents, focused on integrated, systems-oriented strategic change. But it was not implemented as the outcome of one specific, predetermined model. The change process itself was conceived and implemented as a more fluid and responsive process, and it was assumed that it would change in response to new and unforeseen issues.

The change managers conceived of the organization as a set of highly interdependent elements, interacting as parts of an open system with each other and the environment. They believed, in the words of Nadler, that "organizations will be most effective when their major components are congruent with each other" (1981, p. 194). Congruence has been managed as an ongoing issue, both within the various elements of the agency and as an aggregate outcome of the overall change.

Six subsystems have been identified for purposes of explaining the change and the new organization that would result from it. Each posed its own class of problems in the transition process, and strategies and interventions were implemented to address each within the overall change effort. Figure 20-1 presents a chart to identify these organizational elements and the primary management strategies by which change was enabled. It was assumed that not all strategies could be implemented successfully. Nonetheless, the effectiveness of the change process was (and is) dependent on the degree to which all were managed to ensure relative balance or congruence, as well as consistency.

The perspective of Beckhard and Harris (1977) provided substantial guidance in planning and understanding the orga-

Figure 20-1. Organization and Change Management in Labor and Industry.

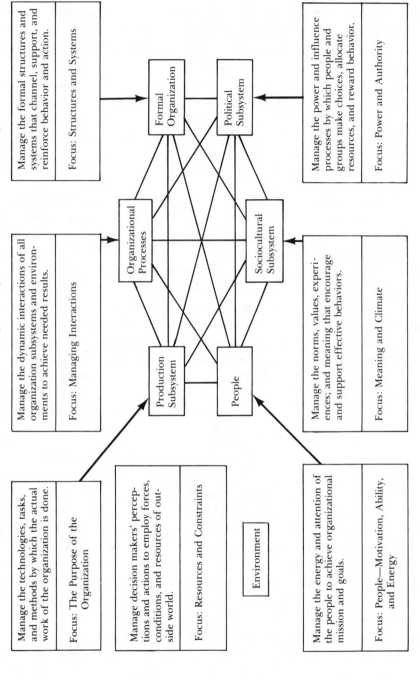

nizational transition process as a comprehensive approach to change. They emphasize the need to design and implement, in a careful and intentional manner, the actual intervention process so as to support and ensure a full and effective transition to the new state. A critical element of this concept is to recognize and manage the transition state as a discrete and separate organizational state, linked to but different from the prechange and postchange states. As a result, it must be managed separately. The transition management issues for each element are described in Table 20-1. Maintaining congruence, in the change managers' perspective, was critical throughout the transition phases, as well as for the postchange state.

This congruence was simultaneously assessed and managed from two vantage points. The elements were managed to be congruent with the desired end result of the change in organization. They were also managed to remain in balance throughout the transition process. In other words, the elements of the organization could not be allowed to become radically unbalanced at any time during the change process. This was very important since the organization's clients continued to require consistent service throughout the change process.

These models successfully addressed the technology of change, but they only implied what came to be the most intense and challenging elements of this government organization change. Culture, resistance, and individual and group dynamics were all critical variables that required continuous, sensitive, and careful management. Underlying these variables was a basic integrative fact: the content of the transformation involved a major shift in the fundamental values and perspectives of the organization and would unseat the existing paradigm. To do this was to challenge the essence of the organization, and a new paradigm could be implemented only to the degree that all organizational support systems and infrastructure were recast in the new mode. There could be no half-way state. Either the change would succeed, or the organization would drift back in the direction of the old system but without having the benefit of the supports that held that system together. As a matter of ethical responsibility, as well as effectiveness as a change agent, it

Table 20-1. Transition Management Issues at Labor and Industry.

Transition Management Elements	Illustrations of Change Actions
Formal Organization: Manage the formal structures and systems of the organization to support and reinforce appropriate behavior and results.	Reorganize structure and create new functions and roles (especially to integrate processes), delete unsupportive functions. Redesign the performance appraisal process to reward action, promote certain communication. Implement comprehensive strategic planning process with objectives setting/monitoring phases and budget function. Redesign facilities and other infrastructural systems, including fiscal management forms, approvals, processes.
Production Subsystems: Manage the tasks, methods, and technologies by which the basic work of the organization is accomplished to ensure that the right work is completed efficiently, effectively.	Redesign the work flow of the organization, overall and within the individual sections. Identify, develop, and implement new technologies and methods in the work flow. Develop and incorporate new knowledge and decision systems into work, especially information management systems.
Political Subsystems: Manage the power and authority relationships (formal and informal) among all stakeholders to ensure they support and reinforce appropriate individual and group behavior toward the organization's goals.	Allocate resources to effective, results-oriented units and leaders (including increased decision power) and keep control of noncompliant unit resources in top management. Reinforce and legitimate most effective decision methods (and have systems for recognizing them). Create collaborative, involvement decision processes. Reinforce participation, incorporate stakeholders, and develop training to produce recognized leaders in organization.
Sociocultural Subsystems: Manage the internal climate, culture, and experiences to develop meaning and identity and comfort with organizational goals and values.	Create new communication mechanisms to focus attention, promote new, and explain meaning of changes (from staff meetings to training to demonstration projects). Create events and symbols that reinforce meaning and value of new systems, and encourage commitment, appreciation (such as rewards and award programs, new stationery and logos). Explain values, incorporate into all activities, and ensure consistency among organization systems (for example, compensation decisions, promotion decisions).

People: Manage the energy and attention of the people in the organization to address their needs and encourage, enable, and support those behaviors that contribute to goal performance.	Create personal development, transition, and coping programs and methods, particularly via training program. Redesign the reward systems to reflect new values. Create individually focused events to encourage commitment, motivation, satisfaction through involvement (such as wellness, safety, education, and career programs). Redesign overall training system to support new roles, provide knowledge and skills for new responsibilities.
Organizational Processes: Manage the dynamic interactions of all organization elements and environment to enable and promote effective and efficient performance and results.	Develop clear leadership at top of organization, via roles and explicit values and strategies that focus action. Develop new decision, planning, and linking mechanisms to focus action at appropriate levels (for example, put planning and budget decisions at appropriate levels, and require some concurrence from interdependent units' managers). Teach and reinforce effective conflict resolution methods that are consistent with new values goals, such as dispute resolution at lowest activity levels possible. Create roles that focus on coordination of action. Actively review, redevelop, or build vertical and lateral communication and feedback systems (such as staff meetings, task forces, objectives evaluation/feedback activities, newsletters and publications on goals, and office automation systems that connect and encourage interaction among managers, supervisors, and key staff roles). Plan carefully the timing of changes, and sequence to build "layers" of changes to form foundations and synergy for future actions (for example, build the systems and structures that guide future action before expecting decision makers to implement the actions).
Environment: Manage the way in which key decision makers perceive and employ the conditions and resources external to the organization to achieve mission, goals, objectives.	Create boundary-spanning roles and functions (such as a research and education unit, legislative liaison, staff positions to interact with external regulators). Establish ongoing, structured linkages to maintain relations with key stakeholders (such as advisory councils, update workshops). Create and use trend and issues assessment processes that incorporate feedback from spanners, managers, and so on). Train and otherwise redevelop decision and analysis abilities of management team to understand and use information from the environment in planning, review, strategy development.

is crucial that the changing organization not be left stranded in such condition. Because the change of Labor and Industry has been so intensive and extensive, it has been critical that the transition be managed to address this issue on an ongoing basis.

The department's transformation was triggered by severe external pressures for change and internal conditions reinforced the need for major organizational change. The department's model for change, then, has been to manage the entire organization as a system and to manage the change transition as a discrete stage apart from prechange and postchange stages. In managing the organization as a system, it has been critical to keep the forces and elements of the organization relatively balanced. It has been particularly important to be attentive to and manage the less visible elements of the department, such as its culture, informal organization, and the entrenched bureaucratic infrastructure.

One of the most critical linking elements of the entire transition process has been leadership. While the commissioner provided the overall vision and promoted most strategies for the transition, the change managers and top-line managers provided for the actual implementation. Hundreds of individual interventions were designed and coordinated (not always successfully) to be congruent with this model and the emerging values of the organization.

Managing Commitment and Change

As noted earlier, the transformation of Labor and Industry began with the legislation of the workers' compensation reform law. This law redesigned all strategic and many specific components of the system and therefore redefined the primary task of the agency. Some of the desired core values were demonstrated early in the process of designing the legislation through the use of involvement and participation at all levels of the agency. Further, it was in this process that the commissioner first demonstrated active (and sometimes dramatic) leadership on behalf of the new system, a role that was reinforced by relatively frequent and prominent media coverage of the legislative process.

To manage the transition process within the agency, it was necessary to develop a number of infrastructure subsystems that would support and enable the change. New roles were created, and many specific management strategies and procedures were adopted. These initiated the transition as a separate phase of organizational action. A new role was created for a change and planning facilitator — a manager of organization development. The commissioner was the entrepreneurial visionary in the change process. The assistant commissioner and the manager of organization development worked closely with him to further define, focus, and plan ways to act on the agenda for the future of the organization; these two were the key change agents.

Getting consensus on the change from a systems perspective, as would be theoretically desirable, was not immediately accomplished. The commissioner conceptualized and valued the change process in ways different from those of the two change agents, whose perspectives were based on systems theories and values. As a result, the transformation process was more incremental and evolutionary than the change agents alone would have designed. Much of the creativity and organizational effectiveness of these roles, however, grew from the creative tension of these differences. So, too, did some troublesome role conflicts and tensions that became part of the transformation life cycle. As much of the emerging literature on the transition of entrepreneurially led organizations continues to document, there exist some practical and paradigmatic differences that complicate the collaborative management efforts of entrepreneurs and professional managers. These created occasional conflicts and observable inconsistency of behavior that sometimes worked against the transformation process.

The transition strategy that was most immediately experienced by everyone in the organization was a strategic planning process. This process was a vehicle for involving all employees in both diagnosis and design for the future organization, as well as a means for values clarification at all levels. It was expected that through this type of involvement employees would recognize many of the problems of the organization and that such recognition would produce support for the change process. The planning process was, in reality, the first coordinated activity of the transition state itself.

This strategic planning process formalized the expectations of the commissioner and executive staff, enabling the change agents to chart the vision, implicit values, mission, goals, and key strategies of the new organization. The strategic planning process encouraged explicit communication and assessment simply by pulling together the collective organizational knowledge of the executive team and getting these key actors to tell each other what they believed and hoped about the change and the work of the organization. The process also incorporated, through specific development activities, the opportunity for the top management team to develop awareness of and sensitivity to their own interpersonal concerns, issues, and styles.

The planning process was operated in parallel manner, simultaneously gathering information by means of top-down and bottom-up methods. Every employee in the organization participated in discussing how his or her work and the work of his or her division related to some sort of overall or agency mission. The meetings were facilitated by the change managers for the combined purpose of promoting and explaining the change themes and enabling planning. The top management team and commissioner used the information as additional input into their process of identifying the mission, key organizational goals, and long-term strategies for the organization. The resulting strategic planning document explained these to the agency, and group meetings were held to promote and explain the resulting vision to all employees. In addition to the strategic planning process, a number of ongoing information-gathering and diagnostic methods were implemented. The methods included an organization assessment instrument, group meetings on the labor climate and labor relations, focus groups, externally conducted evaluations, and interviews, document analysis, and unobtrusive data collection methods.

At no point in this transformation program was an all-inclusive formal plan put on paper. The strategic planning document explained, in essence, the content of the organization's transition. But it provided only an implicit and between-the-lines glimpse of the means by which the department management team would manage the transformation.

The top management approach to managing the transformation had been agreed upon in principle, particularly in the context of planning. Specific strategies and components were consistently under revision in response to new, unforeseen, and inappropriately addressed contingencies. As Beckhard and Harris (1977) state, there are usually several locations at which transition interventions may be implemented, including top management, "hurting" units, staff units, new program areas, and units that appear most ready for change. Based upon existing conditions, resources, and the priorities of the plan, all these locations ended up being addressed at Labor and Industry. The pressures that first enabled the changes, however, promoted attention in two key areas: workers' compensation reform and organizational management effectiveness.

As a political reality, workers' compensation reforms had to be well in place before the conclusion of this administration's term. As a practical matter, the change in the management system would also need to be firmly in place if the transformation were to stabilize and become institutionalized. The continuing strategy that underlay the change effort was to professionalize the management corps and decentralize the authority and responsibility for the development and operation of individual units to the managers of those units. Unfortunately, few managers were prepared or able to facilitate the change effort in their units. The overall management system was severely underdeveloped.

Generating and maintaining commitment to change at Labor and Industry were, and continue to be, a major challenge. Most models for managing transformation focus on issues of commitment, controlling resistance, and generating support for the image of the future. This is a critical issue in any organization, but it has been especially so for the entrenched bureaucracy of Labor and Industry. Within the department, the change process has demonstrated the clash of prechange conditions with anticipated values, philosophies, and management styles. It tended to clarify the distinctions between the new, change-oriented appointees and the permanent civil service employees and managers. This created occasional but significant conflicts that had to be productively managed.

Such issues as the legitimacy of the change agenda, the right of external actors (for example, the legislature) to dictate change, and the role of top management as advocates for or against existing modes of agency operation were all debated. Many actions were taken to challenge change-oriented strategies and events. Since so many elements of the old organizational system seemed under fire, there tended to be little discussion of these issues by employees and managers who questioned the change. Norms and values were in transition, and it was thought to be much safer to wait out the change cycle. The assumption about outcomes was explicitly stated: "These things have been tried before, but they never take hold."

An extensive effort was implemented to build constituencies, at least for parts of the future image, if not for the entire grand scheme. A number of commitment strategies were employed simultaneously, and, where possible, these strategies addressed both commitment and other elements of the change effort to seek some level of synergy. The strategies included:

1. group events in which participants worked with change agents to identify positive future conditions for their own unit and problems to be solved.

2. training and education programs and events created to address operational problems. The change agents would focus attention on the vision and how to get there. Training events were structured with the obvious assumption that change was happening, and the training was to help people cope and succeed. Training on how to behave in new ways was implemented, including explicit discussions on norms and values.

3. changes that were targeted, early on, at units that had obvious problems that bothered the rank and file. Suc-

cessful small-scale "repairs" were implemented in ways that emphasized involvement and encouraged unit members to see how the new methods helped them.

4. changing certain elements of the reward system, such as reestablishing an achievement award system to recognize and reward innovative future-oriented behavior. This was done at the individual, work group, and division levels.

5. encouraging and training top-level managers, especially the commissioner, to model or demonstrate the appropriate behaviors for the future in the ways they accomplished their everyday work. This meant using new methods, new technologies, and new styles of management and explaining the utility of the new. This also helped crystalize commitment among top management members.

6. using a corrective discipline process in a few cases where obvious resistive behavior was demonstrated. This began with coaching an employee on more appropriate behaviors but included actual discipline where resistance was explicit insubordinate behavior.

7. positive involvement events, structured whenever possible; events in which employees could readily see peers demonstrating new behaviors with recognized success.

8. changing and publicizing, through involvement meetings with employees and union officials, organizational policies and programs to meet the growth and development expectations of rank-and-file employees.

9. public relations and celebratory events created to explain changes and upcoming positive events and to publicly recognize "old culture members" who had contributed to the success of new changes. These occasionally bordered on "pep rallies" and included social events that brought people together in the name of the new system.

The commitment events usually included reminding people of the need to work together toward the future, so that external forces could not be brought to bear on the agency in ways that would be punitive or take away its control of the change process. It has been essential that all these strategies remind people that they are still in charge of the organization.

Targeting the Change Sites

Implementing the change program in the department required a combination of careful decision making and planning, capitalizing on logical opportunities, taking emergency measures to save a subunit about to collapse, and so on. The nature of the transformation and the values that undergird the new vision dictated how the change agents approached and initiated specific intervention strategies. Further, in an organization as bureaucratized as a state government agency, there are many highly formalized maintenance systems that support the organization's annual and biennial life cycle. These systems have well-defined points at which intervention is more likely to succeed. The culture and informal organizational subsystems in which leverage was needed are quite complex and slow to change.

Therefore, the interventions sequence was not as negotiable as the change agents might have wished. Once the new strategies had become an integral part of these systems, however, maintenance of them became easier, and resistance seemed less likely to impede the changes. Many of the opportunities to intervene did arise in rapid order, and the change process began to move at a rate faster than desirable, according to the current literature on change rates in complex organizations.

These issues and conditions reinforced the perspective that the group in the organization that provided some of the best early opportunities for successful intervention was the staff group known as Administration Operations. Given that a major management theme was to decentralize decision-making authority and responsibility to individual division managers, the Administration Operations group's role relative to these divisions would have to change. Further, it was going to have to be ready to support the new needs of division managers, so they would be able to learn and implement these new areas of authority. Administrative Operations brokered and managed the resources required by all divisions. Their infrastructure had to be recreated to support the decentralized management system, yet at the same time it had to encourage program effectiveness and cost effectiveness. This required redesigning the policies and procedures that gave authority for decision making, creating new information-sharing modes to support lower-level decision processes, and redefining and reestablishing all the human resource management systems.

Therefore, Administrative Operations was an integral component in the longer-term departmentwide diffusion of the change, and it also provided a high-leverage location to begin the process. When these people were "on board" they would help maintain the systems that would reinforce and support changes elsewhere in the organization. For better and for worse, governmental organizations are greatly dominated by their staff functions and the accountability/control systems of which these staff functions are a part. When these units adopt a style of operation, they influence, in multiple systemic ways, the culture of the entire organization.

For several reasons, it was also easier to focus on Administrative Operations for the initial changes. One key change manager, the assistant commissioner for administration, was the line manager directing the operations of these divisions. Therefore, he had relatively greater contact with, understanding of, and control over the day-to-day operations of these units. The entire Administrative Operations group was closely linked with but separate from all other divisions, so the events and changes occurring there could be observed without being an immediate threat to the other operating divisions. The successes of this group would be observed, discussed, felt, and appreciated by all other units of the organization, and the time lag to implementation elsewhere would allow some additional time for the personnel in other units to get used to the changes to come.

Administrative Operations was also a small section, and it was easier for the change managers to monitor the results and problems of the change process there than it would have been in larger units. Finally, the Administrative Operations group was the group that supported all other organizational units by facilitating and enabling the flow of essentially all the resources that they needed to function. This presented at least an implicit need for the rest of the organization to follow through on the methods and strategies that this group implemented.

In the typology of power bases that French and Raven (1959) posit, this organizational group had the capacity to exercise all types of power on behalf of the transformation process: expert (on administrative and management matters), referent, legitimate, and reward and punishment forms of power are all present in the relationship between Administrative Operations and the other divisions and their managers. This had value in reinforcing the various types of commitment that the change agents were seeking as the strategies were expanded to include the department as a whole.

The historical behaviors and traditions of the Administrative Operations units were not particularly supportive of the new strategies. While many of the old and comfortable roles that the members of these units played in the department would continue and even be strengthened, some roles and behaviors were being eliminated. For example, staff units frequently made unilateral decisions to shift funds, equipment, and interagency political support or influence based on their own assessments of various divisions' circumstances. Rarely did these decisions reflect petty personal jealousies. But they did reflect the staff units' assessment of needs, priorities, interdivisional equity and equality, and related elements of the appropriateness of managers' administrative behavior. Since the prechange organization had no explicit strategic plan or shared goals and priorities, these decisions were merely an extension of staff biases that might or might not have contributed to the overall effectiveness of the organization. Fast local decisions also made staff jobs easier. Since information about options and choices was often not shared with divisional personnel, resources were being allocated beyond the awareness of most decision makers.

In place of this, the change process shifted decision-making power to individuals outside of the group. Some issues or priorities were shifted to the commissioner's office (when the strategic plan did not guide action), while most of the day-to-day operational decisions became the turf of individual managers. Since the managers would be held more accountable for their performance in managing their resources relative to the program goals, they needed the authority to redirect those resources (to the extent that this authority rested anywhere within the department). To encourage, facilitate, and support this change of organization philosophy, effective strategies had to be implemented within this group. Ineffective intervention would cripple the chances for the organizationwide shift toward decentralization.

There were several other areas in which the change process was initiated early. These units tended to be the sections of the department with critical performance problems that threatened the overall success of the workers' compensation reform effort. The interventions in these areas tended to be focused on immediate deficiencies in unit management and function, and they were designed to address both the immediate problems and to begin to inculcate elements of the long-run change process. This was intended to capitalize on logical points of entry, that is, areas where staff and managers were more likely to recognize that performance was poor enough to warrant and legitimate a major change strategy. Such interventions also served to reinforce an explicit value of the commissioner and his administration: Poor performance was unacceptable and would not be tolerated.

The diffusion of the change process has been structured from the top of the organization, and the sequence of divisions and units to become actively involved has been set by the commissioner and his staff based on general assessments of the health of organizational subunits. The level of change has been very intensive in those units that have undergone development, and generally only two or three sections or divisions have experienced development at any one given time. This diffusion strategy was primarily a response to resource issues. Given the small size of the core support group assisting the change process, only a limited number of projects could be handled at one time. Further, the change agents deemed it more effective, on an organizationwide basis, to focus on developing to the fullest those units that they could work with in what might be a limited time frame (that is, the single four-year term of a governor).

Since the change process continues at the time of this writing, we can discuss only the concept of evaluation that is being used. The change managers in this effort are committed to implementing an evaluation process that focuses on the transformation goals and outcomes. The change process itself included an element of evaluation that the change managers have sought to institutionalize as a part of the ongoing planning, budgeting, and individual performance management support subsystems. Increased attention has been placed on documenting performance and establishing and monitoring effectiveness criteria at the divisional or program level.

Critical Issues in Transforming the Department

The transformation process in Labor and Industry is still young, with much remaining to be accomplished. There have been dramatic successes in some areas, including increases in effectiveness and productivity gains of up to 40 percent. But there have also been critical problems that have inhibited the effectiveness and rate of change of the transformation process. It is too early to draw conclusions about the organizationwide impacts of the process. Moreover, at this time in the transformation process, it is more significant to review the challenges, problems, and issues. They will provide the next phase of diagnostic insight that will be used to refine, refocus, and maybe even revitalize the transformation. They inform us to where the organization should next place its energy.

From this point on, six types of issues appear to be critical to the continuation of the success of the change effort at Labor and Industry:

1. Leadership and managerial style
2. Resistance to change efforts
3. Environmental pressures and influences
4. Resource management in a systems effort

5.   Communications, information systems, and technology
6.   Energy demands in a changing system

All these issues surfaced in some way or another in earlier discussions and they are noted here for their relevance to the transition state at the present time.

Leadership and managerial styles have been critical positive and negative influences on agency change. Clarity of vision and the ability to see and *communicate* the future of the organization are essential — and not only at the beginning of the change. A certain degree of malaise is likely to set in when the leader becomes less visible, less confident, or less clear about the future of the organization. And this is even more of a problem in government: the responsible leader cannot guarantee any permanence to the present vision. It becomes a critical motivation issue as well. Much more emphasis will be put on addressing this issue in the future.

A second aspect of this issue is the creation of expectations within the organization. In attempting to motivate, encourage, and support, leaders and the people whom they influence create their own expectations, which need to be positive but realistic. Entrepreneurial leaders often overpromise outcomes and underestimate the time needed to achieve observable results, and they successfully sell these promises. The costs in resulting disenchantment and disillusionment can be great, and need to be carefully controlled. Excessively high expectations have caused such problems in parts of Labor and Industry, and much future attention will be paid to tempering enthusiasm with "realistic optimism."

Resistance is an issue and a continuing factor in the change effort at Labor and Industry. Two elements of resistance control that need further attention in the agency's change program are conflict management/problem solving and recommitment. New modes of commitment and renewal are necessary when change stretches over several years, and these must continue to build involvement and ensure full communication. Where resistance collides with fast-moving change in certain divisions, it must be addressed and controlled or eliminated.

The methods and effectiveness of conflict resolution or management strategies are very important to the future of the change and to the acceptance of the values of the change. The issue overlaps with labor relations issues, as well, when unionized employees find that competing organizations are seeking their commitment, support, and energy. Unions sometimes find it useful to encourage conflicts to ensure themselves a continuing role in the organization's future. Their meaningful involvement throughout the transition and postchange states must be ensured and communicated to encourage an ongoing and collaborative relationship.

Environmental pressures and influences are often uncontrollable, but the change process must continue to help people identify, understand, and cope with them. In some cases, effective change strategies can mediate environmental influences (for example, those coming from a legislature), and Labor and Industry will be focusing additional resources on such strategies during the next year. Politics will be an active factor in change. It is important to recognize and differentiate which areas can and which cannot be changed and to continuously reintegrate this information into both transition and ongoing organizational planning and action.

Resource management continues to affect the success of the change, and this, again, is an area that requires consistency and careful attention in the middle of the change process. Detractors often look at resource allocation decisions (especially on where top management spends its time) to assess whether there is continued commitment to the change process. Initial strategic decisions require clearly demonstrated follow-through, including resource support. This issue interacts with leadership and energy demand issues.

A critical resource in the modern organization, especially in a governmental bureaucracy, is information. As change has caused events in the agency to move faster and faster, the frequency, intensity, and quality of information has not kept up. Necessary strategies include such mechanisms as cross-functional and staff meetings, and more technological methods such as computerized information and office automation systems. Complete support for full and effective communication, including support structures and training, is critical to sustaining a change process and addressing such other problems as commitment and leadership. This includes setting open communications norms, demonstrating these in management, and providing resources.

The amount of effort required to implement change also becomes a critical issue. For the organization as a whole, for the individuals who are part of the transformation, and for the change leaders and managers themselves, the demands for enough energy to keep the changes and systems moving can be overwhelming. This is especially true when the organization is running prechange and transitional systems simultaneously and individuals have multiple roles to serve.

A particularly ironic dimension of this problem concerns the perspective of the effective change manager. As described earlier, it is important to work from a systems perspective in managing the transformation program. Yet this very awareness exacerbates the energy problem, for it leads the change manager to attempt to monitor and orchestrate every piece of the organization—and to do so is impossible! It is essential to set and apply a priority system that focuses leaders' energies on the interventions with the highest leverage, and the organization must actively encourage and support coping, stress management, and renewal opportunities.

Change leaders need to retain perspective on the time frame for the overall change process. Burnout and loss of commitment become increasingly serious concerns as the organization change processes stretches out over years. Managing these energy resource demands is critical to the success of the change and to the well-being of the organization and its people. This is especially true in governmental organizations, which almost never have the resources to maintain 100 percent effort on both the maintenance and transition systems.

Since there is also an intensive interaction among all these issues, they must be collectively managed to sustain and achieve the transformation. All are increasingly difficult to address when change spreads more extensively across the organization, and the rate of transformation and diffusion must be managed to retain the balance or congruence that the organiza- tion requires. It has been useful at Labor and Industry to re- develop the strategic plans as a basis for making choices and targeting activities to achieve synergy and success in the highest leverage locations.

Conclusion

Because there are so many forces for stability and organi- zational maintenance at work in the government organization, both intentional and de facto, the change manager must actively incorporate and redeploy as many of the organizational and environmental subsystems as possible on behalf of the change. To succeed at transformation in this setting calls for creativity, perceptiveness, and a well-grounded understanding of the changing organization. This often means that governmental leaders and change managers must do the best they can under less than enabling circumstances. They must welcome and build on serendipity and also accept that there will be frequent set- backs. The government change manager must forge ahead with a strong guiding vision and sense of purpose, including an ethical perspective against which the transformation strategies and outcomes must be judged.

These characteristics appear to be less and less unique to governmental organizations. As the environments in which all organizations function become more information-intensive, networked, decentralized, issue oriented, and intrusive into the strategic management of the organization, the dynamics and challenges of governmental change will become increasingly applicable to all large-scale complex bureaucracies, public and private. The challenge is to institutionalize adaptiveness and responsiveness, so that these organizations can effectively serve the interests of their stakeholders.

The process of managing the transformation of this gov- ernment organization has been intensive and challenging, and the effort will take several years to bring to conclusion. The Minnesota Department of Labor and Industry has implemented the transformation process using methods and techniques advocated in the research and academic literature with a reasonably high degree of success. Yet many critical issues, including some of those that were successfully addressed at the outset of the change process, require continued and renewed consideration as this change process progresses into its fourth year.

Whether the effectiveness of this organization will continually improve remains to be judged. A critical variable will be consistency in the leadership, top management, and change team of the agency. Just as an election caused the change program to be initiated, it may displace it. However, enough stabilizing elements have been built into the organization to maintain a relatively constant level of performance, and even the levels of transformation and revitalization achieved to date are an exceptional improvement over the prior state of agency effectiveness. The Department of Labor and Industry is better able to address the needs of its clients and stakeholders than ever before, both for today and for the long-term future.

References

Argyris, C. "Theories of Action That Inhibit Learning." *American Psychologist*, 1976, *31*, 638–654.

Beckhard, R., and Harris, R. T. *Organizational Transitions*. Reading, Mass.: Addison-Wesley, 1977.

Deal, T. E., and Kennedy, A. A. *Corporate Cultures: The Rites and Rituals of Corporate Life*. Reading, Mass.: Addison-Wesley, 1982.

French, J. R., and Raven, B. H. "The Bases of Social Power." In D. Cartwright (ed.), *Studies in Social Power*. Ann Arbor: Institute for Social Research, University of Michigan, 1959.

Galbraith, J. *Designing Complex Organizations*. Reading, Mass.: Addison-Wesley, 1973.

Kanter, R. M. *The Change Masters: Innovation for Productivity in the American Corporation*. New York: Simon & Schuster, 1983.

Katz, D., and Kahn, R. L. *The Social Psychology of Organizations*. New York: Wiley, 1966.

Knowles, M. *The Adult Learner: A Neglected Species*. Houston: Gulf, 1978.

Lawrence, P. R., and Lorsch, J. *Organization and Environment.* Cambridge, Mass: Harvard University Press, 1967.

Nadler, D. "Managing Organizational Change: An Integrative Perspective." *Journal of Applied Behavioral Science,* 1981, *17,* 191–211.

Nadler, D., and Tushman, M. "Organizing for Innovation." *California Management Review,* 1986, *28,* 74–92.

O'Toole, J. *Vanguard Management: Redesigning the Corporate Future.* New York: Doubleday, 1985.

Schein, E. *Organizational Culture and Leadership: A Dynamic View.* San Francisco: Jossey-Bass, 1985.

Steiner, G. *Strategic Planning.* New York: Free Press, 1979.

Tichy, N. *Managing Strategic Change: Technical, Political, and Cultural Dynamics.* New York: Wiley, 1983.

Anthony F. Buono
James L. Bowditch
John W. Lewis III

21

The Cultural Dynamics
of Transformation:
The Case of a Bank Merger

Organizational transformation — whether through mergers, acquisitions, restructuring efforts, or attempts to change a firm's culture — can be viewed as a strategic response to environmental change and uncertainty. From the perspective of top management, such adaptation is often seen as a means to exploit new opportunities, as part of an organization's long-term growth, or even as a necessary strategy for survival. However, while such transformations may facilitate the accomplishment of these goals, they also create a number of uncertainties and tensions for organizational members since they typically involve a change in the nature, shape, or character of the organization (Beckhard, 1984). Indeed, these individuals often experience high levels of ambiguity and uncertainty concerning organizational goals and rewards (Ackerman, 1982), as well as concerns about the emergent organization's structure, culture, and the roles that they will eventually fulfill (Buono, Bowditch, and Lewis, 1985).

Although the costs and pressures associated with organizational transformations increase with the level of threat to organizational members (as in hostile takeovers), even supposedly nonthreatening transformations (for example, a friendly merger) can take their toll on these individuals (Buono, Bowditch, and Lewis, 1985). Such major organizational changes and the uncertainties related to the transformation can precipitate high levels of stress, tension, anxiety, and resentment on the part of many organizational members (Ackerman, 1982; Kahn and others, 1964; Nadler, 1982). Yet, despite the magnitude of the changes and outcomes involved, organizational transformations have been criticized as being generally "undermanaged," especially at the human resource level (Kimberly and Quinn, 1984; McCaskey, 1979).

As a specific type of organizational transformation, mergers can so change the nature, orientation, and character of one or both of the merger partners that five to seven years are typically needed for employees to feel truly assimilated in the merged entity (Stybel, 1986). During a merger, of course, some employees may find that little has actually changed. For a number of other organizational members, however, behaviors that were once sanctioned by the firm may no longer be rewarded or approved and may, in fact, be punished. Still others may find that their services are no longer valued or needed. The result may very well be lowered organizational commitment and satisfaction along with behaviors that work against what the organization is attempting to accomplish. The significance of such attitudes and behaviors is underscored by recent research that indicates that despite seemingly favorable strategic, financial, and operational assessments made during premerger feasibility studies, mergers have less than a fifty-fifty chance of being successful (Louis, 1982; Pritchett, 1985). This lack of postmerger success is increasingly being attributed to human factors and ineffective management of the transformation (Buono, Bowditch, and Lewis, 1985; Sales and Mirvis, 1984; Mirvis, 1985).

This chapter explores the consequences of managerial actions over the course of a merger. Based on a longitudinal study carried out between 1979 and 1985, it examines (1) the attitudes and perceptions of organizational members before and after the merger, (2) the processes and outcomes associated with the merger, and (3) the uncertainties involved in the transformation. Our main purpose is to formulate an empirically based model of the merger process that underscores the types of problems and difficulties that can emerge during such a large-scale change effort. The chapter concludes with a discussion of the human resource implications of organizational transformation and some of the ways in which managers may facilitate this process.

Study Design and Methodology

This study focuses on the processes and outcomes of a friendly merger between two approximately equal-sized savings banks. Bank A was the fourth largest savings bank in the state, with approximately $600 million in assets and 325 full-time employees. Due to the urban location of its headquarters and branches, the institution served a largely blue-collar clientele. It operated with a divisional structure, and was rather bureaucratic in nature, with clearly defined and bounded jobs at all levels.

Bank B was the fifth largest ($500 million in assets) mutual savings bank in the state, with approximately 275 employees. In contrast to bank A, this merger partner had both its headquarters and all branches in suburban areas and chiefly served white-collar and professional customers. The institution operated with a centrally controlled functional organization, but individual jobs were more loosely defined, particularly at the professional and managerial levels, than in bank A.

A multimethod approach employed in a longitudinal framework was used to gather data on the two premerger banks from 1979 to 1980, on the merger process itself in 1981, and on the postmerger experience from 1982 to 1985. Through a serendipitous research opportunity, climate surveys with the populations of both banks were administered during late 1979 and early 1980, *prior to* any merger-related discussions. The survey used in bank A ($N = 325$) was part of an internally developed quality of work life and organization development program (see Bowditch and Buono, 1982), while bank B ($N = 188$) used a nationally developed survey form. Both surveys focused on employee perceptions about various facets of organizational life, including organizational commitment, job satisfaction, interpersonal relations, job security and advancement, organizational policies, management and supervisory behavior, and compensation. The data-gathering processes for information on premerger organizational climates differed in that bank A relied on a more participatory approach by having small groups of employees provide input to the formulation of the survey, while bank B used a standard, commercially available questionnaire. In spite of the different approaches, however, there were a number of identical or very similar questions, so that clear climate profiles of the two premerger institutions were obtained.

Additional information on the premerger banks was obtained through in-depth interviews with organizational members and observations and archival data gathered throughout the study period. The physical settings (for example, office location and decor, consistency of decor across departments and levels) of both banks were studied, as were each institution's own statements about itself (annual reports, copies of the house organ, internal memos, and so on). Lengthy interviews with the CEOs, upper-level managers, and employees throughout both organizations focused on such items as (1) personal descriptions of the organization, (2) organizational history, (3) types of people working at the firm, (4) type of place the bank is to work at, and (5) other facets of organizational life. Following grounded theory (Glaser and Strauss, 1967) and phenomenological approaches to organizational research (see Sanders, 1982), we examined transcripts of the interviews for concepts and themes that could be used to characterize the two banks. These "emergent hypotheses" were then tested in discussions with members of the research team and the two firms to develop shared perceptions of each organization's culture.

Information on the merged bank was obtained through a similar process. Beginning in early 1982, data on the new institution were obtained through a study of changes in physical settings, self-reports, archival data, and in-depth interviews with a stratified random sample of organizational members (the two former CEOs of the merger partners, ten members of former bank A, ten members of former bank B, and six new employees who joined the institution following the merger). The interviews covered such areas as the types of management style before and after the merger, policy and procedural changes, working conditions and atmosphere, general organizational changes, the merger process itself, and outcomes of the merger.

Data on the organizational climate of the merged bank were collected through survey questionnaires administered in 1982 and 1984. The instruments were developed to reflect the climate items covered by the earlier surveys and were given to a stratified random sample of postmerger bank members (1982: former bank A = 45, former bank B = 45, new employees = 10; 1984: former bank A = 50, former bank B = 50, new employees = 40). Finally, a questionnaire was mailed in 1983 to all employees who left the organization following the merger ($N = 90$; response rate 65 percent). Phone interviews with twenty-eight of these individuals were subsequently undertaken to provide further qualitative information on their perceptions of the merger experience.

Overall, uniformity of data collection efforts was attempted throughout the study period. Analysis was guided by what Lawler (1985) has referred to as *participative research,* in which key organizational members assisted in interpreting the data. Although a limitation of the data concerns differences in the methods used to obtain organizational climate data for bank A and bank B during the premerger period, the information generated still provides a basis for comparative analysis. Combined with the interviews, observations, and archival information, these materials provide a clear picture of the two banks prior to the merger and of the new institution during the postmerger integration period.

Overview of the Merger Process

A basic difficulty that complicates the construction of a general model of the merger process concerns the range of such transformations. The Federal Trade Commission, for example, classifies mergers into four broad types—horizontal, vertical, product and market concentric, and conglomerate. Each type will typically involve different dynamics and synergies. Thus, in conglomerate mergers, where financial rather than operational integration is the goal, the processes and outcomes may very well be quite different from those in mergers whose main goal is to gain operating synergies between the two firms (see Jemison and Sitkin, 1986; Lubatkin, 1983). Accordingly, the present framework focuses on related-business mergers rather than conglomerate cases.

Based on the data gathered in the present study, a descriptive model of the various phases of the merger is outlined in Table 21-1. Since this model is based on a single longitudinal study, each phase, of course, might not appear as distinct as the model suggests or may be only partly observable in other merger situations. These different stages, however, do seem to capture many of the dynamics that occur during related-business mergers and are supported by developmental theories of conflict and group formation (Pondy, 1967; Tuchman, 1965), recent conceptualization of the merger process (Jemison and Sitkin, 1986) and descriptive accounts of other mergers and acquisitions (Darlin and Guiles, 1984; Levinson, 1970; O'Boyle and Russell, 1984; Sinetar, 1981).

During the *premerger* phase, the uncertainty in the larger environment (in the form of banking deregulation, increased competition between financial institutions, growing use of electronic funds transfer and automatic teller networks, growing sophistication of consumers, and so forth) created a number of strategic uncertainties for bankers. Brenner and Shapira (1983) argue that such market uncertainties and the specific uncertainties that confront individual firms contribute significantly to merger decisions.

In the present study, the *merger planning* period began as part of an informal discussion between the CEOs of the two banks during a return trip from an industry association meeting in mid 1980. Interview data revealed that during their talk, the two presidents agreed that industry and general economic conditions were making it very difficult for even medium-sized savings banks to survive. They continued their discussion over

Table 21-1. The Merger Process.

Stage	Characteristics
1. Premerger	Degree of environmental uncertainty (technological, market, sociopolitical) may vary, but respective organizations are relatively stable and members are relatively satisfied with the status quo.
2. Merger Planning	Environmental uncertainty increases, and this precipitates discussion concerning merger/takeover possibilities; fears rise that unless the firm grows, larger companies will destroy it, organization will become less competitive or even fail; the firm is still relatively stable, and discussion is confined to top executive level.
3. Announced Merger	Environmental uncertainty continues to increase and this influences merger decision; organization is still relatively stable, and while members have mixed emotions concerning the merger, expectations are raised.
4. Initial Merger Process	Organizational instability increases and is characterized by structural ambiguity (high) and some cultural and role ambiguity (low); although members are generally cooperative at beginning, goodwill quickly erodes.
5. Physical-Legal Merger	Organizational instability increases as structural, cultural, and role ambiguities increase; mechanistic organizations take on some organic characteristics for a period; conflict between organizational members increases.
6. Merger Aftermath	High organizational instability, lack of cooperation, and "we-they" mentality exist; violated expectations lead to intraunit and interunit hostility; structural ambiguity decreases, but cultural and role ambiguity remains high; dissenters leave the organization.
7. Psychological Merger	Organizational stability recurs as ambiguities are clarified, expectations are revised; renewed cooperation and intraunit and interunit tolerance become evident; this whole process is time consuming.

the next several months and finally agreed that a merger between their two organizations would be a good idea. Since the
banks were not in immediate competition with each other either by territory or clientele, were roughly the same size, and
had similar perceived goals, the CEOs reasoned that a merger
would not only create a stronger, more competitive institution
but in the long run could significantly expand the bank's sphere
of influence as well.

In early 1981, the employees of both banks were informed
about the merger plans at meetings held at each institution
(*announced merger* period). Interviews at the time determined
that although a number of employees expressed reservations,
doubts, and fears about the merger, most employees of bank A
were initially quite favorable toward the merger since they felt it
would give their organization (an urban bank) the opportunity
to expand into the more prosperous suburban communities.
Members of bank B, by contrast, were less enthusiastic about the
proposed venture since they felt that their organization had less
to gain, although a number of these individuals felt that the
merger would provide it with a more solid base of operation.

During the open discussion of the merger, it became
increasingly clear that while industry conditions and competitive considerations were of paramount interest to the CEOs
of the two banks, members further down the hierarchies were far
more concerned with internal organizational interactions. A
significant barrier to the merger, which was initially overlooked
but later acknowledged in interviews with the CEOs, concerned
the cultures of the respective institutions. Although both companies were approximately equal-sized savings banks operating
in the same standard metropolitan statistical area, each bank
employee group saw itself as being quite different from the
other. Members of bank A perceived the institution to be a
people-oriented and egalitarian, if also rather bureaucratic,
type of organization whose CEO and upper-level managers had
encouraged a participative managerial style. Employees of bank
B, by contrast, characterized their organization as more task
oriented and as an authoritarian sort of workplace whose CEO
was the key source of power and decision making. The state

banking commissioner (at the time of the merger) even described the two banks as being "as different as you could possibly get — [bank A] very collegial and consensual and [bank B] totally autocratic."

Although the cultures of these two savings banks were almost extreme types, the premerger climate data summarized in Table 21-2 indicate that both employee groups were quite accepting of their respective organizations. Similar proportions of employees reported pride in working for their organization, as well as satisfaction with their systems of compensation and advancement, the context of their work, and interpersonal relations. Conceptually, it is important to note that while culture is concerned with the *nature* of beliefs and expectations about organizational life, climate is an indicator of *whether* those beliefs and expectations are being fulfilled (Burke, 1985; Schwartz and Davis, 1981). Thus, favorable response on like items of the *premerger* climate surveys suggests that expectations about what it *should* be like to work in each organization were being met. Despite the different realities of organizational life in the two banks, the conditions had existed for an extended period of time, shaped and were shaped by quite divergent values, beliefs, traditions and priorities, and were viewed as "the way things should be." Due to the acceptance of and satisfaction with these different organizations by their respective workers, the initial merger between the two institutions has been described as a literal collision of cultures in which seemingly rational requirements for effecting organizational, procedural, and other merger related changes were strongly resisted because of the threats to the existing cultures (see Buono, Bowditch, and Lewis, 1985).

During the *initial merger process* stage, for example, a number of joint committees were formed to resolve potential operating and procedural differences between the two organizations. These meetings continued over several months, but little was resolved. Additionally, numerous "merger memos" were written by top management and distributed to organizational members detailing what was to take place in preparation for, and following, the merger. Experimental transfers of employees between the banks prior to the merger were attempted, but

Table 21-2. Organizational Climate Comparison: Premerger and Postmerger Periods.

| | 1979 to 1980 Premerger | | 1982 Postmerger | | | | 1984 Postmerger | | | |
| | | | | Prior Affiliation | | | | Prior Affiliation | | |
Selected Items	Bank A (N=325)	Bank B (N=188)	Merged Bank (N=100)	Bank A (N=45)	Bank B (N=45)	New (N=10)	Merged Bank (N=140)	Bank A (N=50)	Bank B (N=50)	New (N=40)
Organizational Commitment										
Sense of pride	90	86	46	34	50	78	74	68	80	76
Good customer service	75	na	43	30	44	83	73	65	80	75
Job-Related										
Overall job satisfaction	73	na	54	49	52	89	75	78	76	67
Job challenge	72	54	56	64	43	66	74	77	79	59
Satisfactory work hours	84	86	92	90	90	94	90	93	94	79
Amount of work reasonable	72	60	77	71	81	83	84	81	82	87
Job worthwhile and important	87	na	79	86	86	78	88	89	92	83
Job Security and Advancement										
Job secure if performed well	91	89	58	46	64	77	74	64	74	89
Say what I think without fear	58	61	54	64	36	72	57	45	66	63
Advancement opportunity	71	72	41	37	37	72	58	58	57	59
Promotions deserved	50	55	37	37	28	73	36	30	65	40

Percent Favorable

	1	2	3	4	5	6	7	8	9	10
Compensation										
Paid fairly	43	39	48	53	42	50	50	49	52	44
Good benefits	86	86	88	86	90	83	82	73	98	72
Supervisor										
Supervisor is fair	83	90	79	79	81	56	88	86	86	91
Available when needed	75	na	82	77	85	83	87	92	84	83
Capable of doing job	na	93	84	85	82	78	91	93	90	87
Lets me know what is expected	79	76	78	79	72	72	90	90	91	87
Ensures employees are well trained	64	73	66	61	63	78	73	65	86	76
Management										
Employee oriented	72	74	38	32	36	72	40	32	46	46
Opportunity to interact with	47	74	36	29	39	50	47	49	52	43
Training effectiveness	50	73	44	38	41	77	62	57	64	67
Organizational Cooperation										
Departmental cooperation	44	48	31	27	27	67	57	52	54	66
Co-workers do their share	73	74	77	76	73	72	81	81	79	86
Good communication	36	67	27	17	29	61	46	41	47	52

individuals were reluctant to go to the "other" bank, allegedly because of an increase in commuting time. Although these efforts focused on specific concerns such as which computer system, forms, and operating procedures the merged bank would use, the discussions were largely characterized by defensiveness on the part of each group concerning why "our way" was better. While a content analysis of all merger-related memos during this period and interviews with organizational members suggested that no problems or potential problems were publicly anticipated, in retrospect it is clear that little of substance emerged from the interbank meetings and employee transfer program because of the cultural differences between the two banks and related ethnocentric feelings.

As the *physical-legal merger* took place in August of 1981, organizational members experienced growing uncertainty with respect to the structural changes and emergent culture of the new institution and the roles they would fulfill. Although these individuals—managers and employees alike—initially felt that they had relatively clear perceptions of what would transpire during the merger, they began to discover that the images they held were quite different from the images held by their co-workers. As these perceptions were shared, the resulting ambiguities and organizational instability rapidly eroded the initial feelings of excitement and the potential for cooperation.

The physical-legal merger created a "storming" atmosphere in the organization. As a number of structural aspects of the organization were still unclear (for example, how were communication linkages to be established, who held legitimate power in different departments), the predominantly mechanistic structures of the two institutions seemed to take on organic characteristics in an effort to resolve these ambiguities. In the functional units, for instance, two supervisors (one from each merger partner) were initially "in charge." Rather than resolve this staffing issue at the beginning, top management allowed for role ambiguity as to who would be named to head a combined function. The competitors from each bank jockeyed for position to take over a particular role, but without clear signals from the top as to who was favored. While this might have

been a useful managerial selection mechanism from the perspective of top management, it had the unintended dysfunctional effect of contributing to the cultural and role ambiguities
at the operating level of merged departments. The influence of
this process can be seen in the fact that employees continued to
identify with their prior departments and supervisors long after
functions were formally merged.

The *merger aftermath* period was characterized by a "we-
they" feeling. Soon after the merger actually took place, each
parent organization was seen by the employees of the other bank
as an "invading enemy" rather than as an equal partner (despite
the relatively equal size of the banks). Although one might
expect a honeymoon period between the two organizations,
especially considering the initial acceptance of the merger, the
differences in organizational cultures led to almost immediate
competition and conflict between the employee groups. As
would be predicted by Schein's (1980) characterization of what
happens between competing groups, there were distorted perceptions about and feelings of hostility toward this "enemy."
Members of both organizations reported that "they [the other
bank] took us over." Employees from the two firms circulated
negative stories regarding the merger partner. Responsibility
for why things were not going as well as they should, why
communication was so poor, or why "I" or "my boss" was not
treated fairly were routinely attributed to the other bank.

People also tended to become nostalgic about their prior
bank affiliation during this stage. Interview and survey data (see
Table 21-3) indicate that employees displayed active dislike of
their merger partner counterparts, the "other bank's" managers,
and its policies and culture, findings consistent with the process
of relative deprivation (Crosby, 1984; Martin, 1981). Prior to the
merger, each group was satisfied with their organizational situations. Once they came face-to-face with people with different
cultural orientations, policies, and procedures, however, each
group felt that the merged entity resembled the merger partner
too closely, and this contributed to their growing dissatisfaction
(see Bowditch, Buono, Lewis, and Nurick, 1985). Frequently
mentioned complaints by respondents from *both* merger part-

Table 21-3. T-Tests on Merger-Related Survey Questions by Former Bank
of Employment: 1982 Postmerger Survey.

	Percent in Agreement	
Question	Bank A	Bank B
All things considered, the merger should not have taken place.	47	28[a]
My former bank's philosophy is the dominant one since the merger.	26	37[b]
There has been an improvement of policies and procedures in the new (merged) bank compared to those in my premerger bank.	20	38[a]
There is a lingering feeling of resentment between the employees of the merger partners.	78	57[b]
There is a lot of friction between former bank A and former bank B employees.	64	36[a]
The atmosphere at the bank is becoming similar to the "good old days."	10	22[b]
My department has been strengthened by the merger.	24	53[b]
I feel that employee benefits have improved as a result of the merger.	66	83[b]
A majority of the employees have come to accept the merger as a necessary and worthwhile step.	36	58[a]
Most people are afraid to open up their feelings about the merger.	74	37[a]

[a] $p < .01$
[b] $p < .05$

ners were the loss of family atmosphere, freedom, camaraderie, and accessibility to management, a disruption of social ties and communication patterns, and decreased cohesion and organizational commitment.

Most of the initially favorable expectations held by employees (for example, the merger would open up greater personal opportunities, and result in a stronger organization) were not fulfilled as organizational members underscored the realities of the merger (fewer advancement opportunities, layoffs, no growth, and breakdown of communication). As indicated in Table 21-2, in the *1982 postmerger* survey, variables reflecting "hard" organizational factors and characteristics (for example, compensation, hours and amount of work, supervision) did not significantly decline, while items reflecting the subtler aspects of organizational life, such as organizational commitment, feelings of job security, feelings toward upper management, job satisfaction, and customer service, showed marked declines. Paradoxically, during a merger upper-level managers typically focus most of their attention on the procedural and material aspects of the organizations in question, while the more subjective, cultural aspects of organizational life are neglected. Moreover, it is important to note that those employees who joined the bank after the merger were generally and significantly more favorable about organizational conditions than either of the merger partners (see Table 21-2). This finding can be explained by the fact that these individuals did not have any allegiances to the preexisting cultures or administrative systems. The change and resulting ambiguity experienced by members of the premerger firms, however, seem to polarize existing attitudes (Lord, Ross, and Lepper, 1979), leading to increased antagonism and resistance between members of merging firms (see Jemison and Sitkin, 1986).

During this period, members of both firms felt betrayed by their top leaders, each of whom publicly assured his employees that they would be secure in their membership in the new organization. Both CEOs repeated earlier public statements that there would be no merger-related layoffs as long as people did their jobs well. Subsequent management decisions to lay off organizational members—even though nonperformance factors in the situation supported such action—resulted in a profound and widespread distrust of the new leadership and the organization. Since people interpret such acts as symbols of what is important to an organization, they can significantly affect the shared beliefs about the firm and its leadership (Nystrom and Starbuck, 1984). The layoff, which occurred in mid December, quickly became known as the "Christmas massacre." The office of former bank B's CEO was subsequently referred to as "murderer's row" since most employees — especially those from bank A — attributed the layoffs to his influence on the new institution.

As employees became increasingly antagonistic toward the merged bank, a significant number of dissenters voluntarily resigned their positions. While one would predict that individuals choosing to or being asked to leave an organization would report less favorable attitudes toward their job and the company compared to those remaining in the firm (whether they were expressing their true feelings or rationalizing their situation), the before-after attitudinal comparison of the "leavers" indicates the powerful impact that such an organizational transformation can have on individuals (see Table 21-4).

Although both CEOs expressed concern that the merged institution should reflect a true blend of the two banks ("a merger of equals"), it was becoming increasingly apparent that the emerging structure and culture of the new institution more closely resembled the slightly smaller bank B than it did bank A. For instance, while the logo and location of its headquarters were a hybrid of the two original banks, the merged institution retained the name of bank B, as well as many of its systems and orientations — important symbols of organizational identity. The merger also resulted in dual top management: the former CEO of bank A assumed the role of CEO and focused predominantly on external industry and environmental concerns; bank B's CEO assumed control of internal decisions as COO and was substantially more visible than his bank A counterpart. While this was the preferred set of activities for both individuals, extending back to their presidency of the premerger banks, many bank A employees felt that their former president had "sold them out." Thus, although the leavers from banks A and B were both quite critical about the postmerger period, the growing influence of bank B on the merged bank is reflected in the greater number of bank A employees who left the new institution.

Following a merger between two organizations, there is a mourning or grief period similar to that experienced when a family member dies (Fried, 1963; Sinetar, 1981) as the dissolu-

Table 21-4. Premerger and Postmerger Attitudes: Organizational "Leavers."

| | Percent Favorable | | | | | |
| | Premerger | | | Postmerger | | |
Selected Questions	(N = 90)	Bank A (N = 69)	Bank B (N = 21)	(N = 90)	Bank A (N = 69)	Bank B (N = 21)
Organizational Commitment						
Sense of pride	88	92	76	27	27	26
Good customer service	92	94	86	36	36	33
Job Related						
Overall satisfaction	84	87	76	26	24	31
Job worthwhile and important	87	89	81	44	43	48
Management						
Top management paying sufficient attention to bank's future	73	74	71	44	44	43
Top management maintained credibility throughout merger	55	58	45	19	21	12
Bank hires well-qualified people	85	86	81	52	56	38
Lack of necessary information	57	57	58	61	60	65
Compensation						
Paid fairly re: others inside bank	75	73	81	56	56	55
Paid fairly re: others outside bank	76	80	62	66	67	62
Job Security and Advancement						
Job was secure if performed well	92	93	88	41	37	52
I could say what I thought without fear	76	77	71	30	24	49
People were afraid to "open up" about their feelings	66	71	52	74	76	69

tion of familiar work surroundings and the slow but steady exit of close friends and associates signals the "end of what was." In the present study, only gradually and over a relatively long period did many of the cultural and role-related ambiguities become resolved as norms and roles began to stabilize and a "refreezing" into new routines began to take place. However, as indicated by the *1984 postmerger* climate survey (Table 21-2), although there was a steady improvement in employee satisfaction and these attitudes were closer to the attitudes held by new employees, these perceptions have still not reached premerger levels *a full three years after the merger*.

Thus, while many employees reported that the cultural issues and problems were "behind them," indicating that there had been movement toward a *psychological merger* between the two institutions, that is, movement toward renewed organizational stability, interpersonal tolerance, and revised expectations, it is clear that this process is not yet complete. Interestingly, the respondents who indicated that the psychological merger has taken place were largely in upper-level positions. Those organizational members who reported continued resistance and animosities were predominantly from the branch and operations job clusters — those areas where integration of merger partner personnel took longer. As one of these individuals, who reflected the attitudes of many of his co-workers, said, "Since the merger the entire atmosphere has changed. The 'family' feeling no longer exists. After more than two years, a 'merged' feeling still has not been achieved. We have become a more consistent organization since the merger, but we have lost the high-spirited morale that both organizations shared."

Implications and Conclusions

Obviously, a merger between two previously autonomous organizations involves an enormous adjustment to change in a relatively compressed period of time. Even a friendly merger introduces a high degree of conflict and tension along a number of different dimensions into the lives of organizational members. In fact, it may very well be that regardless of how delicately and thoughtfully human resource issues are handled, some turmoil is inevitable (see O'Boyle and Russell, 1984). There are, however, a number of implications for both practitioners and interveners involved in such transformations that may minimize these problems.

First, as the preceding discussion suggests, the merger involved a number of stages in which some types of uncertainties and ambiguities were more salient than others (see Table 21-5). The literature on ambiguity in the workplace, however, has largely focused on role ambiguity in terms of two dimensions: unpredictability of outcomes of an individual's behavior and the degree of information deficiency in a particular role (Kahn and others, 1964; Rizzo, House, and Lirtzman, 1970; Pearce, 1981). Environmental and structural change and uncertainty are largely viewed as antecedents to such ambiguity. Based on the data in this study, it appears that on one level such environmental and structural change do lead to ambiguities at the role level. However, they also seem to have differential effects in and of themselves. This finding corroborates earlier criticisms concerning the global nature of the role ambiguity concept and the argument that different individuals may experience different types of ambiguity in the workplace (Breaugh, 1983; Connolly, 1977; Miles, 1976).

Second, the human resources dimension of mergers should be considered formally at the outset of the merger process with the same emphasis and level of attention given financial, legal, and procedural issues. Just as experts in finance are needed to deal with financial planning and lawyers with legal concerns, human resource and organization development professionals are needed to work with managers to develop a plan for dealing with the various uncertainties and concerns faced by organizational members.

Third, at a very broad and general level, there is a need for what Tichy and Ulrich (1984) refer to as a "transformational leader." Such individuals must be able not only to create a new vision out of the old but to develop and communicate that vision to others in an effort to secure organizationwide commitment to the change. As a start, the central concepts of equity, power, and

Table 21-5. Types of Ambiguity.

Level	Type	Manifestations
External (macro)	Environmental	*Technological* (for example, automation, changes in work process) *Market* (for example, competitive structure, consumer preference) *Sociopolitical* (for example, values, legal changes, work force diversity, regulation/deregulation)
Organizational (meso)	Structural	*Patterned* (for example, structural considerations such as reporting relationships and communication patterns; policies and procedures are in flux)
	Cultural	*Normative* (for example, anomie, norms in flux, absence or disruption of social ties)
Individual (micro)	Role	*Positional* (for example, job and status)

personal freedom, along with the dynamics of the decision-making process, must be understood, especially as they are reflected through the different stages and ambiguities of the transformation process. In the present study, it was clear that the majority of organizational members looked initially to their top managers for support and guidance but then came to feel betrayed by and isolated from these individuals.

Fourth, the importance of a high level of communication about the transformation cannot be overstressed. In the present study, although both CEOs thought that they "over met" about the merger, organizational members felt that communication concerning the merger was too infrequent, that the exchanges between the two groups prior to the actual merger raised more issues than they resolved, and that the process did not involve enough representatives from each bank. Although it has been suggested that initial merger negotiations be carried out in secret to minimize uncertainty among personnel (Graves, 1981), it seems that the creation of formal, internal communication mechanisms as early as possible in the process may limit the anxiety that will otherwise be fueled by rumors, the grapevine, or even outside news reports (see Marks, 1982). In the present study, during the merger aftermath period (November 1983) a personnel-based communications committee composed of a cross section of eleven employees and supervisors was formed. This committee met with the vice-president of human resources every two months for the purpose of bringing up problems, discussing solutions, and passing on information to upper-level management and the employee population. Interview data indicate that this group has had a positive effect on the movement toward a psychological merger by focusing on and working through cultural as well as operational concerns. Such transition management structures should be created as early as possible to identify and deal with the unique issues that arise during each stage of the transformation process (see Ackerman, 1982).

Fifth, it is important to develop mutual understanding and respect across the two organizations. In the present study, the initial involvement of organizational members centered on joint committees that took up operations and procedural issues. Yet, due to tensions between the sets of employees, their strong cultural identities, and their ethnocentric attitudes, few positive results were achieved. If such interactions focus initially on the identification of the major *human* problems and concerns raised by the transformation, however, it seems that organizational, operational, and procedural concerns can then be more easily resolved. A recognition of cultural differences through intergroup mirroring interventions, followed by team-building efforts, is applicable here. Intergroup mirroring attempts to bring to the surface the root causes of conflict between two groups and to create conditions under which mutual problem solving can occur. Each group develops and shares an image of itself and the other in an attempt to elicit the stereotypes and assumptions that naturally exist about "them" and "us." The groups then focus on their uniqueness, differences, and similarities as they work through their perceptions of the others' image, motivations, and competencies (Plovnick, Fry, and Burke, 1982). By drawing out the goals of the new organization, the roles that organizational members will play, and the process through which groups will interact, stronger team identities can begin to be established (Beckhard, 1971). Since the emerging culture of the new institution evolves slowly over time as a product of shared experience, the greater the number of these shared experiences that can be produced early on in the process, the faster a set of symbols and shared meanings will develop with which group members can begin to identify.

Sixth, there is the need to develop a problem-solving attitude among organizational members. A main problem with managing organizational transformations is knowing what the future state and its problems will be (see Nadler, 1982). Since such uncertainty typically brings about resistance and anxiety, as well as a longing for the past, managers should have a high awareness of such resistance and the need to work with it. It is also important to realize that the constantly building tension that surrounds mergers may reduce tolerance for ambiguity and increase pressure for the rapid completion of merger-related deliberations. Such premature closure can reduce opportunities for more careful and dispassionate analysis and understanding of the internal dynamics of the process (Jemison and Sitkin, 1986). If people are involved in the change process and are allowed to contribute to solutions as well as to raise problems (as was done with the postmerger Personnel Communications Committee), they can develop a more realistic set of expectations about the transformation and what it will take to resolve the resultant difficulties. Communication efforts should be directed at such issues as: What kind of organization do we want to be? What is our mission? What are the values of the organization? What are some of the transitions that our firm might undergo? How might we deal with such change? One way to accomplish this would be an open systems planning procedure (McCaskey, 1974). However, the basic nature of such change as a human process—with its inherent problems, interactions, and ramifications—must be underscored.

Finally, it is necessary for managers to approach organizational transformation with flexibility and tentative frameworks of thought. In this chapter, we have attempted to outline the various stages and uncertainties involved in a related-business merger. As the discussion points out, even a friendly merger involves a time-consuming and ambiguous process, replete with anxiety-provoking, disruptive, and antagonistic interactions. People view such transformation as a significant life change. Given this situation, managers need to communicate and interact with their employees in ways that recognize the various uncertainties and tensions associated with the process and that enable them to tolerate such ambiguities. If mergers, acquisitions, or other cultural change efforts are to be successful, these intricacies dictate the need for a focused diagnosis, as well as a systematic understanding of the difficulties involved and the human problems inherent in bringing about such change.

References

Ackerman, L. S. "Transition Management: An In-Depth Look at Managing Complex Change." *Organizational Dynamics*, Summer 1982, 46–66.

Beckhard, R. "Optimizing Team-Building Efforts." *Journal of Contemporary Business*, 1971, *1* (3), 23–32.

Beckhard, R. *Organizational Transformation: Fad or Imperative?* Paper presented at 44th annual meeting of Academy of Management, Boston, Aug. 1984.

Bowditch, J. L., and Buono, A. F. *Quality of Work Life Assessment: A Survey-Based Approach*. Dover, Mass.: Auburn House, 1982.

Bowditch, J. L., Buono, A. F., Lewis, J. W., and Nurick, A. J. "Paradise Lost: Violations of the Psychological Contract as a Friendly Merger By-Product." *Proceedings of the Association of Human Resources Management and Organizational Behavior*. Boston, 1985.

Breaugh, J. A. *The Measurement of Job Ambiguity*. Paper presented at 43rd annual meeting of Academy of Management, Dallas, Aug. 1983.

Brenner, M., and Shapira, Z. "Environmental Uncertainty as Determining Merger Activity." In W. H. Goldberg (ed.), *Mergers: Motives, Modes, and Methods*. Aldershot, England: Gower, 1983.

Buono, A. F., Bowditch, J. L., and Lewis, J. W. "When Cultures

Collide: The Anatomy of a Merger." *Human Relations*, 1985, *38* (5), 477–500.

Burke, W. W. *Organizational Culture and Climate Are Not the Same.* Paper presented at 45th annual meeting of Academy of Management, San Diego, Aug. 1985.

Connolly, T. "Information Processing and Decision Making." In B. Staw and G. Salancik (eds.), *New Directions in Organizational Behavior*. Chicago: St. Clair, 1977.

Crosby, F. "Relative Deprivation in Organizational Settings." In B. Staw (ed.), *Research in Organizational Behavior*. Vol. 6. Greenwich, Conn.: JAI Press, 1984.

Darlin, D., and Guiles, M. G. "Whose Takeover?" *Wall Street Journal*, Dec. 19, 1984, pp. 1, 20.

Fried, M. "Grieving for a Lost Home." In L. J. Duhl (ed.), *The Urban Condition*. New York: Basic Books, 1963.

Glaser, B. G., and Strauss, A. L. *Discovery of Grounded Theory: Strategies for Qualitative Research*. Hawthorne, N.Y.: Aldine, 1967.

Graves, D. "Individual Reactions to a Merger of Two Small Firms of Brokers in the Reinsurance Industry." *Journal of Management Studies*, 1981, *18*, 89–113.

Jemison, D. B., and Sitkin, S. B. "Corporate Acquisitions: A Process Perspective." *Academy of Management Review*, 1986, *11* (1), 145–163.

Kahn, R., and others. *Organizational Stress: Studies in Role Conflict and Ambiguity*. New York: Wiley, 1964.

Kimberly, J. R., and Quinn, R. E. *Managing Organizational Transitions*. Homewood, Ill.: Dow Jones-Irwin, 1984.

Lawler, E. E. *Theory and Practice in OD*. Paper presented at 45th annual meeting of Academy of Management, San Diego, Aug. 1985.

Levinson, H. "A Psychologist Diagnoses Merger Failures." *Harvard Business Review*, 1970, *48* (2), 139–147.

Lord, C. G., Ross, L., and Lepper, M. R. "Biased Assimilation and Attitude Polarization: The Effects of Prior Theories on Subsequently Considered Evidence." *Journal of Personality and Social Psychology*, 1979, *37*, 2098–2109.

Louis, A. M. "The Bottom Line on 10 Big Mergers." *Fortune*, May 3, 1982, pp. 84–89.

Lubatkin, M. "Mergers and the Performance of the Acquiring Firm." *Academy of Management Review*, 1983, *8* (2), 218–225.

McCaskey, M. "A Contingency Approach to Planning." *Academy of Management Journal*, 1974, *17* (2), 206–218.

McCaskey, M. "The Management of Ambiguity." *Organizational Dynamics*, Spring 1979, pp. 30–48.

Marks, M. "Merging Human Resources: A Review of Current Research." *Mergers & Acquisitions*, Summer 1982, pp. 38–44.

Martin, J. "Relative Deprivation: A Theory of Distributive Justice for an Era of Shrinking Resources." In B. Staw (ed.), *Research in Organizational Behavior*. Vol. 3. Greenwich, Conn.: JAI Press, 1981.

Miles, R. H. "Role Requirements as Sources of Organizational Stress." *Journal of Applied Psychology*, 1976, *61*, 172–179.

Miles, R. H. *Macro Organizational Behavior*. Santa Monica, Calif.: Goodyear, 1980.

Mirvis, P. H. "Negotiations After the Sale: The Roots and Ramifications of Conflict in an Acquisition." *Journal of Occupational Behavior*, 1985, *6*, 65–84.

Nadler, D. A. "Managing Transitions to Uncertain Future States." *Organizational Dynamics*, Summer 1982, pp. 37–45.

Nystrom, P. C., and Starbuck, W. H. "Managing Beliefs in Organizations." *Journal of Applied Behavioral Science*, 1984, *20* (3), 277–287.

O'Boyle, T. F., and Russell, M. "Troubled Marriage: Steel Giants' Merger Brings Big Headaches." *Wall Street Journal*, Nov. 30, 1984, pp. 1, 20.

Pearce, J. L. "Bringing Some Clarity to Role Ambiguity Research." *Academy of Management Review*, 1981, *6*, 665–674.

Plovnick, M. S., Fry, R. E., and Burke, W. W. *Organization Development: Exercises, Cases and Readings*. Boston: Little, Brown, 1982.

Pondy, L. R. "Organizational Conflict: Concepts and Models." *Administrative Science Quarterly*, 1967, *12*, 296–320.

Pritchett, P. *After the Merger*. Homewood, Ill.: Dow Jones-Irwin, 1985.

Rizzo, J. R., House, R. J., and Lirtzman, S. I. "Role Conflict and Role Ambiguity in Complex Organizations." *Administrative Science Quarterly,* 1970, *15,* 150–163.

Sales, A., and Mirvis, P. "When Cultures Collide: Issues in Acquisition." In J. R. Kimberly and R. E. Quinn (eds.), *Managing Organizational Transitions.* Homewood, Ill.: Dow Jones-Irwin, 1984.

Sanders, P. "Phenomenology: A New Way of Viewing Organizational Research." *Academy of Management Review,* 1982, 7 (2), 353–360.

Schein, E. *Organizational Psychology.* Englewood Cliffs, N.J.: Prentice-Hall, 1980.

Schwartz, H., and Davis, S. M. "Matching Corporate Culture and Business Strategy." *Organizational Dynamics,* Summer 1981, pp. 30–48.

Sinetar, M. "Mergers, Morale, and Productivity." *Personnel Journal,* Nov. 1981, pp. 863–867.

Stybel, L. "After the Merger." *New England Business,* June 2, 1986, pp. 67–68.

Tichy, N., and Ulrich, D. O. "The Leadership Challenge — A Call for the Transformational Leader." *Sloan Management Review,* 1984, *26* (1), 59–68.

Tuchman, B. "Developmental Sequence in Small Groups." *Psychological Bulletin,* 1965, *63,* 384–399.

22

Ralph H. Kilmann
Teresa Joyce Covin

Conclusions: New Directions in Corporate Transformation

The early 1980s showed an unprecedented interest in the management of organizations, as witnessed by the large number of management books on the best-selling list: *Theory Z* (Ouchi, 1981); *In Search of Excellence* (Peters and Waterman, 1982); *Corporate Culture* (Deal and Kennedy, 1982); *Megatrends* (Naisbitt, 1984); *A Passion for Excellence* (Peters and Austin, 1985). The recurring theme in all these books is: Establish a healthy organization that actively encourages all members to be innovative, market driven, productive, and adaptive in a world turned upside down. The consensus is that the organizations that were successful in the past few decades are not suited for excellence in today's world. But how should managers, workers, and consultants actually go about *changing* the old form of an organization to a new one? Most of the best-selling books were silent on the question of implementing change, which left action-prone managers at a loss on what to do next.

In the mid 1980s, however, due to increasing competitive pressures, organizations were forced into swift action ("Surge in Restructuring...," 1985). Whether labeled downsizing, rationalizing, streamlining, or restructuring ("Rebuilding to Survive...," 1987), top executives began slashing levels of management, closing down unprofitable plants, selling flagging business units, and reducing overall head counts in order to improve bottom-line results. While this new obsession with efficiency is certainly refreshing, restructuring simply does not go far enough to ensure *long-term* prosperity. Essentially, restructuring is a short-term financial solution to a long-term behavioral problem: Reducing costs will not automatically stimulate adaptive, market-driven, and innovative behavior. Stated differently, restructuring improves bottom-line results primarily through financial adjustments; it ignores the long-term consequences of disrupting the human side of the enterprise.

The principles of corporate transformation, as discussed by the authors in this book, provide what many of the best-selling management books have ignored (methods to bring about organizational change) and supply what the financial approaches have overlooked (methods to manage the human fabric of organizational life for long-term success). Corporate transformation can improve top-line *and* bottom-line results through a carefully planned approach to organizational change, which prepares all organizational members for the new ways of perceiving, thinking, and behaving required for success in a fast-paced, competitive world.

While this book presents the most up-to-date material on the topic of corporate transformation by leading experts in the field, we recognize that much more work needs to be done to revitalize organizations for a competitive world. The purpose of this concluding chapter is to examine two limitations that we feel must be overcome in order to break an organization's proclivity for choosing short-term financial results over long-term organizational health. First, management must embrace the principles of corporate transformation as a new way of managing and not as a "program" to fix the organization. Second, management must gain control over more than the human resources and strategic aspects internal to organizations; the external educational, governmental, financial, legal, technological, and international dynamics and forces must be managed as well. Better controlling the latter external forces will help to ensure long-term prosperity for our organizations.

Transformation as a New Way of Managing

Many of the discussions on corporate transformation think in terms of a *program* for large-scale organizational change. Generally, the program is initiated when individuals (either key executives or enlightened workers) realize that the old ways are no longer working and that an improvement effort is required for organizational success. Often, some preliminary diagnostic work is performed to unearth the particular problems facing the organization; at other times, top management already is convinced of the need for particular changes. Some program for planned change is then implemented with or without the aid of outside consultants. At various points along the way, evaluations are conducted to ensure that the program is having its desired effects. Such programs for corporate transformation may last anywhere from one to ten years.

As discussed in Chapter One, it is difficult to cite a case of organizational transformation that has been brought to a conclusion. There are several reasons for this. First, corporate transformation is still a rather new phenomenon for contemporary organizations. Therefore, even if numerous companies have started such an effort, one could not expect many of these programs to be completed for several more years. Second, some companies might not be publicizing their efforts at transformation so as to keep a competitive advantage over other firms still struggling with the difficulties of bringing about major organizational change. Third, the world does not sit still long enough for any program of planned change to reach completion—just as one major adjustment is made, the need quickly develops for additional strategic or structural adjustments. Thus, in a dynamic and turbulent world with continuous technological, social, economic, political, and cultural change on a worldwide basis (Scott and Lodge, 1985), it seems unrealistic to think of catch-up "programs." Instead, corporate transformation should be reframed as a continuous, ongoing approach to managing organizations—not as a separate, special activity to be undertaken just when there are signs of trouble.

Viewing transformation as a primary responsibility of

line management, particularly senior executives, one must consider how this management function can be organized and performed on an ongoing basis along with other kinds of strategic and operational decision making. Several recommendations can be offered here under the categories of management development and organizational systems.

Management Development: Managers must be trained to conduct organizational change. In the past, line managers have relied on internal human resource specialists, other staff groups, and outside consultants to help them facilitate change. While these line managers might have taken courses on organizational change and perhaps have read numerous books on the topic, they generally have not spent the time or effort needed to learn the *skills* for conducting change. In the worst cases, line managers have been rather naive about how organizational change can be effected, believing that clever speeches and articulate memorandums will inspire employees to make fundamental changes in their behavior. When the spoken or written word is unsuccessful in bringing about the intended result, the response of these traditional managers is simply another round of formal communications.

The primary responsibility of management is to keep the organization in tune with a changing environment and ahead of the increasingly competitive pressures in the marketplace, and managers cannot rely on others to do this job for them. Managers, therefore, should be selected and trained to conduct organizational change; they must be made aware of the complexities of the task and must acquire the specific skills needed to bring about behavioral change (Tichy, 1978). If the educational institutions (undergraduate, graduate, and executive development programs) do not provide the necessary material and skills training (perhaps because the colleges and universities are still preparing students for the more stable world of the 1960s), then organizations must develop their own educational programs to supplement the deficiencies in these institutions.

In addition to the analytical, technical, and administrative skills taught by corporate training and development programs, managers would be taught to be change agents; that is, to sense the need for change, to diagnose the multiple causes of complex organizational problems, to gain member involvement in discovering or inventing solutions to identified problems, to implement these solutions in a carefully planned manner that takes into account human fears and anxieties about change, and to evaluate how well the implemented solutions resolved the problematic situation. Furthermore, in addition to learning how to address problems *after* they have resulted in unfavorable outcomes, managers would be trained to anticipate emerging issues *before* these developed into severe problems requiring immediate and reactive attention. Learning proactive approaches that anticipate problems and opportunities certainly would ease the difficulties of major organizational change. More specifically, managers can be taught to outline all the things that could go wrong in the current situation, to examine all their underlying assumptions, and to consider how various environmental changes might overturn these assumptions. Managers must also learn to look for early warning signals of impending trouble for the organization, to mobilize task forces to investigate the implications and consequences of possible future developments, and to create contingency plans so that the organization is able, willing, and *prepared* to act regardless of which one of several scenarios actually becomes reality (Mitroff and Kilmann, 1984).

Organizational Systems: These systems can be designed to facilitate environmental scanning for corporate transformation. It is not enough for managers to be skilled in conducting *internal* organizational change; managers must also know what *external* events, trends, and dynamics are critical to the success of the organization and how they should respond to them. Instead of happenstance or individual initiative determining whether organizational members will work to appreciate and understand their environment, organizational systems can be designed to ensure that environmental information is comprehensive, systematized, and utilized for all important strategic and operational decisions.

Market intelligence, business intelligence, and strategic intelligence systems are all special organizational systems that can be used to facilitate ongoing transformation. The strategic intelligence system (SIS) is an organized effort to obtain data, information, and intelligence that relate to relevant opportunities and problems that occur outside of the organization (Kilmann and Ghymn, 1976). This system is used to appraise information bit by bit, to piece it together so that it forms clear patterns, and to disseminate it to appropriate persons or subunits, enabling them to understand more clearly the external environment within which the organization exists (Doz, 1980; Porter, 1986). For example, strategic intelligence includes information about foreign countries and competitors and their probable intentions, capabilities, and vulnerabilities. Strategic intelligence thus represents the critical information that decision makers must have to guide their corporations in a changing world (Prescott and Grant, forthcoming).

The organization can also design task forces to aggressively pursue critical information. These task forces consist of managers and members throughout the organization, including senior executives. Perhaps as many as 50 to 100 persons would spend five to ten hours per week in the SIS, with the remainder of their time being spent on their primary work assignment. Thus, the task forces are not composed of full-time staff persons who are removed from the day-to-day activities of the firm and who must recommend (sell) their proposals for action to line management. Instead, the members on the various SIS task forces represent all the business units in the organization and consist of line managers and other key employees. As a result of this arrangement, information and recommendations that derive from the SIS translate naturally and effectively into organizational action.

Consider an SIS designed for an international company that must keep abreast of a tremendous variety of national and international dynamics. The intelligence relevant to key strategic decisions can be organized into these categories: economic and legal, financial, social, political, marketing, and technical. One task force for each of these categories would be designed into action. For example, the task force concerned with monitoring economic and legal issues would seek to better understand the legal system of the host country, the host government's attitude toward foreign investment, the demand and supply conditions for the firm's product, tax laws, and restrictions on ownership or on imports and exports. Similarly, the task force concerned with monitoring political issues would focus on the host government's political system, the level of political instability, relations with neighboring countries, relations with supranational organizations (such as the United Nations), political factions, the attitude of the political opposition toward foreign investment, and the military's power in the government. The members in each task force would be selected on the basis of several criteria. They would, of course, have to be interested in the topic and have the ability to understand and monitor it. The members would also have to be representative of each business unit in the organization. Finally, they have to be seen as key decision makers or employees in the organization.

One member from each task force would serve on a coordinating board to ensure the effective functioning of the SIS. Attention would be given to discover new ways to involve more organizational members in the SIS activity, perhaps on a rotating basis. It would also be important to consider what training could be provided to the members of the SIS to facilitate their application of the most up-to-date set of skills for complex problem identification and information management. Discussions would be held on just how to present the acquired intelligence to the appropriate persons or subunits in the organization in order to increase the likelihood that the information will be taken seriously and acted upon. A critical issue in the effective use of the SIS design is that decision makers throughout the organization (in addition to the line managers actually involved in the SIS) really do alter the strategic and operational parameters of their business units as a result of what is learned. Too often, relevant information is considered valid only when it fits with the preconceived notions of the decision maker, which is contrary to the intentions behind the SIS. (See Barabba, 1984, for an elaborate discussion on the design and functioning of a market intelligence system at Eastman Kodak).

For the SIS to work, decision makers must create the organizational changes as implied by the intelligence acquired—not impulsively, but by deliberate and thoughtful assessments. But creating the SIS and teaching managers to conduct change are still not sufficient to guarantee ongoing transformation. Other organizational systems must be altered or designed to support this new way of managing (Schuler and MacMillan, 1984). Specifically, the performance appraisal system could reward the members of the SIS for their contributions to the organization above and beyond their everyday job performance. If they received an increase in salary or in incentive compensation or were recognized in special ways, this would certainly make other members of the organization aware of the importance of a manager's doing well on his SIS job. Furthermore, a management information system that is especially designed to update and transfer strategic intelligence to appropriate decision spots in the organization would facilitate the efficient processing and use of this valuable information (El Sawy, 1985). Last but not least, discussions on corporate values and corporate culture could include the importance of scanning and responding to key environmental signals, not just by the members of the SIS but by all organizational members. A shared value could be placed on remaining current with industrial and international affairs—the norm being, keep an eye and ear to the outside world and stand ready to respond with changes inside the organization (Davis, 1985).

Broadening the Concept of Transformation

As mentioned in the opening chapter of this book, the philosophy and methods of corporate transformation have their primary roots in the field of organization development. Traditionally, organization development has focused on the human aspects of the organization (for example, on team-building activities) and has been concerned with single groups or divisions of the organization. Corporate transformation, however, combines the strategic and business aspects with human and psychological issues, and seeks to create fundamental changes in the way all members and groups in the organization perceive, think, and behave.

As the various chapters in this book attest, many efforts at corporate transformation are based on a behavioral science approach to change. In our view, however, the future of transformation must lean more heavily on the business side of the equation, and the concept of transformation must be broadened to include other variables that managers can control.

In order to facilitate more successful transformations in the future, managers must consider the broader technological, educational, financial, economic, legal, political, cultural, and international forces that impact on organizational success. Just as the SIS design can be used to *monitor* international events, managers must find ways to *impact* on these events in the first place. Rather than attempt to cover all the critical forces acting on today's organizations, we will offer three examples for purposes of illustration. Specifically, three important forces to consider are (1) technology, (2) education, and (3) unions. As will be seen, the recurring theme in addressing these environmental forces is the need for interdepartmental and interorganizational cooperation to achieve what one unit or one organization cannot achieve on its own. The same philosophy applies to addressing the great variety of other dynamics challenging the organization. Transorganizational development (Cummings, 1984) and *meta*transformation will be key approaches to achieving competitiveness in the future.

Technology: How can transformation increase the development and use of new technologies? It has often been claimed that investments in research and development are critical for most firms seeking to be competitive in a global economy; at the same time, however, such expenditures do not translate directly into improved products and services (Frohman, 1982). The missing link appears to be the leadership and system of organization needed to mesh increased efforts at research and development with the strategic and business aspects of the organization. Unless an organization creates the necessary linkages between what consumers need and what the new technology can provide, it is unlikely that new technological developments will find their way to the marketplace. Specifically, the leadership of the organization must recognize how the objectives and activities of the technical people in the organization can be integrated with the objectives and activities of the business functions (including production, finance, human resources, and marketing). For most organizations, such an integration of market-driven and technologically focused efforts requires a corporate transformation, and yet transformation can hardly be expected to occur if this integration has not taken place.

Corporate transformation can support the integration of technological and business objectives by selecting and/or training senior executives to value both sides of the competitiveness coin (Schuler and MacMillan, 1984). Discussions on corporate values and corporate culture can emphasize the importance of bringing technological improvements to the marketplace and the need for technical and business people to put their two heads together in corporate decision making. Teams and task forces can be established for the explicit purpose of bringing together all the relevant expertise from different business and technical areas and providing forums where diversity in viewpoint would be valued, sought after, and utilized. These task forces would provide an appropriate forum for information that typically falls between departmental cracks, as was true of the SIS discussed earlier. In addition, the formal documents (for example, objectives of business units and job descriptions of key executives) could be revised to emphasize the expanded role of technology development and transfer. Finally, the reward system can be modified to include incentives for developing and supporting the interface between technology and business. Performance appraisals that explicitly recognize management behavior that is supportive of this interface would send the appropriate signals to the rest of the membership.

Education: Can the educational system be revitalized to develop professional managers for the future? As indicated earlier in this chapter, if the educational system does not provide the necessary skill training to teach managers to be change agents, then the corporation should seek to fill the void. However, there is more to education than teaching change agent skills, and it probably is not cost effective for each organization to do what the colleges and universities should be doing. For example, for each organization to mount its own equivalent of a professional masters in business administration (MBA) program is expecting too much.

The opportunity exists, nevertheless, for organizations to influence curriculum changes in graduate schools of business and management. In most cases, senior executives of firms do participate on the board of advisers of the major business schools and thereby can exert some influence if they organize to do so. Certainly, these executives are consumers of the educational systems through their hiring of MBA students; perhaps the universities need to be reminded periodically who their clientele is. Furthermore, corporations might find it advantageous to provide substantial gifts to local universities on condition that they implement new or modified graduate programs for developing the type of professional manager needed to foster and function well in a transformed organization. Thus, a joint venture between universities and corporations, in which each contributes its own special area of expertise, could provide the necessary formula for preparing managers for a competitive world (Bloch, 1987).

The newly designed academic programs that might result from a joint venture between executives and educators surely would include experiences to develop leadership, communication, inspirational, political, and interpersonal skills—the sort of things that are rarely taught in a content-focused MBA curriculum (Zoffer, 1986). It seems that most colleges and universities concentrate on the cognitive skills needed to solve structured problems in an analytical way. The new world of business, however, calls for managers who can sense and define critical problems before turning to analytical methods for their solution. And regardless of how well the chosen solution seems to address the identified problem, moving the solution—from paper—into the mainstream of organizational life is anything but an analytical or mechanistic activity. The effective implementation of solutions in a complex organizational system is precisely why change agent skills are mandatory and need to be supplemented by political, interpersonal, and leadership skills.

Naturally, curriculum questions must focus on how much emphasis to place on cognitive material relative to efforts designed to teach leadership skills. In addition, questions must be answered concerning *what* cognitive and behavioral skills should be taught and *how* these can be taught most effectively. Should the business schools adjust their criteria for admission, from selecting primarily those students who meet the traditional academic standards to selecting only those students who demonstrate innate leadership qualities and exhibit interpersonal competence? How can the latter qualities be assessed and integrated with the more traditional assessments of analytical capacity and academic achievement? In all likelihood, only a joint effort between business leaders and educators can hope to construct an effective system for selecting and training the next generation of transformational leaders.

Unions: How can union-management relationships be transformed to improve productivity and innovation? Most discussions in the field of organizational development and the new field of corporate transformation focus on *one* organization: the primary corporation in question. Not much attention has been given to revitalizing the union organizations that play a significant role in organizational success, especially in cases where collective bargaining agreements dictate work policies, procedures, and wages for organizational members for a period of several years (Schuster, 1984). If these kinds of union-management agreements are not made with foresight or do not have a certain amount of built-in flexibility in mind, changes in technology and the marketplace can render them obsolete in a short period of time—a severe obstacle to corporate adaptiveness and competitiveness, as witnessed in the American automotive and steel industries. To transform an entire organization requires that the union organization and union-management relationships be transformed as well; otherwise, one more obstacle to success will limit what an organization can accomplish.

During the 1950s, 1960s, and early 1970s, the major labor unions achieved unprecedented gains in wages and security with inflation-contingent clauses. During the worldwide recession of the middle and late 1970s, however, the folly of not tying wages directly to gains in productivity became apparent. By the early 1980s, unions found it necessary to grant unprecedented wage concessions in order to retain jobs and keep their organizations alive. Numerous joint experiments in union and management cooperation were fueled by the need to be competitive in an international, and not just a domestic, marketplace (Solberg, 1985, discusses the example of General Motors). Now that the U.S. economy has recovered, one might wonder if the number of creative union contracts formed in the recent past (see, for instance, Kuttner, 1985, on Eastern Airlines) will continue to grow without having to be spurred on by another severe economic crisis.

The recent power shift away from labor and toward management and capital suggests that management must take the lead in forming creative partnerships—versus adversarial relationships—with union organizations (Mondy and Preameaux, 1985). With a backdrop of general economic pressures and a spirit of wage concessions, management is in a very good position to put the past aside and initiate creative approaches to the interconnected problems of job security, productivity, innovation, and adaptability. Perhaps union organizations will initiate their own efforts at transforming *themselves* as they witness the benefits of transformation for their employer's organization. If both unions and employers were in the process of transformation, joint committees of key corporate executives, union leaders, and the employees could explore alternative agreements for the future. Solutions could be created that seek to satisfy the objectives of both the corporation and the union and that treat each as an equal partner. Thus, the superordinate goal of long-term economic prosperity can replace the former goals of short-term security and self-containment.

Conclusion

The forgoing discussion argued that corporate transformation (1) should be viewed as a new, ongoing way of managing organizations in a dynamic world and (2) could be expanded to include cooperative efforts across traditional organizational boundaries, thereby enabling a corporation to exercise greater control over its environment. The first point can be addressed through management development efforts and the design of an SIS to monitor a global economy. The second point recognizes that transformation must include more than the cultural and strategic aspects *within* one organization; rather, it must include all the technological, educational, union, governmental, and other external factors that flow across organizations and nations. The initiation of joint ventures by organizations and institutions will help them to transcend their individual limitations, just as a single organization enables its members to overcome their own inherent limitations. Corporate transformation, in this context, offers promise for further extending mankind's reach for a better life.

References

Barabba, V. P. "How Kodak's Market Intelligence System Cuts Risk, Speeds Decisions." *Management Review*, Aug. 1984, pp. 8–13.

Bloch, E. "Economic Competition: A Research and Education Challenge." *Research Management*, Mar.–Apr. 1987, pp. 6–8.

Cummings, T. G. "Transorganizational Development." *Research in Organizational Behavior*, 1984, *6*, 367–422.

Davis, S. M. "Culture Is Not Just an Internal Affair." In R. H. Kilmann, M. J. Saxton, R. Serpa, and Associates, *Gaining Control of the Corporate Culture*. San Francisco: Jossey-Bass, 1985.

Deal, T. E., and Kennedy, A. A. *Corporate Cultures: The Rites and Rituals of Corporate Life*. Reading, Mass.: Addison-Wesley, 1982.

Doz, Y. L. "Strategic Management in Multinational Companies." *Sloan Management Review*, Winter 1980, pp. 27–46.

El Sawy, O. A. "Personal Information Systems for Strategic Scanning in Turbulent Environments: Can the CEO Go On-Line?" *MIS Quarterly*, Mar. 1985, pp. 53–60.

Frohman, A. L. "Technology as a Competitive Weapon." *Harvard Business Review*, 1982, *60* (1), 97–104.

Kilmann, R. H., and Ghymn, K. "The MAPS Design Technology: Designing Strategic Intelligence Systems for MNCs." *Columbia Journal of World Business*, 1976, *11* (2), 35–47.

Kuttner, R. "Sharing Power at Eastern Airlines," *Harvard Business Review*, 1985, *63* (6), 91–101.

Mitroff, I. I., and Kilmann, R. H. *Corporate Tragedies: Product Tampering, Sabotage, and Other Catastrophies*. New York: Praeger, 1984.

Mondy, R. W., and Preameaux, S. R. "The Labor-Management Power Relationship Revisited." *Personnel Administrator*, May 1985, pp. 51–55.

Naisbitt, J. *Megatrends: Ten New Directions Transforming Our Lives*. New York: Warner Books, 1984.

Ouchi, W. *Theory Z: How American Business Can Meet the Japanese Challenge*. Reading, Mass.: Addison-Wesley, 1981.

Peters, T. J., and Austin, N. K. *A Passion for Excellence: The Leadership Difference*. New York: Random House, 1985.

Peters, T. J., and Waterman, R. H., Jr. *In Search of Excellence: Lessons from America's Best-Run Companies*. New York: Harper & Row, 1982.

Porter, M. E. "Changing Patterns of International Competition." *California Management Review*, Winter 1986, pp. 9–40.

Prescott, J. E., and Grant, J. H. "Manager's Guide to Competitive Analysis Techniques." *Interfaces*, forthcoming.

"Rebuilding To Survive: Special Report on Corporate Restructuring." *Time*, Feb. 16, 1987, 44–45.

Schuler, R. S., and MacMillan, I. C. "Gaining Competitive Advantage Through Human Resource Management Practices." *Human Resource Management*, 1984, *23*, 241–255.

Schuster, M. "Cooperation and Change in Union Settings: Problems and Opportunities." *Human Resource Management*, 1984, *23* (2), 145–160.

Scott, B. R., and Lodge, G. C. (eds.). *U.S. Competitiveness in the World Economy*. Boston: Harvard Business School Press, 1985.

Solberg, S. L. "Changing Culture Through Ceremony: An Example from GM." *Human Resource Management*, 1985, *24*, 329–340.

"Surge in Restructuring Is Profoundly Altering Much of U.S. Industry." *Wall Street Journal*, Aug. 12, 1985, pp. 1, 12, 13.

Tichy, N. M. "Current and Future Trends for Change Agentry." *Group and Organizational Studies*, 1978, *3* (4), 467–482.

Zoffer, H. J. "How One Dean Would Change the Business Schools." *Management Review*, May 1986, pp. 60–61.

Name Index

Subject Index